RIGHTING RELATIONS AFTER THE HOLOCAUST AND VATICAN II

For Sam, Alison +
Bella

with all my love
and appreciation
for a memorable
visit,

Michael
Sept 23, 2018
Aladistair

Studies in Judaism and Christianity

Exploration of Issues in the Contemporary Dialogue between Christians and Jews

EDITORS

Michael McGarry, CSP
Mark-David Janus, CSP, PhD
Yehezkel Landau, DMin
Peter Pettit, PhD
Elena Procario-Foley, PhD
Ellen M. Umansky, PhD
Rabbi Stephen Wylen

 A STIMULUS BOOK

RIGHTING RELATIONS AFTER THE HOLOCAUST AND VATICAN II

Essays in Honor of
John T. Pawlikowski, OSM

Edited by
Elena G. Procario-Foley
and
Robert A. Cathey

A STIMULUS BOOK

Paulist Press ◆ New York ◆ Mahwah, NJ

Cover image: Photo courtesy Philip A. Cunningham; sculpture located at St. Joseph's University, Philadelphia, PA. *Synagoga and Ecclesia in Our Time* by Joshua Koffman was commissioned by Saint Joseph's University in Philadelphia to mark the 50th anniversary of the Second Vatican Council declaration *Nostra Aetate*. It depicts Synagogue and Church as study partners; the sculpture thus illustrates the words of Pope Francis that "There exists a rich complementarity between the Church and the Jewish people that allows us to help one another mine the riches of God's word."

Cover and book design by Sharyn Banks
Frontispiece courtesy of Catholic Theological Union

Library of Congress Cataloging-in-Publication Data
Names: Pawlikowski, John, honouree. | Procario-Foley, Elena, editor.
Title: Righting relations after the Holocaust and Vatican II : essays in honor of John T. Pawlikowski, OSM / edited by Elena G. Procario-Foley, Robert A. Cathey.
Description: New York : Paulist Press, 2018. | "A Stimulus book."
Identifiers: LCCN 2017058863 (print) | LCCN 2018026231 (ebook) | ISBN 9781587687013 (ebook) | ISBN 9780809153350 (pbk. : alk. paper)
Subjects: LCSH: Judaism—Relations—Christianity. | Christianity and other religions—Judaism. | Holocaust (Jewish theology) | Holocaust (Christian theology)
Classification: LCC BM535 (ebook) | LCC BM535 .R495 2018 (print) | DDC 261.2/6—dc23
LC record available at https://lccn.loc.gov/2017058863

ISBN 978-0-8091-5335-0 (paperback)
ISBN 978-1-58768-701-3 (e-book)

Published by Paulist Press
997 Macarthur Boulevard
Mahwah, NJ 07430

www.paulistpress.com

Printed and bound in the United States of America

*To all the members past and present of the
Christian Scholars Group on Christian-Jewish Relations
(1969–present) who have worked creatively, courageously,
and tirelessly on behalf of righting relations
between Jews and Christians*

CONTENTS

Contents

PART II: HOLOCAUST STUDIES

PART III: INTERRELIGIOUS STUDIES

Contents

FOREWORD

—⁓—

Judith H. Banki

It is almost impossible to summarize Father, Doctor, Professor John Pawlikowski's monumental contribution to Jewish-Christian under-standing and rapprochement, Holocaust studies, and the theological, historical, and ethical dimensions of our joint and separate teaching traditions in the space allotted. His condensed biography on the Scarboro Missions website, however, makes an excellent attempt at saying it all:

> It is hard to find an English-language book on Jewish-Christian relations written in the last 30 years that does not either reference, or include a contribution from, Servite Father John Pawlikowski...one of the most prolific and respected contemporary writers and speakers on the Holocaust, and on the dramatic change in Christian attitudes toward Jews in the decades since the Second World War.[1]

So rather than catalogue his achievements, I have tried to imagine what our field, indeed, our world, would have been like if Fr. John Pawlikowski had not happened along. From the perspective of an observer and an activist in the field of Jewish-Christian relations, it would have been a very different place.

Since he was not ordained until 1967, it is very likely that *Nostra Aetate* would still have been adopted and promulgated. Evidence of the nearly two-millennia tradition of negative, hostile, even combat-ive teaching about Jews and Judaism had been documented for Catholic scholars and leaders involved in planning the Second Vatican Council for years before it opened. The damage to Jewish life and limb engendered by this hostility had also been spelled out. The work of Jewish scholars and activists—including my own—and the contributions of Catholic *periti* had convinced most of the 2,500 bishops attending the Council of the need for an authoritative statement repudiating what the French scholar Jules Isaac tellingly summarized as the teaching of contempt.

But few in the Catholic community could have undertaken the task of looking squarely at Christian antisemitism, implementing the recommendations of *Nostra Aetate* and others that followed from Rome and from the bishops' conferences of many Western nations, interpreting them to generations of students, exploring the theological questions raised in the ensuing dialogue, and challenging Jewish religious and communal leadership to rethink their own attitudes to Christianity. How many combined the essential knowledge, the theological training, the dialogic temperament, the historical awareness, the patience and good will, and the professional opportunity to use these gifts in the service of reconciliation?

Of course, Fr. John was not the only Catholic leader to advance this goal. Monsignor John Oesterreicher played a significant role during Vatican Council II, and many members of the American hierarchy spoke out on behalf of a strong and unambiguous declaration repudiating the charge of deicide attributed to the Jewish people. Father Edward Flannery and Dr. Eugene Fisher—the first and second secretaries of Catholic-Jewish Relations for the United States Conference of Catholic Bishops—lent their talents and energy to expand understanding of Jews and Judaism among Catholics. Fisher conducted a post–*Nostra Aetate* study of Catholic textbooks, published under the title *Faith without Prejudice*, and lent his own expertise and experience to the drafting of many significant statements issued by the bishops. However, joining the faculty of the Catholic Theological Union in 1968, becoming professor of social ethics as well as the director of both CTU's Cardinal Bernardin Center for Theology and Ministry and its Catholic-Jewish Studies program afforded Fr. Pawlikowski a very broad canvas for his work. And work he did, for the next fifty years, during which he wrote a slew of books and articles, and was appointed a founding member of the United States Holocaust Memorial Council by President Jimmy Carter, an appointment renewed by Presidents George W. Bush and Bill Clinton. He has also won a bounty of awards (over two dozen and counting), among which are three honorary doctorates, top awards from Jewish human rights organizations such as the AJC and ADL, a variety of honors from academic societies and universities across the globe, and high-level recognitions from international cities and governments, including Poland (more than one) and Montevideo, Uruguay.[2]

There is probably no one presently active in the field of interreligious dialogue, Jewish-Christian studies, or Holocaust education who has not been touched by John Pawlikowski's teaching, his scholarship, his wisdom, his personal outreach, his friendship. Other contributors to this volume have worked with him more closely, but I doubt if anyone has worked with him longer. When I joined the staff of the American Jewish Committee (AJC) late in 1959, I was given an intriguing assignment: to familiarize myself with the researchers and findings of a series of religion textbook studies that the AJC had stimulated and for which it had secured funding. It should come as no surprise that Jews were concerned about how Christians depicted them in their religious education materials. Many believed that a deeply rooted tradition depicting Jews as deicides, rejected by God and doomed to eternal servitude and misery, was a potent source of antisemitism across the ages. Therefore, it was critical that these were self-studies, conducted by scholars from within the religious community whose materials were studied, and that their funding and findings were independent of AJC control. The Protestant self-study was carried out at Yale University Divinity School (1952–59), by a Methodist scholar, Dr. Bernhard Olson. His study, published as *Faith and Prejudice*, was groundbreaking.[3]

In the United States, the Catholic textbook self-study was carried out at St. Louis University by three religious sisters who examined Catholic social studies textbooks, Catholic literature materials, and finally, Catholic religion and church history materials. This latter study—the only one that showed significant problems of prejudice in the materials—was undertaken by Sr. Rose Thering, OP. It was Fr. John Pawlikowski who, at her own suggestion, summarized and evaluated her findings in book form in *Catechetics and Prejudice: How Catholic Teaching Materials View Jews, Protestants, and Racial*

Minorities.[4] This was my first experience working with Fr. John. I am grateful that it was the first of many.

The essays that follow echo the admiration and respect in which John Pawlikowski is held by his colleagues in academia, religion, Holocaust studies, and interfaith dialogue. They include Christians, Jews, Muslims, clergy and laypersons, men and women representing several generations. Each has been touched by John Pawlikowski's personality, his writings, his teaching, or simply his presence. They speak for themselves.

I recall how one serendipitous, unexpected meeting with him blossomed into a memorable conference, a rich and mind-changing exchange of facts and feelings, of history and theology, and a noteworthy volume. In January 1998, the Vatican issued its long-promised and long-awaited statement on the Holocaust: *We Remember: A Reflection on the Shoah.* It was immediately criticized by some Jewish commentators, and some Protestant and Catholic spokespersons as well, as a self-serving document that inflated Catholic resistance to Nazi genocide, minimized collaboration, and, most seriously, failed utterly to acknowledge any role in creating and promoting the anti-Judaism and antisemitism that culminated in the Shoah. My own view of the document was somewhat more nuanced. I believed that while much of the criticism was justified, it overlooked important affirmations within the document, and ignored or dismissed the social and political pressures underlying its self-defensive tone. In fact, I was mentally drafting an article to that effect intended for *Commonweal* magazine. En route to an ICCJ conference (International Council of Christians and Jews) in Erlbach, in the former East Germany, I had taken a few days to explore Dresden. Suddenly, on the street ahead, John Pawlikowski materialized in front of me! Of course, he was going to the same conference.

That happy coincidence did not go to waste. Traveling together on the train, we agreed that both *We Remember* and the multiple responses to its publication required an in-depth exploration by Catholic and Jewish scholars of the Holocaust, historians of Jewish-Christian relations, communal leaders, clergy and nonclergy, and academics and nonacademics consulting together in a "safe environment" (i.e., free from outside pressure) for several days. Our conversation bore fruit in a three-day consultation at the Catholic Theological Union, cosponsored by the Tanenbaum Center for Interreligious Understanding and CTU's Cardinal Bernardin Center. The consultation was attended by Edward Cardinal Cassidy, then head of the Vatican commission under whose auspices *We Remember* had been issued. Perhaps the finest tribute to the quality of the dialogue at that meeting was his assertion that if he had heard the discussion before *We Remember* was issued, it would have been a different document.

I still recall that meeting as one of the most stimulating of a long professional career in interreligious affairs, an encounter that would not have been possible without John Pawlikowski's skills and the regard in which he was held by colleagues here and abroad. No one invited to the consultation declined an invitation from him! It also afforded me the opportunity to coedit with him a volume emerging from that event, *Ethics in the Shadow of the Holocaust*. In addition to this book (he wrote or edited fourteen more), we also published side-by-side articles in *Commonweal* magazine, offering separate—but usually not conflicting—commentaries on contentious issues between Christians and Jews. Our distinctive comments on *We Remember* and later, on the newly approved and revised Good Friday prayer (for the Tridentine liturgy) by Pope Benedict XVI (2008) remain memorable for me.

John Pawlikowski's writings, teachings, and public presentations have had a profound influence on generations of post–Vatican II Catholics and the broader Christian and Jewish communities. His friendship has been a blessing for all who have worked with him. We can only be grateful that he came along when he did, that he did what he did, and pray that he will keep doing it. We live in dangerous and divisive times; the voices of reason, of thoughtful discussion of tendentious issues, the capacity to hear the other side of a disagreement, the gift of empathy, and civility in argument are threatened by the reemergence of group hatreds and paranoid fantasies we thought we put to rest years ago. Our times desperately need the mindfulness, the balance, the civility of discourse of a host of John Pawlikowskis. Alas, there is but one. May he go from strength to strength!

Notes

1. See Scarboro Missions: A Canadian Roman Catholic Mission Society, "Rev. Dr. John T. Pawlikowski, OSM," accessed May 11, 2018, www.scarboromissions.ca/interfaith-dialogue/jewish-christian-relations/rev-dr-john-t-pawlikowski-osm.

2. Awards excerpted from the curriculum vita provided to the editors by Pawlikowski.

3. Bernhard Emmanuel Olson, *Faith and Prejudice: Intergroup Problems in Protestant Curricula* (New Haven, CT: Yale University Press, 1963).

4. John Pawlikowski, *Catechetics and Prejudice: How Catholic Teaching Materials View Jews, Protestants, and Racial Minorities* (New York: Paulist Press, 1973).

INTRODUCTION

—m—

Elena G. Procario-Foley

Inviolable human rights. These three words stand at the center of John Thaddeus Michael Pawlikowski's mind and heart. They drive his teaching, writing, and ministry as a Roman Catholic priest of the Servite Order. One volume alone cannot adequately do justice to the depth and breadth of his contributions to "righting relationships," healing suffering, and creating a culture of dialogue in a world too long riven by ideological, religious, racial, and economic polarization. His contributions to Jewish-Christian relations alone could fill volumes.

Ordained a priest in 1967, a year later Pawlikowski began his fifty-year-long distinguished teaching career at the Catholic Theological Union in Chicago. He is the intellectual and moral giant on whose shoulders so many of us stand. Beginning a life of teaching and ministry just after the conclusion of the Second Vatican Council, he has labored to make real the vision of the Council. Among students of the Council, it is well known that Belgian bishop Emil Josef de Smedt famously criticized an early draft of *Lumen Gentium*, Dogmatic Constitution on the Church, as triumphal, clerical, and juridical. Pawlikowski's writings have, on the other hand, embodied the ideals of the Council (sometimes captured by the phrase "the spirit of Vatican II") that returned the draft to committee for major revision—the vision of the church as humble and dialogical, as a pilgrim journeying toward the reign of God, and as a servant of all peoples. Pawlikowski's work consistently demands that all members of the church fulfill the goal of the council to be a church that joins itself to the "joy and hope, the grief and anguish" of the world at large, that works for "the common good, which is the sum total of social conditions which allow people, either as groups or as individuals, to reach their fulfillment more fully and more easily," and that honors what is "true and holy" in other religions.[1] The hope for transformation engendered within the ecumenical Christian world by the Second Vatican Council provides one context for and impetus to Pawlikowski's thought.

His tremendous scholarly contributions and his work as a public intellectual are also stimulated by the tragedy of the Holocaust, the Shoah. As the Roman Catholic Church at Vatican II was engaging questions of modernity and seeking aggiornamento, the world was riveted by the capture and trial of Adolph Eichmann. As testimony continued, the world, at least the Euro-American world, could no longer ignore the catastrophe of the nearly successful genocide of their Jewish brothers and sisters. Nations, governments, and religious bodies had to face themselves squarely in the mirror and take account of their culpability for a barbaric and senseless tragedy. To be sure, the process of self-reckoning among Christian religious groups had begun at least as early as the emergency meeting on antisemitism in Seelisberg, Switzerland, in 1947 (and others in this volume will take up aspects of that history). But, in the 1960s, the Eichmann trial forced attention on the brutal and systematic mass murder of a people simply because they were Jewish.

Human rights, therefore, are the guideposts at the beginning and end of any assessment of ethical issues for Pawlikowski. Questions of theology are examined through the critical lens of human rights. Whether religious or political, if the decision cannot pass the test of inviolable human rights, then it holds no ethical credibility.

We have chosen the idea of "righting relations" in history and creation as a particular articulation of the concept of justice and as the broad theme that runs through many of Pawlikowski's contributions to different fields of religious-ethical reflection. The aftermath of both the Holocaust and Vatican II calls us to reflect on relationships, both personal and institutional. How do we repair wounded relationships? What is the nature of relationships with integrity? How does one treat the other? How do groups in conflict tell the truth to each other? What resources and inspiration do such groups have for reconciliation? Pawlikowski's work as a social ethicist, scholar of the

Holocaust, and specialist in Jewish-Christian dialogue (with attention to multilateral religious dialogue) is fundamentally based on the pursuit of right relationships. This volume, therefore, is divided into three sections: ethics and theology, Holocaust studies, and interreligious studies. These areas of course are not so neatly divided and questions from one area inevitably overlap with another. Results in each field challenge the methods in the other to serve the cause of human rights more adequately.

Jewish, Christian, and Muslim, European and American, lay and ordained, our contributors all enjoy some sort of professional or personal connection to Pawlikowski. At minimum, we have all been schooled by his wisdom, challenged by his keen acumen, and make our contributions in the wake of his trail-blazing career. We represent different generations of those concerned with relations among religions, ethics, and theology after the Holocaust and Vatican II. Judith H. Banki (foreword) and James Carroll (afterword) have known Pawlikowski since the beginning of his career, have shared his passion for Jewish-Christian relations, and are colleagues of that courageous first generation (post-Shoah, post–Vatican II) forging new paths of respect between Jews and Christians.

We asked our contributors to reflect on the theme of righting relationships from the perspective of their particular subdisciplines. Incidentally, we were advised against the use of an earlier draft title— "renewing relationships"—on the strength of the fact that there were no appreciable corporate relations between Jews and Christians before Vatican II that could be "renewed." That conversation of advisors from both faiths was itself an act of dialogue demonstrating respect for the other and progress in Jewish-Christian relations.

Based on the theme, contributors were asked to build on their own work. Praise is surely due Pawlikowski but his concern was never for himself but always for the wounded other. A sentimental collection of encomia was not, therefore, an appropriate honor. Rather, critical essays that demonstrated how far the work has come and what yet remains to be done were in order so that the book could function both as an introduction and as a constructive contribution to the state of the field. Our contributors have provided us with chapters that do just that. All of them, in different measure, respond to the question of how to make relationships right and just. They do so from historical, biblical, liturgical, pastoral/practical, and systematic perspectives. While Pawlikowski's fifteen-plus books and countless articles can range from Jewish-Catholic relations to Holocaust to economic injustice to the environmental crisis—to name but a few of his specialties—he did not write for theory's sake but to guide action for righting relationships and for the common good. The last chapter in each section, therefore, is a shorter contribution from the perspective of the pastoral and pedagogical implications of his work. We intend for this book to be useful for teachers and students, clergy and laity, who seek to be informed by the history and creative advance of Christian-Jewish relations to bring its insights to bear on the public and religious issues of our times.

With the conclusion of Pawlikowski's formal teaching career with his retirement from the Catholic Theological Union in June 2017, it is instructive to look back at the beginning of his career. On April 13, 1968, he wrote a comprehensive letter to Judith H. Banki, assistant director of the Interreligious Affairs Department of the American Jewish Committee, that proposed the basic structure and themes of a book that the AJC had asked him to consider writing. He wrote,

> The book, as I conceive it, would deal only with the areas of Christian-Jewish Relations. I feel this is the most neglected of the areas (at least next to the Indian problem)....The book is to be a practical as well as a theological one. I would like it to be an introduction to all aspects of the problem since most people are really unaware of it. Obviously, there has to be some introduction to the theological aspects of the problem even though the book is not to be a formal theological study.[2]

A complete chapter outline of the book (with the proposed title "Judaism and Catholic Education") was enclosed.[3] In fact, he had outlined the agenda for fifty years of work. There were middle chapters about (1) the "Second Vatican Council and Judaism," focusing on the deicide charge and the erroneous portrayal of Judaism as a legalistic religion, and (2) "Problems Not Answered by the Council"—among them "the continuing validity of Judaism as a living religion," "the question of Israel and Christian religious attitudes," and "the problem of reading the New Testament in the liturgy" (a section noting especially the passion narratives and biblical translations). The final chapter in the outline, before the conclusion, was titled "The Importance of Judaism in Christian Education." Of the seven areas that he proposes for this chapter, one in particular stands out: "What Should Be Done: Integration of Judaism into the Core of the Curriculum at All Levels." And then on the typed text he added in handwriting and in parentheses, "grammar, college, seminary, etc." Everything that his outline proposes in this chapter as well as the chapters on the Vatican Council is still a work in progress, as this volume will demonstrate. Pawlikowski's prescient call, however, for consistent and systematic teaching about Judaism at all levels of Catholic education (and one that ecclesial, ecumenical, and interreligious bodies have repeated since) has been the one least heeded. It seems, then, that the best way to honor his five decades of dedicated labor on behalf of righting relations between Jews and Christians is to continue the work and to make real his hope of "making American religion [*sic*] pluralism something truly creative." The talented contributors to this volume show us the way.

* * *

Thanks are due to all our friends in the Christian Scholar's Group on Christian-Jewish Relations who supported this project as authors or advisors. We thank the Rev. Dr. Peter Pettit of Muhlenberg College who first received and shared our proposal of a book in honor of Fr. Pawlikowski. We thank Fr. Michael McGarry, CSP, president of the Stimulus Foundation of Paulist Press for encouraging the creation of this book. We owe a debt of gratitude to our excellent editor, Christopher M. Bellitto, whose good humor, timely insights, and steady hand have guided so many a project to publication. He is a superb scholar and a cherished friend. Robert Cathey expresses his appreciation to Fr. Pawlikowski for sharing his wisdom, friendship, and theological creativity with a Presbyterian, and to the trustees and faculty of McCormick Theological Seminary who provided a sabbatical for the preparation of this volume. Finally, we thank our families and colleagues who were patient and understanding during the process of editing and writing.

Notes

1. The first two quotations are from Vatican Council II, *Gaudium et Spes*, Pastoral Constitution on the Church in the Modern World, §§1, 26 (December 7, 1965), http://www.vatican.va/archive/hist_councils/ii _vatican_council/documents/vat-ii_cons_19651207_gaudium-et-spes _en.html; and the last is from Vatican Council II, *Nostra Aetate*, Declaration on the Relation of the Church to Non-Christian Relations, §2 (October 28, 1965), http://www.vatican.va/archive/hist_councils/ii_vatican _council/documents/vat-ii_decl_19651028_nostra-aetate_en.html.

2. The letter and book outline from which these quotations and those of the next paragraph are taken can be found in the American Jewish Committee archives, Box 96, Folder 8, "St. Louis Study-Pawlikowski (1969)."

3. Pawlikowski incorporated the results of Sr. Rose Thering's doctoral dissertation, which studied the representation of Jews and Judaism in Catholic textbooks, into this book, making her highly technical analyses accessible in a more popular vernacular. Her research provided the foundation for the early chapters of this book, which would be Pawlikowski's first.

ABBREVIATIONS FOR TITLES OF BOOKS BY JOHN T. PAWLIKOWSKI, OSM

Catech. Prej. = *Catechesis and Prejudice: How Catholic Teaching Materials View Jews, Protestants, and Racial Minorities.* New York: Paulist Press, 1973.

Cath. Jews = *When Catholics Speak about Jews: Notes for Homilists and Catechists.* Chicago: Liturgy Training Publications, 1987.

Challenge Holocaust = *The Challenge of the Holocaust for Christian Theology.* New York: Center for Studies on the Holocaust, Anti-Defamation League of B'nai B'rith, 1978, 1982.

Christ Light = *Christ in the Light of the Christian–Jewish Dialogue.* New York: Paulist Press; Eugene, OR: Wipf and Stock Publishers, 1982.

Epistle Hom. = *Epistle Homilies.* Milwaukee: Bruce Publishing Co., 1966.

Jesus Israel = *Jesus and the Theology of Israel.* Wilmington, DE: Michael Glazier, 1989.

Pope John Paul II = *Pope John Paul II on Christian–Jewish Relations: His Legacy, Our Challenge; The Inaugural Annual John Paul II Lecture on Christian–Jewish Relations.* Boston: Boston College Center for Christian–Jewish Learning, 2012.

Restating Church's Rel. = *Restating the Catholic Church's Relationship with the Jewish People: The Challenge of Super-Sessionary Theology.* Lewiston, NY: Edwin Mellen, 2013.

Sinai Calv. = Sinai and Calvary: A Meeting of Two Peoples. Beverley Hills, CA: Benziger, 1976.

WATSA Christ. Jewish = What Are They Saying about Christian-Jewish Relations? New York: Paulist Press, 1980.

Part I

ETHICS AND THEOLOGY

CHAPTER ONE

"*QUO VADIS* HUMANITY?"

Reinhold Niebuhr and John Pawlikowski on Social Ethics in a Global Age

—ᴍ—

Mary Doak

The human race faces major challenges in this still-young twenty-first century. Global economic and communication systems are knitting the people of this planet together to the point that we now affect each other as never before. Isolationism is no longer an option, and socio-economic and political problems must be resolved on global as well as local, regional, and national levels.

These trends toward globalization offer the possibility of sharing our talents and resources so that progress raises the quality of life for all. Globalization, however, also threatens to unfold instead as a winner-take-all system that disrupts local economies, enriches a small global elite class at the expense of the majority of humanity, and imposes a uniform culture on the whole world. Additionally, we are in the midst of a massive human migration, as economic and climate shifts along with wars are unsettling the communities that hemorrhage members as well as those communities that must reconfigure themselves to integrate large numbers of people seeking a secure and sustainable life in a new place. Perhaps most serious of all, this global economy with its orientation toward continual growth and consumption is unleashing a comprehensive climate change that is drastically altering the conditions of life on this planet.

Was there ever a time when social ethics mattered more? Humanity now has the power to do great good or great harm on a global level. As John Pawlikowski has aptly observed, the technological

3

powers at our disposal present us with the question, "Quo Vadis Humanity?"[1] Where is humanity going, and what future are we choosing? Will we direct these global processes toward a sustainable common good, or will we strive against each other, seeking to secure our own privilege regardless of the cost to others or even to the planet itself?

Despite their very different theological contexts, both Reinhold Niebuhr and John Pawlikowski contend that Christianity has valuable resources to contribute to the development of a social ethics adequate to our global responsibilities. Niebuhr, who already in the 1940s is aware of the ethical challenges of globalization, seeks to recover neglected Christian doctrines and symbols as the basis for a more subtle and politically responsible social ethics. Christianity, he insists, has more to offer than the simplistic idealism that many rightly reject as unhelpful and inadequate in the face of the grave and complex problems of contemporary geopolitics. Pawlikowski builds on this Niebuhrian foundation of nuanced Christian social ethics, especially with his emphasis on the revision of traditional Christian beliefs that teach contempt for Jews. As Pawlikowski's work demonstrates, Niebuhr's enduring insights into the value of Christian social ethics are incomplete—and Christian efforts in this global age seriously flawed—unless Christianity is able to overcome the seeds of violence within the Christian tradition.

REINHOLD NIEBUHR AND THE IMPOSSIBLE NECESSITY OF WORLD COMMUNITY

Reinhold Niebuhr is a giant among Christian social ethicists of the twentieth century, and he continues to be a major and unusually influential Christian thinker. Indeed, President Barack Obama has called Niebuhr "one of my favorite philosophers."[2] Emphasizing the human inclination to sin, Niebuhr is perhaps best known for advocating a responsible Christian realism that eschews both the utopianism of seeking the perfect reign of God in history as well as the cynicism of accepting current injustice as the best we can do. Rejecting both these extremes, Niebuhr emphasizes instead the importance of creating social institutions that acknowledge and strive to mitigate the power of sin in society, especially through democratic structures that prevent any unchecked power. Democracy, he affirms, is possible because people are able to rise above their self-interest in order to work for the common good, but democracy is also necessary because all people are tempted to use unchecked power for their own self-interest.[3]

Central to Niebuhr's perspective is his emphasis on the biblical view of human history as having a meaning fulfilled beyond history. This, he argues, is a key contribution of the biblical tradition. Affirming that history has an ultimate—religious—significance discourages the escapism that refuses to take the sociopolitical challenges of our time seriously. Our institutions and the political choices we make about them really do matter! At the same time, believing that history finds its fulfillment only beyond history counters the dangerous fanaticism that considers some particular political project the final goal of history. As Niebuhr insists, no political struggle is absolute.[4]

Rejecting a simple progressive view of history, Niebuhr retrieves the often-ignored Christian eschatological symbols of the antichrist and the second coming of Christ, which he interprets as representative of the reality that good and evil both grow in history until its end. This is true, according to Niebuhr, because while human capabilities generally grow in history, every advance can be corrupted and all forms of power can be used for either good or evil.[5] As the twentieth century has made all too clear, technological progress can be directed to healing or to killing, to providing better nutrition or to devastating the environment.

A further contribution of the biblical tradition is its recognition of the dignity of the person, which must be balanced against the needs of the community. As Niebuhr contends, freedom is essential to the personal growth that allows individuals to flourish and to enrich their communities. At the same time, individual freedoms must be limited in order to safeguard the communities on which all depend.[6] It is worth noting here that Catholic social thought in the mid-twentieth century articulates a similar defense of the dignity of persons-in-community, seeking like Niebuhr to correct the extremes of both

5

Western individualism and Eastern communism.[7] For both Catholic social thought and Reinhold Niebuhr, Christianity calls for as much freedom as possible for the individual, along with as much restriction as necessary for the well-being of the community, because personal and community development are mutually dependent.

These ideas come together in Niebuhr's account of the particular challenges of globalization. Writing in the midst of the second international war in fewer than twenty-five years, Niebuhr draws attention to the fact that, already in his day, the world has become so obviously interconnected that a global community is our "final possibility and impossibility."[8] A world community is a possibility and even a necessity, he argues, because technological, communication, and economic systems now interconnect nations so thoroughly that isolationism is no longer possible (already in 1944!). We have no choice but to learn how to govern these relationships. Additionally, he observes, most ethical systems, including religious ones, have developed the moral imperative of concern for all of humanity.[9] Both ethics and economics have thus advanced to the point that global systems of justice are now indispensable.

Nevertheless, Niebuhr warns that a true world community remains an impossibility beyond our grasp. The governmental structures that would organize a just and participatory democracy on a global level, with sufficient checks and balances to limit the abuse of power, require a complex level of political organization—one that we still have not mastered three-quarters of a century after Niebuhr published this argument.[10] Furthermore, as Niebuhr insightfully reminds us, community requires a sense of common identity. Without a shared history or some particular identity to bind people together, they lack the mutual commitment that inspires people to sacrifice their own good for the greater collective good. Rational arguments are seldom sufficient to persuade people to put a global common good above the needs of themselves and the communities to which they are bound by deep ties of identity and emotion.[11] Reasoned discourse was not effective against Nazi rhetorical appeals to patriotic and emotional sentiments ("blood and soil") in Niebuhr's time, nor is a dry logic of universalism likely to stem the tide of tribalism today.[12] It is unlikely that Niebuhr would be surprised by the strong—and often violent—

passion for racial, ethnic, religious, and national identity that is rising again today in response to the twenty-first century globalization that seems to undermine the local communities to which people give their primary allegiance.

Even though religions too often reinforce these tribal loyalties, Niebuhr believes that religions can also contribute significantly to the development of an ethics of universal moral concern based on the equal dignity of all human beings.[13] Since religious traditions provide values to orient public as well as private lives, Niebuhr cautions against banning religion from the public sphere lest our politics lose its depth of meaning and orientation to the greater good of humanity.

We must not, however, overlook the very real danger of religious absolutism, since absolute claims in a religiously pluralist society (and world) will result in conflict that can only be resolved with the complete privatization of religion, removing it from political life. The solution to public religion in a pluralistic context, Niebuhr argues, is to be found in the religious humility that eschews such absolutism, recognizing instead the fallibility of all positions and so remaining open to correction from others.[14]

While many today seem to think that such humility in religious matters betrays a lack of faith, Niebuhr maintains that belief in a truly transcendent source of value, such as the infinite God of the Abrahamic traditions, leads instead to recognition of the fact that all human expressions and applications of religious values fall short of the transcendent itself. Religion ought to make political judgments more humble, Niebuhr contends, rather than less so.[15]

For Niebuhr, globalization is thus an ongoing challenge that humanity will never quite meet, which is consistent with the Christian belief that the reign of God is fully achieved only at the end, and not within, history. Jesus' crucifixion stands as a reminder to Christians that perfect love remains suffering—not triumphant—love in history.[16] Nevertheless, history does matter, and so Christians have a responsibility to commit themselves to making globalization as just as possible while avoiding the religious absolutism that refuses compromise. In contrast to the many Christians who still believe today that Christian social ethics demands an absolute purity without concession to the limitations of our real-world conditions, Niebuhr retrieves a nuanced Christian anthropology based on the recognition of sin and grace. Christian wisdom about sin and the limitations of history, he argues, provides the basis for a politics that eschews a naïve—and dangerous—perfectionism in favor of a Christian commitment to seeking the least unjust political alternatives possible.

PAWLIKOWSKI, GLOBAL ETHICS, AND CHRISTIAN ANTISEMITISM

John T. Pawlikowski was born nearly fifty years after Reinhold Niebuhr, and these two theologians differ considerably in context as well as in the focus of their thought. Niebuhr did his groundbreaking work before and during the Second World War, though he continued to write insightfully about the challenges of communist Russia and the nuclear stalemate through the 1950s and 1960s. Pawlikowski's career began after Niebuhr's ended, and Pawlikowski has concentrated on the one deeply provocative mid-century challenge that Niebuhr paid little attention to: the significance of the Shoah for Christian life and thought. Yet their differences emerge perhaps most starkly when we consider that Niebuhr, a Protestant minister, is most known for his neo-Orthodox retrieval and defense of traditional Christian doctrines (especially the doctrine of original sin), while Pawlikowski, a Catholic priest, has devoted his life to the doctrinal revisions needed to overcome the contempt for the Jews embedded in the Christian tradition.

Notwithstanding these differences, Pawlikowski builds on the Niebuhrian legacy to provide a Christian response more adequate to the ethical issues of our day, especially those raised by globalization. Since he has paid serious attention to the Nazi use of technology and bureaucracy to facilitate mass murder and genocide during the Shoah, it is not surprising that Pawlikowski agrees with Niebuhr about the need for ethical maturity to direct our growing powers away from evil and toward the good. Pawlikowski considers globalization to be an especially powerful force that poses great dangers, as well as promises considerable benefits, to humanity. As he states,

> To the extent that the globalization process enables us to break down cultural, ethnic, and religious barriers and brings us into increased human understanding and solidarity, it is a good thing. Insofar as it becomes a generator of cultural and economic hegemony by rich and powerful nations over other peoples, it deserves strong condemnation.[17]

Pawlikowski thus shares Niebuhr's general theology of history along with its consideration of ambiguity and its caution against thinking that the reign of God is a historical possibility. "We have to have some sense that we are actively contributing to the emergence of that kingdom," Pawlikowski acknowledges. Yet he further argues that the belief that God's reign will come in history and directly through our efforts "is naïve and certainly goes contrary to the data of history."[18] As Pawlikowski knows well from his study of the Shoah, there is enormous evil alongside the good, and there is no simple progress in history. Our best historical achievements are necessarily finite; the emergence of a greater injustice or oppression is an ever-present danger. For Pawlikowski as for Niebuhr, what we accomplish in history matters somehow, but not directly, to the final and necessarily posthistorical reign of God.

It is worth noting here that Pawlikowski's involvement in Jewish-Christian dialogue has made him aware of the need for a Christian theology of history that includes a theology of the land, a point David Tracy has also argued.[19] Christian thought has largely ignored the theological significance of the promised land in the Hebrew Bible. However, insofar as the Christian covenant is theologically inseparable from the Jewish covenant in which the promise of land is central, then Christians too must consider land to have some theological significance (though not necessarily the same significance it has in Jewish theology).[20] History takes place somewhere, and location is surely a part of the particularity of historical events.

It is arguable that further Christian attention to the Jewish concept of land might strengthen the Christian response to our grave environmental challenges. Pawlikowski has noted that Christianity could learn much from the rich Jewish liturgical and exegetical traditions that value nature as God's creation.[21] A theology that integrates

9

concern for the land into its account of the significance of history would surely provide a more robust foundation for a Christian celebration of nature as integral to, rather than separate from, the history of redemption. Informed by Jewish resources for interpreting the biblical heritage Christians also share, Christianity might better inspire active resistance to human abuse of nature.

Pawlikowski further agrees with Niebuhr that globalization requires a developed ethics of universal moral concern. During the Shoah, many institutions, as well as individuals, put their own concerns ahead of the survival of others outside their communities— these outsiders were considered "unfortunate expendables."[22] Pawlikowski rejects this approach and insists instead that human rights must be at the center of all religious traditions: the dignity and rights of all people, not the self-preservation of the religious community or tradition, is the fundamental concern of all religions.[23] Only then will religious traditions be clearly and consistently forces for global unity, working together to direct the economic and technological forces of globalization toward a true world community rather than contributing to further tribal divisions.

A full religious commitment to the centrality of human rights would also strengthen awareness that there are some things we simply must not do, certain moral standards that we must not fall below. This point may be especially important now that the current global economy has become so massive that it seems beyond anyone's control.[24] If effective resistance is felt to be impossible, then it is all the more tempting to acquiesce in oppressive economic structures (think of the consumption of luxury goods likely produced by slave labor). Are we not often inclined to respond like the German businessmen who disagreed with Hitler's genocidal plans but, as Pawlikowski reminds us, cooperated with his government all the same, shrugging and musing to themselves, "What else can I do?" Pawlikowski insists that we must learn instead to ask ourselves, "What must I never do?"[25] Religious traditions focusing on essential human rights, he argues, could and should be crucial sources of moral formation, training people to recognize the limits of what may be accepted as expedient. This might also prevent an acknowledgment of the need for Niebuhrian compromises from being used to justify a self-serving capitulation to injustice.

Pawlikowski also shares Niebuhr's awareness that efforts to develop a world community are hampered by the lack of a unifying shared identity. Pawlikowski, however, suggests that advances can be made toward greater (though not perfect) global community through international religious communities. To be sure, religious communities remain particular; yet Pawlikowski (who has considerable experience with global Catholicism) argues that international religious bodies such as the Catholic Church could play an important role in forging transnational bonds of support.[26] While this would not be the full identification with a world community that Niebuhr has argued is ideal but not possible, surely any strengthening of community across national boundaries is a step in the right direction.

At the same time, faith communities function at the grassroots level. This makes it possible for religious institutions to channel global resources to local communities in need, particularly since religious leaders may have greater credibility and better knowledge of the needs at the local level. Indeed, Pawlikowski argues that the best hope for economic justice in this global economy at this time is through partnerships between international organizations and faith-based communities.[27]

If international religious organizations like the Catholic Church are to play the significant global roles that Pawlikowski thus defends (and that in many cases they already are playing), we need to consider whether such religious organizations must develop the checks and balances that Niebuhr contends are essential to avoid corruption. Though further exploration of this point is beyond the scope of this chapter, certainly the recent pedophilia crisis in the Catholic Church suggests that Niebuhr's argument for checks on all forms of power applies to religious institutions as well as state governments.

Another issue of religious reform, and one that is central to Pawlikowski's work, is the importance of overcoming the violence within religious traditions. While religious institutions have at times explicitly incited violence, they have often implicitly encouraged violence through the use of religious rhetoric that demeans or even demonizes other people. Religious traditions can do much good (especially in inspiring people to rise above self-interest for the common good, as Niebuhr argues). However, without significant soul-searching and reform, religious traditions may also do much harm, even to the point of "softening up a society for genocide," as Pawlikowski points out.[28]

This is why Pawlikowski maintains (correctly) that involvement in religious dialogue and in overcoming antisemitism are central to developing a Christianity adequate to the challenges of globalization.[29] Interreligious dialogue encourages global concern and cooperation by fostering relationships, overcoming stereotypes, and increasing appreciation for the inherent value of those others from whom we are willing to learn. Of course, this means that we need to engage real people who are members of other religions, and not merely encounter their religious traditions as disembodied texts. This is especially the case with Judaism, which is too often reduced to the Hebrew Bible, as though the Jewish tradition ended with the coming of Jesus.

In his commitment to interreligious dialogue, Pawlikowski is again building on one of Niebuhr's insights. As discussed earlier, Niebuhr considers religious humility, especially as expressed in a willingness to learn from others, to be indispensable if religion is to contribute to political values-formation in pluralistic contexts. As both Pawlikowski and Niebuhr recognize, religious humility about our finite and fallible judgments follows from—rather than denies—faith in a transcendent God. Pawlikowski exemplifies this religious humility in his willingness to learn from others in interreligious dialogue. In doing so, he also demonstrates the value of others who, in their diversity of perspectives, contribute to our human quest for greater truth.

In addition to his engagement in religious dialogue, Pawlikowski has also devoted his career and impressive intellectual energy to overcoming Christian supersessionism and contempt for Jews. The Shoah starkly revealed the inherent violence of the anti-Jewish ideas deeply rooted in Christianity. Even while it is important to recognize that the Nazi ideology was not Christian, we must also acknowledge that Nazi claims about and treatment of Jews mirror many ideas and practices in the long, sad, and violent history of Christian contempt for Jews.[30] Ideas, as the Shoah reminds us, have consequences!

Alas, overcoming Christian antisemitism is no easy task. Contempt for Jews is embedded in classic Christian texts, including the New Testament and the writings of many of the most influential early Christian thinkers. Reading the gospel depictions of Jesus as the Messiah who fulfilled Jewish prophecy, Christians commonly conclude that Judaism is now outdated, replaced by Christianity. When the Gospels portray the Pharisees as legalistic, hypocritical, and blind to the true meaning of their own Jewish faith, many presume this description applies to all Jews who continue to observe the Torah. Perhaps most damaging, the Gospels' emphasis on the responsibility of Jewish authorities (or simply "the Jews") for the Roman crucifixion of Jesus renders the Jewish people as not merely ignorant but actually evil, willfully and murderously opposing God. Even though many churches have officially repudiated the supersessionist teaching that God has taken the covenant from the Jews, these scriptural and traditional christological teachings continue to reinforce contempt for the Jews as hypocritical opponents of God who cling to an empty faith.[31]

Pawlikowski is quite right to identify anti-Judaism as a significant barrier to an adequate Christian social ethics. The global challenges we face today require that we act with concern for the dignity of all persons, and that we see diversity (including diversity of religions) as a potential source of mutual enrichment. We cannot build the world community Niebuhr recognized as essential in a global age without rooting out Christian assumptions that Judaism is an exhausted if not morally bankrupt religious tradition, one that is often identified by church fathers as the source of major Christian heresies and, as David Nirenberg has shown, is considered by later Western thinkers as a threat to Western civilization itself.[32]

Some of the anti-Judaism in the New Testament can be overcome by better translations and education, according to Pawlikowski.[33] However, constructing a Christology that is truly Christian without being supersessionist is not so easy. Drawing on the resources of Paul's later epistles and the Gospel of John, Pawlikowski defends an "incarnational Christology" as an alternative to the prophecy/fulfillment Christologies of the Synoptic Gospels. Instead of continuing to distort the meaning of the Hebrew Bible so that its texts predict

Jesus of Nazareth, an incarnational Christology emphasizes that Jesus reveals God's unity with humanity.[34] This is a specifically Christian revelation (though it builds on aspects of first-century Judaism) that reinforces the dignity of each person as somehow part of a God who has united Godself to humanity. An incarnational Christology thus supports a Christian focus on universal human rights, and so is a key part of the kind of Christianity Pawlikowski has argued is essential in this global age.[35] Interestingly, Pawlikowski finds this incarnational approach to Christology grounding a Christian commitment to human rights in the writings of Pope John Paul II (especially in his 1979 encyclical *Redemptor Hominis*).[36]

An incarnational Christology as outlined by Pawlikowski allows for the distinctiveness of the revelation in Jesus without denying the ongoing validity of Judaism and of the Jews themselves.[37] Jesus did not bring the awaited Jewish messianic age, as a simple look at the world around us will show. Jewish hopes are not yet fulfilled—and neither are Christian hopes, as the doctrine of the second coming reminds us.

Instead of the Christian covenant replacing the Jewish one, then, Pawlikowski defends a two-covenant approach along the lines developed by James Parkes.[38] In this perspective, both covenants remain valid, and both religions are part of the divine plan. Indeed, the two covenants are mutually complementary, since the Christian covenant emphasizes the dignity of the person, while the Jewish covenant focuses on the importance of community. Together they ensure that the value of the individual is balanced against the needs of the community, a point that Niebuhr also emphasizes, as we saw earlier. Serious engagement with Judaism, as Pawlikowski maintains, can thus provide a helpful correction to the Christian tendency toward individualism.[39]

Dialogue with the more communally oriented Jewish tradition can also help Christians negotiate the relationship between justice and love, another concern that Pawlikowski shares with Niebuhr. A major part of Niebuhr's "Christian realism" is his argument that, even though justice is oriented to and completed by love, the infinite demands of love generally surpass what is possible in society. Instead, we must seek to achieve the best justice possible relative to the competing rights and needs of multiple parties. As Niebuhr notes, "As soon as a third person is introduced into the relation even the most perfect love requires a rational estimate of conflicting needs and interests."[40]

Pawlikowski similarly rejects the tendency to identify Christian ethics with love and Jewish ethics with laws, since this dichotomy distorts both traditions. He also criticizes overly general Christian ethics focused on appeals to love and freedom (especially freedom from the law); he insists instead that "a notion of freedom that does not bring us directly into the realm of concrete, human living, as the Torah process does, will prove terribly ineffective in the long run in terms of the actual realization of freedom."[41] The complexity of seeking justice in a global age surely requires all the practical wisdom we can muster and, as Pawlikowski reminds us, the Jewish tradition has much to teach Christians about rigorous practical reasoning.

Niebuhr's emphasis on seeking imperfect justice rather than perfect love has sometimes been criticized as a failure to recognize the power of God's redemptive love in history.[42] I believe this is a misunderstanding of his argument, since Niebuhr's point is not that God's love is irrelevant to, or removed from, history but rather that divine love is redemptive in history as a suffering rather than a triumphant love.[43] Pawlikowski likewise argues for replacing the idea of an all-powerful, commanding God with the concept of a compelling, vulnerable God who suffers with humanity. For Pawlikowski, this compelling God who seeks not to suppress human freedom but to inspire humanity to resist injustice is more appropriate to the experience of the Shoah as well as to our experience of current human powers for good and evil.[44] Recognizing that God suffers in the victims of history surely stands as a reminder of the dignity of each person, and that there are some things "we must never do."

CONCLUSION

Humanity faces unprecedented challenges in this twenty-first century. We have no choice but to learn to negotiate our new global reality and, lest we descend into a war of each against all, we must figure out how to direct the enormous power at our disposal for the good of the whole human community and the planet on which all of us depend.

Reinhold Niebuhr retrieves valuable Christian insights for this global age, especially in his articulation of a theology of history that recognizes human limitations, acknowledges the reality of sin, and encourages Christians to work for the imperfect justice that is possible rather than to adhere to an irresponsible perfectionism in society. Niebuhr's work also, of course, reminds us that we are deceiving ourselves if we fail to recognize the injustice in all of our institutions and efforts for justice. Christianity has much more to offer the complex process of constructing a more just globalization than the general platitudes about love and humanity that are too easily rejected as unhelpful or—worse—cited to cover self-aggrandizing oppression by dominant groups.

Yet Niebuhr does not go far enough in critiquing the systemic distortions within Christianity. John Pawlikowski has shown that Christians must question their classic texts and rethink their fundamental beliefs to excise the rhetorical violence implicit therein. If Christianity is to contribute to a global peace with justice and dignity for all humanity, Christians must first cast out the plank of anti-Judaism from their own tradition. Pawlikowski's incarnational Christology is particularly promising in this regard, as it is grounded in Scripture, upholds the specificity of Christian revelation, and affirms the dignity of all humanity without denigrating Judaism (or other religions).[45] Of course, care must be taken to ensure that this incarnational Christology does not emphasize the value of humanity to the point of denying the intrinsic worth of nature, an issue about which Pawlikowski himself is well aware.

Religious dialogue, as a practice and not merely a theory, is especially crucial to this global age. While Niebuhr acknowledges the necessity of such dialogue, Pawlikowski's work exemplifies, and benefits from, actual engagement in interreligious dialogue. It is through the insights gained in dialogue with Jewish scholars, for example, that Pawlikowski is able to make concrete suggestions not only for overcoming Christian anti-Judaism but also for developing a theology of the land and liturgical celebrations of nature to strengthen

Christian resistance to environmental degradation. Notwithstanding the importance of these insights, interreligious dialogue is of value in itself, as Pawlikowski knows, and as an example of how to further unite (rather than divide) humanity by fostering relations of mutual respect across differences.

Both Niebuhr and Pawlikowski hold out the hope that religion, and especially Christianity, will be a force for peace and justice in history despite the ever-present temptations toward violence and oppression. The revelation of a compelling and vulnerable God who is present in suffering (including the suffering environment) may be key to Christian efforts in this global age to ensure that our enormous power alleviates rather than causes greater suffering.

Notes

1. John T. Pawlikowski, "Creating an Ethical Context for Globalization: Catholic Perspectives in an Interreligious Context," *Journal of Ecumenical Studies* 42, no. 3 (Summer 2007): 372.

2. David Brooks, "Obama, Gospel and Verse," *New York Times*, April 26, 2007, http://www.nytimes.com/2007/04/26/opinion/26brooks.html.

3. Reinhold Niebuhr, *The Children of Light and the Children of Darkness: A Vindication of Democracy and a Critique of Its Traditional Defense* (New York: Charles Scribner's Sons, 1944), esp. xiii. Interestingly, Robin Lovin has argued for the continued relevance of Niebuhr's Christian realism on the grounds that our current time needs less a Niebuhrian caution against the excesses of political ideals and more expansion of our hope and political imagination, which he finds also in Niebuhr's approach. See Robin W. Lovin, *Reinhold Niebuhr and Christian Realism* (New York: Cambridge University Press, 1995), 244–48.

4. Niebuhr develops this argument throughout his corpus. See especially Reinhold Niebuhr, *Faith and History: A Comparison of Christian and Modern Views of History* (New York: C. Scribner's Sons, 1949) and his *The Nature and Destiny of Man: A Christian Interpretation*, vol. 2, *Human Destiny* (New York: Charles Scribner's Sons, 1943), 287–301.

5. See especially Reinhold Niebuhr, *The Nature and Destiny of Man: A Christian Interpretation*, vol. 1, *Human Nature* (New York: Charles Scribner's Sons, 1941), ix; and Niebuhr, *Human Destiny*, 316–19.

6. Niebuhr, *Children of Light*, esp. 54–55, 63–64, 73.

7. Michael J. Himes and Kenneth R. Himes, *Fullness of Faith: The Public Significance of Theology* (New York: Paulist, 1993), 36–46.

8. Niebuhr, *Children of Light*, 187.

9. Niebuhr, *Children of Light*, 154.

10. Niebuhr, *Children of Light*, 177–80.

11. Niebuhr, *Children of Light*, 165–66.

12. Pawlikowski develops this point in his "God: The Foundational Question after the Holocaust," in *Good and Evil after Auschwitz: Ethical Implications for Today*, ed. Jack Bemporad, John Pawlikowski, and Joseph Sievers (Hoboken, NJ: KTAV Pub. House, 2000), 62.

13. Niebuhr, *Children of Light*, 155–56. See also the recent defense of Niebuhr's approach as the basis for a religious pluralism that can better negotiate the tensions of American public life in Tony L. Richie, "A Politics of Pluralism in American Democracy: Reinhold Niebuhr's Christian Realism in a Post-9/11 World," *Journal of Ecumenical Studies* 45, no. 3 (Summer 2010): 471–92.

14. Niebuhr, *Children of Light*, esp. 137, 150–51.

15. Niebuhr, *Children of Light*, 134–35.

16. Niebuhr, *Human Destiny*, 49.

17. Pawlikowski, "Creating an Ethical Context," 363.

18. Alan L. Berger, David Patterson, with David P. Gushee, John Pawlikowski, and John K. Roth, *Jewish-Christian Dialogue: Drawing Honey from the Rock* (St. Paul, MN: Paragon House, 2008), 229.

19. John T. Pawlikowski, "Land as an Issue in Christian-Jewish Dialogue," *Crosscurrents* 59, no. 2 (June 2009): 204.

20. Pawlikowski, "Land as an Issue in Christian-Jewish Dialogue," 205. See also John Pawlikowski, *Jesus Israel*, 95–97.

21. John T. Pawlikowski, "The Challenge of *Tikkun Olam* for Jews and Christians," in *Seeing Judaism Anew: Christianity's Sacred Obligation*, ed. Mary C. Boys (Lanham, MD: Rowman & Littlefield Publishers, 2005), 234.

22. Pawlikowski, "Challenge of *Tikkun Olam*."

23. John T. Pawlikowski, "The Significance of the Christian-Jewish Dialogue and Holocaust Studies for Catholic Ethics," *Political Theology* 13, no. 4 (2012): 455.

24. Pawlikowski, "The Significance of the Christian-Jewish Dialogue," 454.

25. Pawlikowski, "Challenge of *Tikkun Olam*," 234.

26. Pawlikowski, "Creating an Ethical Context," 370.

27. Pawlikowski, "Creating an Ethical Context."

28. Pawlikowski, "Creating an Ethical Context," 366.

29. John T. Pawlikowski, *WATSA Christ. Jewish*, 146. See also John T. Pawlikowsi, *Christ Light*, 151–54.

30. John T. Pawlikowksi, "Christology after the Holocaust," *Encounter* 59, no. 3 (1998): 347–48.

31. See especially John T. Pawlikowski, *Catech. Prej.*, 75–86.

32. For an especially developed version of this perspective, see David Nirenberg, *Anti-Judaism: The Western Tradition* (New York: W.W. Norton, 2013). See also Rosemary Radford Ruether, *Faith and Fratricide: The Theological Roots of Anti-Semitism* (New York: Seabury, 1974).

33. Pawlikowski, *Catech. Prej.*, 87–114.

34. Pawlikowski, *Jesus Israel*, 70–87. See also Pawlikowski, *Christ Light*, 108–20.

35. Pawlikowski, *Christ Light*, 118.

36. Pawlikowski, *Christ Light*, 120.

37. See also the argument developed in the more recent John T. Pawlikowski, *Restating Church's Rel.*, esp. 95–99.

38. Pawlikowski, *Restating Church's Rel.*, 19–20.

39. Pawlikowski, *Restating Church's Rel.*, 121–23. See also Pawlikowski, *Jesus Israel*, 88–91.

40. Niebuhr, *Human Destiny*, 248.

41. Pawlikowski, *Jesus Israel*, 91. See also Pawlikowski, "Challenge of *Tikkun Olam*," 228–30.

42. For a concise description of the opposing positions on Niebuhr's account of God's role in history, see Kevin Carnahan, "Reading Reinhold Niebuhr against Himself Again: On Theological Language and Divine Action," *International Journal of Systematic Theology* 18, no. 2 (April 2016): 192–94.

43. See, e.g., Niebuhr, *Human Nature*, 142–43.

44. Pawlikowski, "Christology after the Holocaust," 359–61. See also Pawlikowski, "God," 53–66.

45. It is worth noting that others have argued that it is precisely the lack of a truly incarnational Christology that prevents Niebuhr's theological ethics from being an adequate Christian perspective for today. See especially the astute analysis in Paul R. Kolbet, "Rethinking the Christological

Foundations of Reinhold Niebuhr's Christian Realism," *Modern Theology* 26, no. 3 (July 2010): 437–65. For a somewhat different interpretation of Niebuhr that nevertheless agrees that his thought needs a more robust Christology, see John Marsden, "Reinhold Niebuhr and the Ethics of Christian Realism," *International Journal of Public Theology* 4 (2010): 483–501.

CHAPTER TWO

PAWLIKOWSKI'S CHRISTOLOGY AS A CHALLENGE TO REFORMED CHRISTOLOGY

―∞―

Robert A. Cathey

INTRODUCTION

Some Presbyterians in North America see our theology as more "reformed," liberal, or progressive than official Roman Catholic theology.[1] For example, take issues like the following:

- Ordination of women and GLBTQI candidates to church offices

- Marriage of gay and lesbian couples in congregations

- Embrace of critical biblical exegesis in preparation to preach and teach

- Providing leadership for ecumenical and interreligious movements

- Revising the doctrines of creation, providence, and eschatology in light of new scientific knowledge

A very important exception (among others) to this common Presbyterian self-understanding is the adoption of *Nostra Aetate* at Vatican II. In 1965, official Roman Catholic theology leapt ahead of other forms of Christian theology by embracing new understandings of Jews and Judaism in ways that Presbyterians have, for the most part, not officially taught in their confessions of faith.

This is a challenge to the self-understanding of some Presbyterians. Whereas Roman Catholics have moved ahead in a new kind of reformation of church doctrine and practice that has changed many for the better, some Presbyterians seem to fall behind in a pre–Vatican II world of Christian superiority to Jews and Judaism.[2]

My wager is that Pawlikowski's revisionary Christology provides a challenge to Reformed Christology whether Presbyterian and Reformed denominations adopt it or not. Furthermore, Reformed theologians can also provide constructive criticism for Pawlikowski's project without diminishing its impact for Christian-Jewish relations.

But why should Reformed theologians care about Pawlikowski's Christology? In conversation John has spoken with me about his indebtedness to Reinhold Niebuhr's theology and social ethics, which he studied at the University of Chicago Divinity School in the 1960s. There is an empirical dimension to his theological method and a return to history in light of the Holocaust that resonates with some Reformed theologians—for example, his use of historical Jesus studies as a significant element of christological revision. Certainly, the centrality of revision in the light of history for his theological method, and in the Reformed conviction that "the church Reformed is ever reforming," signifies a potential openness to revising inherited Christologies, be they Catholic or Reformed. Reformed theology, in partial distinction from Luther's theology and some other Protestant theologies, has more fully included the Hebrew Bible and its primary symbols of God's activity in terms of creation, covenant, law, commandment, election, peoplehood, sanctification, and eschatology. When Pawlikowski seeks the renewal of Catholic theology in attention to both the Tanakh ("Old Testament") and history of Jews and Judaism since biblical times, he offers an implicit challenge to Reformed theology. In light of his theological writings, Reformed theologians could give greater attention to the differences (and similarities) between Reformed uses of biblical symbols like covenant and their meanings for Jews since the parting of the synagogue and the church in early Christianity.

A "PERSONAL" CHRISTOLOGICAL "JOURNEY"

A survey of Pawlikowski's writings since the 1970s shows that Christology has been the most creative locus of his theological labors.[3] His essay "Christology and the Jewish-Christian Dialogue" summarizes his convictions about the person and work of Christ, and how Christian understandings of this doctrine should change in light of the Holocaust and *Nostra Aetate*. In this section, I summarize Pawlikowski's Christology in the form of theses for discussion.

I arranged Pawlikowski's Christology into five preliminary theses and six core christological convictions, along with related qualifications. Other arrangements might be offered, but these articulate in his own words what I find to be his essential affirmations.

PRELIMINARY THESIS 1: "If Jews are now seen as remaining in a covenantal relationship with God after Christ, then Christological statement today needs significant reformulation. But it must be a reformulation that protects a continued universal dimension for the actions of Christ."[4]

PRELIMINARY THESIS 2: "There will be no final resolution of the Christological question in the Christian-Jewish context until Christians fully acknowledge the Jewish 'No' to Christianity's original messianic proclamation as a positive contribution to the understanding of biblical revelation."[5]

Pawlikowski seeks to retire the prophetic-fulfillment type of Christology one finds in the canonical Gospels (e.g., Matthew's Gospel) and other New Testament writings. This retirement poses a challenge not only to Christology but also to most of Christian liturgy. John has spoken about the difficulty of attending Christian services of worship in the season of Advent when the lectionary pairs up "Old Testament" prophecies with fulfillments in the birth narratives about Jesus, because his life, death, and resurrection were not the fulfillment of Jewish hopes for a messianic figure to redeem Israel. Therefore, Christians are not distinguished from Jews as the people who recognize Jesus as the promised Messiah while Jews are blinded by the sins of their ancestors.

PRELIMINARY THESIS 3: "Jesus' uniqueness lay in his making God more 'transparent' [Paul van Buren's term]....A focus on the incarnation offers the best option for developing a Christology that allows for continued covenantal inclusion of the Jewish People."[6]

PRELIMINARY THESIS 4: "The continuing link to the Jewish people in Christian self-identity involves seeing Judaism as important not only for interpreting Jesus' specific teachings but also for the basic theological understanding of the Christ Event as well. The permanent link to Judaism remains a constant check against the ever present gnostic tendencies in Christological interpretation."[7]

PRELIMINARY THESIS 5: "The challenge in Christology is to link together interiority and history."[8]

Pawlikowski faces here a challenge to all modern Christology: What is the relation of the Jesus of history (an object of historical research carried out by Christians, Jews, secular scholars et al.) to the Christ of faith (the "risen Sovereign" who encounters Christians in the proclamation of the gospel, the Eucharist, and forms of spirituality)? Or, what is the relation between the human named "Jesus of Nazareth" and the figure "Jesus Christ" whom Christians worship as "Sovereign and Savior"?

Pawlikowski's Core Christological Vision:

THESIS 1: "From a historical perspective the resounding Jewish 'no' to Jesus represents a much needed, continuing source for what I would term 'Christological purification' within Christianity.... Given the depth of the corruption of Christology, something we continue to see evident in newer, supposedly 'progressive' forms of Christological expression, this burden will remain for the foreseeable future."[9]

THESIS 2: "Any articulation of Christology in light of the relationship with Judaism must regard the Hebrew Scriptures, the Jewish literature of the Second Temple period, and later postbiblical Judaism as indispensable resources for understanding the significance of the Christ Event....Any attempt to build a Christology solely on the New Testament represents a truncated version of Jesus' actual message for humanity."[10]

THESIS 3: "Christological consciousness within the church represented a gradual development, not instant revelation."[11]

THESIS 4: "Incarnational Christology is the best approach to understanding the Christ Event that leaves legitimate theological space for Judaism."[12]

THESIS 5: "What ultimately came to be recognized with clarity for the first time through the ministry and person of Jesus was profoundly how integral humanity was to divine biography. This is turn implied that each human person somehow shares in divinity. Christ is the theological symbol that the Church selected to try to express this reality....This humanity existed in the Godhead from the very beginning....We can say with Paul that God did not become man in Jesus. God always was man: humanity was an integral part of the Godhead from the beginning. The Christ Event was crucial, however, for the manifestation of this reality to the world....The Christ Event in this perspective gave greater transparency to the human-divine link."[13]

> QUALIFICATION 5.1: This "vision" of the Christ Event "does not mean to equate God with the totality of humanity....A gulf remains in my perspective between God and the human community that is forever impassable."[14]
>
> QUALIFICATION 5.2: "Humankind remains equally conscious of the fact that this God is the ultimate Creator of the life that is shared with men and women as a gift."[15]
>
> QUALIFICATION 5.3: "Nor does it mean that there was not a uniqueness about the manner in which humanity and divinity were united in Jesus. Humanity could never have come to the full awareness of the ultimate link between itself and God without the express revelation occasioned by the Christ Event. While

this event will allow us to experience a new closeness with the Creator God, our humanity will never share the same intimacy with the divine nature that existed in the person of Jesus."[16]

THESIS 6: The "reign of God" is central to Pawlikowski's "vision" of Christ, who makes "transparent the full linkage between humanity and divinity. It is the revelation of this linkage that makes possible the proclamation that the kingdom is already in our midst, even if not yet fully realized. The presence of the kingdom can be perceived within both human consciousness and human history."[17]

> QUALIFICATION 6.1: "The new transparency with respect to divine presence that I regard as the core of the Christ Event's revelation should not be taken as a full and complete vision of human salvation by itself." Alongside this vision stands "the absolute centrality of the immersion of God in history and creation, the hallmark of the revelation at the core of the Jewish covenantal tradition." These two "core" visions continue "to play off each other, both 'blessed' by God...until the end of days. Both cores bear a universal significance in terms of the body of humanity."[18]

PAWLIKOWSKI'S CHALLENGE TO REFORMED CHRISTOLOGY

For the global Reformed family of churches, our theology seeks to be faithful to Scripture, past ecumenical and Reformed creeds and confessions of faith, and to the most important challenges facing Christian churches today. Creeds and confessions of faith (and the church councils that produce them) are viewed as fallible, so the authority of these documents are not elevated above Scripture. As already noted, one theme shared among many of these denominations is *ecclesia reformata sed semper reformanda*, which is Latin for "the church reformed, but always being reformed."

Some themes and issues in Reformed Christology include the following:

- The person and work of Christ should not be falsely separated (e.g., Calvin wrote of Christ's threefold office as Prophet, Priest, and King)

- The influence of the Nicene (325 CE) and Chalcedonian Creeds (451 CE) with the later creed's emphasis on the unity of Christ's persons in two natures, human and divine

- In modern times, the recognition of differences between the more functional christological languages of the New Testament in comparison to the more metaphysical terminology of the ecumenical creeds and some sixteenth- and seventeenth-century Protestant confessions—thus the distinction between Christologies "from above" that proceed from God's side of the divine/human relationship and Christologies "from below" that begin from the human side of the relationship with the historical Jesus.[19]

Given the global expansion of the Reformed churches over the centuries, today there is a wide variety of different Reformed Christologies responding to different cultural contexts and spanning the theological spectrum from classic to the revisionary.[20]

Among the challenges to Reformed churches and their Christologies today is whether they have had their own *Nostra Aetate* moments in theology comparable to the revolution in Catholic-Jewish relations at Vatican II. On one hand, the ecumenical creeds and early Reformed confessions left the teachings of Christian anti-Judaism in place without revision. On the other hand, the interest among some Reformed theologians since the nineteenth century in Christology "from below," the impact of historical-critical study of Scripture in Presbyterian-Reformed institutions, and the interest in ecumenism and interfaith relations creates an opening to hear the challenge of Pawlikowski's Christology.

In the next three sections I bring Pawlikowski into conversation with three modern Reformed theologians, Karl Barth, Peter Hodgson, and George Hunsinger.

IN CONVERSATION WITH KARL BARTH

Without equating their theological visions or arguing for some form of influence, I call attention to a well-known lecture given by Karl Barth in 1956, translated under the title "The Humanity of God" (in German: "Die Menschlichkeit Gottes").[21] There are important points of convergence and points of divergence between Barth's Christology and Pawlikowski's. In this section, I concentrate on two possible points of convergence.

The title of Barth's lecture referred to "God's relation to and turning toward man."[22] In it, he compared his theme of "the humanity of God" to his bold proclamation of God as "wholly other" in his *The Epistle to the Romans* (1919; 1921). In the nineteenth-century Protestant theology in which Barth was educated, theological reflection took as its subject matter human forms of piety and religiosity, not God in God's deity. The political and social crises of World War I were the occasion for Barth to discover as a young pastor that the Bible's theme is "God's *deity*," which means "God's independence and particular character...God's absolutely unique existence, might, and initiative, above all, in His relation to man."[23]

However, Barth criticized the rhetorical excess of his earlier theology that seemed "to make *God* great for a change at the cost of *man*."[24] The "wholly other" God of his early writings "showed greater similarity to the God of the philosophers than to the deity of the God of Abraham, Isaac, and Jacob."[25] The corrective to this idea of God is found in the Bible's revelation of God's covenant partnership with humanity: "who God is and what He is like in His deity He proves and reveals not in a vacuum as a divine being-for-Himself, but precisely and authentically in the fact that He exists, speaks, and acts as the *partner* of man, though of course as the absolutely superior partner."[26] God is free to create and redeem humanity for partnership with God. In fact, "it is precisely God's *deity* which, rightly understood, includes his *humanity*."[27]

Barth reframed the deity and humanity of God, and the meaning of human being, in the context of Christology: "In Jesus Christ there is no isolation of man from God or of God from man....Jesus Christ is in His one Person, as true God, *man*'s loyal partner, and as true *man*, God's."[28] Following terms reminiscent of the Creed of Chalcedon, Barth wrote,

> [Christ] is both [humanity and God's partner], without their being confused but also without their being divided; He is wholly the one and wholly the other.[29]...[Jesus Christ] is in His Person the covenant in its fullness, the Kingdom of heaven which is at hand, in which God speaks and man hears...exactly in this way, Jesus Christ, as this Mediator and Reconciler between God and man, is also the *Revealer* of them both.

So for Barth the proper theological question is, "Who and what is God in *Jesus Christ*?"[30] Likewise, theological knowledge about humanity is disclosed in the biblical witnesses to Jesus.

According to Barth, the Bible attests to a sequence and order of priority in its testimony to Jesus: "In the existence of Jesus Christ, the fact that God speaks, gives, orders, comes absolutely first—that man hears, receives, obeys, can and must follow this first act....As the Son of God and not otherwise, Jesus Christ is the Son of Man. This sequence is irreversible."[31] Thus he spoke of God in Christ as "this concrete deity," not a "universal deity" open to conceptual discovery by human inquiry alone.[32]

This "concrete" God disclosed in Jesus embodies loving freedom.

> God's high freedom in Jesus Christ is His freedom for *love*....God's deity is thus no prison in which He can exist only in and for Himself. It is rather His freedom to be in and for Himself but also with and for us, to assert but also to sacrifice Himself...not only judge but also Himself the judged, not only man's eternal king but also his brother in time. And all that without in the slightest forfeiting His deity.[33]

In the light of Jesus Christ, "God's deity does not exclude but includes His *humanity*."[34] In fact, "His deity *encloses humanity in itself.*" The revelation of God in Christ means "that God does not exist without man."[35]

This divine cohumanity does not emerge out of God's "need" for a "partner" to realize Godself in the world. It is rather a matter of who God has eternally willed to be for us in Jesus Christ:

> In this divinely free volition and election, in this sover-eign decision (the ancients said, in His decree), God is *human*. His free affirmation of man, His free concern for him, His free substitution for him—this is God's human-ity....Is it not true that in Jesus Christ, as He is attested in the Holy Scripture, genuine deity includes in itself genu-ine humanity?[36]

Here Barth invoked a mirror metaphor for the knowledge of the humanity of God: "In the mirror of this humanity of Jesus Christ the humanity of God enclosed in His deity reveals itself."[37]

Barth drew out five consequences from this revealed knowledge of God, two of which I highlight here. The first is the most well-known passage from this lecture, and shows the ethical consequence of Barth's Christology:

> On the basis of the eternal will of God we have to think of *every human being*, even the oddest, most villainous or miserable, as one to whom Jesus Christ is Brother and God is Father; and we have to deal with him on this assump-tion....On the basis of the knowledge of the humanity of God no other attitude to any kind of fellow man is possi-ble. It is identical with the practical acknowledgement of his human rights and his human dignity. To deny it to him would be for us to renounce having Jesus Christ as Brother and God as Father.[38]

This is one of the most important points of convergence between Barth's Christology and Pawlikowski's ethics. This consequence undermines the foundation of every form of racism, xenophobia, antisemitism, and ideology that divides humanity into privileged and disinherited groups, factions, tribes, and nations, and that corrupt the life of the churches.

The fourth consequence takes up our awareness that human culture testifies to a different understanding of our being. Rather than humanity as the responsive partner of God, history shows that "man is *not* good but rather a downright monster."[39] We find in ourselves and others the evidence of rebellion, sloth, and hypocrisy.[40] In spite of the godlessness of our human-isms, the "humanity of God" proclaims a different ultimate perspective on our being. For according to Barth's account of the doctrine of election in the light of Christ, on behalf of sinful humankind (not merely for Christians), Jesus underwent God's judgment of our sinfulness on the cross, and God's vindication in the resurrection. Finding such good news in the doctrine of election had provoked Barth's critics. They said he taught the heresy of salvific universalism. Barth replied, "We have no theological right to set any sort of limits to the loving-kindness of God which has appeared in Jesus Christ. Our theological duty is to see and understand it as being still greater than we had seen before."[41] This is another point where Barth's Christology and Pawlikowski's critique of Christian triumphalism aimed at Judaism and other religions appear as potential partners.

IN CONVERSATION WITH PETER HODGSON

When Pawlikowski emphasizes "seeing history and human consciousness as profoundly intertwined," he notes, "Call me an old Hegelian here if you want."[42] Perhaps no contemporary Reformed theologian in the English-language world is more closely associated with Hegel than Peter Hodgson.[43] In his one-volume constructive theology, he takes up Jewish-Christian dialogue in the chapter on Christology. He credits Pawlikowski with the "most ambitious attempt [as of 1994]" to work through the question, "whether we can allow for 'significant new experiences of God to come through Christ' without falling into a 'supersessionary' posture."[44] Pawlikowski engages the dilemma: "On the one hand, Christians can no longer claim that Jesus Christ has fulfilled the Jewish messianic prophecies or inaugurated the messianic age; while on the other hand, if no unique features are recognized in the revelation in Christ, Christianity would have no claim to being a major world religion."[45] How does Pawlikowski respond?

According to Hodgson, first Pawlikowski emphasizes Jesus' continuity with the Judaism of his day by linking "Jesus very closely with Pharisaic Judaism....Jesus furthered, indeed radicalized, the reforming tendencies present in Pharisaism, and many of the characteristic features of his message were already germinally present in Pharisaism."[46] Second, Pawlikowski elaborates the "uniqueness of Jesus in terms of a revised theology of incarnation" in ways that Hodgson finds "both suggestive and puzzling."[47] The "suggestive" side he locates in Pawlikowski's claim that "what ultimately came to be recognized with clarity for the first time through the ministry and person of Jesus was how profoundly integral humanity was to the self-definition of God."[48] But Hodgson is puzzled by Pawlikowski's "claim that the Christ-event represents a culmination of the process of creation, 'in which a part of the humanity of the Godhead broke out into a separate, though not fully separated existence.'"[49] For Hodgson, Pawlikowski's revised Christology results in "a mystical identity of the divine and human that goes beyond the possibilities inherent in Judaism."[50] Hodgson agrees with Peter Haas and Rosemary Ruether's critique of this revised Christology. According to them, Pawlikowski's

> suggestion that Pharisaism is the group that has "seeded" Christianity implies "that while Christianity is thus the mature result of the seeding, Pharisaism (read Judaism?) is but the prior seed." In other words, Christians tend to think of Judaism as locked into a permanently archaic stage and do not really relate to it as a living, changing religion.[51]

This leaves Hodgson with the question whether it is possible "to recognize a *difference* between Judaism and Christianity that does not become supersessionist."[52]

This leads up to Hodgson's overall critique of Pawlikowski's Christology:

[Pawlikowski's] version of incarnation doctrine, as much as his interpretation of Pharisaism, subverts his intentions. He holds onto the *hapax* [once and for all], stressing the ontologically unique and miraculous union of God and humanity through the incarnation of the "humanity in the Godhead," the divine Son or Logos, in a "separate existence," that of Jesus of Nazareth. A more plural and social understanding of the incarnation, one that recognizes a multiplicity of shapes in which God appears, seems more promising. The shape of Christ itself is not one but many, and it does not supersede other shapes. Should we then say that Christianity actualizes *one* of the possibilities inherent in Judaism, but that there are other, equally authentic possibilities within Judaism, resources to which Judaism itself has turned in its ongoing historical evolution?[53]

Briefly I sketch Hodgson's constructive alternative to both classical and supersessionist Christology in his revision of incarnational theology, followed by some questions. He finds three things needed for a more revisionary Christology. First,

the connection between "Jesus" and "Christ" must be loosened or opened up....."Jesus is the Christ" but not that "the Christ is (simply) Jesus." What we mean by "Christ" is shaped in a definitive way by the concrete historical figure of Jesus of Nazareth, but what we mean by it is not limited to this figure and in fact is enriched and extended by encompassing more than this figure.[54]

Second, Hodgson seeks a way to avoid "supernaturalism, patriarchialism, and docetism of the Logos-flesh Christology, of moving beyond the impasse of the two natures doctrine entirely, and of preserving the full humanity of Jesus while at the same time affirming God's incarnate presence in him."[55] This move takes Hodgson beyond Barth's retention of some of the classical christological concepts found in the ancient Christian creeds.

Third, Hodgson seeks to explain

how this "incarnation" is redemptive, that is, how it confronts and provides resources for dealing with the profound problem of human sin and its destructive consequences. The classical doctrine of substitutionary atonement, based on the juridical metaphor (guilt, penalty, satisfaction) and the assumption that it is primarily God who is injured by sin, is as little credible today as the classical doctrine of incarnation.[56]

Hodgson proposes the concept of a "Christ-Gestalt" as "an Incarnate Praxis":

> God is redemptively present in the world, not as an individual human being (a "divine man") performing miraculous deeds (the traditional Christological picture), nor as a distinctive sort of God-consciousness (Protestant liberal theology), nor as a uniform inspiration, lure, or ideal (… some forms of process theology), but rather in specific *shapes* or *patterns of praxis* that have a configuring, transformative power within historical process, moving the process specifically in the direction of the creative unification of multiplicities of acts into new wholes that build human solidarity, enhance freedom, break down systemic oppression, heal the injured and broken, and care for the natural world.[57]

Much depends on Hodgson's concept of "shape" or "gestalt." "A 'gestalt' is a pattern arranged, shaped, or structured from parts, producing a living, organic, plural unity—a unity of consciousness or spirit—as opposed to a dead, mechanical identity."[58] He gives the example of the U.S. civil rights movement of the 1960s. How is this concept helpful for reimagining the incarnation?

> A shape or gestalt is not as impersonal as a universal influence or an abstract ideal since it connotes something dynamic, specific, and structuring, but it avoids potentially misleading personifications of God's action. What God

"does" in history is not to intervene in the sequence of causes and effects in the form of special acts, or to become a god disguised in human flesh, or to speak literally through human speech, but to "shape"—to shape a multifaceted transformative praxis. God does this by *giving, disclosing, engendering*, in some sense *being*, the normative shape, the paradigm of such a praxis. This divinely given gestalt, in which God is really present, shapes the historical gestalts by which structures of freedom, compassion, solidarity, wholeness are built up. This gestalt is not a person or personal agent but a transpersonal structure of praxis that grounds personal existence and builds interpersonal relations since it itself is intrinsically relational, social, communicative in character.[59]

So Jesus and his movement are the gestalt of an emancipatory Christic praxis, but that Christic gestalt is not simply reducible to the historical Jesus. Using this new conceptual framework, Hodgson develops a new "Wisdom Christology":

The "Christ-gestalt"...is for Christians the definitive shape of God in history. If we wish to ask how God is active in this..., the Christ-gestalt is engendered by the Wisdom of God, which is a mode of God's spiritual presence in the world. God shapes spiritually and ethically, by indwelling, moving, empowering, instructing, inspiring human individuals and communities.[60]

The Christ-gestalt is incarnate in the embodied personhood of Jesus, in the bodily as well as ethical/spiritual dimensions of his being....The most radical Christian claim is that it is *God* who dies on the cross, God who takes the negation, suffering, and death of the human condition into God's very being. God is in Jesus as the Christ precisely in his *not*-Godness, his naturalness, his suffering and death, his contingency and limitation. In this sense his bodiliness is of significance for his identity as the Christ, as are his maleness and Jewishness, which are likewise aspects of his embodiedness.[61]

So Hodgson reimagines the incarnation in a nonexclusive conceptual framework of shape or gestalt to overcome the problems of traditional christological schemes, including supersessionism.

> The Christ-gestalt is a shape or structure of incarnate praxis, the praxis of redemptive love and reconciliatory emancipation. This gestalt formed in and around the person of Jesus; his person in some sense became identical with it, and by means of it after death he took on a new communal identity. The Christ-gestalt empowers the distinctive being of human being, which is a way of being in the world as a communion of free persons before God; hence the more radically Jesus is the Christ the more radically he is human....But Jesus' personal identity did not exhaust this shape, which is intrinsically a communal, not an individual shape.[62]

Here I wonder what Hodgson's new set of concepts have to do with God's activity in ancient Israel, the Second Temple Judaism of Jesus' era, and beyond? Was there a "Sinai-gestalt" that preceded the Christ-gestalt, and if so how are they related? Was there a "rabbinical-gestalt" that followed the destruction of the Second Temple? In regard to Christian supersessionism, what about the appearance of false gestalts in history or the corruption of the Christ-gestalt by alien concepts and practices?

IN CONVERSATION WITH GEORGE HUNSINGER

In a provocative essay, Presbyterian theologian George Hunsinger draws upon and goes beyond Barth's theology of Israel. His opening assertions are convivial with Pawlikowski:

- Christianity enters into profound self-contradiction whenever it is anti-Judaic, as it regrettably has been throughout most of its history.

- Christianity cannot love Jesus Christ without also loving the Jews, who are his people, and…when Christianity does not love the Jews, it corrupts its love of Jesus Christ at the very core.[63]

Hunsinger advocates for a version of "philo-semitism or Judaeophilia" that is centered in Christ. Following the terminology of David Novak, he names his position "soft supersessionism," which means "the new covenant does not replace the old covenant, but it does fulfil, extend and supplement it, while also fundamentally confirming it."[64] This position affirms that "there is only one covenant, and thus only one people of God, and yet there are also two faiths. The presence of two faiths…represents a festering wound in the one people of God….Only God can heal it."[65]

He acknowledges deep Christian complicity in the Shoah and the need for Christian "contrition, confession and…reparations."[66] But he seeks more than an "uncritical" "solidarity" between Christians and Jews. "More than solidarity [the gospel] requires love. Christ must be loved and honored in the Jews, because the Jews must be loved and honored in Christ…precisely because he has made them his own."[67]

Assuming Christians as his primary audience, Hunsinger asserts, "[Christ] encounters us as God's self-revelation, as the reconciliation of the world with God and as the proper object of our worship. He himself is the Saviour of the world." Then he qualifies this claim: "According to Christian faith, however, [Christ] is what he is as the world's Saviour only because he is also Israel's long-awaited Messiah."[68]

Hunsinger assumes without argument that the Jewish no to Christian messianic claims for Jesus and the undermining of prophetic-fulfillment Christology by historical criticism can be somehow overridden, or do not constitute positive data for his theology. Here his "soft supersessionism" collides with the insights of Pawlikowski's Christology.

Further assumptions are made: "Soft supersessionism is unavoidable, because there is only one covenant and only one people of God. It is impossible to read Holy Scripture in any other way."[69] But who is the implied reader here? In fact, aren't there multiple ways of reading and construing the Bible within Judaism and Christianity? What Hunsinger takes as self-evident is exactly what was disputed between the early Christians and Jews, and has been disputed among Christians with the incorporation of historical-critical scholarship into the work of theology (which shows there are multiple covenants in the Bible and different kinds of covenants).

Rejecting Christian triumphalism, on the one hand, Hunsinger appeals to a related norm: "According to apostolic authority, God's covenant with Israel is fulfilled in Jesus Christ for the sake of the world....[That covenant cannot] be overturned by well-meaning Christians today in their quest for meaningful repentance."[70] Nevertheless, Hunsinger has to admit, "there is only one indivisible people of God—and yet everywhere it is riven into factions."[71] He appeals to a form of Christian eschatological idealism to trump the pluralities of history: "*Sub specie aeternitatis*, what is true *de iure* in Christ overrides all that exists to the contrary in history, and what is not yet true in history will be severely judged and forgiven, transcended and overcome, at the end of all things."[72] This marks one of the most important methodological differences between Hunsinger and Pawlikowski, for Hunsinger, in part, appears to reject the "return to history" in post-Holocaust theology.

In a footnote, Hunsinger observes that the Nicene Creed omits any reference to the exodus of the Hebrew slaves from Egypt. "The absence of Israel from the creed reflected the general disappearance of Jews and Jewish consciousness from the churches."[73] He fails to mention that the Jewishness of Jesus, his mother, the apostles, and many Christian communities before 70 CE was also erased by the creed.

Hunsinger asks, "Would it be possible for Jews to become Christians without ceasing to be Jews?"[74] In part, he answers: "The emergence of messianic Judaism in our own day is an important and unexpected sign that it might still be possible for some Jews to become Christians without ceasing to be Torah-observant Jews....[But] Messianic Judaism is a sign, not a model."[75]

Thus, Hunsinger seeks to follow a "narrow path" between anti-Judaism, on the one hand, which he decries, and what he calls "anti-Evangelicalism" on the other. A theological position would be "anti-Evangelical if it compromised on the imperative that Jesus Christ be recognized for who he is as confessed by faith. In principle, as I see it, this imperative is incumbent upon all peoples, the Jew first, as Paul put it, and then also the Greek."[76]

However, if the rejection of historic Christian anti-Judaism requires significant revision of our Christology, as Pawlikowski has argued, those revisions will influence our understanding of the gospel and any imperatives our Christian forebears derived from the gospel.

CONCLUSION

As evidence that the challenge of Pawlikowski's Christology is being heard by some within the Presbyterian-Reformed world, I close with a selection from "'...In Our Time...' A Statement on Relations between the Presbytery of Chicago and the Jewish Community in Metropolitan Chicago."[77] This document was composed in recognition of the fiftieth anniversary of *Nostra Aetate*, asking Presbyterians, "What must we confess and do in our relations with Jews and Judaism in this new century?"

> *In our present day*, as Presbyterians, can we see the need to affirm, positively and proactively, our present spiritual kinship with the Jewish people, to rediscover the Jewish dimension of our own tradition, and to engage with the Jewish people in causes of mutual concern?
>
> Jesus sought the well-being of the Jewish people, and through this, the renewal of the world. By following the teaching and practice of Jesus, Presbyterians not only "love our neighbor as ourselves," but fulfill God's call to discipleship which comes through him. In this context, a Reformed theology of Presbyterian relations with the Jewish people...
>
> - *Humbles* Christians as we are reminded that we are not alone in the sacred story of salvation;
> - *Reminds* the Church of the witness of God's plan for all people through the existence, integrity, and perseverance of Israel as a unique covenantal people,

called to be "light of the world" and a "blessing to the nations;"

- *Preserves* the Jewish roots and context of which Jesus was a part;
- *Grounds* Christian theological reflection on 2,000 years of a dynamic and vital Jewish civilization, which continues to this day with the independent and changing lives of a real and living Jewish people;
- *Provokes* the church to repentance from the hubris and historic contempt and actions toward the Jewish people;
- *Sustains* a transformative partnership even when there is irreconcilable disagreement about messianic fulfillment (in Jesus of Nazareth) or a yet unrealized expectation for a messianic age (full realization of God's promises to the people Israel and with it the world);
- *Gives witness* to the One God, to the commandments, and to the ethics that flow from them;
- *Awakens* Christians to the evolving nature of our understanding of God's activity by learning the history of the people Israel in its historic and modern embodiments.[78]

Notes

1. For a brief introduction to Reformed theology, see John Leith, *Introduction to the Reformed Tradition: A Way of Being the Christian Community* (Atlanta: John Knox Press, 1977), chap. 4. For a global history of Reformed churches, see D. G. Hart, *Calvinism: A History* (New Haven, CT: Yale University Press, 2013).

2. E.g., was an assumption of Presbyterian ethical superiority publicly displayed in the divestment debates between Presbyterians and Jews from 2004 to2014 regarding Israeli occupation of Palestinian territory?

3. See, e.g., John T. Pawlikowski, *WATSA Christ. Jewish* (1980); *Christ Light* (1982); *Jesus Israel* (1989); *Restating Church's Rel.* (2013).

4. John Pawlikowski, "Christology and the Jewish-Christian Dialogue: A Personal Theological Journey," *Irish Theological Quarterly* 72 (2007): 147.

5. Pawlikowski, "Christology and the Jewish-Christian Dialogue," 149.

6. Pawlikowski, "Christology and the Jewish-Christian Dialogue," 150.

7. Pawlikowski, "Christology and the Jewish-Christian Dialogue," 153.

8. Pawlikowski, "Christology and the Jewish-Christian Dialogue."

9. Pawlikowski, "Christology and the Jewish-Christian Dialogue," 156.

10. Pawlikowski, "Christology and the Jewish-Christian Dialogue," 157.

11. Pawlikowski, "Christology and the Jewish-Christian Dialogue," 159.

12. Pawlikowski, "Christology and the Jewish-Christian Dialogue."

13. Pawlikowski, "Christology and the Jewish-Christian Dialogue," 160.

14. Pawlikowski, "Christology and the Jewish-Christian Dialogue."

15. Pawlikowski, "Christology and the Jewish-Christian Dialogue."

16. Pawlikowski, "Christology and the Jewish-Christian Dialogue." About this thesis one might ask, "Why not?" What is the unique-making factor about Jesus' intimacy with God that we can't share in? Is it the conviction that Jesus was the first Jewish human being whose life and vocation made the deep relationship between divinity and humanity "transparent" for other Jews, and also for Gentiles? Did Jesus not only proclaim the "reign of God" in his preaching and teaching but embody God's reign in his life and witness such that his disciples and those who came after became conscious of God's divine activity among them in new ways?

17. Pawlikowski, "Christology and the Jewish-Christian Dialogue," 161.

18. Pawlikowski, "Christology and the Jewish-Christian Dialogue."

19. For a brief historical overview of Christology in the Reformed tradition, see Peter Toon, "Christology," in *Encyclopedia of the Reformed Faith*, ed. Donald McKim (Louisville, KY: Westminster John Knox Press, 1992); reprinted in Donald McKim, ed., *The Westminster Handbook to Reformed Theology* (Louisville, KY: Westminster John Knox Press, 2001).

20. For a sample of the wide variety of christological thought in Reformed theology today, my colleague Professor Anna Case-Winters recommends Douglas F. Ottati, *Jesus Christ and Christian Vision* (Louisville, KY: Westminster John Knox Press, 1989), chaps. 3 and 5; C. S. Song, *Jesus and the Reign of God* (Minneapolis: Fortress Press, 1993); Peter Wyatt, *Jesus Christ and Creation in the Theology of John Calvin* (Allison Park, PA: Pickwick Publications, 1996), chaps. 1 and 2; Kathryn Tanner, *Jesus, Humanity and the Trinity: A Brief Systematic Theology* (Minneapolis: Fortress Press, 2001), chap. 1; Cynthia Rigby, "Scandalous

Presence: Incarnation and Trinity," chap. 4 in *Feminist and Womanist Essays in Reformed Dogmatics*, ed. Amy Plantinga Pauw and Serene Jones (Louisville, KY: Westminster John Knox Press, 2006); Cynthia Rigby, "Redeeming Words: Hypostatic Union and the Reading of Scripture," and D. R. Sadananda, "The Johannine Logos: Interpreting Jesus in a Multi-Religious Context," chaps. 23 and 24 in *Reformed Theology: Identity and Ecumenicity II: Biblical Interpretation in the Reformed Tradition*, ed. Wallace M. Alston Jr. and Michael Welker (Grand Rapids: Eerdmans, 2007).

21. Karl Barth, "The Humanity of God," in *The Humanity of God*, trans. John Newton Thomas (Atlanta: John Knox Press, 1960), 39–65.

22. Barth, "The Humanity of God," 37. For historical accuracy, I have left the English translation in its noninclusive language for gender.

23. Barth, "The Humanity of God," 41.

24. Barth, "The Humanity of God," 43.

25. Barth, "The Humanity of God," 45.

26. Barth, "The Humanity of God."

27. Barth, "The Humanity of God," 46.

28. Barth, "The Humanity of God."

29. Barth, "The Humanity of God," 47.

30. Barth, "The Humanity of God."

31. Barth, "The Humanity of God," 48.

32. Barth, "The Humanity of God."

33. Barth, "The Humanity of God," 48–49.

34. Barth, "The Humanity of God," 49.

35. Barth, "The Humanity of God," 50.

36. Barth, "The Humanity of God," 51.

37. Barth, "The Humanity of God."

38. Barth, "The Humanity of God," 53.

39. Barth, "The Humanity of God," 54.

40. Barth, "The Humanity of God," 60.

41. Barth, "The Humanity of God," 62.

42. Pawlikowski, "Christology and the Jewish-Christian Dialogue," 161.

43. Peter C. Hodgson, ed., *G.W.F. Hegel: Theologian of the Spirit* (Minneapolis: Fortress Press, 1997); Georg Wilhelm Friedrich Hegel, *Lectures on the Philosophy of Religion*, 3 vols., ed. and trans. Peter C.

Hodgson et al. (Berkeley: University of California Press, 1984, 1985, 1987).

44. Peter C. Hodgson, *Winds of the Spirit: A Constructive Christian Theology* (Louisville, KY: Westminster John Knox Press, 1994), 241.

45. Hodgson, *Winds of the Spirit*, 241–42.

46. Hodgson, *Winds of the Spirit*, 242.

47. Hodgson, *Winds of the Spirit*.

48. Hodgson, *Winds of the Spirit*, quoting Pawlikowski, *Christ Light*, 114–15.

49. Hodgson, *Winds of the Spirit*, 242, quoting Pawlikowski, *Christ Light*, 115.

50. Hodgson, *Winds of the Spirit*, 242.

51. Hodgson, *Winds of the Spirit*, quoting from Peter Haas and Rosemary Radford Ruether, "Recent Theologies of Jewish-Christian Relations," *Religious Studies Review* 16, no. 4 (October 1990): 319. Note that Haas and Ruether qualify their criticism of Pawlikowski: "Now while it is historically true that early Christianity started off as a sect of Judaism, it is something different to cast this in terms of the seed-plant metaphor. Let me hasten to say that Pawlikowski never says this" (ibid.).

52. Hodgson, *Winds of the Spirit*, 243.

53. Hodgson, *Winds of the Spirit*.

54. Hodgson, *Winds of the Spirit*, 249.

55. Hodgson, *Winds of the Spirit*.

56. Hodgson, *Winds of the Spirit*.

57. Hodgson, *Winds of the Spirit*, 250–51.

58. Hodgson, *Winds of the Spirit*, 251.

59. Hodgson, *Winds of the Spirit*, 251–52.

60. Hodgson, *Winds of the Spirit*, 252.

61. Hodgson, *Winds of the Spirit*.

62. Hodgson, *Winds of the Spirit*, 252–53.

63. George Hunsinger, "After Barth: A Christian Appreciation of Jews and Judaism," chap. 5 in *Conversational Theology: Essays on Ecumenical, Postliberal and Political Themes, with Special Reference to Karl Barth* (New York: Bloomsbury Academic, 2015), 93.

64. Hunsinger, "After Barth," 93–94.

65. Hunsinger, "After Barth," 94.

66. Hunsinger, "After Barth"

67. Hunsinger, "After Barth," 94–95.

68. Hunsinger, "After Barth," 95.

69. Hunsinger, "After Barth."

70. Hunsinger, "After Barth," 96.

71. Hunsinger, "After Barth."

72. Hunsinger, "After Barth," 97.

73. Hunsinger, "After Barth," 97n3.

74. Hunsinger, "After Barth," 98.

75. Hunsinger, "After Barth," 101.

76. Hunsinger, "After Barth," 99.

77. "'…In Our Time…' A Statement on Relations between the Presbytery of Chicago and the Jewish Community in Metropolitan Chicago" was adopted unanimously by the presbytery on November 21, 2015. The longer statement may be read at: http://www.chicagopresbytery.org/wp-content/uploads/2008/07/in-our-time-Final-2.pdf, accessed August 8, 2017. Two of the original four drafters of this statement were influenced by Pawlikowski's dialogical ministry. This is a statement of one local governing body (the presbytery of Chicago), not a statement of the Presbyterian Church (USA), the national denomination, at this time.

78. "…In Our Time…," 8–9.

CHAPTER THREE

A THEOLOGY OF JEWISH-CHRISTIAN RELATIONS

Construction of the Common Good

—˜—

Edward Kessler

I have come to know John Pawlikowski personally over the last three decades and feel privileged to be counted as a friend and colleague. Like many of my generation, I first came across him when I was a student through his writings, and was deeply influenced by his courageous and prophetic contributions. His ability to listen and engage on substantive issues are deeply impressive, as were those occasions when he was Visiting Fellow at the Woolf Institute and brightened up the Cambridge classrooms, enlivening our proceedings. It is with great pleasure that I offer these reflections in his honor, and they represent a small token of my appreciation.

***

Imagine a critic, or even a child of yours or mine, asking, "How do you solve the problem that has led people to kill one another in the name of God since the birth of human civilization? At the end of the day, each religion claims to be true: Judaism, Christianity, and Islam, all claim to be true. They conflict. Therefore, they cannot all be true. At most, one is. If Christianity is true, Judaism and Islam are false. If Islam is true, both Christianity and Judaism are false. It follows that these religions are bound to conflict whenever their devotees take their truth claims seriously."

"I, for my part," my critic continues, "take this as sufficient evidence that all are false. For how could the God of all humanity

45

command his followers to deny the full and equal humanity of those who conceive him differently? I would rather live with the uncertainty of doubt than the certainty of faith, for it is that very certainty that leads people, convinced of their righteousness, to commit unspeakable crimes."

How can we live peaceably together while at the same time honoring the commitments of our respective faiths? The life and writings of John Pawlikowski seek to answer this question: living together requires that our ethics and morality need to become both relational and covenantal. I would describe this as the practical construction of the common good.

In contemporary Western society, it is sometimes claimed there is no shared understanding of the common good; rather, individuals will have their own individual and distinct ideas about what this means and what it means for them. What is shared, at a basic level, is merely the rule of law, and as long as people follow it, individuals should be free to make their own choices about the nature of the good life. For many, this is the bare essence and furthest extent of the common good; yet, influenced by John's concern for Catholic social teaching, I argue that it means much more.

The common good recognizes that human beings are characterized by interdependence, and that living together confers on each individual civic responsibilities toward one another as much as personal rights. This means it consists of values that encourage a sense of solidarity with others that strengthens a sense of shared responsibility and accountability, and leads people to seek the good of the whole and not of an interest group. This is fundamental to a society's health.

How, practically might this understanding of the common good be achieved? In 2013, the Woolf Institute in Cambridge convened a two-year Commission on Religion and Belief in British Public Life, which published its report, entitled *Living with Difference*, in 2015.[1] The Commission recommended that faith leaders should initiate a national conversation on the political and personal values that all faiths and ethical traditions have in common with each other. The goal is to create a shared understanding of the fundamental values of our many traditions as well as to engender equal and mutual respect. This does not just mean toleration, in the sense of permitting various practices and beliefs; rather, it involves the welcoming of difference with an emphasis that all in society, with their divergent views, are involved in and share the national narrative.

Living peaceably together can be portrayed in another way. Sometimes, my philosophical- and scientific-minded colleagues and friends in Cambridge tease me, saying they seek to answer the big questions: What is knowledge? What is truth? What is really there? They tell me that a statement and its opposite cannot both be true. Either there is or is not a table in this room. Either the universe did or did not have a beginning in time.

This works well for facts and descriptions. It does not work at all well for what Viktor Frankl called "humanity's search for meaning."[2] Meaning is not to be found in scientific facts, pure reason, or physical description. Even Richard Dawkins notes in *The Selfish Gene* that scientific facts entail nothing about how we should or should not act: "We, alone on earth, can rebel against the tyranny of the selfish replicators."[3]

Meaning, I suggest, is found not in systems but in stories; not in nature but in narrative—the stories we tell ourselves about who we are, where we came from, what our place in the universe is, and what, therefore, we are called on to do. That is why the Hebrew Bible and the New Testament (and many other scriptures, including the Qur'an) are examples of a search for meaning and written in the form of narrative. Narratives contain multiple points of view. They are open—essentially, not accidentally—to more than one interpretation, more than one level of interpretation. The validity of one story does not exclude another. Stories offer interpretations of the world. They attempt to make sense out of the raw data of events.

What is true of our stories is true of our relationships, which are multifaceted in a way that physical facts are not. I either am or am not (mainly) black-haired, short-sighted, and bespectacled. But I am, simultaneously, a child of my parents, the father of my children, and husband of my wife. I have colleagues, friends, neighbors, and coreligionists. I am a citizen of England, the United Kingdom, and Europe as well as belonging to humanity as a whole. Each of these relationships is covenantal in the sense that it involves reciprocal obligations. These obligations can conflict. Should I accept a speaking invitation or spend the evening with my wife and children? I am torn between my responsibilities as a leader in interfaith relations and my duties as a father and husband. The truth of one does not entail the falsity of others. Indeed, the very words *true* and *false* seem out of place here.

The scientific question is this: What can I know about the world? The theological question for those of us, like John Pawlikowski, who seek to combine faith with the pursuit of knowledge is this: How should we act and expect others to act if we are to achieve together what none of us can do alone? The former generates narratives of displacement. If I am convinced that I possess the truth while you are sunk in error, I may try to persuade you. But, if you refuse to be persuaded, I may conquer or convert you, imposing my view by force in the name of truth. This thinking leads to the attitude, "I'm right; you're wrong; go to hell."

If all this is difficult, which it is, it can be said another way. My wife and I have three children. We love them equally and unconditionally. They are very different from one another. They have different strengths, skills, interests, temperaments, and emotional needs. If we favored one at the cost of the others, we would have failed as parents. Still more would we have failed if, having loved our firstborn, we then withdrew that affection on the birth of our subsequent children, transferring it each time to the youngest. Such behavior would have damaged them all deeply, creating rivalries, insecurities, and a sense of rejection.

If that is true of human parents, how much more is it true of God? Can I really believe that God, having set his love on, and made a covenant with, the children of Israel, then rejected them when they continued to honor that covenant by choosing not to follow the new faith, Christianity? Jesus says in the Gospel of John that "I have other sheep that do not belong to this fold" (John 10:16). Can I make sense of the idea that, six centuries after the birth of Christianity and twenty-six after the journey of Abraham, God revealed to the Prophet Muhammad that Jews and Christians had been mistaken all along and that their religious destiny was other than they had believed it to be? The Qur'an also embraces the diversity of the human family, stating, "We have created you male and female, and have made you nations and tribes that you may know one another" (Qur'an 49:13).

I can perfectly well understand that first Ptolemy, then Copernicus, then Newton—perhaps even Einstein—were shown to be wrong in their scientific beliefs and that if religion is like science, it is open to such refutations. But that is to think God is a concept rather than a parent. Our narratives, as men and women of faith, invite us to reflect not in a theoretical exercise but in a real encounter and to engage not in a concept but in a relationship.

How might we engage in a genuine religious encounter? We would do well to turn to our Scriptures and especially biblical interpretations and commentary. There is an argument going on. In fact, in the surrounding small print there are arguments about the arguments about the arguments. If I were to describe the literature of the Jewish and Christian faiths, the best I could come up with is that it is an anthology of arguments, or even a millennial chat room.

But, let me push this description further. What do we call those arguments? Arguments for the sake of heaven. And the question is not just, why do we argue? I suppose everyone argues. The question is, why is argument central to the religious experience? Why is it the very structure of religious thought? According to Jonathan Sacks, it has to do with an opposition to a fundamental principle of logic: the "law of contradiction."[4] The law of contradiction says that a statement and its negation cannot be true at the same time. Logic says it cannot be both Tuesday night and Friday morning.

A story is told about the Jewish philosopher from Columbia University, called Sidney Morgenbesser, who was attending a class on logic in which the lecturer pointed out the logical asymmetry between negation and affirmation, and that two negatives make a positive but that two positives don't make a negative. Sidney, at the back of the room, shouted, "Yeah, yeah." He wanted to show that the fundamental principle of logic does not always apply.

Similarly, the law of contradiction does not apply to the theology of Jewish-Christian dialogue because we reject the idea that truth is two-dimensional. Very often it is not a matter of either true or false. Two conflicting propositions may both be true! It just happens to depend on where we are standing and what our perspective is. Famously, the Nobel prize-winning scientist Niels Bohr suggested, "The opposite of a simple truth is a falsehood. The opposite of a profound truth is very often another profound truth."[5] In other words, a theology of Jewish-Christian dialogue (indeed, a theology of interfaith dialogue in general) not only emphasizes pursuit of the common good but requires us to engage both sides of what often looks like a contradiction.

When everything is seen in terms of two dimensions, it is either true or it is false. And there can only be one perspective! That is what I reject. There is always more than one perspective. If I am writing this chapter seated here at my desk, things look different from what you see if you are reading it seated at your desk. We are seeing the world from different perspectives. Following in the footsteps of Pawlikowski, the goal is to confer dignity on how the world looks to me and how the world looks to you. There is, in other words, an attempt to do justice to the fact that there is more than one point of view—more than one truth.

Now, suppose you and I see things differently. We have different perspectives on reality. Is that it? What can we do under those circumstances? We can meet and talk. We can engage and converse. You can tell me how the world looks to you. I can tell you how the world looks to me. We can have a dialogue, an encounter. We can, through that dialogue, learn what it feels like to be different. We can bridge the distance between two perspectives.

One might protest that this is fine in theory, but ask, "How might this dialogue work in practice?" Let me turn to the United Kingdom for an example, where the religious landscape has been transformed in the last two generations and has become three-dimensional, consisting of

a) The historic Christian tradition and culture, though with increasing numbers of people who neither believe its theology nor belong to its institutions (often called "cultural Christians");

b) The prevalence of nonreligious worldviews and beliefs (often termed "secular");

c) Increasing religious pluralism, where minority faiths now represent 10 percent of the population (a tenfold increase since 1950).

Britain has a distinctive mix of these three dimensions, as do other Western societies.[6]

In sum, the United Kingdom is less Christian, less religious, and more diverse. The Established Church of England is no longer the dominant host religion; a previously intrinsic relationship is being weakened and belonging to a minority is the norm. The church no longer holds the kind of authority that it once did because the number of people identifying themselves as Christian has declined from 71 to 59 percent in ten years (from 2001 to 2011).[7] The privileged position of the Church of England, as the Established Church, is being questioned, which has major political implications, including questions about the automatic inclusion of twenty-six bishops who sit in the United Kingdom's second chamber, the House of Lords, as well as the future role of the monarch as Head of the Church.

Post–World War II immigration means that Christianity itself is becoming more diverse, and immigrants from the Caribbean and, later, from West Africa, have resulted in thousands of black-led churches and a major black presence, for example, in the Anglican diocese of London. Between 2008 and 2013, six hundred new Pentecostal churches were started, of which four hundred were black majority-led. The number of members of Orthodox churches also rose—by seventy thousand—due to migration from Eastern Europe.[8] This has an earlier precedent with Irish immigration in the nineteenth and twentieth centuries.

One practical response to the changing religious landscape was articulated by the Head of the Church of England, Queen Elizabeth II, during a speech in Lambeth Palace in 2012. The church's role, the monarch said, is not to defend Anglicanism to the exclusion of other religions. Instead, "the Church has a duty to protect the free practice of all faiths in this country. It certainly provides an identity and spiritual dimension for its own many adherents. But also, gently and assuredly, the Church of England has created an environment for other faith communities and indeed people of no faith to live freely."[9]

51

This represents a positive and practical response to the growth of non-Christian religious communities. More than one generation of Muslims, Hindus, and Sikhs (Jews have a longer British history, returning in 1656 under Cromwell) have grown up knowing no other place to call home than Britain and regard themselves as belonging to the country; they do not view themselves as hosted "outsiders." It also represents an attempt by the Head of the Church of England to map out how Christians can be true to their own faith and identity while at the same time create an environment in which differences enrich society and contribute to the common good. This means all communities should feel a positive part of an ongoing national story and share society's values.

Nevertheless, it is clear that society today is facing significant challenges, often of a religious nature. In many countries around the world, leaders are using religious ideology to polarize communities, generate fear, and garner political support. When combined with the socioeconomic factors of nationalism, terrorism, and economic uncertainty, we are now facing increased introspection, insecurity, and intolerance. In this turbulent and unpredictable environment, increasing tension and outbursts of violence, both within and between faith communities, is feeding antisemitism, Islamophobia, anti-Christian hatred, and other forms of prejudice. The growth of anti-Christian hatred overseas, notably in the Middle East, is also having an impact on Christian communities in the West, who are feeling under increased pressure to support their coreligionists. It is noticeable that Pope Francis is increasingly vocal in this area.

Adding to the complexity is the rise of radical (often but not only far-right) political groups and their use of religion, particularly anti-Islamic rhetoric, to advance secular ideological goals. In France, especially in urban areas, what may appear a diverse society when proportions of population are examined solely according to statistics, is in reality a predominately mono- or bicultural environment. North African Arab citizens (primarily Muslim) live parallel lives without actually encountering other French communities. There remain significant barriers, which prevent interaction and mutual trust. Since the Paris attacks in January and November 2015, government measures have been implemented that show a shift toward more authoritarian governance and differentiation along ethnoreligious lines. In these circumstances, it is relatively easy for extremists, of whatever persuasion, to develop myths and misinformation and stir up race and religious hatred.[10]

Bigotry has no place in a civilized society and yet we remain afflicted by it. Across the world, people of all faiths and none are persecuted because of their beliefs, or rather, because of other people's misconceptions about them. Ignorance breeds fear, which in turn lies at the heart of religious discrimination. Fear fosters hatred and conflict, dehumanizing those we do not know or understand. This makes the work of those engaged in interreligious dialogue urgent and pressing. As Reverend Dr. Martin Luther King Jr. said, we live in "the fierce urgency of now,"[11] because there is the danger that as a new generation emerges, it is unwilling to giving a respectful hearing to the other side and take seriously and engage in differing views. When that happens, violence is waiting in the wings.

Our task then is more than logical: it is dialogical and seeks to give dignity to the multiple perspectives from which we perceive reality. And the way we can handle that is by meeting, having a dialogue, learning how to disagree, and managing difference in order to live peaceably together in a world where there is an irreducible multiplicity of perspectives. There is, in other words, the view of Hillel. But there is also the view of Shammai. There is the view of Jacob. But there is also the point of view of Esau. There is the point of view of Isaac but also Ishmael. There is also the point of view of Adam but also Eve. And, ultimately, there is the point of view of us down here and there is the point of view of God up there. Ours is an attempt to do justice to the fact that there is more than one point of view.

The theology of Jewish-Christian dialogue, in other words, can only succeed when it does justice to more than one point of view. Jews and Christians proclaim the unity of God and the diversity of human existence. The dialogue should therefore proclaim not that out of the many come one but rather that out of the one come many. Dialogue should speak to the Other with a full respect of what the Other is and has to say. Such a quest is never easy because it is not merely about the Other; it is also about how the Other differs from us.

This experience was expressed by the early twentieth-century philosopher Franz Rosenzweig, who emphasized not the subject matter that connects the speaker with the listener but the I confronting the Thou. This means that dialogue was dependent on the presence of another person. In a letter in 1913, Rosenzweig reflected on the maxim in the Gospel of John (14:6) that "no one comes to the Father except through me." He did not condemn this saying, but asserted that it was true for the millions who have been led to God through Jesus Christ. However, he continued, "The situation is quite different for one who does not have to reach the Father because he is already with him." In 1916, in a similar reflection, he asked, "Shall I become converted, I who have been chosen? Does the alternative of conversion even exist for me?"[12]

Rosenzweig became one of the main sources out of which Martin Buber developed his idea of the "I and Thou" relationship. He maintained that a personal relationship with God is only truly personal when there is not only awe and respect on the human side, but when we are not overcome and overwhelmed in our relationship with God. The world of "faith" is treated as valid and genuine; it is not an "it" to be carelessly set aside but a distinctive value of belief. An I-Thou relationship is a meeting not of religions but of religious people.

A theology of dialogue, therefore, involves a respect that takes the Other as seriously as one demands to be taken oneself. This is an immensely difficult and costly exercise. It is all too easy to seek common ground or approach interfaith relations solely as a field of study. This is what Buber would have called a fictitious dialogue and not a genuine religious conversation.[13]

Similarly, for Wilfred Cantwell Smith, religion should not be treated as a system, an "ism," a simplistic and sterile, overly conceptualized, static entity that has little to do with the personal and historical reality that we label *religion*. Understanding religion does not lie in religious systems, he argues, but in persons. "Ask not what religion a person belongs to but ask rather what religion belongs to that person," he famously wrote.[14]

Smith assigns priority to faith as a category of understanding religion. Faith for him is much like Martin Buber's "Between," that sense of essential connectedness that underlies all apparent me-and-thems, us-and-theys, that transforms the objective "I-It" attitude toward the world into an "I-Thou" attitude. Therefore, interfaith dialogue should be directed toward the "inter": from faith to faith. Like Buber before him, Smith affirmed that the distinctive quality of the human being was faith (Hebrew *emuna'*) rather than his or her holding a set of beliefs ("the alleged ideal content of faith"), and that therefore dialogue was always from faith to faith, or in Buber's words, from "one open-hearted person to another open-hearted person."

One way to strengthen spiritual and intellectual security within a society is to oppose the attempt to impose my truth, my culture, my way of doing things on you. And that is what I find so convincing (and courageous) in the life and writings of John Pawlikowski, for whom no religion or people is entitled to force its beliefs on any other. Rather, the task is to educate and preserve the lives of this and the next generation so that they are better equipped to create a society based on the principle of the common good—create a narrative to which all contribute and belong. This will generate the tolerance and dignity that the world needs. But those of us following the example of John Pawlikowski know that we must do more than we are doing and more than we have done in order to sustain those visionary horizons that we need in order to remain human in a society that somehow seems obsessively to want to be less than human.

Notes

1. "Living with Difference: Community, Diversity and the Common Good," report of the Commission on Religion and Belief in British Public Life, Woolf Institute, 2015, http://www.woolf.cam.ac.uk/assets/file-downloads/Living-with-Difference.pdf.

2. Viktor Frankel, *Man's Search for Meaning: From Death-Camp to Existentialism*, rev. and updated ed. (New York: Washington Square Press, 1985).

3. Richard Dawkins, *The Selfish Gene* (Oxford: Oxford University Press, 2006), 2–3.

4. Jonathan Sacks, public lecture, February 26, 2000 (accessed from http://rabbisacks.org/faith-lectures-what-is-faith).

5. Niels Bohr, as quoted by his son Hans Bohr in "My Father," published in *Niels Bohr: His Life and Work*, ed. S. Rozental (Oxford: North-Holland, 1967), 328.

6. See "Living with Difference," 6, and appendix A, which uses figures from the Office of National Statistics and the British Social Attitudes Survey.

7. "Living with Difference," from the Office for National Statistics.

8. "Living with Difference," 18. Further details from Peter Brierley, *UK Church Statistics 2: 2010 to 2020* (Tonbridge, UK: ADBC Publishers, 2014).

9. Elizabeth II (2012), "The Queen's Speech at Lambeth Palace, 15 February 2012," https://bpdt.wordpress.com/2012/02/16/the-queens -speech-at-lambeth-palace-15-february-2012/.

10. See https://woolfinstitute.wordpress.com/2016/05/19/a-french -terror-politik/ (accessed May 11, 2018), by Sami Everett, Woolf Institute researcher undertaking research on community relations in Paris.

11. Rev. Martin Luther King Jr., "Beyond Vietnam: A Time to Break Silence" (April 4, 1967), http://www.hartford-hwp.com/archives/45a/ 058.html.

12. Franz Rosenzweig, *Der Mensch und sein Werk in Gesammelte Schriften* I–IV (Den Haag/Dordrecht: Martinus Nijhoff Publishers, 1976–84), 132ff.

13. For the references to Martin Buber and Wilfred Cantwell Smith, see Kenneth Cracknell, "Viewpoint: Dialogue: A Call to Friendship," *Journal of Hindu-Christian Studies* 14 (2001): 37–38.

14. Cracknell, "Viewpoint: Dialogue," 37–38.

CHAPTER FOUR

"LOVE YOUR NEIGHBOR: THIS IS YOURSELF!"

An Essay on the Interpretation of the Commandment of Love of Neighbor (Lev 19:18) from the Perspective of Lévinas's Philosophy of Alterity

—m—

Martin M. Lintner, OSM*

INTRODUCTION: THE DOUBLE COMMANDMENT TO LOVE GOD AND ONE'S NEIGHBOR AS THE HEART OF ANY JEWISH-CHRISTIAN ETHICS

The double commandment to love God and one's neighbor is the heart of any Jewish-Christian ethics. To love God is seen as the most important and greatest commandment, followed by the second commandment to love one's neighbor. According to the teaching of Jesus

---

* The author is honored to contribute to this festschrift for John Pawlikowski and wishes to express his friendship and esteem for his fellow Servite (OSM). This contribution is the English translation of "'Liebe deinen Nächsten: das bist du selbst'. Eine alteritätsphilosophische Lektüre des Gebotes der Nächstenliebe," in *Aus Liebe zu Gott—im Dienst an den Menschen. Spirituelle, pastorale und ökumenische Dimensionen der Moraltheologie, Festschrift für Herbert Schlögel*, ed. Kerstin Schlögl-Flierl and Gunter Prüller-Jagenteufel, Studien der Moraltheologie, neue Folge, vol. 2 (Münster: Aschendorff Verlag, 2014), 93–101. This English version has been revised for this volume and additions have been included in sections 3.2 and 3.3. The author wishes to thank specially Dr. Brian McNeil for the correction of the English text, and the publishing house Aschendorff, Münster, for their kind consent to the translation and republishing of this article.

Christ (Matt 22:36–40; Mark 12:31–33), the second one belongs to the first, and therefore is also most important. To obey these two commandments means to follow a path to eternal life (Matt 19:16–19; Luke 19:25–28). In the Old Testament, hereafter referred to as the Hebrew Bible,[1] these two commandments are not associated immediately, but can be found separately in two different passages (Deut 6:4–5; Lev 19:18). In the New Testament, they form a dynamic unit.[2] It is, however, worth noting that already in Leviticus 19:18 there exists an internal coherence between the love for one's neighbor and the love for God. The commandment of love of neighbor is seen as the essence of the whole Jewish law[3] and is given a theological foundation by the use of the phrase that serves as the (so-called) self-introduction, of God: "I am the LORD."[4]

In the entire Christian tradition of interpretation of the double commandment, the relationship between the love of God and the love of the neighbor was never actually called into question, but often it was forgotten that there is a third person present in the two commandments, namely the loving subject itself: "you shall love your neighbor as yourself." To love one's neighbor was understood as *amor benevolentiae*, as a selfless love for others, through which the loving subject becomes free from selfishness and does not look for his own interests, but dedicates himself unconditionally and without reservation to the other person. Love for oneself was seen as selfish, and therefore had to be overcome through self-denial. Contrary to this tradition, this biblical verse is interpreted (for instance, from a psychotherapeutic perspective) as the requirement that love for oneself and for the other should stand side by side, and ideally should be in balance.[5] Love for oneself means acceptance of oneself. This is a basic precondition, if the subject is to be able to devote himself freely to the other person for his or her own sake. Even in the sense of self-giving to the other, the self must have been developed previously.[6]

In the present essay, the author intends to reflect on two questions: (1) In what does the dynamic of unity and difference of love for God and the neighbor, a dynamic that forms the basis of the tradition of both commandments in the Jewish Scripture, consist? (2) How must the relatedness of love for neighbor and for oneself be understood? And, more precisely, what does "as yourself" mean? Exegetical reflections on Leviticus 19:18 will lead to a better understanding of the Jewish philosopher Emmanuel Lévinas's interesting reflections on this biblical verse.

EXEGETICAL REMARKS ON LEVITICUS 19:18

Leviticus 19:18: Love the Adversary, Not the Neighbor

The commandment "You shall love your neighbor as yourself" is part of a collection of cultic and social demands in Leviticus 19 that are put under the title "You shall be holy, for I the LORD your God am holy" (Lev 19:2).[7] The various parts of this collection are separated by means of the phrase that introduces God: "I am the LORD." The repeated use of the phrase serves as an element of structure and as an affirmation of the commandments. The concrete series of commandments, into which is integrated a commandment of love for one's neighbor (Lev 19:11–19), concerns various forms of social behavior. The more limited context, framed by the formula of self-introduction, is verses 17–18:

> [17a]You shall not hate in your heart anyone of your kin; [b]you shall reprove your neighbor, or you will incur guilt yourself. [18a] You shall not take vengeance [b] or bear a grudge against any of your people, [c] but you shall love your neighbor [d] as yourself: [e] I am the LORD.[8]

In this immediate context, the commandment of love does not yet mean the general moral rule of an unlimited love for everybody, but refers to behavior toward one's fellow citizen, the member of one's own nation[9] who has incurred guilt in relation to me. In a strict sense, the neighbor is not every member of my own people, but the one who has harmed me and has done evil, the one who is hostile toward me. We must therefore approach with skepticism the interpretation that verse 18 means a limitation of love for one's neighbor to the love of one's tribesman, and that it is only in verse 34a[10] that we can find the extension of the commandment of love to include the foreigner (in Hebrew, *ger*—a sojourner, proselyte) who is resident in my country. Verse 18 does not refer simply to any tribesman or neighbor, but only to those who have committed an injustice against me. With regard to this person, the commandment of love means, "Do not hate him, but correct him in order to change him for the better and in order that you yourself may not sin against him. Do not take vengeance, and do not bear a grudge against him." Furthermore, the love for one who has sinned against me does not consist only in the denial of hatred, vengeance, or an unforgiving attitude. It demands more. Love demands that I turn to a person in a positive way. The Hebrew verb *'ahab* (love) means to affirm the other positively, to act as his friend, to have an affective relationship with him that is capable of enduring and of bearing tensions.[11] The fact that love is more than a denial of vengeance is also expressed by the conjunction *wᵉ* in verse 18c, translated with "but." This term introduces a kind of antithesis to the whole of verses 17a–18a–b, and excludes negatively the corresponding forms of behavior toward those who have sinned against me, pointing implicitly to an opposite form of behavior. If all that I do is to renounce hatred or vengeance, even though I would be entitled to behave in such a way, this would nevertheless not mean that I love the other. We find an implicit reference to this interpretation already in verse 17b, because the reprimand that is opposed to the hatred serves to correct and improve the other person, as well as preventing me from committing a sin because of him. In this way, the vicious circle of a guilt that generates more guilt, of a violence that provokes counterviolence, is to be broken.

"As Yourself"?

Of particular interest for the present essay is the meaning of verse 18d: Love your neighbor "as yourself" (Hebrew, *kamôka*). Jewish exegetes and philosophers—such as Martin Buber, Franz Rosenzweig, Hermann Cohen, and others[12]—point out with some emphasis that the translation of *kamôka* (in the LXX, ὡς σεαυτόν) as "as yourself" is wrong. They present two principal arguments in favor of their position: (1) "as yourself" cannot be found in any other passage in the Hebrew Bible with this meaning. Where this meaning is intended, for instance in the description of David's love for Jonathan, we find another expression: love him "as his own soul" (see 1 Sam 18:1, 3; 20:17); (2) the Hebrew Bible does not know the concept of self-love. We can find an allusion to this only in one verse, Proverbs 19:8: "To get wisdom is to love oneself; to keep understanding is to prosper." But this verse does not deal with a general understanding of self-love. It intends, rather, to emphasize the borderline between a correct and an incorrect understanding of self-love: only a person who uses his mind and gathers wisdom can be said to love himself.[13] Although the debate about whether "as yourself" is a correct or at least appropriate and therefore acceptable translation of *kamôka* is still open,[14] the connotations and implications of the translation proposed by the previously mentioned Jewish thinkers are very interesting. Martin Buber and Franz Rosenzweig translate Leviticus 19:18c–d as follows: "Love your acquaintance, as yourself" (German: *Halte lieb deinen Genossen, dir gleich*).[15] The very first time we find a translation like this is in a commentary on Leviticus by Naphtali Herz Wessely, published in 1782: "For he [the neighbor] is like you, he is your equal, similar to you." (German: *Denn er [der Nächste] ist wie du, er gleicht dir, er ist dir ähnlich.*)[16] Buber, who refers to Wessely, gives a number of reasons for this translation of *kamôka*. *Kamôka* should not be understood as a kind of "unit of measurement" for love, as if love for the other ought to be measured by the love one has for oneself. Rather, the love for oneself should be related to the other: the other is like you, he is equal and similar to you; he needs to be loved just as you need to be loved.[17] In this sense, the commandment can be interpreted as an anthropologically profound form of the Golden Rule: the love you need and for which you are hoping, you should not deny to the other who needs and hopes for the same love.[18]

Buber supports his interpretation with a reference to verse 34, wherein love for the foreigner is given the following foundation: "You shall love the alien as yourself, for you were aliens in the land of Egypt."[19] Buber is not positing a relationship between love for the other and love for oneself; he is positing an immediate relationship between the other and oneself. In order to love the other, it is not necessary to love yourself first. But you must acknowledge your own need for love. Accordingly, you will treat well the other who also needs love; you will not treat him worse than you yourself would wish to be treated.[20] The self and the other are human beings of equal rank with the same needs and experiences of misery. Elsewhere, Buber writes that this passage speaks of the "being made in the image of God" of every human being.[21] Wessely had already explained why the other is "like you:" "For he too is created in the image of God....And this includes every human being because everyone is created in the image of God."[22] According to Rosenzweig, the deeper meaning of "equal to you" is that the other should not remain a "third person" for you, an "it." The other should become a "you," because he is like you: the other is a you as you are a you, and therefore an "I."[23] Here, we see clearly the fundamental idea of the philosophy of dialogue, in which the "I" is taken out of its self-relatedness and the "you" is prevented from being subsumed by the thinking subject.[24]

THE REFLECTION OF EMMANUEL LÉVINAS ON LEVITICUS 19:18

During a colloquium at the University of Leiden on May 20, 1975, Lévinas was challenged by the question whether the biblical imperative "Love your neighbor as yourself" should not be understood in the sense that moral experience could be translated as an experience of the other who is identical to oneself.[25] Against the background of the Lévinasian approach to the philosophy of alterity, the provocative character of this question is quite clear. In his answer, Lévinas refers explicitly to the previously mentioned translation of Leviticus 19:18 by Buber and Rosenzweig. He explains that these authors refused to translate *kamôka* with "as yourself" because this ultimately would mean to love not the other, but oneself in the other, and, consequently, to love oneself more than the other, to love oneself most.[26] Then, separating the two parts of the verse by a colon, Lévinas proposes the following reading and interpretation of this biblical verse: "Love your neighbor: this work is yourself"; this means, "The love for the neighbor is yourself."[27]

"Love Your Neighbor: This Work Is Yourself"

Lévinas is aware that this version would present an "extremely audacious reading";[28] nevertheless, he tries to justify it. Like Buber and Rosenzweig from the second edition of their biblical translation, Lévinas, too, separates verse 18d *kamôka* from verse 18c by inserting a colon.[29] In that case, Lévinas argues, verse 18d refers not only to verse 18c, but to the whole text of the Bible:

> It is not at all the two or three verses that precede or follow the verse on which one comments! For the absolute hermeneutic of a verse, the entirety of the book is necessary! Now, in the entirety of the book, there is always a priority of the other in relation to me. This is the biblical contribution in its entirety. And that is how I would respond to your question: "Love your neighbour; all that is yourself; this work is yourself; this love is yourself." *Kamokhah* does not refer to "your neighbour," but to all the words that precede it.[30]

This passage can be understood in its depth and importance only if we consider Lévinas's philosophy of alterity.[31]

Some Fundamental Aspects of the Lévinasian Philosophy of Alterity[32]

Lévinas radically dethrones the absolute, self-centered, and self-sufficient subject. The encounter with the other breaks the totality of the subject that appropriates the world and the other through an assimilating mode of thinking. The face-to-face relationship marks an openness of the subject, an event of no return to itself. Lévinas unmasks the nominative subject as totalitarian and inhumane. Lévinas puts the question of subjectivity in a different way, namely as a question about the humanity of the subject. Humanity displaces the totalitarian subject insofar as the subject is called to go out of itself, to become a stranger to itself through the encounter with the other who calls the subject to responsibility. According to Lévinas, the subject finds itself originally not as self-consciousness but as object and as accused. It is a *sub-iacitum*, a subjugated one that finds its original identity only through inescapably being put into question, being accused by the other. Being called into question does not mean that the subject has to answer, but that the subject finds itself as responsible. The other frees the subject to humanity, to a freedom that is not an original, but a forced freedom. The other does not kindly ask permission: he makes demands. It is not up to the subject to decide whether or not to assume responsibility for the other; the subject is forced to exercise this responsibility and therefore to relate to the other and at the same time to itself. The self-relatedness of the subject is both interrupted through the encounter with the other and is enabled by it. But the way in which the subject faces this being forced by the other—whether in a diaconical or in an appropriating mode— determines the humanity of the subject, its becoming a subject.

The ethical dimension is inscribed from the very outset in an irreducible manner on this process of subjectification. Responsibility is "the essential, primary, and fundamental structure of subjectivity."[33] This means that in Lévinas, the question concerning humanity or human being is not the question of the human being ("What or who is a/the human being?"), but of the subject who finds its subjectivity and proper identity through and thanks to the other. "In fact, it is a matter of saying the very identity of the human I starting from responsibility, that is, starting from this position or deposition of the sovereign I in self-consciousness, a deposition which is precisely its responsibility for the other."[34] It concerns the constitutive meaning of alterity and the relatedness to otherness as the *conditio humana*, as subject-constituting: How can the subject be a human being at the sight of the other who, on the one hand, calls the subject into question, summoning it out from itself and out from its autonomous subjectivity, and, on the other hand, enables the subject to find its humanity not without the other, but only in the face of the other? Humanity arises from assuming responsibility for the other. It is a question of becoming a subject through relatedness to alterity. Lévinasian ethics do not serve the self-assurance of the subject, but provoke and disturb the acting subject. Lévinas shakes and awakens the good conscience that self-righteously tries to fall asleep in the bed of a normal morality. Moral acting can never escape the absolute and infinite responsibility that makes excessive demands of the moral subject, and this means that moral acting is characterized inevitably by becoming guilty and remaining guilty. Feeling disturbed and being guilty reflect the inadequacy of the moral subject and its finitude. The infinite responsibility makes excessive demands of the finite subject. For the subject, this means distress and misery and, at the same time, vocation and grace: vocation, because the call comes from the other and frees the subject to its very identity, and grace, because acknowledging the finitude of the subject means recognizing its humanity.

This requires a rethinking of the relationship between moral autonomy and heteronomy, insofar as the moral subject is brought into freedom by the other. Autonomy is not original, but is enabled heteronomously. Its origin lies in the heteronomous experience of the encounter with the other. To be brought into freedom by the other means to be freed for responsibility by him. Moral autonomy meets responsibility for the other in the sense of a forced freedom. The subject is not free to be free, it cannot *not* respond, but is forced to exercise its freedom in assuming (or not) responsibility for the other. "Here it is impossible to free myself by saying, 'It's not my concern.' There is no choice, for it is always and inescapably my concern."[35] For Lévinas, responsibility is a fundamental choice to recognize the otherness of the other and to translate this choice into a basic attitude of respecting the other's alterity, his uniqueness and singularity. The previously mentioned "priority of the other in relation to me" is not primarily a moral appeal, but has to be understood as the origin of ethics and as the event of the subject's birth.

The Identity-Descriptive Character of the Lévinasian Reading of Leviticus 19:18

According to Andreas-Pazifikus Alkofer,[36] we find in Lévinas an essential shift of emphasis from the neighbor to the other,[37] a shift that is already prepared by Buber, Rosenzweig, and others when they say that the other has to be respected as an autonomous person, as "you" that is different from me, but at the same time equal to me: this is why he must be respected and loved. Lévinas goes beyond this position. He emphasizes the absolute alterity of the other and the need to respect the insurmountable difference between the subject and the other. For morality arises in the situational encounter with the other. Its beginning is not an ethical demand, but the concrete and original passive experience of responsibility. This reading tones down to some extent the appellative character of the moral commandment and expands it through an identity-descriptive dimension.[38] The singularity and identity of the subject consist in the impossibility to withdraw from the other, to slip away from the other. "As long as there is no other, one cannot speak of freedom or of nonfreedom; there is not yet even identity of the person, which is an identity of the 'undiscernable,' internal to what is unique by dint of not being able to evade the other."[39] This means that the other has to be acknowledged as the condition for the "I," as constitutive for its identity and morality.[40]

Protecting the alterity of the other is a source of humanity for the subject itself, and violating the other's alterity leads the subject into cruelty and a loss of humanity. In this sense, Lévinas's revised commandment—"Love your neighbor: this [work] is yourself"—reveals that the subject brings to light its very identity through accepting and assuming positively its inescapable responsibility for the other. Lévinas brings the question of understanding the subject down from abstract ideas into a concrete experience of encounter with the other. Ethics is no longer a matter of abstract ideas, but of being concerned actively with the concrete concerns of the other. Accordingly, ethics is not understood primarily as the moral reflection of an autonomous subject, but as an original break, as the inescapable breaking of the totality of a subject through the encounter with the other, and as such as the subject's exodus out of its broken totality. This exodus is original in the sense of a precognitive experience, of an event that happens without being conditioned by any knowledge. This is why ethics, for Lévinas, is "first philosophy."[41] He argues that ethics has priority over ontology or metaphysics because the original form of the subject's being is not self-relatedness, but relatedness to the other—and therefore an ethical form. It is only from acknowledging the priority of the demand of the other that the necessity of normative distinctions is derived. Alkofer interprets this as a spearhead against a normative-reductive understanding of moral norms and as apologetic in favor of a correctly understood situational ethics that is rooted in practice and concrete acting.[42] A kind of casuistry is requested that recognizes the very singularity and uniqueness of the other as well as of every situation, which can never be reduced and understood as a special case of a general principle or norm.

CONCLUDING REMARKS

The "God-Likeness" of the Human Being

Lévinas recognizes the priority of the other in relation to me as a golden thread that runs throughout the Bible. If one interprets the commandment to love one's neighbor as the essence of all the biblical commandments, while reading it not primarily as a moral demand, but as an identity-giving ability of the subject—who cannot be thought of without this fundamental alterity-relatedness—such an interpretation enlightens also the understanding of the biblical notion of "God-likeness." The human being is created in God's image "according to our likeness" (Gen 1:26–27). As "God's image," the human being represents God, but the specification "according to our likeness" marks a radical difference between God and the human being.[43] Paradoxically, therefore, the human being is both the locus of God's presence and at the same time a real sign of God's absence. The human being is God's placeholder, who holds free and empty God's place in space and time. The concept of "God-likeness," linked to the mandate to exercise dominion (Gen 1:26), indicates the human being's function in the midst of creation, a function of responsibility for life and for all living beings. The order to exercise dominion is an order to take care of and to assume responsibility for creatures and humankind in the name of God. The moral law reminds the human being constantly to assume this responsibility for creatures and humankind, not as a general principle, but as a concrete action. Therefore, in some rabbinic traditions, the revelation of the law at Sinai represents the completion of creation.[44] The law is antecedent to the human being, because he is not God, but since he is like God, he can recognize the law, and distinguish between good and evil (see Gen 3:22). If he obeys the law, he is not only fulfilling a moral norm, but is also manifesting the true greatness of his "God-likeness." When he admits the concrete situation of encounter with the other's face, which orders him, "You shall not kill (me)," he recognizes his very identity: "I am able to love and to assume responsibility for the other's life." In the words of Lévinas, "To love the other: that's myself." If law is fulfilled from this perspective, it is no longer a burden, but becomes a vocation and a divine calling. This ethical view overcomes a fixation on the letter of the law understood as a normative-ethical restriction. It also supplants a wrongly understood casuistry that identifies the concrete only as a particular case of a general principle, thereby fostering entanglement in questions of detail while losing sight of the essential question: assuming responsibility for the concrete other.

The "Samaritan Turn" in Understanding the Commandment of Love of Neighbor (Luke 10:29–36)

When Jesus once was asked by a lawyer who one's neighbor would be, he replied with a parable and then put a counterquestion: "Who proved to be a neighbor to the other?" This counterquestion clarifies the correct understanding of the commandment of love of one's neighbor: for the question is not, "Who, in which situation, would be my neighbor?" What matters is that I am pressured to justify my denial of responsibility for the unique other in a concrete situation. This "Samaritan turn" exemplifies what is meant by "Be merciful, just as your Father is merciful" (Luke 6:36). Through the care for the other, which is not restricted to compliance with the legal requirements, the absolute other, God, comes into view—or, as Lévinas says, "comes to mind." This is precisely the location both of the unity of the love for God and for one's neighbor and of the difference between the two.

Notes

1. The author understands that what Christians call the "Old Testament" and the Jewish community calls "the Hebrew Bible" or "TaNaK" are not equivalent texts. For a brief introduction to the distinction see S. Daniel Breslauer and Celia Deutsch, "Bible," in *A Dictionary of the Jewish-Christian Dialogue*, ed. Leon Klenicki and Geoffrey Wigoder, exp. ed. (Mahwah, NJ: Paulist Press, 1995), 15–21.

2. See Karl Rahner, "Über die Einheit von Nächsten- und Gottesliebe," in *Schriften zur Theologie*, vol. 4 (Einsiedeln: Benzinger, 1968), 277–98.

3. See Hubert Frankemölle, *Matthäus Kommentar*, vol. 2 (Düsseldorf: Patoms, 1997), 354–55.

4. All biblical quotations, unless otherwise noted, are from the New Revised Standard Version.

5. Alexander Susewind, "Liebe deinen Nächsten, er ist wie du… Anmerkungen zur psychologischen Rezeption einer zentralen biblischen Weisung," 2 (quoted from http://www.beziehungsraeume.de/sites/default/files/sites/beziehungsraeume.de/files/Liebe deinen Nächsten - Psychologische Anmerkungen....pdf [accessed November 11, 2016]).

6. See Susewind, "Liebe deinen Nächsten," 2.

7. See Hans-Peter Mathys, *Liebe deinen Nächsten wie dich selbst. Untersuchungen zum alttestamentlichen Gebot der Nächstenliebe (Lev 19,18)*, Orbis Biblicus et Orientalis 71 (Freiburg/Göttingen: Universitätsverlag and Vandenhoeck & Ruprecht, 1986), 57–81; Erhard S. Gerstenberger, *Das 3. Buch Mose: Leviticus*, ATD 6 (Göttingen: Vandenhoeck & Ruprecht, 6th ed. 1993), 238–49.

8. Subdivisions of the verses are added by the author.

9. V. 18b employs the Hebrew term *re^a'* (= friend, companion, fellow). Vv. 17a and 18a speak of "brother" and "children of thy people." The question of who precisely would be one's neighbor arises only in the New Testament in Luke 10:29 (see Mathys, *Liebe deinen Nächsten*, 29).

10. "The alien who resides with you shall be to you as the citizen among you; you shall love the alien as yourself."

11. See Mathys, *Liebe deinen Nächsten*, 12–28; Mathys develops this interpretation by comparing the commandment of love with some parallel verses (Deut 10:19; Prov 17:17; 19:18) and with the pericope of the intimate friendship between David and Jonathan: "The soul of Jonathan was bound to the soul of David, and Jonathan loved him as his own soul"

(1 Sam 18:1, 3; 20:17); see also Gudrun Guttenberger, *Nächstenliebe* (Stuttgart: Kreuz, 2007), 18–19.

12. See Mathys, *Liebe deinen Nächsten*, 6–7. Various texts by Jewish thinkers are compiled in Berndt Schaller, *"'…denn er ist wie du…' Einer alten Übersetzung auf die Spur kommen"*, in *…denn er ist wie du…*, ed. Deutscher Koordinierungsrat der Gesellschaften für Christlich-Jüdische Zusammenarbeit, Themenheft 2001 (Bad Nauheim, 2001), 16–19.

13. See Mathys, *"'…denn er ist wie du…'* Einer alten Übersetzung auf die Spur kommen," 14.

14. Mathys, *"'…denn er ist wie du…'* Einer alten Übersetzung auf die Spur kommen," 7–9, defends the traditional translation "as yourself" and puts forward a number of supporting arguments.

15. *Die Schrift verdeutscht von Martin Buber gemeinsam mit Franz Rosenzweig*, vol. 1: *Die fünf Bücher der Weisung* (Gerlingen: Lambert Schneider, 12th ed. 1997), 326 (English translation by the author). In the first edition (1927), we find the translation, "Love your acquaintance as yourself" (German: *Liebe deinen Genossen dir gleich*). "As yourself" is not yet separated from v. 18c with a colon. We find the colon only from the second edition (1954) onward; see Schaller, *"'… denn er ist wie du …'* Einer alten Übersetzung auf die Spur kommen," 16.

16. See Mathys, *Liebe deinen Nächsten*, 6–7 (Wessely's German text is quoted from: Schaller, *"'… denn er ist wie du …'* Einer alten Übersetzung auf die Spur kommen," 17); English translation by the author.

17. So Buber in his foreword to the commentary in Hermann Cohen, *Der Nächste. Vier Abhandlungen über das Verhalten von Mensch zu Mensch nach der Lehre des Judentums* (Berlin: Dr. Müller, 1935), 6–7.

18. See Mathys, *Liebe deinen Nächsten*, 6.

19. See *Die Schrift verdeutscht von Martin Buber*, 328; Buber, "Vorbemerkung," 6–7.

20. See Erich Neumann, *Tiefenpsychologie und neue Ethik* (Munich: Kindler, 1964), 92.

21. See Martin Buber, *Briefwechsel aus sieben Jahrzehnten*, vol. 2: *1918–1939* (Heidelberg: Lambert Schneider, 1973), 632 (letter of January 27, 1973, to Hans Kosmala, quoted from Schaller, *"'… denn er ist wie du …'* Einer alten Übersetzung auf die Spur kommen," 19).

22. "Denn auch er wurde erschaffen im Bild Gottes….Und dies schließt alle Menschenkinder ein, denn sie alle wurden im Bilde [Gottes] erschaffen." English translation by the author. German text quoted from

Schaller *"'... denn er ist wie du ...'* Einer alten Übersetzung auf die Spur kommen," 19, who mentions other authors, such as Moritz Lazarus and Leo Baeck, who make this strong link between the commandment of love of neighbor and the God-likeness of human beings.

23. See Franz Rosenzweig, *Der Stern der Erlösung*, vol. 2 (Berlin: Suhrkamp, 2nd ed. 1930), 196.

24. See Alfred Schöpf, "Liebe," in *Historisches Wörterbuch der Philosophie*, vol. 5, 290–328, here 327; Andrea Taferner, *Gottes- und Nächstenliebe in der deutschsprachigen Theologie des 20. Jahrhunderts*, Innsbrucker theologische Studien, Bd. 37 (Innsbruck/Vienna: Tyrolia, 1992), 20–21.

25. The dialogue is documented in Emmanuel Levinas, *Of God Who Comes to Mind*, trans. Bettina Bergo (Stanford, CA: Stanford University Press,1998), 79–99, at 90.

26. Levinas, *Of God Who Comes to Mind*, 90.

27. Levinas, *Of God Who Comes to Mind*, 90.

28. Levinas, *Of God Who Comes to Mind*, 90.

29. See above, n. 15.

30. Levinas, *Of God Who Comes to Mind*, 91.

31. For German introductions to Lévinas, see Bernhard H.F. Taureck, *Emmanuel Lévinas zur Einführung*, 2nd ed. (Hamburg: Junius, 1997); Werner Stegmair, *Lévinas*, Herder/Spektrum Meisterdenker (Freiburg i. Br. et al.: Herder, 2002); Andreas Gelhard, *Lévinas*, Grundwissen Philosophie (Leipzig: Reclam, 2005), et al.; English introductions: Roger Burggraeve, "Responsible for the Responsibility of the Other: Emmanuel Levinas Gives to Thought on Psychotherapeutic Counselling as Ethical Relationship," in *Presencing EPIS* 1 (2013): 1–23; Burggraeve, "Sobering Up to the Other: Levinas' Paradoxical View on Mystical Enthusiasm," in *Tattva: Journal of Philosophy* 4, no. 2 (2012): 1–29; Burggraeve, *Proximity with the Other: A Multidimensional Ethic of Responsibility in Levinas*, Dharma Endowment Lectures Faculty of Philosophy DVK, 10 (Bangalore: Dharmaram Publications, 2009); Burggraeve, "The Other and Me: Interpersonal and Social Responsibility in Emmanuel Levinas," in *Revista Portuguesa de filosofia* 62 (2006): 631–49.

32. This paragraph represents an addition to the original paper. See Martin M. Lintner, "Zur Bedeutung von Emmanuel Levinas für die Moraltheologie. Oder: Was kann eine theologische Ethik von ihm lernen?" in *ET-Studies* 2 (2011): 245–65.

33. Emmanuel Lévinas, *Ethics and Infinity: Conversations with Philippe Nemo*, trans. Richard A. Cohen (Pittsburgh: Duquesne University Press, 1985), 95.

34. Levinas, *Ethics and Infinity*, 100.

35. Emmanuel Lévinas, *Ideology and Idealism*, trans. Sanford Ames and Arthur Lesley, quoted from *The Levinas Reader*, ed. Seán Hand (Oxford: B. Blackwell Publishers, 1989), 247.

36. See Andreas-Pazifikus Alkofer, *Ethik als Optik und Angesichtssache. E. Levinas und Spuren einer theologischen Fundamentalkasuistik*, Studien der Moraltheologie, vol. 3 (Münster: LIT, 1997).

37. See Alkofer, *Ethik als Optik und Angesichtssache*, 195–200.

38. See Alkofer, *Ethik als Optik und Angesichtssache*, 198.

39. Levinas, *Of God Who Comes to Mind*, 92.

40. See Alkofer, *Ethik als Optik und Angesichtssache*, 200.

41. See Emmanuel Lévinas, *Ethics as First Philosophy*, trans. Seán Hand and Michael Templè, in Hand, *The Levinas Reader*, 76–87.

42. See Alkofer, *Ethik als Optik und Angesichtssache*, 199–200.

43. On this, see Walther Zimmerli, *1. Mose 1–11. Urgeschichte*, Zürcher Bibelkommentare AT, Bd. 1.1 (Zurich: Zwingli, 4th ed. 1984), 71–83.

44. See Ursula Peter-Spörndli, *Die Zehn Worte vom Sinai. Die Rezeption des Dekalogs in der rabbinischen Literatur* (Berlin: Pro Business, 2012), 112–14, at 114.

CHAPTER FIVE

WELCOMING JESUS HOME

—〰—

Michael S. Kogan

You don't honor a tradition by endlessly repeating it; you honor a tradition by marching forward in its name.
—Gabriel Vahanian (to the author)

This essay and this volume celebrate fifty years and more of the Christian-Jewish dialogue, as well as the ongoing work of Dr. John Pawlikowski, one of the guiding lights of the dialogue and its greatest chronicler. Over a half-century, his brilliant writings and his passion for Christian-Jewish reconciliation have inspired dialogue among theologians and advanced the progress of a movement of growing mutual understanding and partnership between the two long-estranged covenant communities that grew out of ancient Israel. This volume is an expression of the appreciation, admiration, and gratitude of all participants in the dialogue who look to Fr. John for inspiration and encouragement.

THE FIRST LIE: DEICIDE

There are two great lies that have distorted the relationship between Christians and Jews for two millennia. The first lie, an expression of past Christian malevolence, always rejected by Jews, is the charge that the Jewish people were and are collectively guilty of killing Jesus, their own messiah and the incarnation of God. The second lie, innocently and ignorantly shared to this day by Christians and Jews, is that the Jews "rejected" Jesus.

The churches began to reconsider the first lie following the Shoah, as decent Christians at last confronted the Jew-hatred festering at the heart of their "religion of love," a hatred that had prepared the way for Hitler's "final solution." This Christian reconsideration issued in the Second Vatican Council and its declaration on Catholic relations with the Jews, *Nostra Aetate*, Declaration on the Relation of the Church to Non-Christian Religions (no. 4).

Since the Council, one Protestant church after another has followed the Catholics in rejecting the deicide charge as historical nonsense and theological poison. They also declared that Christians had erred in claiming that they had replaced the Jews as God's people, a designation the Jews had allegedly lost by not accepting Jesus as their messiah. The churches now affirmed that they had not *replaced* the Jews (God's covenant with Israel being eternally valid); rather, they had *joined* the Jews in the worship of the one true God. One might say that the churches had moved from Paul's replacement theology of Galatians to his inclusivist theology of Romans 9—11: "God has not rejected his people whom he foreknew" (Rom 11:2). For the first time in their history, the churches had come to recognize the eternal efficacy of the covenant sealed between God and Israel at Sinai. They had concluded that, even after the Christ event, the faith and people of Israel had a vital role to play in salvation history.

It had proved difficult to banish the charge of deicide from church teaching; there was much debate at the Vatican Council over this issue. But it was accomplished. How deeply this profound shift in doctrine and attitude has penetrated down into the consciousness of the Christians in the pews is another issue; some lectionary readings continue to be accusatory. However, in most areas the churches are doing all they can to maintain this 180-degree turn in their teachings. Their friendship and partnership with their Jewish brothers and sisters is real and deepening.

A number of contemporary Jewish theologians, including me in my book *Opening the Covenant: A Jewish Theology of Christianity*,[1] have responded to these Christian affirmations of the eternal validity of God's covenant with Israel. But long before our time, several rabbis and other leading Jewish thinkers had affirmed the role of Christianity in God's plan of redemption.

HISTORICAL JEWISH STATEMENTS ON CHRISTIANITY

Moses Maimonides (1135–1204) saw Christianity (and Islam) as extending the mission of Judaism by carrying Israel's Torah "to the far isles." The work of Christian missionaries would thus hasten the messianic advent.

In the thirteenth and early fourteenth centuries, Rabbi Menachem Ben Shlomo Ha-Meiri (1249–1315) of Provence included Christians (and Muslims) under the title *Israel*. Both Christians and Jews were "peoples restricted by the ways (the moral precepts) of religion." Both believed in one true God and in his universal ethical demands. Addressing his fellow Jews, he proclaimed that Christians "are with you in [observing] Torah and commandments." They are therefore engaged, together with Jews, in the holy work of building the kingdom of God.

Moses Mendelsohn (1729–86), father of modern Judaism, held that Christians could be "saved" if they lived according to "The Seven Laws of the Sons of Noah," ethical precepts and prohibitions basic to any decent civilized society. He regarded Jesus as an admirable religious teacher and a pious Jew. While disagreeing with the church's divinization of Jesus, he held that Christians could live lives acceptable to God by following the ethical model of the life of Jesus, the Jewish teacher.

Rabbi Elijah Benamozegh (1823–1900) was rabbi of the cosmopolitan city of Leghorn, Italy. He held a positive view of Jesus, a faithful Jew, and saw in the emerging progressive forms of Christianity a fulfillment of God's commission to Abraham to be a blessing to all the world. Together, Judaism and liberalized Christianity could become partners in the work of world redemption.

Franz Rosenzweig (1886–1929) developed a unique theology of the relationship between Judaism and Christianity in which the two faiths need each other to be what each one is. His powerful metaphor is "the Star of Redemption." Picture the "Magen David," the six-pointed star of Judaism. At its center is an eternal flame. This is symbolic of Judaism. It contains the immortal truths revealed by God. Radiating out from the flame in the heart of the star are eternal rays of light shining out into the world and enlightening it. The rays represent Christianity. Judaism cultivates the flame, eternal and unchanging; Christianity brings the flame's rays to all humanity and converts the world. The value of this vision is not that it reflects the reality of today's dynamic Judaism, as active in the world as is Christianity. It does not.

However, Rosenzweig's conception (based on the more insular Judaism of his day), sees Judaism and Christianity as necessary to each other, as part of one redemptive process. A flame is useless without rays of light shining outward; the rays cannot exist without the flame from which they shine. Judaism and Christianity are, thus, equally valid and mutually dependent. Both are necessary to God's plan of world redemption.

Martin Buber (1878–1965), perhaps Judaism's foremost twentieth-century theologian, declined to evaluate the work of Christianity in the world. Of the relationship between Judaism and Christianity, he said only that "every authentic sanctuary could acknowledge the mystery of every other authentic sanctuary." Does he mean that holy Judaism must recognize the holiness of Christianity? Usually he stresses the differences between the two faiths. Christianity declares that the world is already redeemed; the Jew knows that it is not. Redemption is yet to come.

Buber's most poignant contribution to Jewish-Christian under-standing is not found in his reluctant and scattered remarks about Christianity, but in his powerful and suggestive words about Jesus:

> From my youth onwards I have found in Jesus my great brother....And today I see him more strongly and clearly than ever before. I am more than ever certain that a great place belongs to him in Israel's history of faith and that this place cannot be described by any of the usual categories.[2]

Abraham Joshua Heschel (1907–72), in his essay "No Religion Is an Island," wrote of a salvific alliance of Judaism and Christianity to oppose nihilism and godlessness. To do this, each faith must affirm the other. "A Christian ought to realize that a world without Israel would be a world without the God of Israel. A Jew, on the other hand, ought to acknowledge the eminent role...of Christianity in God's design for the redemption of all men."[3] So, like Judaism, Christianity is "of God" and is Judaism's partner in its world-redemptive labors. However, while Heschel says many positive things about Christianity, he is totally silent on the question of the identity and role of Jesus, the personality on whom Christian faith is founded.

"Dabru Emet" (2000),[4] a document produced by a group of Jewish theologians of varied backgrounds, proclaimed that Jews and Christians worship the same God, but were called to that worship by distinct revelations. And it adds, "Jews can respect Christians' faithfulness to *their revelation* just as we expect Christians to respect our faithfulness to *our revelation*" (emphasis mine). So there were divine revelations at the outset of *both* faiths; thus *both* are part of God's redemptive plan and must work together for justice and peace in the world. Both are "of God." But again, this admirable statement omits all references to Jesus, through whom came Christianity's distinct revelation.

In December 2015, a group of leading Orthodox rabbis in Israel, Europe, and America issued a statement on the relationship between Judaism and Christianity. This document marks Orthodox Judaism's entry into the fifty-year-old Christian-Jewish dialogue. Remarkably, it goes beyond earlier statements by Conservative and Reform authorities that spoke of God's affirmation of all peoples, not only Jews, but failed to comment on the question of the divine origin and mission of Christianity. In my opinion, this focus on general humanity is a way to avoid commenting on Christianity in particular and dealing with a revelation that came through Jesus.

But this Orthodox statement titled "To Do the Will of Our Father in Heaven: Toward a Partnership between Jews and Christians"[5] goes further and gets to the heart of the matter:

> Now that the Catholic Church has acknowledged the eternal covenant between God and Israel, we Jews can acknowledge the ongoing constructive validity of Christianity as our partner in world redemption....Neither of us can achieve God's mission in this world alone (§3)....Both Jews and Christians have a common covenantal mission to

perfect the world (§4)....God employs many messengers to reveal his truth (§6).

Thus, both Christianity and Judaism have been called by God to a shared mission. Both are revealed religions and neither can accomplish God's purposes without the help of the other. Again, as in most Jewish dialogue statements, Jesus and his role in God's plan are not mentioned. Even so, after half a century of Jewish-Christian dialogue, the Orthodox rabbis have come on board and affirmed the divine mission of the church. At least, as a first step, "'tis enough, 'twill serve."

Of all the statements quoted, only one, that of Martin Buber, suggests that Jesus might be more than a righteous teacher. Buber affirms that Jesus, his "great brother," has a major role to play in the Jewish understanding of God's plan of redemption that "cannot be described by any of the usual categories." Buber does not suggest a new category under which Jews might come to understand Jesus. In this essay I will suggest two.

THE SECOND LIE: REJECTION

Having offered this overview of past Jewish statements on the role of Christianity in God's redemptive plan, I would like to move to a discussion of the second lie that I mentioned early in this essay. That is the contention that the Jews rejected Jesus.

The record of the Synoptic Gospels tells us the opposite. Jesus was followed by adoring Jewish crowds, even during his last days as he preached in the Temple courtyard. In Mark 12:37, the evangelist tells us that at the Temple "the large crowd was listening to him with delight." The Sadducees, against whom he was preaching, naturally objected to his words and actions that were disrupting the changing of money from Roman to Temple coinage and the selling of animals necessary to the Temple cult of animal sacrifice. But the people hung on his words and did not oppose his radical, prophetic pronouncements and actions. After all, they knew that they echoed the words of ancient prophets, especially Jeremiah, whom he quoted during his

Temple tirade (Mark 11:15–16). The Sadducee high priest wanted to arrest Jesus as he addressed the people. But he was prevented from doing so by his fear of the crowds who were clearly on Jesus' side.

Wanting to avoid "a riot among the people" (Mark 14:2), the high priest required information as to when Jesus would be alone, without his admiring Jewish audience. This is the information Judas supplied to him. The arrest in the garden in the dead of night attests to Jesus' popularity with the Jewish masses. Their attitude toward him was the opposite of rejection.

At Jesus' hearing before Pilate (probably an invitation-only event held in Jerusalem's Antonia Fortress or at Pilate's palace), a small crowd of flunkies chosen by Pilate or the high priest were gathered to yell "Crucify him!" on cue. This charade was designed to shift the blame for killing a popular prophet away from the governor and the high priest. Once again, this was necessary because of Jesus' popularity with the people.

The popular images of vicious, hate-filled Jews abusing Jesus as he carried his cross to Golgotha are flights of evil fantasy conjured up by the medieval Christian imagination. Nowhere in the Gospels do the people of Jerusalem turn on Jesus, certainly not as he approached the cross. The Gospel of Luke tells us that on Jesus' route to Calvary the women of the holy city wept for him (Luke 23:27). They were clearly sympathetic supporters.

JESUS THE PROPHET

In his recounting of the discussion between Rabbi Jesus and his twelve students at Caesarea Philippi, Mark's Gospel tells us that Jesus asked his disciples, "'Who do people [my fellow Jews] say that I am?' And they answered him, 'John the Baptist; and others, Elijah; and still others, one of the prophets'" (Mark 8:27–28).

Now, it is understandable that some Jews would confuse him with John the Baptist; their messages were virtually identical: "the kingdom of God has come near" (Mark 1:15; Matt 3:2). Others might well have believed that this apocalyptic preacher was Elijah, sent to announce the coming of "the great and terrible day of the

Lord" (Mal 4:5). But they add that other Jews who had heard of Jesus assumed, in my view, rightly, that he was a prophet sent to admonish the people and call them to prepare to enter the kingdom. The people's view of Jesus as a prophet is also attested to in Matthew 21:11 and Luke 24:19.

If many Jewish people of Jesus' day saw him as a prophet, they certainly did not reject him. On the contrary, they attached to him the most exalted title possible for a human being: a prophet, speaking to the people words put in his mouth by God, an inspired conduit of the Lord's revealed word to Israel. There was no popular rejection, only affirmation and support in the face of opposition by the high priest who reacted in panic to Jesus' disruption of Temple activities, and the Romans who feared him as a political revolutionary.

If our ancestors, Jesus' fellow Jews of first-century Galilee and Judea, viewed him as a prophet, why should we hesitate to do so? If our forebears did not reject him as a spokesperson for God, why should we? The argument against a Jewish reappropriation of Jesus as the last prophet of ancient Israel is first based on the fact that Jesus has not had any part or played any role in Jewish theology for nearly two thousand years. Perhaps more importantly, Christian persecution during that period is responsible for Jewish reluctance to reconsider our view of Jesus. But how can we hold him responsible for the later misdeeds of those who claimed to be his followers? How sad that Judaism read out of its faith this giant of the prophetic tradition. How and why did this happen?

If Jews did not reject Jesus during his lifetime, but saw him as a prophet, what is it that Jews did reject? They rejected, and must continue to reject the church claims in centuries following Jesus' life that Jesus was the long-awaited Jewish messiah, that he was in a unique way the "son of God," or "God, the son," and therefore divine as well as human, possessing, as did no other, a dual nature (a doctrine echoing earlier Christian thought but formulated officially in 431 at the Council of Ephesus). Judaism reacted to what it viewed as extravagant, even pagan, church claims that Jesus was God in the flesh, by removing him entirely from the Jewish faith tradition. In my view this was an overreaction, losing the human Jesus as well as the later assertions of his unique divinity.

TWO DEFINITIONS OF *SIN*

What can Judaism say about Jesus as messiah? The answer depends on how one defines *messiah*. If, as much of Christianity has it, Jesus as messiah must suffer and die to pay the price for humanity's sins, then Jesus, in the Christian story of salvation, meets that definition. But while this was an understanding of *messiah* adopted by much of the early church at the prompting of Paul, their first and greatest theologian, it has and can have no role in the mainstream Jewish definition of *messiah*. The Christian definition rests upon the Pauline view that when Adam and Eve "fell" in Eden, all the world descended into sin and death. For Paul, the inner nature of Adam became sin, a sin which all human beings inherit: "Therefore, just as sin came into the world through one man, and death came through sin, and so death spread to all because all have sinned" (Rom 5:12) and "by the one man's disobedience the many were made sinners" (Rom 5:19).

For Pauline Christianity, sin is what we *are*. We cannot stop being what we are. Therefore, if we are to be saved from sin and death, another who was unaffected by the fall and possessed of the power to save must accomplish the work of salvation. That other is God who takes on flesh to do for us what we cannot do for ourselves. He lives a sinless life, dies a self-sacrificial sinless death and, for the sake of his righteousness, we unrighteous ones are saved from paying the penalty for our sinfulness. He has paid it. The Jews are right, says Paul: righteousness is the solution to the problem of sin. But the Jews are wrong in believing that it is human righteousness that is called for. According to Paul, righteousness is impossible for humans whose very nature has become sin. The saving righteousness must be God's own as manifest on the cross by Jesus. That righteous, saving work is the function of the messiah as defined by Pauline Christianity. Humans are called on to have faith in "the righteousness of God" (Rom 3:22) shown forth in the life and death of Jesus (Paul emphasized the death) and so be saved.

None of this new Christian definition of the work of the messiah can be accepted by Judaism because the fall of humanity is not part of Judaism's understanding of the world. In the Jewish account of the Eden story, Adam and Eve did indeed sin. But for Judaism, sin is a misdeed by Adam. His nature was not changed by what he did. For Judaism, sin is not what we *are*, but what we *do*. While we cannot stop being what we *are*, we can stop doing what we *do*. In the Jewish conception, we retain our free will after Eden, uncompromised by sin. We are born not "in sin," but as free agents with a good inclination and an evil inclination. We are capable of following the good inclination. A divine intervention into history was required to provide guidance to us as we seek to do the good. That divine intervention was the revelation of Torah. It is God's gift of grace that urges us to follow our good inclination. If for Judaism, sin is what we *do*, not what we *are*, we can, with the guidance of Torah, stop doing evil and start following the good inclination.

Despite this crucial difference regarding the nature of sin, Christianity and Judaism do have some similarities here. For Judaism, Torah is God's word; for Christianity, Jesus is God's Word made flesh. In the synagogue we find God's word, the Torah scrolls, in the ark. In the church we find God's Word enfleshed in the elements of communion in the tabernacle. Both represent divine interventions of grace into human history. But the revelation of Torah is a much less radical act than the incarnation. That is because, for Judaism, sin is a much less radical problem than it is for Christianity. "Sin as what we do" is a very different problem than "sin as what we are." Thus the dominant Christian definition of *messiah* has no place in Judaism, since, for Judaism, there is no "original sin" inherited by humanity that must be overcome.

In the normative Jewish understanding of *messiah*, a royal figure will mount the throne of David and quite literally rule in Jerusalem over a righteous Israel and, ultimately, a righteous world. He is not a divine person, nor does he pay the penalty of original sin, since Judaism has no such concept.

But how does Judaism interpret the verses cited by Christians in Isaiah 53 referring to a servant figure who suffers and dies for the sins of the world and, through his suffering, heals sinners, that is, moves their consciences to forsake sin? Most Jews have historically read Isaiah's verses as referring to the people Israel and their suffering at the hands of a sinful humanity. For Christians, these verses speak prophetically of Jesus. It is time that both faith communities accept that

Isaiah's concept of the "suffering servant" can lead to more than one entity. Christian and Jewish readings of Isaiah's words both "work."

MESSIANIC VISIONS

Many of the Jewish sects that arose before, during, and after the first century produced their own unique conceptions of a messiah. Christianity, one of the sects of late first-century Judaism, produced its own vision of the messiah and his work. This portrait of a saving, suffering, divine-human messiah was by no means invalid. It was as worthy as all the other sectarian interpretations. But ultimately, mainstream rabbinic Judaism rejected most of these theories in favor of the messianic king model of the Davidic tradition. It would be impossible for Judaism to adopt the Christian understanding of the saving work of their messiah, since in Jewish theology such a messiah would have come to solve a nonexistent problem, original sin. For Judaism, Torah-guided "repentance, prayer and righteousness" are sufficient to "avert the severe decree"[6]—Jesus' saving work would be a redundancy.

Christians also view their messiah as "son of God." So does Judaism. But Jews would define that status as Mark's Gospel seems to do in his depiction of the baptism of Jesus. Lacking a virgin birth account or a childhood narrative of any kind, Mark implies that Jesus was an ordinary person until he was anointed king of Israel (messiah, the anointed one) by John the Baptist, as the ancient high priests had anointed the Davidic kings before him. Jesus is anointed king by John as a heavenly voice intones the words of the second psalm, the coronation anthem sung by the Levitical choir at the anointing of a new king: "You are my son; today I have begotten you" (Ps 2:7, cf. Matt 3:17; Mark 1:11; Luke 3:22). The newly "anointed one" is the "son of God," not by birth but by adoption at the moment of anointing. Thus every Israelite king was an adopted "son of God."

Originally, before the Davidic reign, which began in 1000 BCE, it was the people Israel who were seen as the *collective individual* "son of God." Moses demanded that Pharaoh free Israel, God's "firstborn son," so that he might serve his divine Father (Exod 4:22–23). But as

Davidic court theology later developed, "son of God" (by adoption) came to refer to one man, Israel's messiah-king. Eventually several of the prophets perfected this title and projected it into the future so that it no longer referred to the currently reigning imperfect king, but to an ideal king to come in the near or distant future. John anointed Jesus as this longed-for ideal king. But since Jesus did not go on to fulfill the messianic pattern as understood by the royal Davidic tradition of mainstream Judaism, he was not accepted as messiah by most Jews. However he did speak and act like a prophet, and so he was seen by the people.

It should be remembered that Jesus as pictured in the Synoptic Gospels did not publicly claim to be the messiah during his travels around Galilee. Even if he conceived of himself as messiah, this was never at the heart of his public message. His stress was not on himself but on his hearers. He announced, "The kingdom of God is at hand, repent and believe...." His own lack of stress on the messianic title suggests his discomfort with it; he preferred the title "son of man" (as used in Ezekiel to mean a representative human being). This leaves open the question of whether he actually saw himself in the messianic role as defined by Christianity.

Mark's account of the exchange at Caesarea Philippi (cited earlier) includes Peter's confession that Jesus is the messiah, the son of God. But how did Jesus react to Peter's words in this earliest account of the incident? In Mark's Gospel, Jesus does not confirm Peter's affirmation but tells him to be quiet about it. He goes on to speak of the "son of man" and his coming suffering. Does this mean that Peter had the wrong idea about the work of the messiah, that he had in mind the dominant Jewish view of a Davidic messiah-king? Or does it mean that Jesus declined to think of himself under that title, preferring "son of man?" Mark leaves open the question of whether Peter was right or wrong.

Of course, when Matthew rewrote and totally reconceived the scene (Matt 16:13–20), he had Jesus assuring Peter that he is correct: Jesus is indeed Israel's messiah, but not in the mainstream Jewish definition of the title. Matthew's Gospel has Jesus speak of the unique conception of the messianic pattern peculiar to the Christian sect. Did the historical Jesus see himself as messiah in any of its definitions? Who can tell, when Mark and Matthew tell such different stories?

JESUS:
BEYOND THE USUAL CATEGORIES

If the theological Christian-Jewish dialogue of the last fifty years is to move forward, "from mutual respect to mutual influence," a step I called for in essays written three decades ago, we must find a suitable bridge between us. Some years ago I attended a Seton Hall University convocation addressed by Cardinal Kurt Koch. The cardinal was then the Vatican's official representative to the Jewish community. In his remarks he stated that the cross might be the link between Christians and Jews.[7] I was among many in the audience who objected. We pointed out that while the cross was for Christians a suitable symbol of God's all-embracing love, for Jews it had been fatally compromised due to centuries of persecution of Jews living under its sway. We proposed instead that Jesus was a more likely link between us. I still believe this. Jesus was a Jew upon whose life, death, and resurrection, the Christian faith has been established. But while Jews cannot accept the Christian understanding of Jesus, still he can come to have meaning for our faith. I say this as a believing, observant Jew.

The key to understanding the relationship between the two faiths is the parallel between the stories told of the career of Israel, the *collective* "son of God" in the First Testament, and of Jesus, the *individual* "son of God" in the Second. This is no accident. The Second Testament account of Jesus was composed as a repetition and recapitulation of the story of the people Israel.

The parallels between the two narratives have been noted. Both Israel and Jesus are born of miracle births (Isaac to a one-hundred-year-old man and his ninety-year-old wife). This was surely a miracle. Philo of Alexandria pointed out the impossibility of such a birth. He went so far as to claim that Isaac was, in fact, not the natural son of Abraham and Sarah, but was the "son of God."[8] Isaac gave birth to the people Israel, the *collective* "son of God," chosen to witness in the world to God's oneness and to call all peoples to God's service.

For Christianity, Jesus, the *individual* "son of God," was also born in a miracle birth, in this case to a virgin. Israel comes out of Egypt; so does Jesus. Wicked Pharaoh seeks to slay Israel's sons; wicked Herod does the same, leading the holy family to flee into Egypt. Israel is, in Paul's words, "baptized" in the Red Sea; Jesus is baptized by John. Israel is made up of twelve tribes; Jesus chooses twelve disciples. Israel enters the covenant at Mount Sinai; Jesus outlines a new covenant at the Mount of the Beatitudes. Israel spends forty years in the wilderness, being purified for its mission; Jesus spends forty days in the same wilderness wrestling with his coming mission. Israel journeys to the holy land; Jesus leads us to the holy dwelling above. Jesus is slain once for the sins of humanity; Israel is slain repeatedly by a sinful humanity. Both rise again, Jesus once, Israel many times in a long history.

The parallels go on and on. They teach us that Jews and Christians are embarked on closely related missions to fulfill the divine commission to Abraham to bring blessing to all peoples. Once we accept that both faiths are engaged in the same project, we are freed to recognize that we need each other to understand fully who we are and what we are called to accomplish in the world. Neither of us is alone in our redemptive work.

I have said that Jesus can be the bridge between us. But if Judaism cannot see Jesus as *uniquely* possessing divinity or as Israel's messiah, then how can we Jews come to understand him? Buber called for a new Jewish category for Jesus, but did not name it.

I believe that Judaism should come to see Jesus as a great rabbi and righteous teacher of Torah who lived his teachings day by day. He was, in Schleiermacher's words, "the God-conscious man." He was also the last prophet of ancient Israel and the Jew through whose interpreters the covenant between God and Israel was opened to include all humanity. But this understanding would not be adequate for Martin Buber. All the above are versions of "the usual categories."

It seems to me that, in addition to seeing him as the last prophet of ancient Israel, we can look to the Christian doctrine of Jesus' dual nature as both human and divine. However, if we are to do this, we must remember that Jesus came not primarily to tell us who *he* was, but who *we* are. That was his message during his public ministry.

86

A woman in the crowd raised her voice and said to him,
"Blessed is the womb that bore you and the breasts that
nursed you!" But he said, "Blessed rather are those who
hear the word of God and obey it!" (Luke 11:27–28)

Here, as elsewhere in the Synoptics, Jesus turns the focus away
from himself, back to his interlocutor; the issue is who *we* are, not
who *he* is. But Christians have focused so exclusively on who *he* was—
"What do you think of the Messiah?" (Matt 22:42)—that they have
often forgotten that who *we* are was Jesus' focus and should be ours
as well. The dual nature was not exclusive to Jesus.

The dual nature of the human, a finite being containing an
infinite yearning, a consciousness of the infinite, is attested to in our
Torah. In the Book of Genesis, human beings are depicted as the
earthly images of God. No less. To be the image of God, we must
contain infinite as well as finite elements. God reaches beyond himself
and there is man; man reaches beyond himself and there is God. But
are they really reaching beyond their own natures? Self-transcendence
is integral to a Creator God. If God does not create, God is not the
Creator. The Creator creates the creation, but the creation creates the
Creator. No Creator, no creation. But, no creation, no Creator is also
true. Each needs the other to be what each is. Man is the self-
transcendence of God; God is the self-transcendence of man. They
are mutually dependent for the realization of their respective natures.

As it is with the term *Creator*, so it is with all the names we give
to God. They are all relational. They speak of the necessary relationship between the divine and the human. It has been noted that the
Torah contains no *theobiography*, no story of God before God created
the world. God might have preexisted the world, but not as any reality
of which we can possibly conceive. "In the beginning," God and the
world seem to emerge together. As we have said, there can be no Creator
without a creation. And there can be no Sustainer without a world to
sustain, no Redeemer without a humanity to redeem. Can we speak of
the Infinite without contrasting it with the finite, and vice versa? God
and the human become what they are only in relation to each other.

Thus, the finite creation is constitutive of the infinite Creator.
The infinite needs the finite to be what it is. But the reverse is also

true: the finite needs to incorporate the infinite in order to be what it is. A non–self-transcendent God is not God; a non–self-transcendent person is not fully human. We must try to understand these radical implications of the concept of the human as the image of God. What is true for Adam, whose name simply means "earthling," must then be true for us all. He is the first human who represents all the rest of us to come.

The stories of Jacob's two dreams further illustrate this point. Jacob too is a representative man. In his stairway dream (Gen 28:10–17), Jacob comes to understand the necessary relationship between God and humanity. This is illustrated by the stairway linking heaven and earth, with angels, divine beings of human form and aspect, flowing up and down. In this dream God and humanity are necessarily linked. But they do not interpenetrate each other. Jacob awakes and declares, "Surely the LORD is in this place—and I did not know it!"

The second dream (Gen 32:22–32), or dreamlike experience, twenty years later, takes the divine-human connection a giant step further. The text tells us that Jacob "was left alone." Will Jacob be wrestling with himself as all humans must to achieve self-knowledge? Then we are told that "a man wrestled with him until daybreak." Must the human person, seeking self-understanding, wrestle with our fellow humans? But when the unidentified "other" with whom Jacob wrestles changes Jacob's name to "Isra-El" (in Hebrew, "Yisra-El": God-wrestler), this tale takes the human-divine connection "into another intensity."[9] The fully human person, Isra-El, cannot be what he is without discovering the divine within himself. "El," the name of God, is not only necessarily *related* to the human as in the earlier stairway dream, but it is *constitutive* of the human reality. Remember, the dream comes to Jacob, who was "left alone." It reveals, as all dreams do, hidden aspects of himself. Isra-El and his pugilistic partner now interpenetrate each other as intimately joined elements of a shared reality. Emerging from this encounter, Isra-El declares, "I have seen God." God (El) is now revealed as present in his own human nature. His name now incorporates the name (the reality) of God. El is interior as well as exterior to the human. Here the divine and the human touch each other intimately. The name "Isra-El" reveals the dual nature of us all.

Judaism, while not prepared to see Jesus as *uniquely* possessing a dual nature, and remembering that Jesus' message concerned the divine possibilities of every person, can accept the dual nature of Jesus, of Isra-El (both the man and the people), and of all humans. By universalizing the concept, as does our Torah in speaking of Adam and Isra-El as representative human persons, we can appreciate the poignant teachings of Jesus, also a representative human person, a "son of man." *Jesus holds a mirror up to each of us* and focuses on a crucial message of our faith as well as of Christianity. The bridge that we can build between us, symbolized by the man Jesus, is our common understanding of the divine and human aspects of every person, also present in the stories of Adam and Isra-El. Christianity has long looked to those First Testament stories for inspiration. Why should we Jews not deepen our understanding of this theme by opening ourselves to Second Testament expressions of it in its account of the life and words of Jesus? Like all of us, Jesus possessed a dual human-divine nature. But, unlike many of us, he *knew* it and *lived* it and he called us to join him in that knowledge and that life.

Martin Buber predicted that Israel would someday come to see Jesus as occupying an important place in its history of faith, but under a new category that he does not describe. Here I am suggesting that Jesus' role for a Judaism willing to readmit him would be as a "son of man," a representative human being who reveals the divinity in all of us humans. He shows us clearly who we are.

John Pawlikowski, in his brilliant little book *Jesus and the Theology of Israel*,[10] moves from Jesus as Jewish messiah, a category he rejects, to Jesus as incarnation of God. He is trying to formulate a Christology that does not denigrate Judaism. He correctly states that on this definition of Jesus, Christianity and Judaism part ways. Judaism rejected incarnational claims for Jesus long ago, as they seemed too similar to the claims of divinity made by Antiochus Epiphanes in the second century BCE (against whose divine claims the Jews fought an extended war), the Emperor Alexander the Great, the mad Emperor Caligula, and other pagan rulers. In focusing on incarnational theology, Pawlikowski moved beyond the Synoptic Gospels' theology of Jesus' messianic fulfillment that he believes expresses a triumphalist attitude toward Judaism. But he has not formulated an understanding of Jesus that might be acceptable to Jews. He recognizes this. That was never his intention. He was writing to Christians, not to Jews.

But it is my intention. I am writing to Jews. I believe that if we focus on the issue of the dual nature we share with Jesus, this could be a bridge between our two faiths, as long as we remember that what is true of him is true of all of us. Every "son of man" possesses divine as well as human aspects. As ancient Greek philosophers observed, if we can conceive, even imperfectly, of the infinite and eternal, then there must be an aspect of us that is infinite and eternal ("like knows like").

Can today's Jews find in Jesus a rabbi and prophet whose entire life reflects in a poignant and moving way the human and divine elements that meet in all of us? His revelation to us is both old and new, not a contradiction of Israelite themes, but a powerful confirmation of them. I wonder if this formulation of a role for Jesus in our Jewish history of faith would satisfy Martin Buber.

Buber would surely endorse the idea developed here of the necessary connection of the divine and the human in which each becomes what it is only in relationship with the other. In his great work of religious ethics, *I and Thou*, Buber held that the *I* of the *I-thou* relationship was utterly different from the *I* of the *I-it* relationship. When *I* meet *thou* in true reciprocity, recognizing and cherishing the full human dignity and totality of the other, *I* become who *I* truly am in my totality. Without *thou*, *I* cannot be fully who *I* am. Confronting the other as *it* (what Kant would call a "means," not an "end"), *I* see only a fragment of the other, and *I* engage only a fragment of myself.

For Buber, there can be no isolated *I*, but only the *I* of *I-it* or the very different *I* of *I-thou*. These relationships are each other's opposites. How *I* relate to the other is the crucial factor that shapes my self. *How I* relate is in my hands, but one way or the other, relate *I* must. If *I* am altered by the other, then there is a necessary and profound interpenetration of each to each. And if, as Buber wrote, "in every *thou* we address the eternal *Thou*,"[11] then both divine and human natures must arise in relationship, the divine and the human possessing the dual nature of which we speak.

In the wrestling match account in Genesis, of which we have already written, Jacob represents the *I* of the *I-it*, an undeveloped person only marginally engaged in the world, interacting with others of whom he only partially conceives. Thus he uses his brother and father to achieve his own ends. But as he wrestles with himself, with others and with God, he becomes Isra-El, God-wrestler, the *I* of *I-thou*. Following the pugilistic contest, "the sun rose upon him" (Gen 32:31). Enlightened, he discovers that everything has changed. The world has changed. It has become "Peni-El" (the face of God). The divine countenance now shines from every bush, from every stone, from every blade of grass. He has changed. His newly developed human nature now incorporates the name (the reality) of God (the El of Isra-El). And God has changed. El is revealed as present in the human person as the self-transcending human opens to admit the divine. One can no longer utter the name of the human without invoking the name of God; one can no longer say the name of God without naming a necessary element of the human.

In this story, the *I-it* becomes the *I-thou*. Isra-El is the name of the fully human person who includes God in his/her identity. But we do not always act in this fully human manner. Godlessness and sin, both failures of human self-transcendence, are ever-present dangers. The *I-thou* of Isra-El can fall back into the *I-it* of Jacob. Buber reminds us, "This is the exalted melancholy of our fate, that every *thou* in our world must become an *it*."[12] Had Buber ever expressed his thoughts on that new category under which Judaism could include Jesus in its faith tradition, he might have presented him as an exemplar for all who seek to resist this collapse of what Schleiermacher called "God consciousness" into "God forgetfulness," of *I-thou* into *I-it*.

All of us alternate between these two modes of interaction with the others in our lives. Can we look to Jesus as a fully developed "son of man," an *I* for whom all others were forever *thou*? All *thous*, no *its*: a world of *thous* revealing the presence of God, the eternal *Thou*. Thus Jesus would be a model for us, an ideal toward which we must strive. The example of Jesus as the *I* for whom all the world is *thou* could be the new category under which Buber might conceive of Jesus' role in Israel's faith. It is a radically new role that could not have been clearly expressed until Buber's development of his ethical theology of *I and Thou*. But now, in the light of Buber's thought, why should Judaism not be open to seeing Jesus in this way?

Buber often sounded like a mystic, but he always resisted mysticism because its doctrine of full union of the human and the divine in which the human ego is totally eclipsed, seemed to him to be a denial of the reality of our actual life. We might have exalted moments of mystical union with the divine, but in our daily lived reality, the full reciprocity of relationship must be the goal. *I* am altered by *thou*, but *I* am not swallowed up by *thou*. Unless both *I* and *thou* remain, there can be no relationship.

I have not written that the human becomes divine or that the divine becomes human, but have tried to maintain the two aspects of the encounter. By speaking of the dual nature of human beings, I have stopped short of holding that there is a full mystical union of God and the human person. They interpenetrate each other, but they do not become fully one.

Jesus was a giant in the fellowship of enlightened ones sent to reveal to us our true natures, whether in Buber's terms (as the *I* for whom all others are *thou*) or in the role I have envisioned, revealing the dual human and divine aspects of us all, the self-transcendence that makes us fully who we are. And so we have two new categories under which Judaism can readmit Jesus into "Israel's history of faith." Either understanding can work for a newly opened and inclusive Judaism. Jesus was a Jew, one of our own. He should no longer remain a stranger to our, and his, Jewish faith.

Notes

1. Michael Kogan, *Opening the Covenant: A Jewish Theology of Christianity* (New York: Oxford University Press, 2008).

2. Martin Buber, *Two Types of Faith*, trans. Norman P. Goldhawk (New York: Harper Torch Book, 1961), 12–13.

3. Abraham Joshua Heschel, "No Religion Is an Island," *Union Seminary Quarterly Review* 21, no. 2, pt. 1 (January 1966): 124.

4. See *Dabru Emet: A Jewish Statement on Christians and Christianity in Christianity in Jewish Terms*, ed. Tikva Frymer-Kensky et al. (Boulder, CO: Westview Press, 2000), xvii–xx; see also https://www.ccjr.us/dialogika-resources/documents-and-statements/jewish/319-dabru-emet (accessed July 13, 2017).

5. For the text, see https://www.ccjr.us/dialogika-resources/documents-and-statements/jewish/1359-orthodox-2015dec4 (accessed July 13, 2017).

6. The "U'netanah Tokef" is a tenth-century prayer that is part of the High Holy Days liturgy.

7. Kurt Cardinal Koch, "Theological Questions and Perspectives in Jewish-Catholic Dialogue," *Studies in Christian-Jewish Relations 7* (2012), https://doi.org/10.6017/scjr.v7i1.2072.

8. See the phrase, "The Lord has begotten Isaac," in Philo, *Allegorical Interpretations*: 3:77.

9. Cf. T. S. Eliot, "East Coker," in *The Four Quartets*.

10. John Pawlikowski, *Jesus Israel*.

11. Martin Buber, *I and Thou*, trans. Walter Kaufman (New York: Charles Scribner's Sons, 1970), 68.

12. Martin Buber, *I and Thou*, trans. Ronald Gregor Smith, 2nd rev. ed. (New York: Continuum, 2004), 21.

CHAPTER SIX

PEDAGOGICAL/PASTORAL PERSPECTIVE

John Pawlikowski as Pastoral Theologian

—∞—

Jon Nilson

The aim of this essay is to locate John Pawlikowski's work in the context of the massive changes in U.S. Roman Catholic theology from the late 1950s to the present and thereby to assess his accomplishment more precisely. During these decades, Catholic higher education experienced a crisis of identity that has not yet been resolved. Catholic theology, which had migrated from the seminary to the academy as its primary locus in the wake of Vatican II, was also affected by the challenges that its host institutions were facing. These developments, plus initiatives during the pontificates of Popes John Paul II and Benedict XVI to regulate theologians' work, left the Church without the full theological resources it needed to meet the demands of its mission.

Pawlikowski's theology, however, has always been vigorously, responsibly, ecclesially, and ecumenically Catholic. So, this essay will conclude by arguing that his work is a model for U.S. Catholic theologians as they grapple with the multiple challenges involved in giving reasons for our hope today (1 Pet 3:15).

His formal theological education began in the fast-fading shadows of Vatican I and Modernism.[1] Vatican I (1869–70) had declared faith to be a supernatural virtue by which we believe the "things" revealed by God.[2] Without faith, one could not please God and be saved. Theology, or "reason illumined by faith," according to the Constitution, could reach a "very fruitful understanding" of these revealed mysteries. Its role was primarily to explain and defend the church's teaching.

Then, nearly fifty years later, the work of Alfred Loisy, George Tyrrell, and others had been ruthlessly condemned in Pius X's *Pascendi Dominici Gregis* in 1907. This encyclical, plus the anti-Modernist oath imposed in 1910 on seminary professors and others, made theological creativity downright dangerous.[3] While some new theological glimmers from Europe occasionally broke through the gray clouds of neo-Scholasticism (e.g., the liturgical movement), these hardly affected average Catholic thought and practice. In Catholic colleges and universities, theology was a matter of advanced catechetics and moral formation. In seminaries, theology was a matter of manuals and memorization to ensure simply that future priests learned the "what"—not the "why"—of the church's teaching.

Yet some visionary Catholics saw the Depression and two world wars as proof of the terrible consequences of a God-less modernity. They were convinced that their church had the wisdom needed for the nation's new challenges. Sister M. Madaleva Wolff's pioneering theology graduate program for women, begun in 1943, aimed at preparing students to "Christianize the social order," a challenge that demanded strong theology.[4]

Other Catholics, however, considered such a program too insular and "apologetic," in both senses of that word. Their spokesperson became the prominent church historian John Tracy Ellis, whose 1955 article "American Catholics and the Intellectual Life"[5] became the clarion call for reform and renewal of Catholic higher education. He argued for "unremitting labor, prolonged thought, and a sense of the exalted mission of the intellectual apostolate."[6] For Ellis, intellectual honesty demanded that Catholics come to terms seriously with the best of contemporary thought, whether it was Catholic or not. Nothing less than "excellence" would do.

Which was...what, exactly? "Scholarly excellence" could be found nowhere else, it seemed, but in the nation's major secular universities. So, from 1955 on, Sr. Madaleva's model began to fade and Ellis's vision became the ideal. Meanwhile, neo-Scholasticism was fast losing its credibility because its proponents were out of touch with contemporary developments. Within a decade, too, Vatican II had declared that Catholics share the joy, hope, grief, and anxiety of people today and that baptism makes all Christians one family.[7] Non-Christians were not strangers—and certainly not enemies.

Soon Catholic colleges and universities were *Contending with Modernity* and *Negotiating Identity*, as Philip Gleason's and Alice Gallin's book titles summed up the new challenges.[8] Meanwhile, secular models of academic excellence were the only ones on offer. Fewer priests and vowed religious were available to keep the spirit of the religious orders alive in the schools that those orders had founded. Pressures to downplay an institution's religious identity increased, lest it be suspected of proselytizing under the guise of education and thus losing its government funding. The 1967 Land o' Lakes statement demanded complete autonomy for the Catholic university to carry out its mission, while claiming that this autonomy posed no threat to its distinctive identity.[9] Yet what was that distinctive identity of Catholic higher education and of the mission that followed from it? No consensus emerged then and none has emerged since. Chapter 6 of Gallin's book is entitled "Are They Still Catholic?" and her question remains open.

The quest for scholarly excellence sent Catholics to Harvard, Yale, Princeton, and Chicago for their doctorates. There they learned what it meant for theology to be an academic discipline.[10] If Catholic theology was to be "excellent," it had to operate with new criteria and free of control by any authorities external to the institution itself. In no way could it be confessional, apologetic, or proselytizing. The vastness of the field required the theological scholar to be a specialist engaged with other specialists, who alone were competent to judge the quality of the scholar's work. Hiring, tenure, and promotion decisions were their preserve. The legally binding contract of tenure would protect creative theologians from punitive Church authorities, if need be.[11]

Instead of understanding and relating their work primarily to the needs and mission of the Church, theologians now took their issues and standards from their profession as it was practiced in those universities renowned for their "excellence." Academic theology became "real" theology. All other theologies were deemed second rate: insular, confessional, or, at best, simply popularizations of real theology.

This academic theology was a vast improvement over what mostly passed for theology in the United States prior to Vatican II. Now, though, the distinctive identity of Catholic theology became a serious question.[12] When Catholic theologians did speak and write about controversial church issues, they were often accused of ignoring, if not threatening, the authority of the magisterium. Hadn't they gone so far as to construct a new vision of sexuality[13] after telling Catholics to follow their conscience in the wake of Paul VI's *Humanae Vitae* (1968)? Hadn't they challenged John Paul II's *Ordinatio Sacerdotalis* (1994), despite the claim of the Congregation for the Doctrine of the Faith that reserving ordination to males was infallible teaching?[14]

Undaunted, most theologians' loyalties and energies remained devoted to their specializations. Within the academy, theological service to the church might be admirable, but it was not the kind of scholarship that counted toward tenure and promotion. Few theologians played any formal role in the life of the church and these few had to meet churchmen's stringent criteria of orthodoxy. No public disagreement with any church teaching was tolerated. Efforts to establish cooperative relationships between theologians and bishops were few and sporadic.[15]

In 2014, the Catholic Theological Society of America acknowledged the excellence of John Pawlikowski's scholarship with its highest honor, the John Courtney Murray Award. A survey of his bibliography shows that he is unmistakably an ecclesial theologian or, as Karl Rahner puts it, a "pastoral theologian." That is, he has not worked primarily on the questions that arise among specialists, but on issues central and critical to the mission of the church in our time. His bibliography covers war and peace, ecology, economic justice, ecumenism, and, most notably, Jewish-Christian relations.

Rahner described himself as a pastoral theologian, too,[16] unlike laborers in the "ivory tower" of particular—and justified—specializations.[17] Ivory tower theologians focus on questions arising in the academy. Pastoral theologians focus on questions arising from the life of the church. Pastoral theology for Rahner "consists in scientific and theological research into the task laid upon the Church in the present of achieving the fulness [*sic*] of her own nature as Church."[18]

This "does not imply any cheap popularization of the intellectual disciplines involved, nor...any 'adult education courses' in the realm of theology."[19] Rahner's own work is quite demanding, as he himself admits, because the difference between academic theology and pastoral theology is not one of intellectual depth and complexity. No theology should be superficial.

Rahner realizes that certain pastoral questions cannot be answered by pastoral theology on its own. Such questions can and should be posed to academic theology because every genuine theology, even within the ivory tower, is essentially *intellectus fidei*.[20] This does not mean simply that pastoral theology asks questions and academic theology answers them. New questions that have never been considered before in any theology will always emerge. So this interchange promises to extend and deepen academic theology's grasp of the issue at hand.

We can see this process at work in Pawlikowski's reconstructive efforts in Christology and soteriology, to which his pioneering work in Jewish-Christian relations has led him. He has not flinched at the painful question of how we can do Christian theology after Auschwitz. "Supersessionism" (i.e., the notion that "Christians had replaced Jews in the covenantal relationship with God"[21]) was exploited by the Nazis in the Holocaust. It must be thoroughly expunged from the church's teaching and worship.

To do so, however, requires a solution to the problem that, at this historical moment, seems insoluble: *How might we Christians in our time reaffirm our faith claim that Jesus Christ is the Savior of all humanity, even as we affirm Israel's covenantal life with God?*[22] Pawlikowski understands that the church needs nothing less than a radically new Christology. His own proposal involves a turn to and retrieval of "Spirit Christology," which will not simply evade supersessionism but also offer a more "relatively adequate"[23] grasp of the mystery of salvation.[24] This is an extremely difficult, long-term challenge, nothing less than the "beginning of a new beginning," as Walter Kasper observes.[25] Yet, even as he admits the tentative character of his own proposals, Pawlikowski has begun to map a way forward.

Like Rahner's pastoral theology, then, Pawlikowski's analyses of war and peace, ecology, economic justice, ecumenism, and, most notably, Jewish-Christian relations are not simplistic popularizations of academic theology. They are as rigorous and demanding as the church's mission in our time requires. Taken as a whole, his work also suggests a response to that question of the unique identity of Roman Catholic theology: it is that theology that arises from and feeds back into the life of the Roman Catholic Church on its journey through history. Indeed, John Pawlikowski's work over a lifetime shows us the promise of a future where pastoral theology takes its place as the heart and center of all the other theological disciplines.

Notes

1. Space limitations require that I paint the following historical portrait with a very broad brush. The nuances are provided by *The Challenge and Promise of a Catholic University*, ed. Theodore M. Hesburgh (Notre Dame, IN: University of Notre Dame Press, 1994); Philip Gleason, *Contending with Modernity: Catholic Higher Education in the Twentieth Century* (New York: Oxford University Press, 1995); Alice Gallin, *Negotiating Identity: Catholic Higher Education since 1960* (Notre Dame, IN: University of Notre Dame Press, 2000); and *Theological Education in the Catholic Tradition: Contemporary Challenges*, ed. Patrick W. Carey and Earl Muller (New York: Crossroad, 1997).

2. "But the Catholic Church professes that this faith, which is the beginning of human salvation, is a supernatural virtue by which, with the inspiration and help of God's grace, we believe the things revealed [*revelata*] by God to be true, not on account of the intrinsic truth of the things [*intrinsecam rerum veritatem*] as seen by the natural light of reason" (chap. 3), https://w2.vatican.va/content/pius-ix/la/documents/constitutio-dogmatica-dei-filius-24-aprilis-1870.html (my translation), accessed July 13, 2017.

3. Paul VI rescinded the oath in 1967. Before that, St. Mary of the Lake Seminary, which John Pawlikowski and I attended, began its academic year with our professors swearing the oath in front of the cardinal archbishop at the Mass of the Holy Spirit.

4. See Sandra Yocum Mize, "'A Catholic Way of Doing Every Important Thing:' U.S. Catholic Women and Theological Study in the Mid-Twentieth Century," *U.S. Catholic Historian* 13, no. 2 (Spring 1995): 49–69.

99

5. John Tracy Ellis, "American Catholics and the Intellectual Life," *Thought* 30 (1955): 351–88.

6. Ellis, "American Catholics," 387.

7. I refer to the well-known opening sentence of Vatican Council II, *Gaudium et Spes*, Pastoral Constitution on the Church in the Modern World, 1 (December 7, 1965), http://www.vatican.va/archive/hist _councils/ii_vatican_council/documents/vat-ii_cons_19651207 _gaudium-et-spes_en.html.

8. See n. 1.

9. http://archives.nd.edu/episodes/visitors/lol/idea.htm (accessed July 13, 2017).

10. See Matthew L. Lamb, "Will There Be Catholic Theology in the United States?" *America* 162 (May 26, 1990): 523–25, 531–34.

11. Theologians who teach on "pontifical faculties" (i.e., faculties within institutions approved by the Holy See) are not protected by tenure. See the case of Charles Curran in Jon Nilson, "One Man Out," *Notre Dame Magazine* 18, no. 3 (Autumn 1989): 21–24.

12. Thus, the theme of the Catholic Theological Society of America's annual convention in 1974 was "Is There a Catholic Theology?"

13. Anthony Kosnik et al., *Human Sexuality: New Directions in American Catholic Thought* (Ramsey, NJ: Paulist Press, 1977). This text, plus the negative reactions to *Humanae Vitae* and the Land o' Lakes statement mentioned earlier, alarmed some theologians and thus led them to form the Fellowship of Catholic Scholars in 1977. See http://www .catholicscholars.org/indexFCSDocuments_response.php?ID=34 (accessed July 13, 2017).

14. Congregation for the Doctrine of the Faith, "*Responsum ad propositum dubium* Concerning the Teaching Contained in 'Ordinatio Sacredotalis'" (October 28, 1995), http://www.vatican.va/roman _curia/congregations/cfaith/documents/rc_con_cfaith_doc_19951028 _dubium-ordinatio-sac_en.html. See also Jon Nilson, Margaret Farley, and Francis Sullivan, "Tradition and the Ordination of Women: A Question of Criteria," *Proceedings of the Catholic Theological Society of America* 51 (1996): 333–42.

15. See Leo J. O'Donovan, ed., *Cooperation between Theologians and the Ecclesiastical Magisterium* (Washington, DC: Canon Law Society of America, 1982).

16. Paul Imhof and Hubert Biallowons, eds., *Karl Rahner in Dialogue: Conversations and Interviews, 1965–1982*, trans. Harvey Egan (Crossroad: New York, 1986), 192, 334.

17. Karl Rahner, *Foundations of Christian Faith: An Introduction to the Idea of Christianity*, trans. William V. Dych (New York: Seabury, 1978), xiii.

18. Karl Rahner, "The New Claims Which Pastoral Theology Makes upon Theology as a Whole," in *Theological Investigations*, vol. 11., trans. David Bourke (New York: Seabury Press, 1974), 118.

19. Rahner, "New Claims," 122.

20. Rahner, "New Claims," 127, 134.

21. John T. Pawlikowski, *Restating Church's Rel.*, 1.

22. Philip A. Cunningham et al., "Introduction," in *Christ Jesus and the Jewish People Today: New Explorations of Theological Relationships* (Grand Rapids: William B. Eerdmans Publishing Company, 2011), xxii. Emphasis in original.

23. David Tracy's felicitous phrase.

24. "The Holy Spirit: A Possible Foundation for a Catholic Theology of Religious Pluralism," forthcoming.

25. Walter Kasper, "Foreword," in *Christ Jesus and the Jewish People*, xiv.

Part II

HOLOCAUST STUDIES

CHAPTER SEVEN

"GOD ISN'T FIXING THIS"
Righting Religious Differences

—⁂—

John K. Roth

You mustn't believe in your religion. I don't believe in mine.
—Swami Muktananda of Ganeshpuri

A colleague and friend for more than forty years, John T. Pawlikowski has devoted his long and distinguished career as author and teacher, priest and Holocaust scholar, ethicist and interreligious bridge-builder to *righting relations*, the task and challenge aptly underscored by the title of this volume in his honor. Pawlikowski's life and work embody dual meanings embedded in that concept. Personally, he strives to set right—rectify and restore—relations between groups and traditions when those relations have been strained and often violent. In addition, he encourages institutions—ethical and religious, national and international—that exist to make things right. Their emphases on cooperation, mediation, and reconciliation entail courageous resistance against injustice as well as compassionate care for those who are wracked and ruined in harm's way. Typically, Pawlikowski's concerns have been profoundly influenced by the Holocaust, Nazi Germany's genocide against the Jewish people, an event whose reality, implications, and reverberations compel what he has called "a major reformulation of divine and human responsibility."[1]

Building on the theme of *righting relations*, and with an emphasis on the Abrahamic traditions—Judaism, Christianity, Islam—this essay about righting religious differences aims to amplify a sound contemporary understanding akin to Pawlikowski's outlook and work. Advancing such amplification is a project all the more important as a

105

result of Donald Trump's election victory on November 8, 2016, which makes him the forty-fifth president of the United States. In the apt words of the noted journalist and author Masha Gessen, Trump is a man "who has lied his way into power, openly embraced racist discourse and violence, toyed with the idea of jailing his opponents, boasted of his assaults of women and his avoidance of taxes, and denigrated the traditional checks and balances of government."[2] In addition to his misogyny, racism, xenophobic nationalism, problematic business practices, and countless conflicts of interest, Trump's hostility to Islam and Muslims, far from righting religious differences, feeds suspicion, stokes fear, and intensifies hatred. During the first two weeks after his election, for example, the Southern Poverty Law Center recorded more than seven hundred acts of hate or violence targeting minorities in the United States, more than 15 percent of them on university and college campuses.[3]

As evidenced by the Washington, DC, gathering held on November 19, 2016, by the National Policy Institute, a white nationalist think tank, some of Trump's most enthusiastic and steadfast followers openly embraced white supremacy and antisemitism, prompting an immediate response from the United States Holocaust Memorial Museum, which included a telling reminder—"the Holocaust did not begin with killing; it began with words"—and an urgent call for "all American citizens, our religious and civic leaders, and the leadership of all branches of the government to confront racist thinking and divisive hateful speech."[4] Meanwhile, Trump and his inner circle continued to keep alive plans to "register" Muslims within and entering the United States, a prospect that understandably led critics to recall the registries that facilitated the mass murder of Jews during the Holocaust and to worry that Muslim registration might result in new versions of the World War II camps in which Japanese Americans were unjustly imprisoned.

On November 17, 2016, Jonathan Greenblatt, the courageous national director and CEO of the Anti-Defamation League, issued one of the most significant and compelling responses to the registration of Muslims when he closed his opening remarks at Never Is Now: The ADL Summit on Anti-Semitism by pledging "right here and now, because I care about the fight against anti-Semitism, that if one day in these United States, if one day Muslim-Americans will be forced to register their identities, then that is the day that this proud Jew will register as a Muslim."[5] Righting religious differences in the Trump era will take much more courage of that kind. To see further why such responsibility needs to loom so large, it is instructive to consider some religion-related events that took place prior to Trump's election but now need to be seen as preludes to his ascendancy.

HEADLINE NEWS

On the morning of December 3, 2015, the *New York Daily News* ignited a volatile if short-lived firestorm when its inflammatory front-page headline proclaimed, "God Isn't Fixing This."[6] Atop the headline, the *Daily News* announced "14 Dead in California Mass Shooting." Below the headline were words that added fuel to the fire: "As latest batch of innocent Americans are left lying in pools of blood, cowards who could truly end gun scourge continue to hide behind meaningless platitudes."

According to the *Daily News*, the meaningless platitudes, rapidly disseminated wherever the tweets of mainly Republican presidential hopefuls could take them, consisted of expressions that "thoughts and prayers" were with the victims of the mass shooting carried out by Syed Rizwan Farook, 28, and Tashfeen Malik, 29, a married Muslim couple, who opened fire on December 2, 2015, during a holiday party at the Inland Regional Center in San Bernardino, California. The attackers were killed in a gun battle with police, but not before they had murdered fourteen people. Twenty-two others were wounded or injured in the maelstrom.

At the time, Hillary Clinton, Bernie Sanders, and Martin O'Malley were the Democrats running for their party's presidential nomination. In the immediate aftermath of the bloodshed, the three Democrats tweeted against what Sanders called "sickening and senseless gun violence" and urged, as Clinton put it, "action to stop gun violence now." Such tweets—platitudes in their own right—did little, if anything, to change matters, but they spared the Democrats from the *Daily News*'s criticism of the GOP's presidential contenders.

"Conspicuously silent on the issue of gun control," the paper charged, the Republicans instead "were preaching about prayer."

Reaction was prompt, widespread, and pointed. The *Daily News*, the critics maintained, had escalated but by no means won the latest battle in American culture wars by insulting those who opposed gun control, demeaning well-meaning people who expressed sympathy for the shooting victims, and compounding the intolerance and insensitivity by mocking prayer itself. By the evening of December 3, *Daily News* editor-in-chief Jim Rich walked back the implication of the day's front page in a statement contending that the paper was not, "in any way, shape or form, condemning prayer or religion."[7] That statement, of course, was scarcely an endorsement of either prayer or religion, let alone of God and claims about God's providential engagement in history, issues to which we soon will return. Before doing so, however, three related events—all fraught with problems immediate and long-term—need to be remembered.

WHAT IS GOING ON?

First, while details about possible links between the Islamic State (ISIS) and the San Bernardino killers remain unsettled, there was little doubt that, earlier on, ISIS-related terrorists had unleashed an even more devastating attack in Paris on the night of November 13, 2015, when well-coordinated gunmen and suicide bombers targeted a concert hall, a major stadium, restaurants, and bars. The mayhem left 130 people dead and hundreds wounded.[8] Second, on March 22, 2016, a few months after the attacks in Paris and San Bernardino, and only four days after Belgian police captured Salah Abdeslam, the lone suspect in the Paris assaults believed to have survived, Brussels became the next ISIS-related target. The explosions that rocked an airport terminal and a subway station murdered thirty-two persons and injured more than three hundred others.[9] Third, in the context of these three disasters, not only Americans were left to consider the portents of the statement made on December 7, 2015, by Donald Trump, the eventual Republican nominee and presidential victor, who called for "a total and complete shutdown of Muslims entering the United States until our country's representatives can figure out what is going on."[10] Polling results fluctuated when attempts were made to gauge American support for that plan, which Trump tried to moderate on May 10, 2016, by dubbing his earlier call "just a suggestion." *The Hill*, however, probably has stayed close to the mark when it reported in late March 2016 that "50 percent of all American voters support a temporary ban on Muslims traveling to the U.S."[11]

Events such as these did not bode well, but they helped to account for the fact that in a *Vanity Fair* essay called "Why Jewish-Catholic Reconciliation Gives Us Hope for the Future" (December 15, 2015), the French philosopher Bernard-Henry Lévy argued that our troubled world needs "a *Nostra Aetate* for three voices."[12] As he rightly observed, that remarkable 1965 Catholic document "marked the beginning of the end of Catholic anti-Semitism." Fifty years on, and thanks in no small part to the work of John Pawlikowski, relations between Christians and Jews are immensely better than they have been for centuries. As Lévy underscored, however, a third voice—Muslim—needs to be added more than it has been, and indeed more than ever, to the Christian-Jewish dialogue that continues to make valuable progress.

In the wake of the murders committed in Paris and San Bernardino in the late autumn of 2015 by ISIS-instigated terrorists, widespread anti-Muslim campaigns inflamed xenophobic fear and hateful acts of revenge. In the two weeks after the mass shooting in San Bernardino, at least three dozen threats and attacks against Muslim Americans and mosques in the United States were documented by Oren Segal, director of the Anti-Defamation League's Center on Extremism.[13] The number of such incidents thereafter and in 2016 grew larger, and what it will be during President Trump's administration remains to be seen, but there can be no doubt that the imperative for Jews, Christians, and Muslims to stand together in solidarity that resists radicalization and its pervasive violence is ignored at humanity's peril.

Righting religious differences—coping with them well—will not be sufficient to prevent, let alone eliminate, the twenty-first century violence that, in one way or another, cloaks itself in religion. But, to paraphrase Donald Trump, we need to do more to figure out what is going on, a task that also requires discerning what is *not* going on.

That proposition leads back to the headline in the *New York Daily News*—"God Isn't Fixing This"—and also to Swami Muktananda and his admonition not to believe in one's own religion.[14]

SENSES OF THE WHOLE

To follow where those threads lead, consider that *religion*, a broad concept that eludes final definition, often refers to multiple dimensions and expressions—personal and public—of what can be called *spiritual culture*.[15] Following the American theologian William Dean, I interpret this culture to be constituted by and expressed through "myths, rituals, narratives, traditions, and theories," as well as through institutions and communities, all of which inform and mold a society's deepest beliefs and meanings, yearnings and purposes.[16] Following Dean again, I take those *deepest beliefs and meanings, yearnings and purposes* to refer to "a person's or a people's 'sense of the whole,'" to "whatever is ultimately important within 'the whole'" as a person or a people understands it, and thus to what is sacred or divine, or thought to be that way.[17]

As I use the phrase, a "sense of the whole" emerges from a basic human awareness that is widely if not universally shared: we are small but perhaps not insignificant beings within a vast reality. Although reality may not be restricted to history and nature, it at least includes all the powers and processes, individual things and particular persons and communities that history and nature contain. So, the awareness of which I speak entails plurality, "manyness," the sense that reality is vitally full of great variety and particularity. Within that variety and particularity there may be plenty of disconnections and discontinuities, too. Nevertheless, the awareness of which I speak also involves relationships, order, and coherence; it senses that reality hangs together, more or less.

In addition, these varied dimensions of our experience are rich with meanings, purposes, aims, and goals that human decisions help to initiate and actualize. These elements increase religion's diversity. They also make us wonder how all of these ingredients fit together—to the extent that they do. A sense of the whole reflects, expresses, builds upon, and interrogates that wondering. Thus, a sense of the whole is not complete but in process, for reality eludes humankind's full comprehension. We experience horizons that can be approached but never reached; they keep receding as experience unfolds. As we have and ponder these experiences, our sense of the whole expands accordingly, and yet, finite though we are, we can and often do produce a particular sense of the whole, infinite though the whole may be.

Although the infinite whole that we experience partially and incompletely may ultimately be one, the particular sense of the whole that each of us may produce, finite as we are, likely varies over time and differs, at least to some extent, from the sense of the whole produced by other individuals and groups. Thus, to accentuate the mutability, acknowledge our finitude and fallibility, and emphasize the plurality, it is important to underscore that, strictly speaking, there is no single, one-size-fits-all sense of the whole but rather always plural *senses* of the whole instead. By indicating that there can rightly be only senses of the whole, I also stress that no individual's, community's, nation's, or religion's sense of the whole can reasonably claim finality or completeness. Judged in terms of absolute truth, every particular sense of the whole mistakes something, if only by leaving something out. The *mistaking* that inescapably infects every sense of the whole entails, at least to some extent, that each one is in some sense false. More than that, no human sense of the whole exists forever. Coming into existence and passing away, some rightly stand the test of time much better than others, but none—no religion, science, or philosophy—escapes completely the fate of being ephemeral, a fleeting episode in the cosmic scheme of things. Hence, as I refer to a sense or senses of the whole, both concepts entail rejections of every form of totalitarian or exclusively absolutist tendencies. Furthermore, as I refer to a sense or senses of the whole, both concepts entail warnings against violence invoked and unbridled in the name of any and every "revelation" or "truth," "country" or "cause" that calls for and inflicts suffering and death as required not only to eliminate "enemies," but also to prove commitment and obedience to such "ideals." Importantly, however, those rejections expand room for the insight and loyalty that are much needed for righting religious differences.

111

INSIGHT
AND LOYALTY

Notice, next, that while human consciousness can conceive a sense of the whole, nobody is born in possession of any definite understanding of that kind. To speak of a sense of the whole, then, is to refer neither to an innate idea nor to one unrelated to the particularities of experience, including their historical, cultural, scientific, religious, and political contexts. A sense of the whole, moreover, depends on sensing something. To sense something means to perceive, consider, or grasp it, activities that are situated and grounded in social settings. To sense something might also mean to interpret it, even to invest it with meaning or to bestow meaning upon it. Out of such activities, which again are situated and grounded in social settings, insight can emerge. An understanding that focuses on fundamental relationships, insight grows from and develops through the particularities of experience. Through the interaction, interdependence, and intersubjectivity of feeling, imagination, tradition, and reasoning, insight brings a sense of the whole to life.

A sense of the whole begins with and, in turn, informs the particularities of experience. Its primary sources and effects include the loyalties that govern our lives. Those loyalties are not abstractions. They are definite and vital connections that consist of real persons and places, values and virtues, commitments, causes, and communities. Even more specifically, the loyalties that connect with life's profoundest depths are those that transcend the finitude of our individual lives, which is to say that these loyalties are not ones that ever get completely fulfilled and finished.

Loyalty to one's family, to a political cause such as liberty or justice, to scientific inquiry, to one's country or specific religious faith may be like that. Such loyalties can appeal so strongly to us as individuals, as members of a community or tradition, or as citizens that we become willing and even compelled to spend our lives, indeed even to give up our lives, in their service. Human judgment, of course, can be blind, illusory, or deceived about these matters. A feeling or belief that something is worth dying for is not sufficient to make it so.

Nevertheless, such loyalties can both lead and respond to senses of the whole.

The things we human beings care about most as individuals and as members of communities reach beyond the boundaries of our finite lives. Our loyalties make us wonder what will happen next—when our energy is spent or replenished, when our causes are lost or won, when we recognize that history is not ours to control completely, that inquiry can be unending, and that death awaits us. Only through the particular embodiments and expressions of our lives can loyalty exist, but when it is most profound, loyalty shows that, within history and beyond, so much eludes its particular embodiments and expressions. Arguably, religion involves those recognitions and responses to them more than any other aspect of human experience. Indeed, their presence identifies religion, which can both lead and respond to senses of the sacred or divine within the whole.

To speak of the sacred or divine is to identify what remains as most important, valuable, precious, meaningful, and good after critical reflection peels away error and dross. Here, too, human judgment is limited and imperfect. Ongoing evaluation is crucial. As that evaluation takes place, clarity about a central insight emerges. Much does not deserve to be called sacred or divine in these senses, but much that does deserve such identification—take justice, for example, or liberty and life itself—is also fragile, vulnerable, irreplaceable, and often tragically targeted for violent destruction. Thus, our Jewish, Christian, or Muslim senses of the sacred or divine, for example, reflect and intensify loyalties, which, in turn, raise questions and responses pertaining to senses of the whole. How do the things we Jews, Christians, or Muslims care about most deeply fit together, if they do? Especially in a world with the awesome mixtures of success and failure, art and atrocity, joy and grief, faith and despair, good and evil that ours contains, how are we to cope and live well—individually and as members of communities? What lasts beyond the finitude of our private needs and public selves? What is the significance of that reality? What about that reality might be of ultimate importance? How could we relate to that ultimate importance? How should we?

THE SWAMI'S INSIGHT

One place to look for insight about sound responses to those questions is a story that my friend, the Jewish scholar Richard Rubenstein, likes to tell. It features Swami Muktananda of Ganeshpuri. Meeting Muktananda on two occasions in the mid-1970s, Rubenstein was deeply moved by the first words that Muktananda spoke to him, for it seemed, says Rubenstein, that the guru knew instinctively what he needed to hear: "You mustn't believe in your own religion," the swami advised him, "I don't believe in mine. Religions are like the fences that hold young saplings erect. Without the fence the sapling could fall over. When it takes firm root and becomes a tree, the fence is no longer needed. However, most people never lose their need for the fence."[18]

Rubenstein took Swami Muktananda to be a deeply religious man. What, then, did Muktananda mean when he said that he did not believe in his own religion, and that Rubenstein ought not to believe in his? Rubenstein found the Swami's insight particularly helpful because, Rubenstein says, he received it at a time when he was feeling "bitterly pessimistic about almost every aspect of the human condition," a mood that included what he acknowledged as an intolerance toward people in his own Jewish tradition who apparently declined to face what Rubenstein called "the difficulties involved in affirming the traditional God of covenant and election after Auschwitz."[19] As Rubenstein interpreted Muktananda, the swami was urging Rubenstein not to give up his fundamental insights but to use them to look deeper and to see beyond their limited meanings. The point was not that the place where one stands is unimportant. Nor was it to contend that particular religious traditions are insignificant and undeserving of loyalty, finite and fallible, if not ultimately false, though they may turn out to be. On the contrary, the issue is to draw on what is best in a tradition and to filter out what is not. That process rejects what the historian Richard Landes calls "triumphalist religiosity," the term he uses to designate "believers who need to assert their own dominance as a *visible* sign of their superiority, as a *proof* of God(s) 'favor.'"[20] That process emphasizes empathy and reconciliation, not by underestimating, let alone ignoring, violence and destructiveness, especially

when those forces are unleashed in the name of religion, but by recognizing that religion's value depends decisively on the degree to
which religion informs and encourages the best ethical commitments
that critical judgment and ongoing inquiry support.

That proposition, I believe, leads back to the *Daily News* headline: "God Isn't Fixing This." In this instance, we can think of God
as God is identified in senses of the whole that traditionally appear in
Judaism, Christianity, or Islam. Or we can let the term *God* be interpreted more broadly as a way of referring to what is sacred or divine.
In either of those approaches, however, it may well be that the *Daily
News* was on target. When it comes to the multiple shortfalls and
shortcomings of thought, character, decision, and action that tempt
us human beings to betray what is good, right, virtuous, and just,
and incite us to inflict incalculable harm, "God isn't fixing this."
That task falls to us human beings. If we do not rise to that occasion,
nobody or nothing else will. What is sacred or divine will still make
its appeals, such as the commandment "You shall not murder," which
God insisted should be followed but apparently has done too little to
credibly back up the insistence, at least as far as history's slaughter
bench suggests.

THEN WHAT?

If God is not "fixing" our moral and religious failures to the
extent that is needed, if that task is left to us, and we are not able to
fulfill it, at least not completely, then what? My response is that it is
still possible, partly through encountering and welcoming the
stranger, to experience and extend what I like to call an *in-spite-of* joy.
To discern what I mean, recall that in April 1915, a few weeks after
the first use of poisonous gas in World War I, the Ottoman Turkish
regime was about to launch the first state-planned genocide of the
twentieth century by annihilating the Armenian people in their homeland. Thirty years later, World War II came to its European ending,
leaving enormous devastation in its wake. That carnage was evident at
Buchenwald, the Nazi concentration camp liberated by American
troops on April 11, 1945. Among the Jews who had been force-

marched from Auschwitz to that place a few months earlier was a teenaged boy named Elie Wiesel. Eventually the recipient of the Nobel Peace Prize, Wiesel, who died at the age of eighty-seven on July 2, 2016, reminds us that "indifference and resignation are not the answer....If life—mine or that of my fellow man—is not an offering to the *other*, what are we doing on this earth?"[21]

The Armenian genocide and the Holocaust—catastrophes that depended on moral and religious failures, to say nothing of God's absence—took place decades ago. The journalist Jeff Jacoby—the son of a Holocaust survivor—may have gotten it right when his 2016 Yom Hashoah reflection drew the conclusion that for frail humanity "eventually, everything is forgotten. Even the worst crime in history."[22] But the American novelist William Faulkner also had a point when he said that "the past is never dead. It's not even past."[23] It had been hoped that "Never again!" might be more than a slogan, but in April 1994, the Rwandan genocide began and was soon in full cry. In just one hundred days, between five hundred thousand and one million Rwandans, predominantly Tutsi, were killed, most of them hacked to death machete-style. As the violence of ISIS reveals presently, the impulses that lead to mass atrocity crimes—genocide, crimes against humanity, war crimes, ethnic cleansing—continue to wreak havoc and inflict horrific suffering.

The French philosopher Albert Camus thought that even by its greatest effort humanity "can only propose to diminish arithmetically the sufferings of the world." But, he insistently added, "The injustice and the suffering of the world...will not cease to be an outrage."[24] That outlook led Camus to contemplate the fate of Sisyphus, the mythical Greek king who passionately loved life and defied fate by thwarting death itself. The gods condemned Sisyphus to a ceaseless repetition that required him to push a weighty rock up a mountain only to have it roll back to the bottom as he neared the top.

Sisyphus riveted Camus's attention during the return to the bottom, where the burden had to be taken up again. If that descent was "sometimes performed in sorrow," said Camus, "it can also take place in joy. This word is not too much," he contended. "The struggle itself toward the heights is enough to fill a man's heart. One must imagine Sisyphus happy."[25]

The joy that Camus had in mind is not sentimental, occasional, or fleeting. It is scarcely synonymous with feel-good fun. Resistant and resilient, the joy Camus had in mind is an *in-spite-of* joy. Refusing to be driven to despair, such joy encourages resistance against atrocity, even if not always victoriously. Kindled and sustained by friendship, by the help that we give as well as receive, by doing what is right and good, by love, such joy sustains solidarity with those who oppose and limit harm, relieve suffering, and save lives. Declining to give in or give up, *in-spite-of* joy keeps people going even when doing so may seem like a forlorn cause.

In his book *Moments of Reprieve*, the Italian Jew and Holocaust survivor Primo Levi touched on related themes by recalling his friend Lorenzo Perrone, whom Levi credited with saving his life in Auschwitz. Not a Jew but an Italian civilian, Lorenzo, a skilled mason fifteen years older than Levi, was "officially" a "voluntary" worker helping to build the industrial plant that the Germans were constructing at a place known as Auschwitz III. Established in 1942, this sub-camp in the vast Auschwitz complex, also called Buna or Monowitz, housed prisoners—Elie Wiesel and Levi among them—who toiled at the synthetic rubber factory located on the outskirts of a Polish village. In fact, however, Lorenzo was more like a labor conscript, and he despised the German cruelty that he saw at Auschwitz.

After meeting Levi in late June 1944, Lorenzo decided to help his fellow Italian, although it was a crime with grave consequences for Lorenzo even to speak to an Auschwitz prisoner. For months, Lorenzo got Levi extra food, which was the physical difference between life and death. "I believe that it was really due to Lorenzo that I am alive today," Levi would write, underscoring that Lorenzo's help meant much more than food alone. What also sustained him was that Lorenzo

> constantly reminded me by his presence, by his natural and plain manner of being good, that there still existed a just world outside our own, something and someone still pure and whole, not corrupt, not savage, extraneous to hatred and terror; something difficult to define, a remote possibility of good, but for which it was worth surviving.[26]

When liberation came, Levi lost track of Lorenzo, but later he became determined to find out what had happened to his life-saving friend. They reconnected for a short time in Italy after the war, but soon Lorenzo died. At one of their postwar meetings, Levi learned that he was not the only Auschwitz prisoner whom Lorenzo had helped, but Levi's friend had rarely told that story. In Lorenzo's view, wrote Levi, "We are in this world to do good, not to boast about it."[27]

Remote though it often seems, difficult to define though it may be, the possibility that we are in this world to do good remains. More than that, the possibility becomes an imperative if the world is to be less corrupt and savage and more opposed to hatred and terror. I think Levi was right to suggest that it is difficult to define precisely how it is that we are in this world to do good, but it was not difficult for Levi to feel Lorenzo's "presence" and to discern his "natural and plain manner of being good." Lorenzo's presence, his offering to Levi, his ways of being good were oppression resisting, hope sustaining, death defying, and life giving. Resonating with the ancient Jewish wisdom that it is not incumbent upon us to finish the task, but we are not free to desist from it (Ethics of the Fathers, 2:21), such qualities, which abound in the life and work of John Pawlikowski, are the ingredients that inspire and nourish the *in-spite-of* joy that we need to have in our lives every day, especially as we keep seeking, in particular, the best ways to right religious differences and to keep reformulating our senses of divine and human responsibility during the era of Donald Trump and far beyond as well.

Notes

1. John T. Pawlikowski, "The Holocaust: Its Challenges for Understanding Human Responsibility," in *Ethics in the Shadow of the Holocaust: Christian and Jewish Perspectives*, ed. Judith H. Banki and John T. Pawlikowski (Chicago: Sheed & Ward, 2001), 269.

2. Masha Gessen, "Trump: The Choice We Face," *New York Review of Books*, November 27, 2016, http://www.nybooks.com/daily/2016/11/27/trump-realism-vs-moral-politics-choice-we-face/.

3. For further information, see the Southern Poverty Law Center's report, "Ten Days After: Harassment and Intimidation in the Aftermath of

the Election," November 29, 2016, https://www.splcenter.org/20161129/ten-days-after-harassment-and-intimidation-aftermath-election.

4. See the USHMM statement, "Museum Condemns Hateful Rhetoric at White Nationalist Conference; Calls on the Nation to Confront Hate Speech," November 21, 2016, https://www.ushmm.org/information/press/press-releases/museum-condemns-white-nationalist-conference-rhetoric.

5. The text of Greenblatt's speech is at https://www.adl.org/blog/neverisnow-opening-remarks-by-adl-ceo-jonathan-greenblatt, accessed June 12, 2018. In his speech's summation of the antisemitism that swirled around and through the 2016 presidential campaign in the United States, Greenblatt contended that "the American Jewish community has not seen this level of anti-Semitism in mainstream political and public discourse since the 1930s."

6. Images of the December 3, 2015, front page of the *New York Daily News* are embedded in that day's report by Rich Shapiro about the events—and reactions to them—provoking the headline. These items are at http://www.nydailynews.com/news/politics/gop-candidates-call-prayers-calf-massacre-article-1.2453261 (accessed July 13, 2017).

7. For examples of reaction to the December 3 coverage in the *Daily News*, including Rich's remarks, see Jessica Taylor, "'God Isn't Fixing This' Argument Divides Even More in Gun Debate," December 3, 2015, http://www.npr.org/2015/12/03/458312256/god-isnt-fixing-this-argument-divides-even-more-in-gun-debate.

8. For further details, see the BBC report, "Paris Attacks: What Happened on the Night," December 9, 2015, http://www.bbc.com/news/world-europe-34818994.

9. For further details, see Alissa J. Rubin, Aurelien Breeden, and Anita Rachman, "Strikes Claimed by ISIS Shut Brussels and Shake European Security," *New York Times*, March 22, 2016, http://www.nytimes.com/2016/03/23/world/europe/brussels-airport-explosions.html?_r=0. See also Merrit Kennedy and Camila Domonoske, "The Victims of the Brussels Attacks: What We Know," National Public Radio, March 31, 2016, http://www.npr.org/sections/thetwo-way/2016/03/26/471982262/what-we-know-about-the-victims-of-the-brussels-attack. The wave of ISIS-inspired terror continued to expand far and wide during the summer of 2016. On June 12, for example, Omar Mateen, an American motivated

by ISIS, opened fire at the Pulse nightclub in Orlando, Florida. His rampage, the worst mass shooting in modern American history at that time, murdered forty-nine people and wounded fifty-three others. Later, what some called the Ramadan terror campaign took heavy tolls in Turkey, Bangladesh, Iraq, and other Middle Eastern places.

10. See "Donald J. Trump Statement on Preventing Muslim Immigration," December 7, 2015, at https://www.usatoday.com/story/news/politics/onpolitics/2017/05/08/preventing-muslim-immigration-statement-disappears-donald-trump-campaign-site/101436780/. As Jessica Estepa explains in her *USA Today* article (updated May 9, 2017), Trump's campaign website highlighted the December 2015 statement, but deleted it on the afternoon of May 8, 2017, as federal court hearings proceeded regarding the legality of President Trump's plan to restrict travel to the United States from six Muslim majority countries.

11. See Kristina Wong, "Poll: Half of American Voters Back Trump's Muslim Ban," *The Hill*, March 29, 2016, http://thehill.com/policy/defense/274521-poll-half-of-american-voters-back-trumps-muslim-ban. Citing data from a reliable poll conducted by Morning Consult, Wong's article noted that "71 percent of Republican voters supported the ban, 34 percent of likely Democratic voters and 49 percent of independents also did." In addition, *The Hill* went on to report, "almost half of voters—45 percent—also said they support the use of enhanced interrogation techniques, such as waterboarding, against suspected terrorists in order to defeat the Islamic State in Iraq and Syria (ISIS)—another idea touted by Trump." In contrast to Trump's benighted policies on torture, see Leonard Grob and John K. Roth, eds., *Losing Trust in the World: Holocaust Scholars Confront Torture* (Seattle, WA: University of Washington Press, 2016). Still further, the Morning Consult poll showed that 49 percent of American voters—a "virtual majority"—agreed with Ted Cruz's position that American law enforcement should be empowered "to patrol and secure Muslim neighborhoods before they become radicalized." See Katie Zezima and Adam Goldman, "Ted Cruz Calls for Law Enforcement to 'Patrol and Secure' Muslim Neighborhoods," *Washington Post*, March 22, 2016, https://www.washingtonpost.com/news/post-politics/wp/2016/03/22/ted-cruz-calls-for-law-enforcement-to-patrol-and-secure-muslim-neighborhoods/.

12. Lévy's essay, "Why Jewish-Catholic Reconciliation Gives Us Hope for the Future," *Vanity Fair*, December 15, 2015, is at http://

www.vanityfair.com/news/2015/12/jewish-catholic-reconciliation
-muslim-divide.

13. See Caitlin MacNeal, "The Stunningly Long List of Anti-Muslim Hate Crimes since San Bernardino," *TPM* (Talking Points Memo), December 15, 2015, http://talkingpointsmemo.com/news/anti-muslim -attacks-after-san-bernardino.

14. Here I am focusing primarily on Muktananda's proposition, not on the man himself. Suffice it to say that although he continues to be a controversial figure, owing to accusations about his sexual and financial conduct, the Hindu Muktananda (1908–82) nevertheless remains significant as the founder of the spiritual and meditative path called Siddha Yoga. Emphasizing enlightenment and self-realization, Muktananda taught that "God dwells within you as you" and that people can and should "see God in each other." See, especially, the Internet site for Siddha Yoga, accessed July 13, 2017, http://www.siddhayoga.org/teachings/essential. At various times, Muktananda left his native India to travel the world. In the 1970s, he lived and taught in the United States, where he established meditation centers, ashrams, and SYDA (Siddha Yoga Dham Associates), which advance and support his legacy.

15. The discussion in the next several paragraphs draws on my book *Private Needs, Public Selves: Talk about Religion in America* (Urbana: University of Illinois Press, 1997).

16. William Dean, *The Religious Critic in American Culture* (Albany: State University of New York Press, 1994), xiv.

17. Dean, *The Religious Critic in American Culture*, ix. In American philosophy and religious thought, versions of these same concepts can be found in a significant tradition that includes Ralph Waldo Emerson, Henry David Thoreau, Charles Sanders Peirce, William James, Josiah Royce, and Alfred North Whitehead. Dean takes the phrase "sense of the whole" from John Dewey, a magisterial philosopher in that tradition. See, for example, John Dewey, *Human Nature and Conduct: An Introduction to Social Psychology* (New York: Henry Holt and Co., 1922), 264, 330–31, where he writes as follows:

"The religious experience is a reality in so far as in the midst of effort to foresee and regulate future objects we are sustained and expanded in feebleness and failure by the sense of an enveloping whole....Even in the midst of conflict, struggle and defeat a consciousness is possible of the enduring and comprehending whole....Religion as a sense of the whole is the most individualized of all things, the most spontaneous, undefinable, and varied....Within the flickering inconsequential acts of separate selves dwells a sense of the whole which claims and dignifies them."

18. See Richard L. Rubenstein, *After Auschwitz: History, Theology, and Contemporary Judaism*, 2nd ed. (Baltimore: Johns Hopkins University Press, 1992), 293–94.

19. Rubenstein, *After Auschwitz*, 293.

20. See Richard Landes, "Triumphalist Religiosity: The Unanticipated Problem of the 21st Century," *Tablet*, March 31, 2016, http://www .tabletmag.com/jewish-news-and-politics/197151/triumphalist -religiosity?utm_source=tabletmagazinelist&utm_campaign= 17244cba14-Thursday_March_31_20163_31_2016&utm_medium= email&utm_term=0_c308bf8edb-17244cba14-207179709. Triumphalist religiosity, Landes contends, has a long and unfortunate history that has manifested itself especially in monotheistic traditions. "Right now," he emphasizes, "the core element of the jihadi impulse [in militant Islam] is triumphalist."

21. Elie Wiesel, *Open Heart*, trans. Marion Wiesel (New York: Alfred A. Knopf, 2012), 73, 75.

22. See Jeff Jacoby, "'Never Forget,' the World Said of the Holocaust. But the World Is Forgetting," *Boston Globe*, May 1, 2016, https://www .bostonglobe.com/opinion/2016/04/30/never-forget-world-said -holocaust-but-world-forgetting/59cUqLNFxylkW7BDuRPgNK/ story.html.

23. William Faulkner, *Requiem for a Nun* (New York: Vintage Books, 2011), 73.

24. Albert Camus, *The Rebel: An Essay on Man in Revolt*, trans. Anthony Bower (New York: Vintage Books, 1956), 303.

25. Albert Camus, *The Myth of Sisyphus and Other Essays*, trans. Justin O'Brien (New York: Vintage Books, 1955), 89–91.

26. Primo Levi, *Survival in Auschwitz: The Nazi Assault on Humanity*, trans. Stuart Woolf (New York: Simon & Schuster, 1996), 121. For more detail on Perrone, see the Yad Vashem article about him in "The Stories of Six Righteous among the Nations in Auschwitz," accessed July 13, 2017, http://www.yadvashem.org/yv/en/exhibitions/righteous-auschwitz/ perrone.asp. Despite the medical assistance that Levi arranged for him, Perrone, wracked by tuberculosis, died in 1952. Significantly, Levi's daughter, Lisa Lorenza, and his son called Renzo were named after

Perrone. On June 7, 1998, Perrone was recognized by Yad Vashem, the state of Israel's memorial to the victims of the Holocaust, as one of the Righteous among the Nations, a special honor for non-Jews who rescued Jews during the Shoah.

27. Primo Levi, *Moments of Reprieve: A Memoir of Auschwitz*, trans. Ruth Feldman (New York: Penguin Books, 1987), 160.

CHAPTER EIGHT

HASIDEI UMOT HAOLAM ("THE RIGHTEOUS AMONG THE NATIONS")

Gentiles? Christians? Who Were They?
What Were They?
Why Did They Do What They Did?

—ɯ—

Steven Leonard Jacobs

INTRODUCTION

Among the most difficult questions regarding the Shoah/Holocaust[1] is that of *"lessons to be learned"* if Jews and non-Jews alike are to salvage *any* meanings whatsoever from these horrific events. In the last decades of the twentieth century, and early in this twenty-first century, perhaps too many scholars, laity, and organizations alike have focused their efforts on the so-called righteous Gentiles in a wounded attempt to somehow balance the scales of justice and mercy; and then there are the critics who argue "too few, too little, too late." To be sure, such efforts have been furthered, not without controversy, by the good efforts of Yad Vashem in Israel to recognize more than twenty-five thousand such persons, oft-times at the expense of their own lives and those of their families and communities.[2]

With the accuracy of hindsight, it is now time to ask, *What have we learned by their examples? What can we conclude about human behavior in extremis? What is the best collective term to describe these singularly unique persons, their families and friends, and, in rarer*

124

cases, their communities? What do they have to say to those who were the Shoah's primary victims about how Jews should and must now behave in a world where they are, once again, endangered, one where genocide is an all-too-common ongoing reality (e.g., the conflicts in Syrian and Sudan)? And, by extension, what do they have to say to non-Jews, be they Gentiles and/or Christians, in equal measure, in our increasingly frightening world?

Before directly turning to the topic at hand—the *hasidei umot haolam* ("the righteous among the nations")—one needs to frame this entire contribution with what is, perhaps, the most uncomfortable and difficult of all questions when addressing the Shoah: *What would you/I have done?* Three brief vignettes:

In 1979, thirty-four years after the end of the Second World War (usually marked as May 1, 1945, the alleged day of Hitler's suicide together with his mistress-wife Eva Braun [1912–45][3]; or V-E [Victory in Europe] Day on May 8, 1945), Professor Byron L. Sherwin, late distinguished service professor and director of doctoral programs at the Spertus Institute for Jewish Learning and Leadership, Chicago, Illinois, published a largely forgotten and by-and-large neglected but important essay, "Philosophical Reactions to and Moral Implications of the Holocaust."[4] Embedded within that essay was a series of difficult and uncomfortable questions, all based on historical realities, and all subsumed under the rubric "What Would You Do?" Among the difficult questions Sherwin raised were the following:

> Would I as a non-Jew take risks to save a Jew? To what degree? Would I risk my life, the lives of my family, the lives of my fellow villagers?

> Would I as a German Christian defy my church and my government to oppose the regime, to help Jews? At what risk?

> Would I as a citizen of a country occupied by the Nazis join the Resistance or help my Jewish compatriots? To what degree of risk?[5]

Four years before I encountered Sherwin's essay, I attended a lecture in Birmingham, Alabama, by the late Conservative Rabbi

Harold Schulweis (1925–2014) of Valley Beth Shalom Congregation, Encino, California. And while my memory of that talk suggests that it, too, concerned the topic of the righteous, I no longer remember much of what he said. The last line of his presentation, however, has resonated in my own consciousness for more than four decades, and has framed much of my own intellectual journey and work in the academy as well as in the various communities where I have lived. That comment was, "The hardest thing for us Jews to remember is that *not* every Christian is an antisemite and *not* every German is a Nazi!"[6]

Even earlier, during my sojourn in Mobile, Alabama, and my teaching at Spring Hill College (1977–84), where I taught the first-ever undergraduate course in the Shoah, I had the good fortune to befriend an elderly European couple who invited me to their home for *kafe und kuchen* (coffee and cake). After enjoying this treat and stepping back into an earlier culture, she, a concert pianist and committed Roman Catholic, played several pieces, and told me the following story:

> Born a Jew in Germany, she was engaged to a young Roman Catholic who was drafted into the Wehrmacht, only to be killed in one of the early battles after the German invasion of Poland in 1939. Her future in-laws, out of love and concern for her physical safety, as the Nazis ramped up their antisemitism and hatred of Jews inside Germany, hid her and she survived the war, though they themselves did not. After the war, out of her love for her almost in-laws and her deceased fiancé, she converted to Roman Catholicism and embraced it meaningfully, while never distancing herself from her Jewish roots, as she and her Italian-born survivor-husband would attend worship services at the local synagogue regularly.

Here, then, in the aggregate, are lessons that need to be learned, at least initially: life itself is a messy affair; attempts to discern reasonable understandings of the past are difficult, complicated, and equally messy; and monocausal explanations of anything are rarely correct and all too often lead us to draw false conclusions as to what happened and why such-and-such an event happened.

Having provided an interpretive context for my investigation, I proceed to the case of the *hasidei umot haolam*: *Who* were they? *What* were they? *Why* did they do what they did?

A CAVEAT

Historian Peter Jelavich, in a significant 2009 article entitled "Anti-Semitism in Imperial Germany: Cultural Code or Pervasive Prejudice?" raises the following caveat:

> Did every person who rescued Jews in occupied Europe, invariably at the risk of his or her own life, appreciate Jews? Probably not. Some may have disliked Jews, but they hated the German invaders much more; some may have disliked Jews, but they had been taught in their Christian churches that murder is a grievous sin; some may have disliked Jews, but they had the burning belief that, *at a fundamental level*, every human life is so precious that one should imperil one's own life to save another one.[7]

Jelavich's conclusions appear to be borne out by those primary researchers who have distinguished themselves in attempting to fathom why those whom we consider today the "righteous among the nations" did so: Samuel and Pearl Oliner, Eva Fogelman, Nechama Tec, and Kristen Renwick Monroe. Furthermore, his conclusions seemed confirmed by the fact that Yad Vashem in Israel has, as of January 1, 2016, honored more than 26,000 such persons, with Poles (6,620), Dutch (5,516), French (3,925), Ukrainians (2,544), and Belgians (1,707) composing a full 78 percent of the total number of those so honored.[8]

Yet philosopher and ethicist Berel Lang[9] challenges the use of this word *righteous* when reflecting on their deeds, and, even more problematically writes,

This use of the traditional phrase, however, is a misrepresentation of the conduct it is meant to honor as well as of other moral issues related to the Holocaust; furthermore, the weight of its distinctions between Jews and non-Jews and between "righteous" and other Gentiles is invidious and offensive....To judge someone as righteous ordinarily implies that that person has acted as he or she *ought* [emphasis added] to have, presumably meeting their obligations more fully than is usual (otherwise there would be no reason for mentioning it at all), but not necessarily doing more than is required of them or anyone else. To act righteously, after all, is just to do what one *ought* [emphasis added] to....The "Righteous Gentiles" did only what they *ought* [emphasis in the original] to have—and what the much larger majority of their fellow-Gentiles were guilty of not doing....The criterion of "righteousness" remains an inadequate measure—first, of the non-Jewish rescuers of Jews during the Holocaust, but then also of the non-Jewish non-rescuers....*The rescuers now called "Righteous" were by common standards not righteous but heroic* [emphasis added]....The measure of honor due them is not because they did what was incumbent on them, but precisely because it was not....The reduction of heroic acts to only righteous ones diverts attention from a larger group of "un-righteous" acts which had far more significant consequences in the history of the Holocaust.[10]

Andrew Flescher sides with Lang in labeling such persons as "heroic," and writes,

What is distinctive about rescuers is not only their courage, *which makes them heroic*, but also the advantage they have over others in being able to determine what, in the strictest sense, "ought" to be done in a situation in which those around them are either oblivious to, or overwhelmed by, the sheer magnitude of the evil and suffering to which they are exposed....Rescuers are persons with an expanded sense of duty owing to their virtuous character. They are moral exemplars, demonstrations of human beings living the best kind of life, able to see more vividly than those around them both the nature of the evil that confronts them and the kind of human response that such evil warrants. At the same time, rescuers are ordinary persons, not pictures of perfection. The daring and noble life to which they have habituated themselves is one that is in principle accessible to everyone....Rescuers were heroic not so much because they overcame their fear and drive to self-preservation—although this may be how we interpret their heroism—but more because they had the wisdom to perceive correctly the responsibility that life had unexpectedly thrust upon them, as well as had the courage to actually meet the demands of such responsibility in their actions. Through exhibiting wisdom and courage, rescuers were able to flourish fully as human beings.[11]

WHAT THE RESEARCH SHOWS: THE WORK OF THE OLINERS, FOGELMAN, TEC, AND MONROE

Whether one is comfortable with the historic phrase "righteous Gentiles" or this newer evaluation, "heroes," it is equally important to examine the work of these primary researchers—the Oliners, Fogelman, Tec, and Monroe—and their studies and conclusions about why such persons did what they did before concluding with two tantalizing questions: "What, indeed, have we learned?" and "Where do we go from here?" *Christian* scholar David P. Gushee, in 1993, raised the actual and appropriate questions that these researchers were, collectively, trying to ascertain:

Why did the righteous risk their lives to help Jews, when the great majority of their neighbors did not?

What, besides the fact that they rescued Jews, set these people apart?

Were they raised differently?

Were they members of particular social classes or partisans of certain political ideologies?

Were they less (or more) inclined to religious conviction?

What motivated them to do what they did?

Is their involvement in rescue best explained by situational factors?[12]

Let me tentatively and preliminarily answer these questions by citing Philip Hallie's assessment of Pastor André Trocmé (1901–71) of the French Huguenot village of Le Chambon sur Lignon, who motivated his people to save approximately five thousand Jews between 1940 and 1944 "because it was the right—*and Christian*—thing to do":

He was a good man according to the classic conception of good and evil, but he was more. Essential to his goodness, central to his decency, was what he did with and for other people, and what he did against them. In part, he was good because he resisted the people who were doing harm and because he helped save the lives of those they were seeking to do harm, the refugees. He was good because he diminished evil *in the world*. The evil he diminished was harm doing, and the evil he diminished was suffering. His character was important, but that was not all, and it was not the only cause of the goodness he had and the goodness he did.[13]

In 2007, Patrick Henry wrote an important text, *We Only Know Men: The Rescue of Jews in France during the Holocaust*,[14] the title of which was Pastor Trocmé's response to that Vichy official on August 10, 1942, who fully expected him to turn over the Jews hidden in the Huguenot village of Le Chambon: "We don't know what a Jew is. We only know men." Henry succinctly summarizes these significant findings of Tec, the Oliners, Fogelman, and Monroe: *there simply was no* single motivating factor among rescuers of Jews during the Holocaust that can best account for this courageous altruism.

Further summarizing the work, therefore, we may thus outline these factors that led these non-Jewish rescuers—and here I want to emphasize further and again, Lang's and Flescher's term *heroes*—as follows:

A nurturing, loving home where children are taught caring values

Altruistic parents or a caretaker as a role model for altruistic behavior

Tolerance for people who are different

Independence

Self-reliance

Self-confidence

Modern self-esteem

A history of giving aid to the needy

A belief in a common humanity

The ability to act according to one's own values regardless of what others do[15]

TENTATIVE AND FRAGILE CONCLUSIONS: ARE THERE, INDEED, "LESSONS TO BE LEARNED"?

In a world of utter darkness, the *hasidei umot haolam*—whether we call them "righteous Gentiles" or "heroes"—were beacons of light pointing the way in an otherwise damaged and dangerous landscape of horrors unanticipated in the aftermath of the terrors and tragedies of World War I—"the war to end all wars." Survivors Primo Levi (1919–87)[16] and Jean Améry (1912–78)[17] have both weighed in and said to us that "it happened once, it can happen again." That is to say, that which was impossible has now become possible in a world where "Never again" has become a seemingly empty phrase, and genocides of others have followed the Shoah with an all-too-easy regularity.

Surrounded by too many perpetrators and too many bystanders and too many victims, these individuals and their families and communities dramatically drive home—beyond question or doubt—the central importance of child rearing as a moral and ethical responsibility if we are to raise a generation of rescuers. And this is a topic about which the Jewish and Christian religious traditions, for example, have much to say. One cannot help but think of Proverbs 22:6: "Train children in the right way, and when old, they will not stray."

Then, too, Jewish history is a history of communal caring, communal responsibility, and the welcoming embrace of family and community, bar none. *Kol Yisrael arevim zeh bazeh*, "All Israel is responsible one for the other" (BT Shavuot 39a). What the rescuers have taught us is *Kol b'nai Enosh arevim zeh bazeh*, "All *humanity* is responsible one for the other."[18] And that is why Jews and Christians cannot forget the Shoah, cannot remain silent, for example, in the face of the false revisionism and denialism of the Turks who continue to dismiss their historical genocide against the Armenian people, the current genocidal crises in Syrian, the Sudan, and elsewhere.

Only the most naïve would contend that post-Shoah Jewish survival was and is the result of Jewish efforts only. And only the most naïve would contend, that, if another Shoah would rear its ugly head again against the Jewish people, the Jewish people could successfully defend itself against its monstrosities without others.

If the Shoah has taught us anything, it has taught us the interconnectedness of all humanity, both the perpetrators *and* the victims. But it is the *hasidei umot haolam* who continue to remind us by their heroic actions that individuals *do* matter, that one person or a few or a community confronting a terrorizing majority *can* make a difference, and that the potential for good resident in human beings *can* be energized when naked evil, shorn of all pretense, presents its ugly face to our world.

Notes

1. I will use the Hebrew word *Shoah* for the rest of the essay to refer to the historical calamity commonly called the "Holocaust."

2. See http://www.yadvashem.org/righteous/statistics (accessed July 17, 2017), for up-to-date statistics on the righteous.

3. Debate remains about whether they committed suicide before or after midnight on April 30. Even those within the bunker disagree as to when they heard the shots.

4. Byron L. Sherwin, "Philosophical Reactions to and Moral Implications of the Holocaust," in *Encountering the Holocaust: An Interdisciplinary Survey*, ed. Byron L. Sherwin and Susan G. Ament (Chicago: Impact Press, 1979), 448–49.

5. See the appendix for the complete list of questions.

6. Eleven years later, Schulweis would go on to establish the Jewish Foundation for the Righteous, headquartered in New York, which, according to its website, www.jfr.org, provides both much-needed financial assistance to rescuers on a monthly basis, and a national education program. Two of its important publications have been Peter Hayes, ed., *How Was It Possible? A Holocaust Reader* (Evanston, IL: Northwestern University, 2015), and a set of eight posters on rescue entitled "Traits That Transcend," which are available for download. Each poster focuses on two exemplars of one of the following characteristics: compassion, cooperation, courage, ingenuity, integrity, moral leadership, self-sacrifice, and social responsibility.

7. Peter Jelavich, "Anti-Semitism in Imperial Germany: Cultural Code or Pervasive Prejudice?" *Jewish Quarterly Review*, 99 no. 4 (2009): 493. Emphasis added.

8. In a recent article entitled "'Kristallnacht': The Legal Status of the Bystander," Amos N. Guiora makes the following observation:

"History shows relying on both a moral compass and impetus with respect to the 'right thing to do' is insufficient. The Righteous Among the Nations movingly honored at Yad Vashem offer proof of the willingness of individuals to act bravely in risking life and limb. However, the thousands who sought to aid their fellow man (*sic*) pale in comparison to the millions who turned their backs in the fact of both potential and clear harm to others. It is for this reason that I propose imposition of a legal duty to act; relying on moral imperative is simply insufficient." http://www.tabletmag

.com/jewish-news-and-politics/194680/kristallnacht-amos-guiora (November 9, 2015). See also n. 2 for Yad Vashem.

9. See Paul R. Bartrop and Steven Leonard Jacobs, *Fifty Key Thinkers on the Holocaust and Genocide* (New York: Routledge, 2011), 169–74, for a brief discussion of Lang's contributions to this endeavor. Lang is the author of such important works as *Writing and the Holocaust* (New York: Holmes & Meier, 1988), *Act and Idea in the Nazi Genocide* (Chicago: The University of Chicago Press, 1990), *The Future of the Holocaust: Between History and Memory* (Ithaca, NY: Cornell University Press, 1999), *Holocaust Representation: Art within the Limits of History and Ethics* (Baltimore: The Johns Hopkins University Press, 2000), *Post-Holocaust: Interpretation, Misinterpretation, and the Claims of History* (Bloomington: Indiana University Press, 2005), and *Philosophical Witnessing: The Holocaust as Presence* (Walden, MA: Brandeis University Press, 2009).

10. Berel Lang, "For and Against the 'Righteous Gentiles,'" *Judaism* 46, no. 1 (1997): 91–96. The quotations are drawn consecutively from across the entire article.

11. Andrew Flescher, "Characterizing the Acts of Righteous Gentiles: A Matter of Duty or Supererogation?" *Journal of Religion & Society* 2 (2000): 2, 7.

12. David P. Gushee, "Many Paths to Righteousness: An Assessment of Research on Why Righteous Gentiles Helped Jews," *Holocaust and Genocide Studies* 7 no. 3 (1993): 373. See also his *Righteous Gentiles of the Holocaust: Genocide and Moral Obligation*, 2nd ed. (St. Paul, MN: Paragon House, 2003).

13. Philip Hallie, *Lest Innocent Blood Be Shed: The Story of the Village of Le Chambon and How Goodness Happened There* (New York: HarperCollins, 1979), 279. See also Caroline Moorehead, *Village of Secrets: Defying the Nazis in Vichy France* (London: Chatto & Windus, 2014) for the latest telling of this story. An eviscerating and lengthy fifteen-page critique of Moorehead's book, however, was recently posted online by documentary filmmaker Pierre Sauvage (b. 1944), himself a Jewish child of the village of Le Chambon: "Does 'Village of Secrets' Falsify French Rescue during the Holocaust?" *Tablet*, October 31, 2014, http://www.tabletmag.com/jewish-arts-and-culture/books/186652/moorehead-le-chambon. One awaits a response—or not.

14. Patrick Henry, *We Only Know Men: The Rescue of Jews in France during the Holocaust* (Washington, DC: The Catholic University of America Press, 2007).

15. Henry, *We Only Know Men*, 153. A further somewhat tantalizing possibility is that altruism may, in fact, be biologically grounded. See "The Biology of Altruism: Good Deeds May Be Rooted in the Brain," interview, September 22, 2014, https://www.npr.org/templates/transcript/transcript.php?storyId=349639464, and especially the comment by reporter Michelle Trudeau:

"All pretty normal—except for a telltale difference in a part of our brain called the amygdala. It's an almond shaped cluster of nerves; it's our emotional radar. And it was significantly larger in altruists compared to those who'd never donated an organ. Additionally, Marsh [Abigail Marsh, who studies what she labels "extraordinary altruists"] reports that the amygdala in altruists is supersensitive to fear or distress in another's face."

16. Among his many important and well-known texts (in translation) are *Survival in Auschwitz* (New York: Simon & Schuster, 1958), *The Periodic Table* (New York: Schocken Books, 1975), *The Monkey's Wrench* (New York: Penguin Books, 1978), *If Not Now, When?* (New York: Simon & Schuster, 1982), and *The Drowned and the Saved* (London: Sphere Books, 1986). See also Ann Goldstein, ed., *The Complete Works of Primo Levi* (New York: Liveright Publishing, 2015).

17. Born Hanns Chaim Mayer, he is most well-known for his important book *At the Mind's Limits: Contemplations by a Survivor on Auschwitz and Its Realities* (Bloomington: Indiana University Press, 1966). Tragically ironic, he also wrote *On Suicide: A Discourse on Voluntary Death* (Bloomington: Indiana University Press, 1976), and, two years later, killed himself with an overdose of sleeping pills.

18. Douglas Huneke has proposed the term *communal rescuers* to describe those who saved Jews within a somewhat circumscribed circle of helpers, but saved Jews nonetheless. See David P. Gushee, "Learning from the Christian Rescuers: Lessons for the Churches," *Annals of the American Academy of Political and Social Science* 548 (1996): 138–55, and specifically, 146–47. Huneke is also the author of *The Moses of Rovno: The Stirring Story of Fritz Graebe, a German Christian Who Risked His*

Life to Lead Hundreds of Jews to Safety during the Holocaust (New York: Presidio Press, 1990).

APPENDIX

What Would You Do?

- Would I as a non-Jew take risks to save a Jew? To what degree? Would I risk my life, the lives of my family, the lives of my fellow villagers?

- Would I as a businessman in Nazi Germany help increase my profits, satisfy my stockholders, and please the regime by using slave labor? Would I take the economic and personal risks that noncompliance might entail?

- Would I as a German Christian defy my church and my government to oppose the regime, to help Jews? At what risk?

- Would I as a Jew take risks to save a fellow Jew, a non-Jew? To what degree? Would I collaborate with the enemy to secure certain benefits and privileges? To what degree? Would I become a Kapo, a guard?

- Would I as a German soldier obey my superiors when commanded to participate in the deportation and extermination of Jews, Gypsies, etcetera? Would I take the risks which such disobedience might entail? To what degree?

- Would I as a citizen of a country occupied by the Nazis join the Resistance or help my Jewish compatriots? To what degree of risk?

- Would I as a woman save my life by becoming a prostitute in a German brothel?

- Would I as a member of the Resistance kill a Nazi soldier if I knew that retaliation for such an act might entail the deaths of my family or of a group of my countrymen? If captured, would I betray my comrades in order to save my own life?

- Would I as a Jewish leader in a ghetto, aware that transports were sending people to the gas chambers of Auschwitz, inform the inhabitants of the ghetto of this fact? Would I sign transport lists of people selected to go to Auschwitz? Would I put my own name and/or the names of members of my family on these lists rather than sign them? If told by the Nazis that my choice was to compose a transport list of ten thousand names or have twenty-five thousand people arbitrarily chosen and transported by the Nazi authorities, what would I do?

- If I were a parent told by a Nazi officer, "I will kill one of your four children and if you cannot decide which one within a span of 60 seconds, I shall kill all," what would I do?

- If I were a ghetto inmate awaiting transport, would I choose suicide rather than transport?

- If I were a camp inmate or a survivor and a Nazi appealed to me to save his life, would I do so? If a concentration camp guard on his deathbed asked me to forgive him for his crimes, would I forgive him?

- If I were a survivor and the German government offered me reparations for the death of my wife/husband, son/daughter, mother/father, would I accept them?

Byron L. Sherwin, "Philosophical Reactions to and Moral Implications of the Holocaust," in *Encountering the Holocaust: An Interdisciplinary Survey*, ed. Byron L. Sherwin and Susan G. Ament (Chicago: Impact Press, 1979), 448–49.

CHAPTER NINE

THE ETHICS OF INTERFAITH POST-HOLOCAUST ENGAGEMENT

—⚏—

Victoria J. Barnett

The ethical implications of the Holocaust are central to any attempt to understand or memorialize it. These implications emerge not only from the historical record but from the very nature of the event: the phenomenon of millions of human beings who were humiliated, persecuted, and murdered only because of their identity as Jews; the widespread complicity and participation in these crimes by individuals and institutions from all sectors of society, not just in Nazi Germany but from across the European continent; and the failures of the international community and its leaders and institutions in responding to this crisis. In his introduction to *The Failures of Ethics: Confronting the Holocaust, Genocide, and Other Mass Atrocities*, John Roth quoted the French philosopher and Holocaust survivor Jean Améry, who wrote that "the gravest loss" he suffered in the Holocaust was "trust in the world...the certainty that by reason of written or unwritten social contracts the other person will spare me" and that as a result "declarations of human rights, democratic constitutions, the free world and free press" could no longer give him any real sense of personal or social security.[1]

The *Oxford English Dictionary* defines *ethics* as "the moral principles by which any particular person is guided; the rules of conduct recognized in a particular profession or area of human life."[2] The scope of human ethics ranges from the standards that guide individuals to the broader "social contracts" that Améry referenced—the

138

norms and moral values of entire professions, institutions, and societies. In the years between 1933 and 1945, there was a collapse and distortion of ethical norms and human behavior at all these levels, leading the German theologian and resistance figure Dietrich Bonhoeffer, in his unfinished manuscript on ethics, to write hauntingly about "the twilight that the historical situation casts upon good and evil."[3]

Those who study the Holocaust cannot avoid pondering the ethical aspects of what occurred between 1933 and 1945, but assumptions about the ethical implications of this event extend beyond the academic study of the history itself. The very act of studying, teaching, or memorializing the Holocaust is viewed by many scholars and students of the Holocaust as an ethical task, even a duty. The phrase "Never again" expresses an ethical obligation to honor the victims, prevent future such horrors, and wrestle with the ongoing meaning of this historical event in a post-Holocaust world.

All these factors have influenced the post-Holocaust Jewish-Christian relationship. After 1945, the relationship between Jews and Christians entered a dramatically new phase, opening the way for the founding of new organizations, new developments in biblical and theological scholarship, and some remarkable changes in Christian theology. There is now a distinct body of literature that focuses on post-Holocaust Jewish-Christian dialogue. A related body of theological scholarship has taken the Holocaust as the starting point for examining and reformulating Christian teachings, establishing a new relationship to Jews and Judaism. This theological project intersects with the now-extensive body of historical work about how Christian leaders, institutions, and laypeople reacted to National Socialism and the persecution and genocide of the European Jews.

Many of those who became involved in post-Holocaust Jewish-Christian dialogue viewed their work as an ethical duty, a point expressed at the 1947 meeting of the International Conference of Christians and Jews in Seelisberg, Switzerland. The primary document that emerged from this meeting, "The Ten Points of Seelisberg," articulated the theological foundation for removing anti-Judaism from Christian thought.[4] As the preamble to "The Ten Points" made clear, however, those meeting in Seelisberg viewed this task as ethically imperative:

> We have recently witnessed an outburst of antisemitism which has led to the persecution and extermination of millions of Jews. In spite of the catastrophe which has overtaken both the persecuted and the persecutors, and which has revealed the extent of the Jewish problem in all its alarming gravity and urgency, antisemitism has lost none of its force, but threatens to extend to other regions, to poison the minds of Christians and to involve humanity more and more in a grave guilt with disastrous consequences.[5]

The preamble then summoned Christian churches

> to show their members how to prevent any animosity towards the Jews which might arise from false, inadequate or mistaken presentations or conceptions of the teaching and preaching of the Christian doctrine, and how on the other hand to promote brotherly love towards the sorely-tried people of the old covenant.[6]

The post-Holocaust task spelled out at Seelisberg was primarily theological, demanding that Christians acknowledge the roots of their faith in Judaism and confess the extent to which this had been denied and distorted throughout Christian history. It reminded Christians that Jesus of Nazareth was an observant Jew, as were his followers during his lifetime and immediately afterward. His ethical and spiritual teachings came from Judaism, and thus the accounts of his life and teachings in the Christian Scriptures cannot be correctly understood outside the Jewish tradition.[7]

The break between the Jewish community and the followers of the new Christian movement became permanent in the period after the destruction of the second Temple. With the establishment of a Christian empire under the emperor Constantine came a profound shift in the power relationship between the Christian majority and the Jewish minority. In the centuries that followed, anti-Judaism

140

became deeply embedded in Christian theology, scriptural interpretation, and liturgy. Judaism was viewed as an incomplete tradition whose texts and promises had been fulfilled with the coming of Jesus Christ, a tradition that therefore had been superseded and replaced by Christianity. Jews were portrayed as the murderers of Christ; their refusal to convert and recognize Jesus as the Messiah was interpreted either as demonically driven obstinacy or as part of God's mysterious plan to make their suffering a witness that would bring people to Christ. In a majority Christian culture, these theological perspectives had political, cultural, and social consequences for the Jewish minority, and in the centuries that followed, the Jews of Europe suffered under discrimination, persecution, and often open violence. What began as a religiously based prejudice became a broader, widespread cultural prejudice that shaped attitudes toward Jews throughout the Western world and continues to exist throughout the world today.[8]

The antisemitism that was at the core of Nazi ideology was a racialized, pseudoscientific hatred that portrayed Jews and their descendants as genetically inferior, dangerous threats to German culture and society. It was not theologically framed, and indeed there were explicitly anti-Christian elements of Nazi ideology. Nonetheless, there is a general recognition among Holocaust scholars that while National Socialism did not emerge directly out of Christianity, Nazi antisemitism (and the widespread support for this antisemitism among Christians throughout Europe) drew on all too familiar prejudices. Jews throughout Europe suffered under the betrayals of their Christian neighbors and the failure of Christians around them to help them. As historian Yosef Hayim Yerushalmi put it, Christian antisemitism was a "necessary but not sufficient" precondition for the Holocaust.[9]

As a result, those who became involved in Jewish-Christian dialogue after 1945 viewed the task of revising Christian attitudes toward Judaism as "a sacred obligation":[10] "at the heart of this sacred obligation lies Christianity's confrontation with the Shoah."[11] This was coupled with a broader ethical agenda that went beyond simply acknowledging the long history of anti-Jewish hatred: Jews and Christians who engaged in post-Holocaust dialogue saw their ethical task as *tikkun olam*, the "repair of the world." Intrinsic to this was the "righting of relations" between Christians and Jews, a complex task that continues to the present time.

Although Jewish-Christian relations concern a number of issues that are not directly related to the Holocaust, it has been impossible to completely detach this relationship from it. What does this mean today, however, more than seventy years after the end of the Holocaust, in a world that is very different from the world in 1945? What is the significance of the post-Holocaust Jewish-Christian relationship in a highly globalized world, where there are a number of broader interreligious relationships and issues? Where does the "post-Holocaust factor" figure into broader Abrahamic dialogues among Jews, Christians, and Muslims, for example, and is it relevant at all for other interreligious conversations? Is the history of post-Holocaust Jewish-Christian relations, and the accompanying scholarship about it, instructive for these other conversations? Or is the Holocaust—and the related Jewish-Christian conversations—so singular that it is not relevant for these other relationships?

There are related questions about what it would mean *in an ethical sense* to expand this conversation to include other groups. Would such an expansion detract from or even undermine the specific nuances of the Jewish-Christian relationship? With regard to Holocaust history, does such engagement open the door to distortion, false analogies, or even minimizing the nature of the Holocaust? Or might it be possible, even productive, for an interfaith post-Holocaust dialogue to examine the Holocaust and its lessons, acknowledge the unique aspects of the post-Holocaust Jewish-Christian conversation, and bring it into a productive conversation with contemporary interreligious issues?

In reflecting on these issues, I will begin by examining some of the historical and ethical dynamics between 1933 and 1945 that laid the foundation for the specific questions that Jews and Christians addressed in the wake of the Holocaust, and conclude by exploring the broader issues of how this history and its legacy might inform broader interreligious relationships today.

THE INTERSECTION OF ETHICAL, HISTORICAL, AND RELIGIOUS ISSUES DURING THE HOLOCAUST

From the very beginning, there was an ongoing tension in the scholarship about the Holocaust between scholars who viewed this event as an unprecedented rupture in Western civilization and others who focused on the continuities between certain philosophical, political, social, and religious motifs in European history and what subsequently occurred under National Socialism.

There are indeed continuities between Christian anti-Judaism, Nazi antisemitism, and the responses of Protestants and Catholics to the Nazi measures after 1933. In his seminal work, *The Destruction of the European Jews*, historian Raul Hilberg offered a striking example of this in a table ("Canonical and Nazi Anti-Jewish Measures") in which he compared Catholic anti-Jewish laws through the centuries with similar Nazi laws.[12] After 1933, there were numerous other explicit examples of the successful use of Christian anti-Judaism to appeal to popular prejudices. Martin Luther's anti-Jewish texts were used in Nazi propaganda and repeated in Lutheran sermons.[13] Julius Streicher's propaganda tabloid *Der Stürmer* regularly drew upon the deicide charge in various cover illustrations that portrayed the "crucifixion" of Germany by the Jews.[14] Streicher also published a children's book, *Der Giftpilz* ("The Poisonous Mushroom"—the title referring to the Jews) that included an illustration of a mother showing her children a crucifixion scene and reminding them of "the horrible murder by the Jews on Golgatha."[15]

The ways in which leading bishops, clergy, and theologians in both the Protestant and Catholic churches began to revise doctrine, theology, and liturgy to conform to Nazi ideology was more complex and insidious. This process, as well as the public support for the Nazi regime by some clergy and theologians, was influenced not only by theological attitudes toward Judaism, but by nationalism, anticommunism, and other factors. Some of Germany's most distinguished theologians, such as Paul Althaus (a Lutheran) and Karl Adam (a Catholic), emphasized the relevance of ethnicity and nationalism for

143

Christian theology, leading to racialized theologies that offered a kind of intellectual legitimacy to Nazi ideology.[16] The most prominent example of this was the German Christian Faith Movement, a pro-Nazi faction within the Protestant churches that sought the nazification of German Protestantism, including the exclusion of baptized members of Jewish descent.[17] Inevitably this led to distortions of Christian theology, the most extreme example being a group of leading biblical scholars, members of the German Christians, who argued for the "Aryan" nature of Jesus and in 1939 established the Institute for the Study and Eradication of Jewish Influence on German Church Life.[18]

There were figures in both churches who offered outspoken opposition to these developments, the most prominent example being the Protestant Confessing Church, which protested the German Christians' distortion of Christian teachings and their attempt to bring the church under Nazi state control.[19] Neither the Protestant nor the Catholic churches in Nazi Germany produced a coherent theological or political critique of National Socialism or its antisemitism, however, and the church leadership offered little open opposition to Nazi measures. With the exception of a few brave individuals, the Catholic and Protestant churches were silent with respect to the persecution of German Jews.

There were similar patterns in other Christian churches throughout Europe. The German Christian Faith Movement was not the only ethno-nationalist movement to emerge during the interwar period: similar groups emerged in Romania, Hungary, Poland, Italy, and France, combining their respective Christian traditions (these groups included Orthodox, Catholic, and Protestant movements) with open support for antisemitism, fascism, and ethno-nationalism.[20]

The history of the Christian churches during the Holocaust covers a wide and complex range of Christian traditions, institutions, figures, and actions over the twelve years of National Socialism—beginning inside Nazi Germany, extending throughout the European countries that came under Nazi occupation, and including international Christian leaders and church bodies. The record includes actions that were theologically, institutionally, and ethically motivated, as well as responses that were influenced by factors that had little to do with theology or belief. One example was the self-understanding of Christian churches and their leadership with regard to the public role of the church in terms of church/state issues. Was the church's duty first and foremost to preach the gospel and administer the sacraments? What were its obligations to state authority? What were the theological and institutional frameworks for possible opposition and resistance? Church leaders in different European countries arrived at different answers to these questions, but overwhelmingly, church leaders tended toward caution, compromise, and silence with respect to the Nazi authorities and the antisemitic measures.[21] Church leaders often focused on strategic considerations, intended to retain institutional control of the church and avoid direct conflict with the Nazi state and possible repercussions against the church. Resistance and rescue tended to come from the grassroots and the margins, rather than from the top. The precise role played by theological attitudes in all this was often difficult to tease out from other factors. In the wake of the Holocaust, this history awakened a sense of obligation among scholars and interfaith leaders to focus not only on the historical failure of the churches, but on the deeper theological elements that had fed it.

At the same time, however, another body of Holocaust scholarship emerged that, rather than tracing historical and theological continuities, focused more on the inexplicable and shattering nature of what had just happened, and its repercussions for human ethics. The German Jewish philosopher and Holocaust survivor Emil Fackenheim wrote in *To Mend the World: Foundations of Post-Holocaust Thought* that the Holocaust was a rupture "of all things hitherto considered 'human.'"[22] United States Catholic theologian and ethicist John Pawlikowski stated, "The basic challenge of the Shoah lies in our changed perception of the relationship between God and humanity and its implications for the basis of moral behavior."[23]

These scholars emphasized that the Holocaust represented an event that in a sense went beyond history itself: an unprecedented rupture in human history that challenged our very capacity to grasp the nature and scope of the evil. The Holocaust had occurred in the heart of Europe, and for European and North American thinkers the realization was shocking that Germany—a nation noted for its cultural achievements, level of education, and other indicators of "civilization"—had descended into such barbarity. It must be acknowledged, of course, that this was a European and North American perspective, one that ignored other barbarous events in Western history, such as slavery and the genocides of indigenous populations.[24] The notion that wealth, culture, and education inoculate people and cultures against such barbarity is an illusion belied by history. Nonetheless, in the early decades following 1945, the view of the Holocaust as a kind of "rupture" in human history strongly influenced the ethical discourse.

This interpretation was also an ethical declaration of sorts, for it constituted the deliberate repudiation of any rationale or logic that might serve to "normalize" what had just happened: if this horror could be explained, might that not give it some kind of sense, of meaning, even legitimacy? This led to a certain tension between the work of historians and ethicists, but over time the historians won. As horrible as they were, Nazi ideology and policies had a logic and calculus, and under National Socialism, Germans often acted as they did for mundane reasons, not just ideological ones. The historiography gradually moved away from the notion of Holocaust as "rupture," documenting in more detail the factors that had shaped individual and institutional behavior in Nazi Germany. Increasingly, scholars understood the perpetrators not as monsters but as "ordinary people," and Nazi crimes as crimes that any human being might become involved in, given the right circumstances. This new understanding was accompanied by more comparative work on patterns of human behavior and the dynamics of atrocity not only during the Holocaust but in other genocides.

Some scholars who looked specifically at ethical issues argued that Germans under Nazism actually had viewed their behavior not as evil, but as a coherent set of ethical action standards in the purpose of what the Nazis had defined as the greater good. This argument was made most explicitly by Peter Haas, a professor of Jewish studies, in his book *Morality after Auschwitz*, in which he argued that Nazi leaders, as well as professionals and the elites in German cultural, educational, political, and religious professions and institutions, articulated and governed by a "Nazi ethic," one that emphasized values like ethnic purity above more traditional norms.[25] This in itself was a kind of rupture, a reversal of traditional social norms and values. The German theologian and resistance figure Dietrich Bonhoeffer described the result in his 1942 essay, "After Ten Years" (the title refers to the ten years Germans had just spent under National Socialism):

> The huge masquerade of evil has thrown all ethical concepts into confusion. That evil should appear in the form of light, good deeds, historical necessity, social justice is absolutely bewildering for one coming from the world of ethical concepts that we have received. For the Christian who lives by the Bible, it is the very confirmation of the abysmal wickedness of evil.[26]

These discussions went far beyond the parameters of the Jewish-Christian relationship, raising deeper philosophical questions about civilization and human nature itself. Philosopher John K. Roth argued that as a result of the Holocaust "our very understanding of what it means to be human has been radically altered by the organized, persistent, modern, bureaucratic, and brutal murder of millions of those deemed 'unfit for humanity.'"[27]

Such broader philosophical questions may resonate deeply among individuals and groups with no direct relationship to this history, thereby opening the way for new conversations, including multireligious ones. In a 2014 article, in a special edition of the *Journal of Interreligious Studies* that was devoted to the Holocaust's relevance in a multireligious world,[28] scholar Khaleel Mohammed described the impact of a workshop at the United States Holocaust Memorial Museum for Jews, Christians, and Muslims that led him to conclude that "ethics, rather than theological perspectives, should govern interfaith relations."[29]

REFLECTIONS ON THE RELEVANCE OF POST-HOLOCAUST THEMES FOR BROADER INTERFAITH CONVERSATIONS

There were multiple intersecting circles of conversation between Christians and Jews after 1945. In some of them, the starting point was the academic study of the Holocaust; for others, it was a broader philosophical and ethical reflection on what had just occurred. Others focused on explicitly faith-framed conversations with the goal of reconciliation and understanding.

As the historical overview just provided indicates, however, all these post-Holocaust Christian-Jewish conversations carried a number of burdens. While the purpose of interfaith dialogue is usually understood as reconciliation and understanding, post-Holocaust conversations invariably served as the means for multiple processes, including the examination of a long and painful theological history as well as the record of Christian responses during the Holocaust itself. These processes in turn intersected with contemporary issues of contention, notably those surrounding the Israel/Palestine conflict, or with areas of ongoing cooperation on issues like civil rights and ecological issues.

All of these arenas offered the potential for "righting relations" between Christians and Jews. An intrinsic part of that process is not only moving to a new stage of relationship, but the resultant process of change that inevitably occurs within the respective traditions. Interfaith dialogue "facilitates the process of change within traditions....Partners in a dialogue cannot be honest without being changed—and this is true both for individuals and institutions."[30] Such internal changes within the respective traditions are well documented by the long list of statements that have been issued by the different churches since 1945, as well as the joint statements from Jews and Christians.[31]

What does all this mean for broader interreligious relations, and—to return to one of my opening questions, what are the ethics of this? Should the post-Holocaust Jewish-Christian conversation actually be expanded to include other faith traditions, or is it better to see this unique conversation as a foundation that can fruitfully inform some of these other conversations?

In answering such questions, it is necessary first to acknowledge the important distinctions between the Jewish-Christian relationship and other interreligious or multireligious discussions. The first and most important difference is that the inherent theological tension between Judaism as the root of Christianity, and Christianity as a distinct tradition, is unique in the history of religions; the related historical phenomena, including the centuries of anti-Judaism in Western culture and the Holocaust itself, are also singular. At the same time, there are elements within this history that resonate among other religious groups that have suffered discrimination and persecution. Wherever there have been religiously or theologically framed tensions between different religious or ethnic groups, the aftereffects often become embedded in subsequent narratives and memories of the event, thereby gaining a longer influence on subsequent political and religious relationships. The European wars of religion between Protestants and Catholics and within Protestantism itself, the Muslim conflicts and the Ottoman wars, the ongoing conflicts between Hindus and Muslims in Kashmir and India, and the tensions within the Muslim world between Sunni and Shia are just a few examples.

This understanding has led some Muslim scholars, such as Mehnaz Afridi, to find in the history of the Holocaust the potential for a different understanding between contemporary Muslims and Jews; in her book *Shoah through Muslim Eyes*, Afridi analyzed the dynamics of memory and empathy in both groups.[32] There is also a growing body of scholarship about the Holocaust that explores the history of Muslim populations in North Africa and Europe under National Socialism, an avenue of study that could well inform broader interreligious implications of the Holocaust. Holly Robertson Huffnagle traced the pre-Holocaust interrelationships between Jews and Muslims in Poland and examined how that affected patterns of Muslim rescue and resistance after 1939.[33] The Moroccan anthropologist Aomar Boum has studied Muslim-Jewish relations in North Africa in the wake of the Holocaust; he has also studied the cooperation between Muslims and Jews in North Africa before 1945 in fighting for civil liberties and against antisemitism.[34] This new scholarship opens the way both for scholars and for religious people from other traditions to explore the Holocaust's potential for other groups outside the Jewish-Christian relationship.[35]

The clearest analogies that can be drawn between what happened during the Holocaust and the persecution and genocide of minorities in other historical instances, however, may relate to larger ethical questions. These include the perversion and distortion of ethical rules under National Socialism, the ways in which religious communities addressed this and the related human rights issues, the wide range of behavior by church leaders, lay members, and religious institutions, the dynamics of personal and institutional complicity and compromise with evil, and the phenomena of rescue and righteousness. The ways Christianity in Nazi Europe became ideologically driven—leading even prominent theologians and church leaders to become apologists for Nazi ideology—may also be instructive case studies for under-standing how a religious tradition can become an ideological tool. The Holocaust offers a grim case study in the history of persecution, the dynamics of "othering," and the exclusion of minorities. Theologically, the literature on the Holocaust is a rich resource for exploring the universal questions about good and evil, both in human history and with regard to religious teachings.

With the growing focus on interreligious dialogue as a means toward reconciliation, the post-Holocaust literature gives insight into discussions about rupture, trauma, and reconciliation. In particular, the gradual acknowledgment by the different Christian churches of their record under National Socialism and their failures toward the Jews were an important aspect of reconciliation in the decades after the Holocaust. This was a long and complicated process, for in the period immediately following 1945, church leaders throughout Europe often portrayed their role more heroically than it had actually been. Only with the passage of time—and the emergence of more critical historiography—was there a greater acknowledgment of accountability by the leaders of the different churches.[36] As this signi-fies, the documented historical record of ethical failure in all its com-plexity can be crucially important for opening the way to theological and ethical reflection. The extensive literature about the Holocaust, including the literature on Jewish-Christian relations, offers a case study in how "history, done well, helps to keep us ethically honest."[37]

All of these aspects, so central to the history of the Holocaust as well as the related Jewish-Christian relationship, may offer fruitful starting points for other interreligious dialogues that are confronting histories of conflict, tension, and violence. The real service of Holocaust studies, and the extensive literature on post-Holocaust Jewish-Christian relations, might be to serve as a methodological and philosophical model for other such conversations—which might in turn open the way toward a multireligious post-Holocaust dialogue. The history of the post-Holocaust Jewish-Christian relationship illustrates how over time theological and historical tensions can be addressed: not completely, and not (yet) completely overcome, but in the form of decades of dialogue, repentance, statements, theological revisions, new scholarship, and new language that addressed both the religious aspects of anti-Judaism and the larger ethical and philosophical questions.

Inevitably, the fruits of such a multireligious approach will be shaped by new challenges and concerns—yet this was an inherent part of the post-Holocaust project as well. Post-Holocaust Jewish-Christian dialogue was always influenced not just by the history of the Holocaust, but by the subsequent unfolding realities and by the process of dialogue and contention itself. All these things are part of the dialogical process, and the post-Holocaust history of change in the Jewish-Christian relationship attests both to the difficulties, the potential, and the significance of such an endeavor.

Notes

1. John K. Roth, *The Failures of Ethics: Confronting the Holocaust, Genocide, and Other Mass Atrocities* (Oxford: Oxford University Press, 2015), 19.

2. "Ethics," in *The New Shorter Oxford English Dictionary*, reprint, with corrections, 3rd ed. (New York: Oxford University Press, 1993), 856.

3. Dietrich Bonhoeffer, *Ethics*, Dietrich Bonhoeffer Works English Edition (Minneapolis: Augsburg Fortress Press, 2009), 284.

4. See "The 10 Points of Seelisburg," ICCJ, December 31, 1947, http://www.jcrelations.net/An+Address+to+the+Churches.+Seelisberg+%28Switzerland%29+1947..2370.0.html?L=3.

5. "The 10 Points of Seelisburg."

6. "The 10 Points of Seelisburg." See also two articles on the Seelisberg meeting in *Studies in Christian-Jewish Relations* 2, no. 2 (2008): Victoria Barnett, "Seelisberg: An Appreciation," 54–57, and Christian Rutishauser, "The 1947 Seelisberg Conference: The Foundation of the Jewish-Christian Dialogue," 34–53, https://ejournals.bc.edu/ojs/index.php/scjr/issue/view/127.

7. See Clark M. Williamson, *A Guest in the House of Israel: Post-Holocaust Church Theology* (Louisville, KY: Westminster John Knox Press, 1993). See also Amy-Jill Levine and Marc Z. Brettler (eds.), *The Jewish Annotated New Testament*, 2nd ed. (New York: Oxford University Press, 2017).

8. Cf. David Nirenberg, *Anti-Judaism: The Western Tradition* (New York: W. W. Norton & Company, 2011).

9. In Carol Rittner and John K. Roth, *From the Unthinkable to the Unavoidable: American Christian and Jewish Scholars Encounter the Holocaust* (Westport, CT: Praeger, 1997), 48.

10. Mary C. Boys, ed., *Seeing Judaism Anew: Christianity's Sacred Obligation* (Lanham, MD: Rowman & Littlefield Publishers, 2005).

11. Eva Fleischner, "The Shoah and Jewish-Christian Relations," in Boys, *Seeing Judaism Anew*, 5.

12. Raul Hilberg, *The Destruction of the European Jews*, vol. 1, 3rd rev. ed. (New Haven, CT: Yale University Press, 2003), 6–9.

13. Doris L. Bergen, *Twisted Cross: The German Christian Movement in the Third Reich* (Chapel Hill, NC: University of North Carolina Press, 1996), 158–62; and Christopher J. Probst, *Demonizing the Jews: Luther and the Protestant Church in Nazi Germany* (Bloomington: Indiana University Press, 2012), 59–84, 121–23.

14. Probst, *Demonizing the Jews*, 137–38. See also the online German Propaganda Archive created at Calvin College: http://research .calvin.edu/german-propaganda-archive/sturm28.htm (accessed July 31, 2017).

15. This image and the history about it can be found here: https:// collections.ushmm.org/search/catalog/pa1069728 (accessed July 31, 2017).

16. See Robert P. Ericksen, *Theologians under Hitler: Gerhard Kittel, Paul Althaus, and Emanuel Hirsch* (New Haven, CT: Yale University Press, 1985); and Kevin P. Spicer, *Hitler's Priests: Catholic Clergy and National Socialism* (DeKalb: Northern Illinois University Press, 2008).

17. See Doris L. Bergen, *Twisted Cross*.

18. See Susannah Heschel, *The Aryan Jesus: Christian Theologians and the Bible in Nazi Germany* (Princeton, NJ: Princeton University Press, 2008).

19. See Victoria Barnett, *For the Soul of the People: Protestant Protest against Hitler* (New York: Oxford University Press, 1992).

20. This remains a growing but underresearched area of the scholarship. Recent work that examines these developments includes Victoria J. Barnett, "Track Two Diplomacy, 1933–1939: International Responses from Catholics, Jews, and Ecumenical Protestants to Events in Nazi Germany," *Kirchliche Zeitgeschichte* 27, no. 1 (2014): 76–86; Giuliana Chamedes, "The Vatican, Nazi-Fascism, and the Making of Transnational Anti-Communism in the 1930s," *Journal of Contemporary History* 51, no. 2 (April 2016): 261–90; and Paul Hanebrink, "European Protestants between Anti-Communism and Anti-Totalitarianism: The Other Interwar Kulturkampf," in *Journal of Contemporary History* (2017): 1–22, https://doi.org/10.1177/0022009417704894.

21. In addition to the works cited in previous notes, see Michael Phayer, *The Catholic Church and the Holocaust, 1933–1965* (Bloomington: Indiana University Press, 2000); and Kevin P. Spicer, ed., *Antisemitism, Christian Ambivalence, and the Holocaust* (Bloomington: Indiana University Press, 2007).

22. Emil L. Fackenheim, *To Mend the World: Foundations of Post-Holocaust Thought* (New York: Schocken Books, 1989), xxii.

23. John Pawlikowski, "Divine and Human Responsibility in the Light of the Holocaust," in *Humanity at the Limit: The Impact of the Holocaust Experience on Jews and Christians*, ed. Michael A. Signer (Bloomington: Indiana University Press, 2000), 16.

24. Recent works that explore the Holocaust in these larger contexts include Michael Rothberg, *Multidirectional Memory: Remembering the Holocaust in the Age of Decolonization* (Stanford, CA: Stanford University Press, 2009); and Willie James Jennings, *The Christian Imagination: Theology and the Origins of Race* (New Haven, CT: Yale University Press, 2011).

25. Peter J. Haas, *Morality after Auschwitz: The Radical Challenge of the Nazi Ethic* (Minneapolis: Augsburg Fortress Press, 1988).

26. Dietrich Bonhoeffer, *Letters and Papers from Prison*, Dietrich Bonhoeffer Works English Edition (Minneapolis: Augsburg Fortress Press, 2012), 38.

27. John Roth, "Double Binds: Ethics after Auschwitz," in *The Double Binds of Ethics after the Holocaust: Salvaging the Fragments*, ed. Jennifer L. Geddes, John Roth, and Jules Simon (New York: Palgrave Macmillan, 2009), xii.

28. See http://irstudies.org/category/journal/issue14/ (accessed July 31, 2017).

29. http://irdialogue.org/wp-content/uploads/2014/06/JIRS-ISSUE-14-mohammad.pdf (accessed July 31, 2017).

30. Victoria J. Barnett, "Interreligious Dialogue since the Holocaust: Turning Points and Next Steps," in *Learn-Teach-Prevent: Holocaust Education in the 21st Century*, ed. Carol Rittner (Greensburg, PA: Seton Hill University: National Catholic Center for Holocaust Education, 2010), 22.

31. See http://ccjr.us/dialogika-resources/documents-and-statements (accessed July 31, 2017).

32. Mehnaz Afridi, *Shoah through Muslim Eyes* (Boston: Academic Studies Press, 2016).

33. Holly Robertson Huffnagle, "Peaceful Coexistence? Jewish and Muslim Neighbors on the Eve of the Holocaust," *East European Jewish Affairs* 45, no. 1 (January 2015): 42–64, https://www.tandfonline.com/doi/abs/10.1080/13501674.2015.961879.

34. Aomar Boum, *Memories of Absence: How Muslims Remember Jews in Morocco* (Stanford, CA: Stanford University Press, 2013); and Boum, "Partners against Anti-Semitism: Muslims and Jews Respond to Nazism in French North African Colonies, 1936–1940," in *The Journal of North African Studies* 19, no. 4 (2014): 554–70.

35. See Jacob S. Eder, Philipp Gassert and Alan E. Steinweis, eds., *Holocaust Memory in a Globalizing World* (Göttingen: Wallstein Verlag, 2017).

36. See Robert P. Ericksen, "Christian Complicity? Changing Views on German Churches and the Holocaust," Joseph and Rebecca Meyerhoff Annual Lecture, United States Holocaust Memorial Museum, November 8, 2007, https://www.ushmm.org/m/pdfs/Publication_OP_2009-11.pdf.

37. Victoria Barnett, "The Creation of Ethical 'Gray Zones' in the German Protestant Church: Reflections on the Historical Quest for Ethical Clarity," in *Gray Zones: Ambiguity and Compromise in the Holocaust and Its Aftermath*, ed. Jonathan Petropoulos and John K. Roth (New York: Berghahn Books, 2005), 369.

CHAPTER TEN

MUSLIM MEMORY AND RIGHTING RELATIONS WITH THE OTHER

—m—

Mehnaz M. Afridi

In June 2016, John T. Pawlikowski and I sat at the Limelight Hotel, Aspen, surrounded by the beauty of the Colorado Mountains and breathing the wispy oxygen. I had met John several times at various conferences—the United States Holocaust Memorial Museum in Washington, DC, where we sat on a couple of committees together, the Council of Centers on Jewish-Christian Relations, the American Academy of Religion, the Parliament of the World's Religions, and the very special conferences on "Encountering the Other/Stranger" in Aspen hosted by Carolyn Manosevitz, an artist, interfaith organizer, and a wonderful, sensitive thinker. In Aspen, John and I discussed the weather, his health, and the political climate in the United States before the advent of Trump. I sat with a man whom I can only describe as a man of gravitas who exudes a sparkle and a passion from his eyes as the gestures of his hands gently stroke the genius of his words. I am honored to have been included in this book and I am quite new to this group as the youngest representative of the Abrahamic faiths historically and intellectually. Therefore, as Muslims we have a lot to learn from our predecessors.

My recent work has been focused on the Holocaust and Muslims; however, my new work is on Islam and the memory of the "other." John's own work relates to Christianity, the Holocaust, and memory. He is a scholar, teacher, and activist whose work permeates challenging boundaries of dialogue between Jews and Christians; he offers us a way to see both the failings and triumphs of dialogue. I want to use this opportunity to demonstrate and illustrate how Muslims can learn from thinkers and activists like John T. Pawlikowski.

I will address the following questions: How can Muslims look at the transmission of memory of the "other"? What do Muslims recall about early relations with Jews and Christians? How do we understand our own tradition in relationship to others? How do Muslims think about the Holocaust? In my recent book, *Shoah through Muslim Eyes* (Academic Studies Press, 2017), I argue that acknowledgment of the suffering of the "other" is the beginning of dialogue. If Muslims grasp and acknowledge the gravity of the *Shoah* with no hesitation, denial, and relativizing, then perhaps we can have some open dialogue. If Jews can grapple with the historical colonial and political oppression of Muslims and Islam, then perhaps we can recognize in one another a suffering that is different and not at all comparable but *real* for each narrative. This is the kind of deep and critical dialogue that Pawlikowski has outlined in his own work between Jews and Christians about the Holocaust, with a stark focus on the ethics of responsibility of one's own tradition and sacred values. Not only has he called for responsibility but a self-evaluation of faith, sacred texts, and historical beliefs about Jews. This type of analysis is challenging and rare, especially when he pressures Christians to take the words of *Nostra Aetate* beyond Jewish-Christian dialogue and into the larger realm of multilateral interreligious relations.

For many Muslims, post-9/11 Islam has been at the forefront of the global stage as a religion in a deep crisis that has resulted in fringe extremist groups. Islam has been described as hijacked, mistranslated, and at times "uncivilized" because of the violence that has ensued from extreme factions in almost every Muslim country. Words such as *reformation* or *revisions* reverberate with Muslims and non-Muslims. The question of being the last Abrahamic religion and the last revelation has also sparked some debate. The inclusion of Muslims in *Nostra Aetate* along with Jews as accepted religions has made a tremendous difference in Jewish-Christian-Muslim relations. Pawlikowski's question in his essay on "Fifty Years of Christian-Jewish Dialogue—What Has It Changed?" exerts pressure on those involved in dialogue to engage the deeper challenge for a "wider interreligious relations," which is significant in light of Muslims and the relationship with "other" traditions. As he states,

> A substantially new template had been installed in Christian consciousness with regard to Judaism and the other major religious traditions. A new day was dawning. Even a rather conservative leader Archbishop Charles Chaput of Philadelphia, in an address to Jewish representatives in that city, emphasized the transformative effect of *N.A.*: "So I believe we really are living a new and unique moment in Catholic-Jewish relations. And Catholics will never be able to go back to the kind of systemic prejudice that marked the past." The question fifty years later is whether, despite the switch in the basic template for Christian-Jewish and a wider interreligious relation, *N.A.* has lived up to its full promise.[1]

The important question is, as Pawlikowski has demonstrated, how this has been practiced and lived out in the "wide interreligious relations" for Jews, Christians and especially Muslims. As I contemplated Pawlikowski's work, I thought about how Muslims might learn from this and began to reflect on how Muslims imagine the "other." I focus on the word *imagine* because so much of the "religion on the street"[2] stems from political and historical memory and myths of Jews or Christians. This imagination seems to whitewash or deform the vulnerable memory sites of many believers about one another. Islam, as most scholars and believers know, embraces the Gospels, Psalms, and the Torah as the first true revelations from God. The Qur'an echoes that Jews, Christians, and Sabeans are to be promised heaven and paradise. In Surah Al-Baqarah we read,

> Indeed, those who believed and those who were Jews or Christians or Sabeans [before Prophet Muhammad]— those [among them] who believed in Allah and the Last Day and did righteousness—will have their reward with their Lord, and no fear will there be concerning them, nor will they grieve. (Surah Al-Baqara, Al-Qur'an: 2:62)

One would think that since the Qur'an especially accepts Jews and Christians, Islam truly should have embraced Jews and Christians as the people of the Book. I am afraid, however, that this is not always the case. This is the challenge and the growing concern for me as a Muslim, scholar, and educator of Islam and the Holocaust. Pawlikowski's question as a Catholic man and his skepticism about fulfilling a promise as a church should also be the major frame of reference for Muslims, Islamic Centers, and mosques today. Islam stands as the youngest Abrahamic faith but also the most decentralized faith. It does not have a pulpit or a rabbinical council. Muslims must be challenged and need to interrogate what they imagine and remember about their relationship with Christians and Jews. To some Muslims, especially in the rhetoric of extremists, non-Muslims are viewed as outsiders and traitors to Islam and Prophet Muhammad. However, the Qur'an clearly states,

> And We caused Jesus, the son of Mary, to follow in the footsteps of those (earlier prophets), confirming the truth of whatever there still remained of the Torah; and We sent him the Gospel, wherein there was guidance and light, confirming the truth of whatever there still remained of the Torah, and as a guidance and admonition unto the God-conscious. (Qur'an 5:46)

Is the Qur'an not the inimitable word of God? Perhaps. The "religion on the street" has taken over the minds of so many who are left with imprints and impressions of the "other."

INVENTING A TRADITION
AND THE "OTHER"

> Invented tradition is taken to mean a set of practices normally governed by overtly or tacitly accepted rules and of a ritual or symbolic nature, which seek to inculcate certain values and norms of behavior by repetition, which automatically implies continuity with the past.[3]

Hobsbawm's quotation above encapsulates some of the ways in which I am framing how we think of one's tradition as a repetition or retelling of the stories of the past. Pawlikowski, similarly, has pressed for a deconstruction of Christian thought that rethinks and reevaluates the clear antisemitism within the church. Retelling the Christian story in terms of its relationship to Judaism has been at the forefront of his work, but he also asserts that this dialogue could pave the way for dialogue with Islam:

> One added note: In the development of Christianity's dialogue with other world religions, especially Islam, the new perspective on Christian self-understanding emerging from the scholarship involved with the Christian-Jewish dialogue needs to take center stage. We cannot conduct these other dialogues as if the dialogue with Judaism has not significantly altered Christianity's classical self-perception and self-expression. In that sense as well as its surfacing of the basic Christological question, the Christian-Jewish dialogue remains central for all wider interreligious discussions.[4]

Pawlikowski's insistence on a "new perspective on Christian self-understanding" is crucial in my attempt to revisit some larger issues that frame the "other" in the imagination of some Muslims according to both the interpretation of the Qur'an and to the memory of what was and is perhaps lost at a time or period of longing. It is important to analyze the multiple trajectories of Jewish-Muslim-Christian interactions from the beginning of Islam, Qur'anic injunctions against Jews and others, and the recorded Jewish memory of Muslims and their encounter.

The memory of Jews and Muslims began in Arabia of the seventh century, when the new believers of an emerging Islam began to establish their own particular message and view of the world. The Qur'an reports that Prophet Muhammad and his followers came into contact with Jews,

> and this particular contact became extremely important because reactions to it were recorded for posterity in the

159

Qur'an. The only sources for the earliest relations between Jews and Muslims are the Qur'an and its attendant literatures, which, like other sacred literatures, are interested in history only insofar as it helps to define the emerging community and its values and ideas.[5]

This early perception of Jews and Muslims in Medina has also made Holocaust denial and relativism possible in contemporary Muslim communities as this contact was read as hostile and violent. Furthermore, the massacre of the Jewish tribe has lent itself to the sustained image of Muslims as violent in Jewish contemporary communities.

This image perpetuates, however, because the focus on the exclusivist verses or particular verses that are quoted by extremist groups and some Muslim leaders have created a deep division between Muslims and the "other." These verses exist and can be damaging to the future of Islamic relations to others. It is also important to recognize, as Hobsbawm explained, that the invention of a tradition through repetition *is* continuity with the past even if the past tradition was and is invented. The repetition of negative images of the Jew or the Christian becomes the memory of the past. As noted by Hassan Khalil,

> This is evident in the case of certain Medinian Jews: despite their relative proximity to Muslims theologically, some of the Qur'an's harshest criticisms—doctrinal or otherwise— are reserved for these individuals. By the same token, however, the Qur'an includes other Jews among those who may be saved (as in 2:62 and 5:69).[6]

One might note that these early encounters between Jews and Muslims in Medina may not be relevant; however, this early encounter has been revived in a contemporary light and plays a significant role in the imagined early Jewish-Muslim communities. The early perceptions become very immediate and "the perceptions of hostility or even war between Muslims and Jews is sometimes based on references to the Qur'an, which allegedly predicts religious wars on a global scale between Muslims, Jews, and Christians."[7] Similarly, from 1933 to 1945 the churches' antisemitic attitude toward Jews sustained itself during the pre-Nazi, Nazi, and post-Nazi era. The early church condemnation of Jews was sustained in the past as a continuous moral and ritualist belief within the church.

Similarly, the continuity with the past in Jewish memory of the early Muslims is full of terror and fear, and the Muslim encounter that is recorded in the Qur'an is full of mistrust. The tensions of these communities are not so different in the imagination of Muslims today. The Qur'an may clearly accept Jews and Christians, but there is also the underlying tension of contemporary and colonial influences that have imprinted the memory of relations between the "other" Abrahamic faiths and Islam with deep and lasting images of violence and terror. The Qur'an acts as a source for this tension, but the larger framers of memory of the early relations between Muslims and the "other" exacerbate the current relations. For example, some Muslims believe that the Jews were responsible for the killing of Muhammad; nowhere does the Qur'an or Hadith mention such a killing, but this myth variously finds its way into the discourse:

> Nirmal identified those who tried to kill Muhammad as Jewish as "the enemies." His concept of Jihad included the defense against these enemies who are Jewish and all those who threaten Islam or hinder its spread. He also portrayed Jews as those who hinder "everyone" and live "the life which we want." Antisemitic stereotypes of Jews as rich and controllers of the world served to help him maintain that Jews are still a threat. Nirmal transferred the "defense" against Jewish tribes at the time of Muhammad to the present day and included himself in this fight, saying that "we are enemies," and the fights are about territories that "belonged to us Muslims."[8]

During early Islam, it is true that Islam was just gaining some power when the first Muslims encountered Jews in Medina, and the Jews did not accept Islam or Muhammad as their prophet or new messenger (this was also true of Christians). The history of acceptance and rejection becomes central to the time of Muhammad or the imagined new community that was rejected by, in this case, Jews and Christians. This memory returns back to the street as the prominent images of one another reflect early memories of tension between Islam and the "other." Christian early scholarship was also shaped by the churches' own beliefs about Christ, and the new "Mohammedans"[9] were seen as a cult and a new tribal tradition that wanted an equivalent figure like Christ. The memory of being rejected and Muhammad being imagined as a false prophet is recorded by Kecia Ali in her book *The Lives of Muhammad*; she explains how Christians described and depicted Muhammad as a fictional character based on Christ and "that all the boasted equality or superiority of Mohammed to Christ rests on mere fiction, devoid of all foundation in fact."[10] It is also important to note, as Pawlikowski does,

> Responsibility here is surely uneven in comparison with the challenge before the Christian community. Jews never defined themselves over against Christianity in the way that Christianity staked a central part of its self-understanding in terms of the replacement of Judaism, an understanding that bore not only a theological dimension but also practical social consequences for Jews when the churches had overwhelming political power in many European societies.[11]

These depictions of one another but especially of Jews in the mind of Muslims created deep negative myths about Judaism and even the Holocaust. The Holocaust was minimized and relativized because of the parallels made to Palestinian suffering and the many wars in the Middle East. The imagination of such myths can lead to more distance and less understanding, even if there was friction between Jews and Muslims in earlier literatures as the only organized community in Medina.

All negative descriptions of Jews recorded in the Qur'an and the early literatures were a result of the friction between the early Muslim community and the organized Jewish communities (tribes) of Medina. The Qur'an represents itself as a universal teaching, however, so because of this aspect of its rhetorical style it appears to refer negatively to the Jews in general terms. To add to the problem is the fact that to Muslim believers, the Qur'an is inimitable scripture (and the inimitability of the Qur'an is an absolute dogma of Islamic theology), so its portrayal of Jews represents a level of truth that is extremely difficult to question. As scripture, the Qur'an is a powerful foundation for contemporary Muslims' worldviews all over the globe. The conflicts it reflects ensued for only a few years, but the verses of scripture that record them are eternal.[12]

This "foundation for contemporary Muslims' worldviews" becomes highly problematic today in light of the antisemitism that Jews are experiencing from Muslims either through violence or propaganda. The denial of the Holocaust and suffering of Jews is seen as a myth and an imagined reality—a fabricated lie to gain control and power over land in the Middle East. Pawlikowski points out in his essay,

> In terms of the frontal attack on the Jewish community by Hitler I have always argued that it was rooted in two fundamental realities. The first was the continuing legacy of anti-Semitism, including anti-Semitism prompted by Christian religious belief. There never has been a question in my mind that this classical anti-Semitism played a decisive role in defining and supporting Nazi ideology. This is particularly true at the grass roots level where the majority of those who stood on the sidelines or even directly collaborated with the plan for the Jewish extermination did so because they had been influenced by classical negative images of Jews and Judaism, especially within Christian religious literature and Christian art.[13]

The Jewish response to the early encounter with Muslims relies on the fact that many believe that they were massacred at the hands of early Muslims. "From the Jewish side, the response toward Islam could take the form of revolt (Isawiyya); rejection (polemics); debate (in salons, homes and marketplaces); or conversion (Abdallah Ibn Salam)."[14] There was a fear that a new authoritative religion was being set up that could be a threat to Jews.

> According to the sources the Jews of the Qurayza surren-
> dered. Trenches were dug in the marketplace of Medina,
> and Muhammad had the men's heads struck off in those
> trenches as they were brought out in batches. Sources put
> the number of people killed that day to 600 to 900.[15]

This and other stories in the memory of Jews are seen as the first massacres under early Islam. The memory of the negative aspect of the warring Muslims is further exacerbated by the image of the "Ishmaelites," as the Muslims were referred to by Jews.

> Islam is linked to the genealogy of Abraham through Rab-
> binic texts. Isaac is considered to be the true heir of Abra-
> ham; while the descendants of Abraham's other son,
> Ishmael, are depicted in Rabbinic texts as nomadic hunters
> who inhabit a wide swath of the Middle East; sometimes
> they are also called Hagarites. Though there is no direct
> reference to Islam, later Jewish texts associated these peo-
> ple with ethnic representations of the Islamic conquest.
> Through this association, later texts connected to Islam
> the negative image of Ishmael in the rabbinic sources.
> Ishmael, as the negative counterpart of Isaac, is associated
> with the unrighteous descendants of Abraham, as opposed
> to the chosen descendants of Isaac. In Job, "the Ishmael-
> ites" are portrayed as thieves: "The tents of the robbers
> prosper, and they that provoke God are secure since God
> brought them with His hand" (Job 12). He is depicted as
> violating the three cardinal sins of idolatry, sexual immoral-
> ity, and murder (Genesis Rabah 53, PT Sotah 6:6).[16]

These very early perceptions of Muslims and Jews find themselves enveloped in the politics of today's extremist Muslim groups like ISIS and al-Qaeda. Why have these images and memories resurfaced? What are the memories of the "religion on the street"?

RECENT MEMORIES
AND NARRATIVES

Today, religion is back in the public forum all over the world, but serious inquiry into the meaning of religion itself—what it is, where it came from, and where it is going—remains rare within this public forum, and even those engaged in policy discussion regarding religion seem uninterested in asking precisely what it is they are talking about. What type of religious memory are we discussing? Do we as Muslims discuss the diverse positive and negative segments of history since the advent of Islam?

Islam was able to survive after colonialism, but assimilation has proven to be a challenge and in some cases impossible. Yet, at its core, when all the political and social elements and lingering consequences are stripped away, Islam remains a story about people, millions of them, who in their individual quests to change their lives, live their lives, and remember their traditions have made a *nostalgic* turn of historical memory. ISIS (Islamic State of Levant and Iraq), Al-Qaeda, Boko Haram, Al-Shabab, and many other extremists are also claiming something that has been lost, a betrayal, or even a moment that reifies a "pure" and "idealized" time in history. However, if one takes a close look at Christian and European scholarship on Islam, one can find negative depictions of Muhammad that are still remembered by Muslims. The early images of Islam are not so different from the present images. Today, Muhammad is depicted in cartoons and magazines as a terrorist and an immoral man echoing descriptions from the Middle Ages:

> Medieval Christian accounts say little of his birth but get mileage from his (usually humiliating and shameful) death. During the twelfth and thirteen [*sic*] centuries, Christians viewed Muhammad as "disgusting in life and, most of all, in the manner of his death." Authors wrote Muhammad an

undignified death—perhaps drunk or even murdered, in one account, by a cuckolded husband—and lingered on the dismemberment or desecration of his "smelly corpse" by (unclean) animals, often pigs or dogs.[17]

These are some of the ways that religions have interpreted others, whether Christians, Jews, or Muslims. However, this is where the danger lies in seeing the "other" through the lens of one's own imagination, or as I call it, nostalgia. These images and descriptions tend to stay with the people who represent the main voice of each tradition. Pawlikowski would advise that we deal with the attitude and historical memory of religious traditions and their encounter. As he states,

> From the Christian side a number of other issues will certainly challenge the churches as result of the dialogue with Judaism. The first will be the need to deal with the dark side of the church's record with respect to Jews throughout history, in particular during the Nazi era. For those who put a strong emphasis on the church as a transhistorical, transcendental reality apart from history this can prove trying theologically. A number of Catholic episcopal conferences, the French in particular in their declaration of repentance in September 1997 as well as the Germans in 1995 have acknowledged corporate Christian failure during the time of the Holocaust. Pope John Paul II also gave personal support to such moves in the liturgy of confession and reconciliation which took place at the Vatican on the first Sunday of Lent 2000. He added to this initial witness when during his historic visit to Jerusalem he placed the same statement of repentance for Christian antisemitism in the city's sacred Western Wall.[18]

Gunther Jikeli's *European Muslim Antisemitism: Why Young Urban Males Say They Don't Like Jews* provides us with a Muslim example. He finds commonly believed ideas about Jews and the Holocaust by Muslim men that might add to the larger picture of antisemitism from Muslims in general. The various interviews focus on religious tensions that begin with the time of the Prophet Muhammad and range up to the existence of the modern state of Israel. Israel and Jews are viewed as interchangeable and read as the main issue of contention for most of the interviewees. However, the issue of religious tension is more nebulous and is based on hearsay, what these men have heard through their families, friends, and Muslim communities. The interviewees do not provide much evidence for their religious prejudice against Jews, which the author notes in his study. "Sabri emphasized that the enmity was related to religion and mentioned an alleged betrayal of Muhammad by the 'the Jews' but he was uncertain about this event."[19]

The religious tensions described by the interviewees are fueled by the reality that "the perception of hostility or even war between Muslims and Jews is sometimes based on references to the Qur'an, which allegedly predicts religious wars on a global scale between Muslims, Jews, and Christians."[20] These accounts can be disconcerting and even shocking when the interviewer asks questions about the Jews who were killed in the Holocaust.

Some interpretations, explanations, and beliefs about the Holocaust amount to diminishing or even denying it. This often contradicts what interviewees have learned in school. Three interviewees explicitly depicted the Holocaust as a myth or said that far fewer than six million Jews were killed. Haroun, for example, is aware of the disparity of his beliefs and the narrative he was taught in school in France:

> They are saying the Jews were killed and that. I don't know if that's true. This is what I was taught in school that they were deported, killed, some things. But I was told something else that there was an illness called Typhus which spread everywhere and that's why they were burned.[21]

The fact that some of these young men recall myths about the Holocaust is disturbing; equally disturbing is the fact that these myths have become part of the *real* memory of the past that relates to the relationship between Jews and Muslims (and, in some cases,

Christians are equated with the West). The religious imagination of Muslim-Jewish relations remains nebulous but significant when Jikeli notes the following:

> Allusions of Jews being on the side of the devil can be interpreted as part of the perception that Jews are condemned by God. But such allusions were only made in indirect and superstitious ways, for example, by rumors of a "haunted" local synagogue or by allusions that Freemasons are devil worshippers and somehow related to Jews. Another form of accusation against Jews that they rejected Muhammad and God's message is that their holy scripture was falsified. *"Torah [...]. This isn't good. The Qur'an stayed [...] as it was, nobody ever changed it—and the Thora [sic]—there were some who took it"* (Mohammed, Paris).[22]

RIGHTING RELATIONS

In conclusion, Muslim memory of the Holocaust, of Jews and early Islam, and of Christian and Western perceptions of Islam are all in need of a reformist or revisionist review that can speak to the people on the street and create a wider and more nuanced understanding of what types of sacred and historical memories are passed down at significant moments and periods of time. An example of such a revision by Catholics is found in the 1998 promulgation of *We Remember: A Reflection on the Shoah* from the Vatican's Commission for Religious Relations with the Jews. It expresses repentance for the past and hope for the future, directs Catholics to wrestle with the immense evil of the Holocaust, and urges Catholics to come to an understanding of its history and ponder how crimes on such a scale could happen in Christian civilization.

> Pope John Paul II himself has repeatedly called upon us to see where we stand with regard to our relations with the Jewish people. In doing so, "we must remember how much the balance [of these relations] over two thousand years

has been negative." This long period "which," in the words of Pope John Paul II, we must not tire of reflecting upon in order to draw from it the appropriate lessons, has been marked by many manifestations of anti-Judaism and anti-Semitism, and, in this century, by the horrifying events of the Shoah.

Therefore, the Catholic Church wants all Catholics, and indeed all people, everywhere, to know about this. It does so also with the hope that it will help Catholics and Jews towards the realization of those universal goals that are found in their common roots. In fact, whenever there has been guilt on the part of Christians, this burden should be a call to repentance. As His Holiness has put it on one occasion, "guilt must always be the point of departure for conversion."[23]

This, I would argue, would be a way forward for Muslim relations with Jews and Christians, to remember that Muslims were not innocent or pure during the advent of Islam nor in the treatment of minorities—perhaps *Nostra Aetate* could act as a model of deep self-critique and reflection on the acceptance of the Jewish and Christian message as revelations that stand apart from the last Abrahamic message: Islam.

Muslims have to take responsibility for verses that can be read literally to attack or defend the "other" in the very abhorrent fashion taken on by extremists and some moderates. *Righting Relations* is about accepting the deep holes within one's theology and accepting responsibility for past and present acts of violence toward the other. If we confront past trauma and our nostalgia in a way that can right relations, then we can accept our ethical responsibility for our past, present, and future relations with one another. This work is the exceptional work that John T. Pawlikowski has brought to sharp scrutiny within Jewish-Christian relations both nationally and internationally, a determination that all scholars of religion and theology must learn from and implement in their own life and practice.

Notes

1. John T. Pawlikowski, "Fifty Years of Christian-Jewish Dialogue—What Has It Changed?" *Journal of Ecumenical Studies* 49, no.1 (Winter 2014): 99.

2. I use the term *religion on the street* to connote the vernacular or ordinary understanding of the stereotypes of Islam, Judaism, or Christianity that are heavily influenced by their past relations with one another as well as by political images and propaganda. For example, Muslims are violent, Jews are controlling, and Christians are imperialist and immoral.

3. Eric Hobsbawm, "Introduction: Inventing Traditions," in *The Invention of Tradition*, ed. Eric Hobsbawm and Terence Ranger (London: Cambridge University Press, 1983), 1.

4. Pawlikowski, "Fifty Years of Christian-Jewish Dialogue," 106.

5. See more on the Jewish-Muslim Engagement USC website by Reuven Firestone, accessed August 3, 2017: http://cmje.usc.edu/.

6. Mohammad Hassan Khalil, *Islam and the Fate of Others: The Salvation Question* (New York: Oxford University Press, 2012), 138.

7. Gunther Jikeli, *European Muslim Antisemitism: Why Young Urban Males Say They Don't Like Jews* (Bloomington: Indiana University Press, 2015), 140.

8. Jikeli, *European Muslim Antisemitism*, 137.

9. The term *Mohammedanism* was applied to Muslims until the twentieth century. This term is offensive because it assumes that Muslims worship Muhammed in the same way that Christ is worshiped. Islam cannot worship or submit to anyone but God.

10. Kecia Ali, *The Lives of Muhammad* (Boston: President and Fellows of Harvard College, 2014), 75.

11. Pawlikowski, "Fifty Years of Christian-Jewish Dialogue," 103.

12. Reuven Firestone, "Jewish-Muslim Relations," in *Modern Judaism: An Oxford Guide*, ed. Nicholas de Lange and Miri Freud-Kandel (London: Oxford University Press, 2005), 440.

13. John T. Pawlikowski, "Poles, Jews, and the Holocaust: Some Reflections," *The Polish Review* 59, no. 3 (2011): 208.

14. Steven S. Wasserstrom, *Between Muslim and Jew: The Problem of Symbiosis under Early Islam* (Princeton, NJ: Princeton University Press, 1995), 11.

15. Reuven Firestone, *An Introduction to Islam for Jews* (Philadelphia: Jewish Publication Society, 2008), 38.

16. Alan Brill, *Judaism and World Religions: Encountering Christianity, Islam and Eastern Traditions* (New York: Palgrave MacMillan, 2012), 146.

17. Ali, *The Lives of Muhammad*, 20–21.

18. John T. Pawlikowski, "Risk and Renewal in Christianity," *Jewish-Christian Relations: Insights and Issues in the Ongoing Jewish-Christian Dialogue* 592 (January 2, 2009), http://www.jcrelations.net/Risk_and _Renewal_in_Christianity.2975.0.html?page=6.

19. Jikeli, *European Muslim Antisemitism*, 136.

20. Jikeli, *European Muslim Antisemitism*, 140.

21. Jikeli, *European Muslim Antisemitism*, 188.

22. Jikeli, *European Muslim Antisemitism*, 139–40.

23. Edward Idris Cardinal Cassidy, "Presentation of *We Remember*," March 16, 1998, http://www.vatican.va/roman_curia/pontifical_councils/ chrstuni/documents/rc_pc_chrstuni_doc_16031998_shoah_en.html.

CHAPTER ELEVEN

THE PURIFICATION OF MEMORY
A Tribute to John Pawlikowski, OSM

—w—

Katharina von Kellenbach

Fifty years after Vatican II passed *Nostra Aetate*, John Pawlikowski observed that the document's "most far-reaching, initial accomplishment was to wipe clean the classical interreligious slate dominated by highly negative stereotypes of the religious other in the Catholic tradition."[1] Taking his metaphor of cleansing, I want to reflect on common approaches to purification in the context of ideologies of contempt and political histories of violence. All too often, the language of purification supports habits of cleansing that move the dirt of culpable wrongdoing out of sight and out of mind. As Mary Douglas has famously pointed out in her groundbreaking study *Purity and Danger*, "Dirt is the byproduct of a systematic ordering and classification of matter....Dirt offends against order. Eliminating it is not a negative movement, but a positive effort to organize the environment."[2] But how do we eliminate dirt? Where does the dirt go? Can it simply disappear? It is time to think creatively and constructively about dirt and to develop methods of purification that decontaminate, compost, and convert irritating remainders of the past into new perspectives and relationships. Using the principles of ecology, I want to offer the work of John Pawlikowski as an example of successful transformation of Christianity's doctrinal complicity and institutional collaboration with anti-Judaism and the Holocaust.

We cannot simply wipe away material and metaphorical dirt by declaring, as *Nostra Aetate* did, that "no foundation therefore remains

172

for any theory or practice that leads to discrimination between man and man or people and people."[3] *Nostra Aetate* wiped the slate clean, but it took the sustained effort of theologians, such as John Pawlikowski, to turn the refuse of anti-Judaism into new theological thinking and ethical reflection.[4] In fact, the assumption that refuse magically disappears undermines genuine change. Revolutionary paradigm shifts that fail to treat analytically what has been repudiated are not successful, as Pawlikowski noted when he questioned "whether, despite the switch in the basic template for Christian-Jewish and wider interreligious relations, *N.A.* has lived to its full promise."[5]

Nostra Aetate proposes two pathways to move beyond violence and contempt in the past, both of which are problematic because they erase memory. In paragraph 3, which aims to reset the relationship between the Church and Islam, the document calls on both parties to forget:

> Since in the course of centuries not a few quarrels and hostilities have arisen between Christians and Moslems, this sacred synod urges all to forget the past and to work sincerely for mutual understanding. On behalf of all, let them together preserve and promote social justice, moral values, peace, and freedom.[6]

Can new beginnings be built upon oblivion? The text remains vague and unspecific about the particular histories that need to be forgotten. The language of "quarrels and hostilities" obfuscates political accountability and moral agency. Quarrels and hostilities break out seemingly without agents. Such language conceals the ideas and institutions that exert power and act strategically to influence and control communities. Without critical analysis of history, the call to forget serves to suppress memories of theological and political conflict that demand critical reflection and institutional change in order to reconcile after violence.

Paragraph 4, which recasts the relationship between the church and Israel, charts a different memorial strategy. Here (in 4.2) the reader is repeatedly exhorted to remember:

The Church...remembers the bond that spiritually ties the people of the New Covenant to Abraham's stock....The Church, therefore, cannot forget that she received the revelation of the Old Testament through the people with whom God...concluded the Ancient Covenant. Nor can she forget that she draws sustenance from the root of that well-cultivated olive tree onto which have been grafted the wild shoots, the Gentiles....The Church keeps ever in mind the words of the Apostle about his kinsmen....She also recalls that the Apostles...[7]

Which memories are invoked and which ones are overlooked? Numerous commentators have noted that paragraph 4 makes no reference to the Shoah or to centuries of anti-Jewish violence across European Christendom.[8] Furthermore, the text glosses over centuries of church teachings on the Jews. It is remarkable, as Pawlikowski pointed out, that the Council disregarded the entire dogmatic body of church doctrine and instead chose to justify the renewal of the relationship with the synagogue on a radical return to the Pauline roots:

Examining chapter four of *Nostra Aetate* we find scarcely any reference to the usual sources cited in conciliar documents: the Church Fathers, papal statements and previous conciliar documents. Rather, the Declaration returns to Romans 9—11, as if to say that the Church is now taking up where Paul left off in his insistence that Jews remain part of the covenant after the Resurrection despite the theological ambiguity involved in such a statement. Without saying it so explicitly, the 2,221 Council members who voted for *Nostra Aetate* were in fact stating that everything that had been said about the Christian-Jewish relationship since Paul moved in a direction they could no longer support....Given the interpretive role of a Church Council in the Catholic tradition this omission is theologically significant. It indicates that the Council Fathers judged these texts as a theologically inappropriate resource for thinking about the relationship between Christianity and Judaism today.[9]

Does *Nostra Aetate* clean the slate by sweeping centuries of supersessionist doctrine, liturgy, law, and art under the rug? Selective memory that shifts attention to elements of the tradition that express new insight while deemphasizing others that conflict with renewal is certainly legitimate. But what happens to the elements that have been repudiated and excised? Strategic silence not only fails the victims of teachings of contempt, whose suffering remains unacknowledged, but also the perpetrators whose faith must change. Unless the refuse created by a theological revolution such as *Nostra Aetate* receives further treatment, the uncanny return of the repressed remains a risk.[10] Pawlikoswki warned in one of his earliest publications about this shortcoming of *Nostra Aetate*:

> The greatest single defect of Vatican II's decree on the Jews is the failure to make any reference to the sufferings of the Jews at the hands of Christians. This omission probably stems from the fact that the Council Fathers, like most Christians, were simply unaware of the true situation, having learned their history from mutilated books. The Pope had the courage during the Council to ask forgiveness of the Protestant community for any guilt on the part of the Roman Church. Should there not be something similar with regard to the Jews?[11]

It is amazing to realize that a papal apology for the Reformation preceded acknowledgment of the church's role in inciting spasms of anti-Jewish violence over centuries as well as its complicity in the Holocaust. Already in 1967, Pawlikowski understood that the theological revolution initiated by *Nostra Aetate* could not proceed on the basis of a fudged history but required the courage to confront the historical record of Christian anti-Judaism. Pawlikowski embraces a different strategy of purification. Instead of removing and burying the waste of history, he advocates its unearthing and calls for a "much deeper appreciation of anti-Semitism among Christians.... Real theological dialogue cannot begin until anti-Semitism is brought out into the open."[12] Already in 1967, Pawlikowski warns that antisemitism cannot be overcome unless its roots and branches are fully comprehended. A purification of the church that merely condemns antisemitism must fall short because neither our physical garbage nor ideological baggage can simply be expelled into the wilderness of oblivion. Rather, the dirt of history must become the raw material of regeneration and renewal, a transformation that requires sustained scholarly attention to theological doctrines, cultural habits, and political legacies.

When Pope John Paul II prepared the church for the millennium, he made the concept of the purification of memory the central metaphor: "Acknowledging the weaknesses of the past," he announced in the 1994 apostolic letter *Tertio Millennio Adveniente*, "is an act of honesty and courage which helps us to strengthen our faith, which alerts us to face today's temptations and challenges and prepares us to meet them."[13] In his bull *Incarnationis Mysterium* (1998) preparing for the Great Jubilee of the Year 2000, he asserted that the church is "in no way weighed down by the weariness which the burden of two thousand years of history could bring with it"[14] because

> first of all, the sign of *the purification of memory*; this calls everyone to make an act of courage and humility in recognizing the wrongs done by those who have borne or bear the name of Christian....Because of the bond, which unites us to one another in the Mystical Body, all of us, though not personally responsible and without encroaching on the judgment of God who alone knows every heart, bear the burden of the errors and faults of those who have gone before us. Yet we too, sons and daughters of the Church, have sinned and have hindered the Bride of Christ from shining forth in all her beauty. [15]

Purification is key to renewal, evocatively expressed in the image of the young, virginal, untouched bride. This image of purity is problematic not only for its sexual politics but also for its implicit erasure of the old. By contrast, the image of the purity of compost piles draws attention to the transformation of remainders that have been thrown away and reconstituted. Of course, we are not considering benign backyard composts made up of harmless kitchen scraps and organic garden leavings, but rather toxic waste dumps created by traumatic memories and noxious ideologies that require decontamination. The purification of memory should be approached as a Superfund site that needs structured and sustained bioremediation in order to prevent future poisoning.

When the International Theological Commission convened in Rome to discuss the theological implications of the concept of the purification of memory, they distinguished between the facts of history that ought to be remembered and the feelings of hate and trauma that ought to be eliminated. Their 1999 study, *Memory and Reconciliation: The Church and the Faults of the Past*, approved by Cardinal Ratzinger as prefect of the Congregation for the Doctrine of Faith, clarifies the theological, historical, ethical, and pastoral implications of the purification of memory. They note that *Nostra Aetate* and other Vatican II documents did "not add a request for pardon for the things cited" (§1.2) and ask whether "today's conscience [can] be assigned 'guilt' for isolated historical phenomena like the Crusades or the inquisition?" (§1.4). They tried to formulate criteria for what needed to be remembered and what needed to be forgotten:

> Purifying the memory means eliminating from personal and collective conscience all forms of resentment or violence left by the inheritance of the past, on the basis of a new and rigorous historical-theological judgement [*sic*], which becomes the foundation for a renewed moral way of acting. This occurs whenever it becomes possible to attribute to past historical deeds a different quality, having a new and different effect on the present, in view of progress in reconciliation in truth, justice, and charity among human beings and, in particular, between the Church and the different religious, cultural, and civil communities with whom she is related....The memory of division and opposition is purified and substituted by a reconciled memory, to which everyone in the Church is invited to be open and to become educated.[16]

How exactly we are supposed to eliminate disturbing, destructive, and unproductive qualities of the past and separate it from historical memory itself is not clearly spelled out. The process by which the purification of memory distills the historical truth from its personal, cultural, and religious reverberations remains vague, which allows for multiple interpretations.

It is only in the preface to the German translation of *Memory and Reconciliation*, published on the Vatican website, that Gerhard Ludwig Müller explicitly warns against understanding purification as a form of washing away guilty remainders. More than other countries, Germany has employed metaphors of washing and cleansing to force closure on its Nazi past. Here is my translation from the German introduction to the study:

> What is not meant is a washing-oneself-clean, which aims
> at repressing and forgetting the guilt and tries to place a
> line-of-closure [*Schlussstrich*] under the past. The goal is
> the creation of a "reconciled memory" of the wounds,
> which one has inflicted on each other in the past.[17]

In the German context, the term *purification* evoked cultural associations with the Hour Zero, the *Persilschein*, and the *Nestbeschmutzer*. *Persilscheine* were named after a prominent laundry detergent and used in de-Nazification proceedings to testify for the upstanding character of defendants, and they possessed the seemingly magic power to wash away the stains of complicity for Nazi crimes.[18] *Nestbeschmutzer* (the one who soils the nest) referred to mudslinging journalists and prosecutors who dredged up the past and ruined the clean vests of respected West German citizens. In the German context, the term *purification* was thoroughly identified with the promise of washing away traces of guilt in people's biographies.

Germany, more than other countries, was forced to recognize the futility of cleansing and closing off history. Its political culture came to embrace *Vergangenheitsbewältigung* (coming to terms with the past) as a continuing and productive task. Each decade added another layer of conflict and contention: public apologies (Brandt, 1970) and resumption of diplomatic relations (e.g., with Israel, 1965), criminal trials (Eichmann, 1961; Auschwitz trial, 1965) and media events (e.g., the NBC television series *Holocaust*, 1978), restitution

178

negotiations (*Wiedergutmachung*,1952, art work, insurance) and anniversary celebrations (Bitburg, 1985), political scandals (Kiesinger, Waldheim), exhibits (Wehrmacht, 1995) and publications (Goldhagen, 1996). These decades of political, legal, cultural, and personal battles with the Nazi past have become foundational for German national identity. Without romanticizing this postwar experience, the German example shows that the desire for white vests and clean hands must be resisted. Purification is not an event but a process of cultural transformation, ideological decontamination, and political disassociation. This applies *mutatis mutandis* to the church.

Beginning in 1992, the church acknowledged responsibility for past policies of repression, violence, and intolerance, including the prosecution of Galileo Galilei in 1992, involvement in the slave trade in 1993, male domination in 1995, and silence during the Shoah in various national contexts.[19] In 1998, the Pontifical Commission for Religious Relations with the Jews published *We Remember: A Reflection on the Shoah*, which affirmed a duty of remembrance and expressed "deep sorrow for the failures of her sons and daughters in every age [and]...pray[s] that our sorrow for the tragedy which the Jewish people has suffered in our century will lead to a new relationship with the Jewish people."[20]

This formulation caused controversy because it suggested that the church herself had remained pure while culpability adhered only to a few bad apples and black sheep. Strong ecclesiological traditions that view the church as the pure bride of Christ militated against a more unambiguous language.[21] This evasion of responsibility undermined the impact of *We Remember*. The document appeared to misname culpability and to misremember complicity in an effort to preserve the institution's purity, as Pawlikowski argued:

> Surely the authors of *We Remember* were not in a position to resolve ecclesiological tensions within contemporary Catholicism. Nonetheless the statement could have, and should have, made it clearer that the "sons and daughters" of the Church who fell into the sin of anti-Semitism did so because of what they had learned from teachers, theologians (including the Church Fathers), and preachers

sanctioned by the institutional Church. Reading the document in its present form leaves the impression that the sinful "sons and daughters" of the Church who espoused anti-Semitism were led to this pernicious outlook by teachings and teachers outside the context of official Catholicism. This was one of the major criticisms of the document in the Commonweal editorial, which rightly argued that *We Remember* failed to urge the need for institutional self-examination within Catholicism.[22]

On his visit to Jerusalem in 2000, the pope inserted a prayer into the Western Wall that expressed sadness over those "who in the course of history have caused these children of Yours to suffer" and "asking Your forgiveness we wish to commit ourselves to genuine brotherhood with the people of the Covenant."[23] He suggested that the "Church...should kneel before God and implore forgiveness for the past and present sins of her sons and daughters."[24] Again, this powerful gesture was undermined by the appearance of suppressing the facts of institutional failure.

When political scientists Zohar Kampf and Nava Löwenheim reviewed "Rituals of Apology in the Global Arena" in 2012, they cited the pope's "millennial apology" as an "asymmetrical purification ritual," in which the offending party neither offered to "relinquish power and prestige" nor strove "to achieve appeasement and restore balance to wounded relationships.[25] They described the pope's visit to Jerusalem as an example of a unilateral apology aimed at self-exoneration. To the political scientists, the concept of "purification of memory" sounded like a form of whitewashing: "the offender issues an apology in order to purify the dismal past of its group members, but does not necessarily need the forgiveness of a specific offended party in order to achieve its goals."[26] By focusing on the public gesture, the scientists overlooked the theological changes that had occurred internally within the church because of theologians such as John Pawlikowski.

Unlike the public ritual, which appeared to try to protect the purity of Christianity, Pawlikowski has used the memory of anti-Judaism to construct a new systematic theology. His understanding of purification requires a "reformulated expression of that faith:"[27]

I am not the same Christian person I was before my involvement in the dialogue. Hence the need to restate Christological meaning in the light of this experience which I know has also been shared by other Christian men and women involved in the dialogue.[28]

This approach to purification is not committed to cleansing the church in order to restore an original purity. Rather, it uses the dirt—that is, beliefs that need to be shed such as supersessionism and triumphalism—to reformulate the center of Christian faith: Christology. This is an audacious move, not least, because Pawlikowski is not trained as a systematic theologian but as an ethicist. But he took on the task of wrestling with Christology because it lies at the root of theological anti-Judaism. Accepting Rosemary Radford Ruether's conclusion in *Faith and Fratricide* that anti-Judaism constitutes the left hand of Christology,[29] he sets out to develop a Christology that (1) "does not invalidate the Jewish faith" (i.e., supersessionism), (2) does not claim to be superior or the fulfillment of Judaism (i.e. triumphalism), but (3) remains faithful to its Jewish roots by incorporating its "sense of rootedness in history," including the most recent history of the Holocaust and the state of Israel.[30] There are Christian theologians who fear that uprooting anti-Judaism would threaten the systematic integrity of Christianity and concede too much ground on its universal, unique truth. By contrast, Pawlikowski argues that the incarnation does not invalidate the Jewish matrix of Jesus and his followers but expands on Pharisaic teachings about the intimacy between humanity and divinity. Pawlikowski interprets the incarnation as the "manifestation of the divine-human nexus,"[31] which occurred uniquely in the Christ event, which however does not negate that "a gulf remains between God and the human community that is forever impassable."[32] In the "express revelation occasioned by the Christ event," humankind comes into "full awareness of the ultimate link between itself and God."[33] The incarnation is the church's unique and universal message that does not nullify the covenantal validity of the relationship between God and Israel: "The revelation at Sinai stands on equal footing with the revelation in Jesus."[34] This premise of radical covenantal equality spurs Pawlikowski's revisionist

Christology. He argues against a Christology that is built around the passion and resurrection of Christ because it fosters a sense of triumph and inadvertently transmits traditions of deicide that paint Jews as Christ killers from generation to generation. By contrast, the incarnation provides a platform that allows constructive and dialogical conversations about "the sense of intimacy between humanity and divinity revealed through [Jesus'] ministry and person."[35] Pawlikowski aims to purify Christology of habitual postures of supremacy and to transform the purged dirt into new affirmations of faith.

The task of wrestling with anti-Judaism should be accepted as an internal Christian theological affair that occurs concurrent with, if not antecedent to Jewish-Christian dialogue. It is not the task of the Jewish partners in dialogue to educate Christians about antisemitism or to flag anti-Jewish stereotypes. Purification requires self-criticism and introspection before the repair of relationships can proceed. In practice, the sequence of this process often seems to be the reverse. Pawlikowski has pointed out that it cannot suffice when the church condemns anti-Judaism only in statements that specifically address Jewish-Christian relations. For instance, in a 2001 commentary on the Polish bishops' statement on Jews and Judaism, he wrote,

> Thus far, *Nostra Aetate* has had little direct impact on Catholic theology as a whole. One looks in vain for citations from the document in books or articles reflecting on Catholic theological identity. Since in the past this identity has been centrally shaped by a theology of the Church as the fulfillment and displacement of Judaism, Catholic theologians must ask themselves how to define Catholic identity today in the light of *Nostra Aetate* and the many theological statements of Pope John Paul II about the inherent bond between Jews and Christians. Does *Nostra Aetate* have significance only when Catholics are speaking with Jews? Or is it also brought into the picture when Catholics are conversing among themselves? Only if the latter is true can we say that *Nostra Aetate* has been genuinely received within the Christian community.[36]

The failure to move beyond rituals of purification that repudiate but fail to transform anti-Judaism has become painfully obvious in recent empirical studies that detect a higher prevalence of anti-Jewish stereotypes among the Christian faithful than among secular Europeans. When the German Bundestag convened a Commission on Antisemitism in 2012, they invited a Protestant and a Catholic theologian to explain the results of multiple empirical surveys that find a strong correlation between church affiliation and perseverance of antisemitic prejudice.[37] In 2012, Germans who attend churches—a minority, to be sure—displayed greater susceptibility to antisemitic stereotypes than nonobservant, secular Germans. These empirical findings almost fifty years after *Nostra Aetate* are disturbing. Why has Jewish-Christian dialogue, promoted at the highest levels of the church since *Nostra Aetate*, yielded so little change as measured by social scientists?

One explanation given by the Protestant theologian Albert Scherr before the Bundestag is that Jewish-Christian dialogue is practiced among scholars and church leaders but fails to trickle down to the congregations.[38] A second reason provided by Catholic theologian Matthias Blum is that "the many efforts...to describe a Judaism with dignity have apparently failed to generate a verifiable dimension of religiosity that protects against Judeophobia."[39] And he warns that "acceptance of a dictated condemnation of Judeophobia ordered by church hierarchies will only gain traction if the void left by the erasure of anti-Jewish stereotypes is made plausible and transparent by new theological formulations that replace the empty spaces."[40] It is not enough just to get rid of the dirt. It must be decontaminated, composted, and reintegrated into the theological foundations of the church. Rituals of purification such as *Nostra Aetate* and the millennial apologies serve as milestones on the path of Jewish-Christian reconciliation, but without the microbial transformation of anti-Judaism at all levels of the church, the stated intention and promise of purification remains unfulfilled.

Nostra Aetate articulated the Council's wish to "foster and recommend mutual understanding and respect, which is the fruit, above all, of biblical and theological studies as well as of fraternal dialogues."[41] In the immediate post-Holocaust period, dialogue encounters between Jews and Christians were tentative, ritualized, and polite meetings that carefully navigated around the raw emotions and gaping wounds left by the European catastrophe. As Seligman and his coauthors have argued in *Ritual and Its Consequences: An Essay on the Limits of Sincerity*, rituals create a subjunctive world, in which we act "as if" we lived in a polite, respectful, and peaceful world. We say, "I am sorry," "please," and thank you" even though we do not feel sincerely sorry or grateful. Ritualized speech acts help individuals and communities navigate complex, fractured, and transitional situations.[42] The early encounters between Jews and Christians were often ritualized and scripted events in which participants acted "as if" mutual understanding and respect truly existed. It was only over time, and as a result of incremental changes in theology, liturgy, education, and politics, that polite conversations turned into sincere working relationships and genuine friendships.

The bonds of solidarity forged in Jewish-Christian dialogue generate the courage to face facts and the audacity to speak truth. John Pawlikowski has served four terms on the Council of the United States Holocaust Memorial Museum since he was appointed in 1980 because he could be trusted as a reliable mediator between different constituencies, Jewish and Christian, Polish and American. He reliably spoke out when conflicts erupted, including over the Carmelite convent in Auschwitz,[43] scholarly access to the Vatican archives, or the canonization of Pope Pius XII. His integrity with respect to historical facts led him to challenge Pope Benedict XVI's account of the ideological roots of National Socialism while he visited to Auschwitz Birkenau in 2006:

> While the present pope certainly makes clear the horrors of the Nazi period, he attributes these to the emergence of neo-paganism in Europe with at best minor Christian complexity. This is simply incorrect history that will not stand up to the facts of the situation. Such denial compromises the ability of institutional Catholicism to serve as a positive force for moral responsibility in contemporary global society.[44]

Pawlikowski agrees with Pope Benedict XVI that Nazi "bioracism" is a modern, scientific ideology that should be distinguished from Christian supersessionist (mis)representations of Israel as blind, stubborn, and invalid faith. But he never whitewashes the fact that the Holocaust "could not have succeeded, however, as well as it did without the seedbed of traditional anti-Semitism that developed over centuries in Christian societies."[45] In his writings he reflects on the meaning of the fact that the planners of the Holocaust were baptized, had been raised in Christian homes, while others even retained their church memberships, attended services, and celebrated Christian holidays. Unless we accept these historical facts and embrace the questions they raise as challenges to Christian faith practice, we cannot recover the power and integrity of the Christian message.

We should be very careful when using metaphors of purification that suggest rituals of washing. Inevitably, such cleansings are linked to mandates that obligate victims to forgive and forget and that paralyze perpetrators in postures of denial and exculpation. Instead, we could appropriate ecologically enriched metaphors of purification by composting that call for the decontamination of toxic ideologies and the modification of habits of the heart. Pawlikowski's lifelong commitment to theological transformation in light of Christianity's failure during the Holocaust embodies a practice of purification by incremental transformation and gradual repair of relationships in trust and respect.

Notes

1. John Pawlikowski, "Fifty Years of Christian-Jewish Dialogue—What Has Changed?" *Journal of Ecumenical Studies* 49, no. 1 (Winter 2014): 99–106, at 99.

2. Mary Douglas, *Purity and Danger: An Analysis of Pollution and Taboo* (London: Routledge & Kegan Paul, 1966), 2.

3. *Nostra Aetate* 5, accessed August 16, 2016, http://www.vatican.va/archive/hist_councils/ii_vatican_council/documents/vat-ii_decl_19651028_nostra-aetate_en.html.

4. Mary Boys, ed., *Seeing Judaism Anew: Christianity's Sacred Obligation* (Lanham, MD: Rowman Littlefield, 2002).

5. Pawlikowski, "Fifty Years of Christian-Jewish Dialogue," 99.

6. *Nostra Aetate* 4.

7. *Nostra Aetate* 4

8. Stuart Rosenberg, *The Christian Problem: A Jewish View* (New York: Hippocrene, 1986), 194.

9. John Pawlikowski, "Reflections on Covenant and Mission," *Crosscurrents* (Winter 2007): 71.

10. On the uncanny, see Tania Oldenhage, *Parables for Our Time: Rereading New Testament Scholarship after the Holocaust* (New York: Oxford University Press, 2002).

11. John Pawlikowski, "Reflections on Jewish-Christian Dialogue," *The Reconstructionist* (October 20, 1967): 19.

12. Pawlikowski, "Reflections on Jewish-Christian Dialogue," 19.

13. Pope John Paul II, *Tertio Millennio Adveniente* 33, accessed July 17, 2017, https://w2.vatican.va/content/john-paul-ii/en/apost _letters/1994/documents/hf_jp-ii_apl_19941110_tertio-millennio -adveniente.html.

14. Pope John Paul II, *Incarnationis Mysterium* 2, Bull of Indiction of the Great Jubilee of the Year 2000 (November 29, 1998), §11, http:// www.vatican.va/jubilee_2000/docs/documents/hf_jp-ii_doc _30111998_bolla-jubilee_en.html. Cf. *Homily*, First Sunday of Lent, 2000, https://w2.vatican.va/content/john-paul-ii/en/homilies/2000/ documents/hf_jp-ii_hom_20000312_pardon.html.

15. *Incarnationis Mysterium* 11.

16. International Theological Commission, *Memory and Reconciliation* (December 1999), §5.1, http://www.vatican.va/roman_curia/ congregations/cfaith/cti_documents/rc_con_cfaith_doc_20000307 _memory-reconc-itc_en.html.

17. International Theological Commission, *Erinnern und Versöhnen: Die Kirche und die Verfehlungen in ihrer Vergangenheit*, accessed August 16, 2016, http://www.vatican.va/roman_curia/congregations/cfaith/ cti_documents/rc_con_cfaith_doc_20000307_memory-reconc-itc_ge .html#VORWORT_DES_HERAUSGEBERS_.

18. Ernst Klee, *Persilscheine und falsche Pässe: Wie die Kirchen den Nazis halfen* (Frankfurt/Main: Fischer Verlag, 1992).

19. See http://www.humanrightscolumbia.org/ahda/political-apolo gies (accessed August 16, 2016).

20. Commission for the Religious Relations with the Jews, *We Remember: A Reflection on the Shoah* (March 16, 1998), §V, http://www

.vatican.va/roman_curia/pontifical_councils/chrstuni/documents/rc_pc_chrstuni_doc_16031998_shoah_en.html.

21. Johanna Rahner, "Kirche und Schuld: Skizze einer dogmatischen Verhältnisbestimmung aus katholischer Sicht," in *Schuld: theologische Erkundungen eines unbequemen Phänomens*, ed. Julia Enxing (Ostfildern: Grünewald Verlag) , 98–122.

22. John Pawlikowski, "Developments in Catholic-Jewish Relations: 1990 and Beyond," *Judaism* 55, nos. 3–4 (Fall–Winter 2006): 97–109. *The Free Library*, s.v. "Developments in Catholic-Jewish relations: 1990 and beyond," http://www.thefreelibrary.com/Developments+in+CatholicJewish+relations%3a+1990+and+beyond.-a0171034154.

23. John Paul II, Prayer at the Western Wall, Jerusalem, March 26, 2000, http://w2.vatican.va/content/john-paul-ii/en/speeches/2000/jan-mar/documents/hf_jp-ii_spe_20000326_jerusalem-prayer.html.

24. John Paul II, *Homily*, First Sunday of Lent, 2000.

25. Zohar Kampf and Nava Löwenheim, "Rituals of Apology in the Global Arena," *Security Dialogue* 43, no. 1 (2012): 43–60, at 54.

26. Kampf and Löwenheim, "Rituals of Apology in the Global Arena," 54.

27. Pawlikowski, *Christ Light*, 7.

28. Pawlikowski, *Christ Light*, 7.

29. Rosemary Radford Ruether, *Faith and Fratricide* (New York: Seabury Press, 1974).

30. Pawlikowski, *Christ Light*, 34.

31. Pawlikowski, *Christ Light*, 115.

32. Pawlikowski, *Christ Light*, 115.

33. Pawlikowski, *Christ Light*, 115.

34. Pawlikowski, *Christ Light*, 122.

35. Pawlikowski, *Christ Light*, 109.

36. John Pawlikowski, "Honesty Breeds Integrity," *Dialogue & Universalism* 11, nos. 1/2 (2001): 53.

37. Matthias Blum, "Expertise: Katholische Kirche und Antisemitismus," accessed August 16, 2016, http://www.bagkr.de/wp-content/uploads/blum_antisemitismus_katholisch.pdf. Albert Scherr, "Expertise: Verbreitung von Stereotypen über Juden und antisemitischer Vorurteile in der Evangelischen Kirche" (Freiburg i. Br.: Bundestag, 2011), http://www.bagkr.de/wp-content/uploads/scherr_antisemitismus_evangelisch.pdf.

38. Scherr, "Expertise," 91.

39. Blum, "Expertise," 27.

40. Blum, "Expertise," 26.

41. *Nostra Aetate* 4.

42. Adam B. Seligman, Robert P. Weller, Michael J. Puett, and Bennet Simon, *Ritual and Its Consequences: An Essay on the Limits of Sincerity* (New York: Oxford, 2008), 25ff.

43. John Pawlikowski, "The Auschwitz Convent Controversy: Mutual Misperceptions," in *Memory Offended: The Auschwitz Convent Controversy*, ed. Carol Rittner and John K. Roth (New York: Praeger, 1991), 63–73. "The Struggle for Memory and Memorialization at Auschwitz," in *The Continuing Agony: From the Carmelite Convent to the Crosses of Auschwitz*, ed. Alan L. Berger, Harry J. Cargas, and Susan E. Novak (Binghamton, NY: Binghamton University Press, 2002), 137–59.

44. John Pawlikowski, "The Significance of the Christian-Jewish Dialogue and Holocaust Studies for Catholic Ethics," *Political Theology* 13, no. 4 (2012): 444–57, at 449.

45. Pawlikowski, "The Significance of the Christian-Jewish Dialogue," 447.

CHAPTER TWELVE

PEDAGOGICAL/PASTORAL PERSPECTIVE

Choices

—m—

Carol Rittner, RSM

Thinking about the pedagogical and pastoral consequences of Fr. John T. Pawlikowski's many contributions to Holocaust studies reminds me of something former Prime Minister of Sweden Göran Persson (1996–2006) said:

> The Holocaust was no accident of history. The systematic murder of the Jews did not happen by chance. Nor the genocide of the Roma. Nor the mass murder of disabled persons and the persecution and murder of homosexuals and dissidents. It occurred because people willed it, planned it and carried it through. It occurred because people made choices which allowed it to happen. It occurred, not least, because people remained silent.[1]

No doubt, Mr. Persson was thinking about the choices individuals, institutions, and governments made leading up to and during the Nazi era, World War II, and the Holocaust (1933–45): Should we speak out against the Nazis, or keep silent? Should we take in Jewish refugees, or keep them out? Should we do business with Nazi Germany, or boycott them? Should we go to war, or stay neutral? What shall we do? What can we do? What do we want to do?

Prime Minister Persson makes me think about choices governments made during the Holocaust, and Fr. Pawlikowski makes me think about choices the institutional Catholic Church made during the Holocaust: Should we speak out against the Nazis, or keep silent? Should we help Jewish refugees, or ignore them? Should we keep our nuncio in Nazi Germany, or recall him? Should we side with the Allies, or stay neutral? What shall we do? What can we do? What do we want to do? And both men, one a politician and the other a priest, make me think about bystanders during the Holocaust.

BYSTANDERS

Helen Fein's landmark study, *Accounting for Genocide: National Responses and Jewish Victimization during the Holocaust,*[2] shows that the single most important determinant of Nazi success during the Holocaust was not the behavior of the murderers (who sought to destroy Jews everywhere), nor was it the behavior of the Jews (generally unsuccessful when it came to escaping or resisting genocide). The key determinant of murder rates—which varied from 95 percent killed in Poland and the Baltic countries to 95 percent saved in Denmark—was the behavior of bystanders, including individuals, institutions, and governments.[3] There were, of course, other factors that made the Holocaust possible, including the following:

- A long and terrible history of anti-Judaism in Christian theology and its pernicious "fertilizing" effects on the Christian psyche

- The effects of World War I's brutalization and numbing on European populations

- The impact of Nazi ideology propagated by Hitler and his cohort, reinforced in the media and through the German educational system

- Nazi racial laws

- The Nazis' use of terror and fear inflicted on civilian populations in Germany and occupied Europe

The success with which the Nazis carried out the Holocaust represents the outcome of a massive failure by many institutions—political, legal, cultural, educational, and above all, religious. Any mass murder represents a catastrophic failure of a civilization's checks and balances, as well as of the human solidarity and ethics that should have prevented such systematic evil practices from being implemented. And because religions and ethical traditions represent the claims of transcendent meaning and human values, they are particularly wounded by such failures. The Holocaust convicts religions of a failure to teach and create solidarity across religious lines and between people so that they stand together against degradation and murder. It reveals that various religious and ethical traditions treat others as *other*, thereby distancing others from themselves. This lack of respect for those who are different, that is, other than oneself, encourages *bystanding*, encourages those who are not being persecuted to look out only for themselves or for those who are like themselves and to make little or no effort to check the aggressors.

During World War II and the Holocaust, the Germans lacked the power to sustain the so-called Final Solution without the cooperation of non-Jews who were under their domination. The "brave" soldiers of the Nazi Third Reich were busy fighting a world war on two major fronts. In addition, German officials and military administrators also had to administer nearly the whole of occupied Europe. This meant that Hitler and his generals did not have the resources to commit large numbers of their military personnel to their annihilation machinery, but they did not need them. They had plenty of people under occupation—non-Jews—who had been *de-formed* by centuries—two millennia, in fact—of Christian "teaching of contempt" for Jews and Judaism. What the Nazis needed to carry out their Final Solution were *bystanders* who would not interfere with their dirty, rotten killing business. And they found them—millions of them—standing on street corners, peeking out from behind window shades, lurking in dark alleys.[4]

Most bystanders were quiet citizens who wanted nothing more than to get on with their private lives. They were safe enough if compliant enough. They watched as Jewish families disappeared from their apartments in building after building, in city after city. Neighbors watched them go,[5] all of them: the doctors and lawyers, the merchants and grocers, the teachers and rabbis, the mothers and children. Neighbors watched them all go as they stood on the sidelines, fearful, unobtrusive, and compliant.

CONSEQUENCES

During the Holocaust, it was as easy for people to say, "The Jews *are* a problem," as it was to say, "The Jews are not *my* problem." In fact, many people said, "The Jews have nothing to do with me, or mine, or us. I have my own family, myself to worry about." But some people could not say such things. They could not join in persecuting and harassing Jews, much less torturing and murdering Jews. Some people simply could not turn their backs on Jews who were being hunted down all over Nazi Germany, and after 1939, throughout Nazi-occupied Europe. They had to act. They had to do something to help the despised, vulnerable, isolated, and frightened Jews. Why? Because, as Emanuel Tanay, a Polish Jew who was helped by Polish Catholics during World War II and the Holocaust, said, "That's the kind of people they were."[6] They were people who knew their actions had consequences.

Many people today do not believe that what they do makes any difference in our world. The great Jewish political thinker Hannah Arendt (1906–75), an agnostic, was convinced that this loss of belief in the consequences of what one does or does not do had its origins in the process of secularization that began in the Enlightenment (c. 1685–1815). People lost belief in what traditionally had been called in religious terms "the last judgment," and it has had unforeseen consequences over the centuries, even up to our own time.

> If we do not think that our actions have consequences for the worse, then neither will we be convinced that they will make any difference for the better. If we think that the good consequences of our actions depend on the witness or approval of others, then we will remain unconvinced that we can do good, that we can make a difference in our world.[7]

Those who helped Jews during the Holocaust knew that what they were doing had consequences for themselves and for the Jew or Jews they were trying to help if they were caught. Elie Wiesel always said that we need to know about people who helped Jews during the Holocaust, and we need to learn from them.[8] One thing we can learn from them is that our choices have consequences—for ourselves and for others.

During the Holocaust, the people the Jews call "righteous gentiles"[9] (or, to use Ervin Staub's term, "active bystanders"[10]) were a very small minority, not at all representative of the attitudes and responses of the more than 300 million non-Jews under German domination[11] in occupied Europe during World War II and the Holocaust. For me, the righteous Gentiles highlight the power a person has to choose an option when faced with the choice, "Whose side am I on?"

CHOICES AND DECISIONS

Choices and decisions are involved in how people act and react to what is happening around them. People might make their choices and decisions with or without reflection, but they do make them—we all do—and people do decide—we all do—whose side they are on: the victim's or the perpetrator's. As Elie Wiesel has said, "There is always a moment when the moral choice is made."[12] During the Holocaust, individuals, institutions, and governments made choices: either to ignore, collaborate, or resist by helping Jews who were being hunted down by the Germans and their collaborators throughout Nazi-occupied Europe.

For sure, righteous Gentiles were not angels or saints. (For example, if you have seen the film *Schindler's List*, Steven Spielberg makes it clear that Oskar Schindler was not a saint.) Righteous Gentiles were ordinary human beings. Like the Nazi perpetrators, who were neither devils nor monsters but ordinary human beings as well, righteous Gentiles lived in the same moral sphere as the other multiple millions who walked the footpaths and streets of German-occupied Europe. Those who tried to help Jews during the Holocaust breathed the same air, had the same fears, and faced the same challenges as did people in occupied Europe who were passive bystanders, neither helping nor hindering the Germans as they hunted down Jews wherever they could find them.

Just as it is a mistake to make the perpetrators *other* than what they were—*ordinary* human beings—it is also a mistake to make the righteous Gentiles *more* than what they were—*ordinary* human beings. Making that mistake allows us to say, "I'm not like them. I'm just an *ordinary* person, neither a monster (a perpetrator), nor a saint (a righteous). I am neither capable of killing, like the perpetrators, nor of helping, like the righteous." We must not make either the perpetrators or the rescuers *larger* than life. Rather, we must keep them what they were: life-sized during a time when humanity was diminished.[13]

The story of non-Jews who helped Jews during the Nazi era, World War II, and the Holocaust is not simply the tale of single so-called noble acts of letting someone, or many, into one's home for a day or two, or of hiding Jews in one's barn for a few weeks or months, dangerous as that was. Rather, the story of the righteous Gentiles is the story of a continuous struggle against enormous odds to save one or more Jews: men, women, and children; old and young; rich and poor; agreeable and disagreeable (not even all the Jews were saints!). In the case of Irene Opdyke, for example, a young Polish Catholic woman who saved the lives of twelve Jews caught in the Nazi maw of death, choices were constant, never-ending. When given the choice of being a Nazi major's "housekeeper" or remaining a waitress serving other Germans in a big dining room, Irene decided to live with the major, which may have compromised her "morally" but gave her the cover she needed to save human beings from certain death. She hid all twelve Jews in the basement of her SS major's villa. "Upstairs" she cared for the major's needs; "downstairs" she cared for her Jews.[14]

Imagine the many choices she faced, the decisions she had to make every day, not once or twice, but repeatedly for months on end under the very nose of her Nazi lover. Once, when the major arrived home unexpectedly, he discovered Irene and her twelve Jewish guests. "I can still see his chin shaking," she says in the book, *The Courage to Care*, "his eyes glaring with unbelief." She remembers that the major "turned around in silence and walked to his office." What could she do? She had to go and face him. "He yelled at me. He said, 'Irene, how could you do it? I trusted you. I give you such a nice home, protection—why?'" *Why?* Irene Opdyke knew *why*, even if the Nazi major did not. "'Nobody has a right to kill and murder because of religion or race.' He said, 'You know what can happen to you?' I said, 'Yes, I know, I just witnessed what can happen.'"[15] She had just seen Polish families who had been hung with the Jewish families they had tried to help. Still, for Irene Opdyke, the choice was clear: to help and not to harm, even in the face of severe punishment, which in Poland meant death if one were caught helping Jews.

People like Irene Opdyke and Oskar Schindler, people like those who helped Emanuel Tanay and the more than twenty-six thousand[16] other non-Jews in Europe and North Africa honored by Yad Vashem as *hasidei umot haolam* (righteous among the nations of the world) for helping Jews during the Holocaust, not only rescued human beings. They also rescued the concept of the human being as a being capable of *choice*.

Each and every righteous Gentile in Nazi Germany and occupied Europe during World War II and the Holocaust was a witness to what was happening to the Jews. Each and every righteous Gentile made a choice: she or he refused to be a bystander to the Nazi persecution and murder of the Jews of Europe during World War II and the Holocaust. Each and every righteous Gentile "is a reminder of what so many others could have done, of what so many others did not do."[17]

In my view, each and every righteous Gentile during World War II and the Holocaust exemplifies the hoped-for pedagogical and pastoral consequences of Fr. John T. Pawlikowski's many contributions to Holocaust studies: "Whoever saves a single life is as one who has saved the entire world."[18]

Notes

1. Göran Persson, *The Stockholm International Forum on the Holocaust* (Stockholm: Regeringskansliet, 2000), 29–30.

2. See further Helen Fein, *Accounting for Genocide* (New York: The Free Press, 1987).

3. See further the comment about bystanders on the United States Holocaust Memorial Museum website, accessed December 23, 2016,

https://www.ushmm.org/wlc/en/article.php?ModuleId=10008207. Also see further Rabbi Irving Greenberg, "Religious and Ethical Teaching and the Holocaust," in Persson, *The Stockholm International Forum on the Holocaust*, 256.

4. David P. Gushee, *Righteous Gentiles of the Holocaust: Genocide and Moral Obligation*, 2nd ed. (St. Paul, MN: Paragon House, 2003), 5–6.

5. Cynthia Ozick, prologue to *Rescuers: Portraits of Moral Courage in the Holocaust*, by Gay Block and Malka Drucker (New York: Holmes & Meier Publishers, Inc., 1992), xii.

6. Emanual Tanay, in *The Courage to Care: Rescuers of Jews during the Holocaust*, ed. Carol Rittner and Sondra Myers (New York: New York University Press, 1986), 57.

7. Mary Jo Leddy, "The Last Judgement: Living as If Our Actions Have Meaning, *Catholic New Times*, March 8, 1998.

8. Elie Wiesel, in Rittner and Myers, *The Courage to Care*, x.

9. Righteous Gentiles are non-Jewish people who during the Holocaust risked their lives to save Jewish people from Nazi persecution. Today, a field of trees is planted in their honor at the Yad Vashem Holocaust Memorial in Jerusalem, Israel, commemorating their courage and compassion. As of January 1, 2017, 26,513 non-Jews have been so honored by Yad Vashem.

10. Ervin Staub, *The Psychology of Good and Evil: Why Children, Adults, and Groups Help and Harm Others* (New York: Cambridge University Press, 2003), 3.

11. Gushee, *Righteous Gentiles of the Holocaust*, 5.

12. Elie Wiesel, in *The Courage to Care*, x.

13. I am indebted to Mary Jo Leddy for this insight.

14. Irene Opdyke, in *The Courage to Care*, 44–51.

15. Irene Opdyke, in *The Courage to Care*, 48–49, 51.

16. See n. 9.

17. Wiesel, in *The Courage to Care*, x.

18. This teaching from the Talmud is commonly cited as Mishna Sanhedrin 4:5. The Jerusalem/Palestinian Talmud has a variation at 4:1, and there is an additional version in the Babylonian Talmud at 37a. Given John Pawlikowski's concern that Christians engage interreligious dialogue with all religions, it is important to note that Muslims have a version of this teaching in the Qur'an 5:32. When Steven Spielberg used the phrase at the end of *Schindler's List*, a much larger audience became familiar with this teaching.

Part III

INTERRELIGIOUS STUDIES

CHAPTER THIRTEEN

OUT OF THE MYSTERY COMES THE BOND

The Role of Rabbi Abraham Joshua Heschel in Shaping Nostra Aetate

—m—

Susannah Heschel

> *The Church of Christ discovers her "bond" with Judaism by "searching into her own mystery."*
>
> —*Nostra Aetate 4*

Father John Pawlikowski stands in the great prophetic tradition. If the prophet, as my father suggests, holds God and man in one thought at one time, Fr. John Pawlikowski is the prophetic ecumenist, holding Jewish and Catholic faith together at all times. In a dialogue with Rabbi Irving Greenberg in the pages of *Moment* in 1990, he declared, "Jews cannot recover from the deep scarring left on the Jewish consciousness by the bitter history of Christian persecution of Jews."[1] But Pawlikowski also challenged each community to consider how they might be "bonded" to each other. Fifteen years later, in an address to the International Council of Christians and Jews, he reviewed important papal statements concerning the intrinsic importance of Judaism for Christianity, cited Pope John Paul II and Pope Francis, referred back to the *Moment* article, and asked, "Can Christianity speak of an inherent bond with Judaism if no such understanding is to be found in Jewish theological circles? Bondedness cannot be a one-way street."[2] Outspoken as a critic of the centuries of anti-Judaic theological traditions within Christianity, Fr. Pawlikowski is nonetheless not hesitant to demand of Jews a reversal of our long traditions of anti-Christian mockery.

Father Pawlikowski has been our Jewish voice in the Catholic world, not simply explaining Jewish history and religion, but also giving voice to our Jewish perspective, and as such, he has been a noble and loyal Catholic representative of the Jewish people. What marks the distinctiveness of Fr. John Pawlikowski is his unusual ability to hold both Jewish and Catholic experiences together, even when those experiences are different or even in conflict. Rather than trying to make a case for one side *or* the other, he is the supreme reconciler, explaining each side to the other, seeking common ground, scolding each as due, and guiding us gently toward paths of understanding.

The basis for the extraordinary changes represented by *Nostra Aetate* were not historical claims, but theological insights. That the Jews were declared not to be responsible for the death of Jesus was not rooted in the argument of historians that the Romans, not the Jews, practiced crucifixion and held the political authority over first-century Palestine. Rather, the eradication of the charge of deicide emerged from theological considerations raised and debated by Catholic thinkers and clergy, with particular guidance from Augustin Cardinal Bea. Similarly, theological arguments justified accepting the ongoing covenant between Israel and God, which had been denied for centuries by Christian supersessionist theology. Yet the theological debates inevitably became embroiled in Vatican politics, heightened by the efforts of bishops from Arab countries who were anxious not to appear sympathetic to Jewish and Israeli interests. Indeed, the influence of Arab political interests in the deliberations of the Council became so strong that the government of the state of Israel decided to send its own representatives to Rome.

Nostra Aetate has been debated by theologians, with often predictable interpretations of right- and left-wing positions. Father Pawlikowski has been at the forefront of many of those debates, concerned with potential misunderstandings, both of the status of the declaration and its presentation within liturgy, sermons, and catechism. Some Jewish thinkers, particularly the Swiss theologian Ernst Ludwig Ehrlich, participated in the decades following World War II in developing new methods of understanding biblical passages, particularly

Romans 9—11, that could serve as a basis for *Nostra Aetate*, as John Connelly has demonstrated in his important book *From Enemy to Brother*.[3] The story I want to tell, however, concerns the moment itself: the remarkable and unanticipated engagement of my father, Rabbi Abraham Joshua Heschel, in the negotiations, and the unique and unusual spiritual influence that he exerted. Rabbi Heschel was concerned less with doctrinal formulations than with creating a new spirit. For him, the central question was whether the Catholic Church could come to recognize the holiness in Judaism as a source of blessing for Christians. And that holiness could only be recognized if the church abandoned proselytism and instead understood Jews as standing in unbroken covenant with God. Rabbi Heschel was the most prominent Jewish theologian involved in discussion with Catholics during that era. As the historian Joshua Furnal notes, "Without Rabbi Heschel it is doubtful that *Nostra Aetate* would have taken the shape that it did."[4]

What makes Rabbi Heschel's involvement in the Second Vatican Council so remarkable and unanticipated is his personal biography. Abraham Joshua Heschel was born to a distinguished lineage of Hasidic rebbes in Poland. Born in Warsaw in 1907, he received a traditional religious education that he completed at a young age thanks to his brilliance. He studied at the University of Berlin, starting in 1927, and also at the Hochschule für die Wissenschaft des Judentums, also in Berlin, completing his doctoral dissertation just when Hitler came to power. While trying to secure a teaching position outside Germany, he continued to write and publish articles and books about medieval Jewish philosophy. In October 1938, he was arrested along with the other Polish Jews living in Nazi Germany, and deported to Poland. Just weeks before the outbreak of the war, he escaped, thanks to a visa secured for him by the Hebrew Union College in Cincinnati, and arrived in the United States in March of 1940. After teaching at the college until 1945, he joined the faculty of the Jewish Theological Seminary, where he taught until his death in December 1972.

Although he became one of the most admired and beloved Jewish theologians among Catholics, Heschel's relationships with Christians were limited. In his pious life in Warsaw, he lived in a Jewish bubble. When he studied in Berlin, he had Christian teachers at the university, especially in the field of biblical studies, but many of them turned into Nazi supporters. During his years in Germany, Heschel was witness to Christian theologians who declared the Old Testament a Jewish book that had no place in the Christian Bible—and they excised it. Some declared Jesus an Aryan, not a Jew, and claimed that Hitler was fulfilling Jesus' mission of destroying Judaism. In the United States, however, Heschel's work was praised by Christian theologians, and he forged close friendships with several major Christian theologians, including Reinhold Niebuhr and Thomas Merton.

Heschel barely knew English when he arrived in the United States, yet he ultimately became one of the most important leaders of American Jewry by the 1960s, and his many books made him one of the most influential Jewish theological voices of the century. In addition, his new approach to the understanding of religion dramatically altered both Jewish understandings of Christianity and also the trajectory of Christian-Jewish relations that culminated in *Nostra Aetate*, primarily through a relationship he forged with a German Catholic theologian, confessor to Pius XII, Cardinal Bea, as well as a host of other Catholic thinkers. How did this come about?

The Second Vatican Council's sessions in the early 1960s riveted world attention. Although no interest in exploring a new Roman Catholic approach to Judaism and the Jewish people was expressed in the thousands of documents submitted by the bishops of the United States and Europe prior to the opening of the Council, it is the brief statement on the Jews, contained within the larger *Nostra Aetate* document, that altered the course of history. *Nostra Aetate* is the shortest of the sixteen official documents produced by Vatican II. It consists of only five paragraphs. Of these, the fourth, dealing with Judaism, contains just seventeen sentences, yet it has dramatically altered a central feature of Western civilization: how the Roman Catholic Church views Judaism and treats Jews.

After two thousand years of attitudes ranging from ambivalence to hatred, Catholics are now enjoined to repudiate antisemitism, to view Judaism as possessing an ongoing covenant with God, and to cease efforts to missionize Jews. Not all Catholics have embraced *Nostra Aetate*. Reports from Catholics in Asia, the Middle East, and

Africa raise questions regarding the relevance of Catholic-Jewish relations to those parts of the world, and some distinguished conservative Catholic theologians, such as Avery Dulles, have insisted that abandoning mission to the Jews would damage the credibility of the Catholic commitment to salvation through Christ. Dulles writes, "It has been well said that those who withdraw from evangelization weaken their own faith. Once we grant that there are some persons for whom it is not important to acknowledge Christ, to be baptized and to receive the sacraments, we raise questions about our own religious life."[5]

Vatican II not only changed the views of Catholics; discussions over *Nostra Aetate* also stimulated a new Jewish interest in Christianity, bringing about a remarkable shift in the Jewish theological relationship to Christianity. Although *Nostra Aetate* has called for a new kind of relationship between Catholics and Jews, the scholarship on the history of the document does not always reflect that changed relationship. Joshua Furnal has pointed out some of the limitations of that scholarship that have narrated the story of *Nostra Aetate* through an exclusive examination of Catholic efforts, omitting the role of Jewish thinkers.[6] Yet *Nostra Aetate* has exerted a far broader impact on Jewish as well as Christian thought, both during the preparation of the document and in the decades that have followed. One of the most important aspects of its impact has been its influence on Rabbi Heschel to formulate a new Jewish view of Christianity, and it is that remarkable outcome that I will explore in this chapter.

First, I will review some of the steps toward *Nostra Aetate*, with attention to the section on the Jews. Second, I want to describe the relationship between my father and Cardinal Bea, both because their relationship was important to the formulation and widespread acceptance of *Nostra Aetate*, and because of unexpected shared commonalities in their theological outlooks, despite radically different backgrounds, and finally because each was a major figure in that revolutionary moment: Cardinal Bea as the major guiding figure of *Nostra Aetate*, and my father as the Jewish theologian who is most widely acclaimed by both Jews and Catholics.

THE ORIGINS OF *NOSTRA AETATE*

The origins of the ecumenical movement within the Roman Catholic Church were complex, and the church's concern with the Jews should not be reduced to the famous meeting between Jules Isaac and Pope John XXIII. Jerome-Michael Vereb, in his recent book on Cardinal Bea, argues that it was Bea and his colleague, Archbishop Lorenz Jaeger of Paderborn, who initially urged the pope, in a letter of March 4, 1960, to concern himself with ecumenism, that is, the unity of Christians, and the interest in the Jews was simply an outgrowth of that much broader concern.[7] Yet that timing does not seem accurate. Pope Paul VI, writing about his predecessor, notes that Pope John already in 1959 altered the prayer *Pro Perfidis Judaeis* to *Pro Judaeis* during the Good Friday prayers. He also deleted the reference to Islam and the "formerly chosen people" on July 18, 1959, during a consecration prayer to Christ the King.[8] Pope John formed the Secretariat for Promoting Christian Unity and asked Cardinal Bea, whom he elevated to cardinal in 1959, to serve as its first president.

Why was Cardinal Bea selected? Archbishop Louis Capovilla, the pope's private secretary, writes, "Because he was a German." Far more important, I would argue, are Bea's previous, highly influential publications on the question of biblical inspiration. These concern the central question: What is the nature of inspiration that lies behind Scripture? The Thomist tradition was flourishing in the first decades of the twentieth century, and Bea drew on Thomas Aquinas's teaching that the inspired author was an instrument of the Holy Spirit, and in full possession of his faculties wrote down all that the Spirit wanted written. That is, there was no ecstatic experience, loss of consciousness, or neurological seizure that brought about prophecy, in contrast to the rising school of history of religions.[9]

But what is the role of the faithful and our ability to understand and interpret Scripture? On the one hand, Bea writes that the revealed word of God is forever, "without addition and without reduction," but that the church "recognizes a legitimate progress in dogma" not through human agency alone, but with the assistance of the Spirit of truth.[10]

Bea's work on divine inspiration led to his role in drafting the papal encyclical *Divino Afflante Spiritu*, the papal encyclical letter issued by Pope Pius XII on September 30, 1943, that gave permission for Catholic scholars to make use of historical-critical techniques in the study of Scripture, including the study of ancient biblical languages—what Raymond Brown has called the "Magna Carta for biblical progress."[11] Bea's writings on biblical inspiration provided a foundation of authority for the kind of radical change that would be inevitable should Christian unity and a reconsideration of Catholic understandings of other religions come under consideration. Moreover, Bea was more than a theologian and superb Jesuit scholar in the field of Semitics, he was also a highly placed Vatican personality, having served as father confessor to Pope Pius XII, starting in 1945, and a professor at the Pontifical Biblical Institute starting in 1924, rector from 1930 to 1949. What were Bea's experiences of Jews? Probably nonexistent in his childhood and years in seminary in Germany, but quite intense during his time at the University of Berlin in 1913, where he studied with two of the most prominent Jewish Semiticists of the era, Eugen Mittwoch (1876–1942) and Jakob Barth (1851–1914), as well as with Hermann Strack, a leading Protestant scholar of rabbinics. Bea's choice of fields of study would have brought him into circles of Jewish students, and the neighborhood surrounding the university was filled with Jewish immigrants from Eastern Europe, undoubtedly his first experience of such a phenomenon. By interesting coincidence, Mittwoch was also one of Heschel's teachers at the University of Berlin, but some years later, when he was a student from 1927 to 1933.

But why were the Secretariat and Cardinal Bea concerned about Jews? What motivated Cardinal Bea, who persisted in his efforts to formulate a statement concerning Judaism that would satisfy not only Catholics, but Jews as well?

The Second Vatican Council adhered closely to the understanding of biblical inspiration outlined by Bea, first in his book on divine inspiration, published in 1930, and in his many subsequent articles and encyclopedia entries. That same year, 1930, the Dutch Jesuit Sebastian Tromp published a book arguing that "God may provide ideas and even words within the author's mind, but the words on the page are not divinely determined."[12] Bea's theological position was more conservative, arguing that the concept of instrumental causality was not easily transferred to human beings, and that the narrative form in which the divine word is presented is shaped by the historical moment and requires historical truthfulness.[13] The encyclical of 1943, composed mostly by Bea, explains that even the "Sacred Writers" had "certain fixed ways of expounding and narrating, certain definite idioms, especially of a kind peculiar to the Semitic tongues," so that study of "history, archeology, ethnology, and other sciences" was necessary for biblical scholarship.

The statement of the Second Vatican Council reads, "To compose the sacred books, God chose certain men who, all the while he employed them in this task, made full use of their powers and faculties so that, though he acted in them and by them, it was as true authors that they consigned to writing whatever he wanted written, and no more."[14] Thus Scripture was understood as the word of God but as shaped by a human being who transmitted it. Citing *Humani Generis*, an encyclical of Pius XII (1950), Bea wrote that the study of Scripture incorporates "the Catholic principle of tradition," giving theology "a kind of perpetual youth," and distinguishes Catholic exegesis from that of Protestants, who focus on reconciling the unity of the biblical text. What is tradition? Bea writes, "Tradition is found in the living magisterium of the present church, resting on correct foundations," guided by the Holy Spirit from the apostolic age to the present.[15]

Precisely this emphasis on the revelation of God, the shaping of the word by the human beings entrusted with that revelation, and the guidance of the magisterium—or, in Jewish terms, rabbinic tradition—guided by the Holy Spirit, the Shekhinah, the divine presence, forms a common core that my father recognized in his own work with that of Cardinal Bea. Rabbinic Judaism had long recognized that the revelation at Sinai came to the souls of all Jews, present and also future, and that revelation was both past and present. Here is a sample from the widely read *Shnei Luhot Haberit*, by Isaiah Horowitz, 1565–1630, reconciling two statements in the liturgy: "He gave us His Torah of truth" and "He who gives us the Torah" (see Deut 5:22). Horowitz explains, "In truth God already gave the Torah, but He is still giving the Torah and does not stop." The great voice at Sinai contained ideas intended for certain individuals in certain eras. (This is an allusion to the midrash on Ps 29:4, according to which God spoke many messages to many individuals at Sinai, each according to the person's strength and ability to comprehend, so that there are myriads of individual revelations at Sinai.)

> It is not the case, God forbid, that the sages innovated based on their own opinions! Rather, they simply arrived at the conclusion that God had already expressed. Their souls, which stood at Mount Sinai (for at that event all the souls were present), received everything appropriate to the nature of their souls and their generation....It follows that the Holy Blessed One gave the Torah at every time. At every hour the well that pours forth does not stop; what God gives is what God gave in potential.[16]

This understanding has personal implications. The Apter Rav (d. 1825) wrote that a Jew must "always see himself, at every moment, as if he is standing at Mount Sinai to receive the Torah....Every day God gives the Torah to the people Israel....Thus will he achieve a measure of reverence and awe, just as was the case when the Torah was given in fear and in trembling."[17]

What about the human being who receives God's word, then and at every moment? My father's doctoral dissertation, written at the University of Berlin in the early 1930s, was a study of prophetic consciousness, probing precisely what Bea called attention to: What is the human experience of divine revelation, and how does that experience shape God's word? My father explored different classical prophets, and summarized his view of revelation in his book *God in Search of Man*:

> The prophet is not a passive recipient, a recording instrument, affected from without without participation of heart and will, nor is he a person who acquires his vision by his own strength and labor. The prophet's personality is rather a unity of inspiration and experience, invasion and response....Even in the moment of the event he is, we are

told, an active partner in the event. His response to what is disclosed to him turns revelation into a dialogue. In a sense, prophecy consists of a revelation of God and a co-revelation of man.[18]

Aware of their theological affinities, my father wrote a long letter to Cardinal Bea, dated June 11, 1962, in German, outlining for him one of the key arguments he made about revelation in his recently published, two-volume Hebrew book, *Torah min HaShamayim*. In the letter, my father suggested that rabbinic teachings might serve as points of comparison to each section of Cardinal Bea's study, which surveyed historical understandings of inspiration from the New Testament to the present. "I was able, to my great surprise, to determine that [in the rabbinic period] the revelatory nature of the Pentateuch was treated from different perspectives," a mystical standpoint exemplified by the school of Rabbi Akiva and a rationalist school exemplified by the school of his opponent, Rabbi Ishmael. He further suggests that Jewish understandings of revelation may have influenced the early church's understandings of inspiration. For example, referring to an article on inspiration written by Cardinal Bea,[19] my father writes that whereas Akiva believed that Moses was given the divine word literally, to preach and to write it down inerrantly, Ishmael believed that Moses spoke the word of God from his own perspective, shaping it with his own insights. He explained to Bea that no theory of divine dictation of Scripture existed prior to the first half of the second century, and views of revelation differed considerably among rabbinic figures. The orthodox Protestant theories of the sixteenth and seventeenth centuries regarding the literal truth of Scripture, my father suggested, are closely related to the views of Rabbi Akiva. The letter concludes with an offer to send Cardinal Bea the rabbinic sources, both in Hebrew and in German translation.

The answer from Bea was short and disappointing. He was in the midst of the Council meetings and clearly not engaged in academic theological scholarship at that point. He expressed gratitude for the letter, but did not engage the substance of my father's points. It is perhaps not an accident that my father recognized the affinities between his work on revelation and Bea's work on divine inspiration.

Both had studied at the University of Berlin, though many years apart—Bea in 1913, my father in 1927–33—in the same field, Semitics, with at least one of the same professors, Eugen Mittwoch, who was also on my father's dissertation committee.[20] Notable, too, is that in his doctoral dissertation on prophetic consciousness, my father's pen was directed sharply and critically against Protestant biblical scholarship, not Catholic theology, and he made use of philosophical positions associated with Husserl and phenomenology. My father was part of a wider movement in Germany during the 1920s of the second generation of followers of Dilthey and Scheler, who asked how phenomenology could be applied to the study of religion, recognizing that understanding involves reason but also emotion, an engagement and not a conceptual detachment with the phenomenon being studied.

RABBI HESCHEL AND CARDINAL BEA

Let me now review their brief but very intense relationship that continued through 1965. My father was approached by the AJC (American Jewish Committee) in 1961, where his former student, Rabbi Marc Tannenbaum, worked, and he met with Cardinal Bea several times, starting in November 1961. Following that meeting, three of my father's books were sent to Bea, who expressed his thanks in his reply: "A strong, common spiritual bond [exists] between us."

My father's letter to Cardinal Bea was one of many they exchanged since they first met in Rome on Sunday, November 26, 1961, during the preliminary preparations before the Council opened. My father was accompanied by the German Jewish social philosopher Max Horkheimer, who had recently been employed by the AJC as a consultant to undertake a research project on prejudice. Prior to that meeting, my father read two of Bea's books, and also studied the preliminary documents, including the Apeldoorn Statement of August 1960 that, as John Connelly has discussed, shifted attention to Romans as the scriptural basis for Catholic-Jewish relations. At their meeting, my father took up a midrash Bea cited in the introduction to his edition of the Song of Songs, in which Rabbi Akiva says that all of *olam* (world) is not as important as the moment in which the Song of Songs was given to Israel. My father suggested that *olam* here should be translated as "time." We have a prophetic responsibility to time, my father said, because some things are vital in a particular moment, and we have to keep ourselves open to recognizing what is vital for our time, and Pope John XXIII's call for mutual love and understanding is the significant moment in history at this time. Cardinal Bea responded with warmth and friendliness, and the discussion turned to practical matters—Bea's request for a memorandum with suggestions, some discussion of biblical scholarship, and my father's concluding statement that Jews want to be known and understood as Jews (not candidates for conversion).

Responding to his request, the AJC commissioned three memoranda. The first two concerned images of Jews and Judaism in Catholic teaching and in Catholic liturgy. The third was written by my father, "On Improving Catholic-Jewish Relations," submitted in May 1962. He suggested that the Vatican Council recognize "the integrity and permanent preciousness" of the Jews as Jews rather than as potential converts, and urged the Council to recognize antisemitism as a sin that was incompatible with Catholicism. He wrote,

> With humility and in the spirit of commitment to the living message of the prophets of Israel, let us consider the grave problems that confront us all as the children of God. Both Judaism and Christianity share the prophets' belief that God chooses agents through whom His will is made known and His work done throughout history. Both Judaism and Christianity live in the certainty that mankind is in need of ultimate redemption, that God is involved in human history, that in relations between man and man, God is at stake....
>
> The universe is done," he declared. "The greater masterpiece still undone, still in process of being created, is history. For accomplishing His grand design God needs the help of man....Life is clay, and righteousness the mold in which God wants history to be shaped....God calls for mercy and righteousness; this demand of His cannot be satisfied only in

temples...but in history, in time. It is within the realm of history that man has to carry out God's mission.

It is from the inner life of men and from the articulation of evil thoughts that evil actions take their rise. It is therefore of extreme importance that the sinfulness of thoughts of suspicion and hatred and particularly the sinfulness of any contemptuous utterance, however flippantly it is meant, be made clear to all mankind. This applies in particular to such thoughts and utterances about individuals or groups of other religions, races and nations.

He then proposed four goals that he hoped the Council would adopt: (1) reject deicide; (2) stop missionary activity; (3) expose Christians to Jewish life; and (4) establish a church commission to stop prejudice and care for Christian-Jewish relations.

Perhaps it is worth noting that the American Orthodox rabbi Joseph Soloveitchik, published an article, "Confrontation," protesting any theological dialogue between Jews and Christians.[21] His article prompted a great deal of subsequent misunderstanding within the Orthodox community, which assumed that the article was an attack on my father's efforts. However, in a recent article, Reuven Kimelman has demonstrated that the positions of Soloveitchik and my father were essentially identical: the four goals that my father proposed were not concerned with theological principles, and *Nostra Aetate* did not violate the spirit of Soloveitchik's conclusions. The two men, Kimelman concludes, were actually in closer accord than most commentators realize.

Nonetheless, Rabbi Soloveitchik, a highly respected Orthodox rabbi in his day, succeeded in preventing Orthodox rabbis from engaging in the discussions with Vatican representatives, both in the United States and in Europe; the leading Orthodox rabbis of France and Italy, Henri Schilli and Elio Toaff, refused to participate in a meeting in Paris, held in November 1961, to discuss the Apeldoorn Statement. Rabbi Norman Lamm, not yet president of Yeshiva University but a leading Orthodox rabbi in New York City, also polemicized against Jewish involvement in Vatican II. In a sermon delivered in December 1960, he called the Jews engaged in dialogue with the Vatican "sycophants." Lamm compared Catholics to the biblical Esau, citing a midrash that Esau only pretended to kiss his brother Jacob and really wanted to bite him; so, too, the Catholic Church, whose ultimate goal is to convert the Jews but seeks that goal deceptively, through a public relations pretense of friendliness. In a sermon delivered in December 1963 and printed privately, Lamm polemicized against Jews for expressing gratitude for the anticipated changes in the church's attitudes, arguing that Jews should rather congratulate the church for "coming to terms with their conscience."[22] The resentment and arrogance articulated by Lamm captured the mood of a segment of the Jewish population that sent letters to the editors of Jewish newspapers, as well as directly to my father, expressing their contempt for Catholicism and insisting that no Jew should travel to Rome to see the pope; let the pope come to the Jews, they wrote. One prominent Jewish theologian said in public, "When I look at a cross, I see a swastika."

Yet it was that in June 1962 that representatives from Arab countries succeeded, temporarily, in deleting the schema on relations with the Jewish people from the Council agenda. In addition, during that same month an article written by Cardinal Bea on the question of deicide was withdrawn prior to publication in *La Civilta Cattolica*.

Cardinal Cushing of Boston spoke at the opening of the Council meeting on October 11, 1962, and reminded the Council that the "Jewish community and the Protestants have sent their best wishes for our Council's work." Rumors were circulating that Jews were controlling the Vatican via John Oesterreicher and Gregory Baum, both Jewish converts to Catholicism, and the atmosphere was tense. Yet Bea persisted, and declared on October 26 that a schema on the Jews would indeed be included.

On December 7, 1962, the first session ended and Cardinal Bea, in some consternation about the future of the schema, wrote to Pope John for his intervention in reinstating the schema on the Jews as a manifestation of a "purification of spirit and conscience" necessitated by the "appalling crimes of National Socialism against six million Jews." The pope responded and wrote on December 13, "We have read Cardinal Bea's memorandum with care and entirely share his opinion that a profound responsibility requires our intervention." He continued,

> His blood be on us and on our children (Matthew 27:25) did not relieve believers of the duty laid upon them to work for the salvation of all the children of Abraham and, similarly, that of every other human being on earth. Help us, then, we entreat You; help Your servants whom You have ransomed with Your precious blood.[23]

Cardinal Bea made an important trip to the United States in March 1963. This was two months after my father delivered his extraordinary lecture "Religion and Race" at a conference in Chicago, when he first met Martin Luther King Jr. Cardinal Bea's visit to the United States has been called a "crowning point of the cardinal's personal activity in this period."[24] He first spoke at Harvard University to a packed audience in the beautiful Sanders Theatre in Memorial Hall, with an overflow audience watching on closed circuit television. His topic was "Teaching and Research in the Service of Christian Unity." The event was organized by Douglas Horton, a professor at Harvard Divinity School and a Congregationalist. As the invitation to the event stated, this was "the first time that the university, or more precisely its Divinity School, has organized a Catholic-Protestant colloquium,"[25] and it came about because Cardinal Richard Cushing had established a close relationship with Cardinal Bea during the opening of the Council, and Cardinal Cushing was also a close friend of President Pusey of Harvard. Two more lectures by Cardinal Bea followed on two subsequent evenings, both on "The Council and Non-Catholic Christians."

During the course of his stay in Boston, Cardinal Bea is said to have met privately with my father at the residence of Cardinal Cushing, someone my father long viewed as a friend and ally, but that meeting has not been corroborated. Cardinal Bea then traveled to New York City, where he attended meetings with representatives of the World Council of Churches and also with the National Council of Churches. A third set of meetings with Jewish representatives took place on March 31. My father chaired a gathering of rabbis and Jewish leaders

213

at the offices of the American Jewish Committee (AJC). What was discussed? Cardinal Bea wrote,

> In reply to questions which had been included in the program, I first of all clarified from the exegetical viewpoint the matter of the Jews' responsibility for the death of Jesus, that of the meaning of the dispersal of the chosen people among the nations, ruling out, as St. Paul does, any idea that God had rejected or gone so far as to curse his own people.[26]

That night came a formal dinner in Bea's honor at the Plaza Hotel, hosted by the AJC.[27] At that dinner, attended by major religious figures of the United States as well as U Thant, secretary general of the United Nations, Rabbi Heschel addressed the cardinal:

> What will save us? God and our ability to stand in awe of each other's faith, of each other's commitment....This is the agony of history: bigotry, the failure to revere each other's faith. We must insist upon loyalty to the unique treasures of our own tradition and at the same time acknowledge that in this eon religious diversity may well be the will of God.

There are some photographs of that meeting in New York, showing Rabbi Heschel presenting Cardinal Bea with a gift, an edition of the Hebrew midrash on the Song of Songs, a text Cardinal Bea had studied and written about as a text dealing with divine inspiration. Particularly striking in the photographs are the warmth and smiles, not only on the face of Cardinal Bea, but also on my father's face. After all, Cardinal Bea was a German theologian who was publishing theology during the Nazi period, and who served as father confessor to Pope Pius XII. One can well imagine why my father, a refugee from the Nazis whose mother and sisters were murdered, might be uncomfortable, yet the smile is there, indicating the cordiality he felt toward the cardinal.

I also want to add that my father did not act without the encouragement of friends and colleagues. In particular, he consulted his brother-in-law, the Kopitznitzer rebbe, who lived in New York City, and with whom he spoke frequently about his engagement with Vatican representatives.

The night of June 2, 1963, was somber in my parents' home, as we sat in the living room, listening to the radio reports of the illness of Pope John XXIII. On June 4, 1963, Pope John died. Just a week later, George Wallace, then governor of Alabama, blocked the enrollment of two African-American students at the University of Alabama. A day later, on June 12, 1963, members of the Ku Klux Klan assassinated Medgar Evers, field secretary for the NAACP, who had been working to desegregate the University of Mississippi. On June 19, President Kennedy submitted his civil rights bill to Congress and decided to convene a meeting of civil rights leaders at the White House to try to halt the planned March on Washington scheduled for August. My father was among those invited to the meeting and replied with a telegram:

I LOOK FORWARD TO THE PRIVILEGE OF BEING PRESENT TOMORROW AT 4 P.M. LIKELIHOOD EXISTS THAT NEGRO PROBLEM WILL BE LIKE WEATHER. EVERYBODY TALKS ABOUT IT BUT NOBODY DOES ANYTHING ABOUT IT. PLEASE DEMAND OF RELIGIOUS LEADERS PERSONAL INVOLVEMENT NOT JUST SOLEMN DECLARATION. WE FORFEIT RIGHT TO WORSHIP GOD AS LONG AS WE CONTINUE TO HUMILIATE NEGROES. CHURCH SYNAGOGUE HAVE FAILED. THEY MUST REPENT. ASK RELIGIOUS LEADERS TO CALL FOR NATIONAL REPENTANCE AND PERSONAL SACRIFICE. LET RELIGIOUS LEADERS DONATE ONE MONTH'S SALARY TOWARD FUND FOR NEGRO HOUSING AND EDUCATION. I PROPOSE THAT YOU MR. PRESIDENT DECLARE A STATE OF MORAL EMERGENCY. A MARSHALL PLAN TO AID TO NEGROES IS BECOMING A NECESSITY. THE HOUR CALLS FOR MORAL GRANDEUR AND SPIRITUAL AUDACITY.[28]

The change in papal leadership during the summer of 1963 caused alarm; Pope Paul VI was viewed as far more conservative, and it was uncertain if he would support a statement about the Jews and Judaism. However, Pope Paul opened the second conciliar session with a speech in which he spoke of those who believe in God as "the second circle." "Made up of the men who above all adore the one, supreme God whom we too adore. We refer to the children, worthy of our affection and respect, of the Hebrew people, faithful to the religion which we call that of the Old Testament."[29]

On October 17, 1963, *The New York Times* published a preliminary draft of a proposed Council declaration regarding the Jews. My father's response was very positive, calling the draft "an expression of integrity inspired by the presence of God. May the spirit of God guide the work of the Council."

In November 1963, my father made a secret trip to Rome (he was there when President John F. Kennedy was assassinated), concerned that the next draft would include a hope for the conversion of the Jews. In Rome he met with Monsignor (later Cardinal) Willebrands, whom he also held in high esteem and who was serving as Cardinal Bea's secretary at that time. On November 23, 1963, Heschel wrote to Cardinal Bea, expressing his concern that the theme of conversion of the Jews had been introduced into the new text.

Forces of opposition, however, were gaining strength. The second draft appeared with the words the Jews had feared: a hope for the eventual conversion of the Jews to Catholicism. My father's response was cited in *The New York Times* on September 3, 1964:

> It must be stated that spiritual fratricide is hardly a means for the attainment of fraternal discussion or reciprocal understanding. A message that regards the Jews as candidates for conversion and proclaims that the destiny of Judaism is to disappear, will be abhorred by Jews all over the world and is bound to foster reciprocal distrust as well as bitterness and resentment. As I have repeatedly stated to leading personalities at the Vatican, I am ready to go to Auschwitz if faced with the alternative of conversion or death. Jews throughout the world will be dismayed by a

call from the Vatican to abandon their faith in a generation which has witnessed the massacre of six million Jews and the destruction of thousands of synagogues on a continent where the dominant religion was not Islam, Buddhism, or Shintoism.

The statement caused strong reactions—shock, dismay, and, in some, anger. I was a child at the time and terrified by the thought of my father going to Auschwitz.

For my father, the charges of deicide and the effort to convert the Jews were both threats to Jewish life. Deicide had sparked murderous attacks on Jews for two thousand years, and mission to the Jews was, as my father said, a form of spiritual fratricide.

Ten days later, on September 14, 1964, my father met in a private audience with Pope Paul VI, just before Yom Kippur; the meeting lasted thirty-five minutes. He presented a memorandum to the pope:

> Why is so much attention paid to what Vatican II is going to say about the Jews? Are we Jews in need of recognition? God himself has recognized us as a people. Are we in need of a "chapter" acknowledging our right to exist as Jews? Nearly every chapter in the Bible expresses the promise of God's fidelity to his covenant with our people. It is not gratitude that we ask for, it is the cure of a disease, affecting so many minds, that we pray for.[30]

In a private, handwritten note, my father wrote, "In our conversation, I found in the spiritual head of the Roman Catholic Church a sensitive and respectful understanding for the religious position of our people."

He was later informed that after he left, the pope crossed out the statement hoping for the eventual conversion of the Jews.

Some days later, on September 25, 1964, Cardinal Bea addressed the political machinations:

Such renewal is so important that it is even worth exposing ourselves to the danger that some people might prevent this declaration for political ends. It is a case of our duties to truth and justice, our duty to be grateful to God, our duty to imitate faithfully and as closely as possible Christ out Lord and his apostles Peter and Paul. In fulfilling those duties the church and this Council can never allow any political influence or motive to find a place.

Bea stated that the document carried no political overtones, and emphasized that the Jews could not be accused of deicide. Discussion of the document began on September 28, with thirty-five speeches delivered and twenty-seven written memoranda submitted, all about the two-page statement.

What was the opposition? Cardinal Ruffini gave the main speech: he agreed that deicide should be abandoned—"no one can kill God"—and spoke of the many Jews "we" had saved from the Nazis.[31] But he went on to request a quid pro quo: to improve Catholic Jewish relations, he said, the Jews should be exhorted to love Christians. Anti-Christian passages should be censored from the Talmud, and anticlericalism be blamed on "Jewish" Masonry. Other speakers who supported the document suggested it was a proper way to remember Pius XII for having saved Jews from the Nazis.[32]

In October came a bombshell: the statement was to be withdrawn, and a theological commission established that would rewrite the statement concerning the Jews. Cardinal Bea's response was measured: there should be some declaration, regardless of where in the final documents it would be inserted.[33]

Meanwhile, during the third session, in November 1964, the entire schema concerning the Jews was withdrawn to allow antagonisms to quiet down. On November 20, a final revised version of the document was presented and put to the vote, and the cardinals voted overwhelmingly in favor of it. Yet this was not the end of the story.

During the early months of 1965, antagonism toward the schema on the Jews was growing. There were charges that if the Council absolved the Jews of deicide, it would be betraying the gospel; some claimed the document was the result of international

Zionists who had bribed the bishops to support the state of Israel; Catholics in Arab countries were warned of serious consequences, including threats of church fires, if the schema passed. Yet Cardinal Bea remained firm on his position, although during the plenary sessions in May 1965, tensions ran high, "almost as high as if there were a war on."[34] Ultimately, the conclusion was to eliminate the term *deicide*. At the same time, the document on the Jews was integrated into a broader "Declaration on the Church's Relationship with Non-Christian Religions."

The Declaration that circulated starting in May 1965 was a compromise: instead of "deplores, indeed condemns" hatred and persecution of Jews, the new version simply said, "deplores displays of anti-Semitism directed against Jews." The old version warned Christians not to teach anything that could give rise to hatred and persecution of Jews, while the new version urged them not to teach "anything inconsistent with the truth of the Gospel and with the spirit of Christ."[35]

Translating the schema into the minds and speech of Catholics did not happen immediately. Even the pope slipped a bit in his Passion Sunday sermon on April 4, 1965, when he stated, "That people [the Jews] predestined to receive the Messiah, who had been awaiting him for thousands of years...when Christ comes...not only does not recognize him, but opposes him, slanders him and finally kills him."

A new text was presented on October 14, 1965, stating that "the Catholic Church for the first time proposes fraternal dialogue with the great non-Christian religions," Hinduism, Buddhism, and Islam. Regarding the Jews, the document took a strong position against charges of deicide:

> Although the Jewish authorities and those who followed their lead pressed for the death of Christ (John 19:6), nevertheless what happened in his passion cannot be attributed indiscriminately to all Jews then alive, or to the Jews of today. Although the church is the new people of God, the Jews should not be presented as rejected by God or accursed, as if this follows from the Holy Scriptures.

Moreover, the text "deplored anti-Semitism."[36]

Ultimately, the feared hostile reaction did not materialize; church representatives in Arab countries accepted the text, and no violence was experienced. Moreover, the language urging conversion of the Jews was withdrawn. *Nostra Aetate* was welcomed by the Jewish community. My father stated, "The schema on the Jews is the first statement of the Church in history, the first Christian document dealing with Judaism, which is devoid of any expression of hope for conversion. And, let me remind you, that there were two versions."[37]

In his book *The Church and the Jewish People*, published in 1966 and translated into six languages, Cardinal Bea wrote his own commentary on the schema. On the question of deicide, he noted that deicide can only be charged against those who consciously knew they were killing God incarnate in Jesus, which the Jews did not know. Moreover, he continued, only a few Jews of the time participated in the death of Jesus, so the charge cannot be made against all Jews of the time, let alone of all time. Finally, he offers the remarkable insight that in their texts, neither Peter, Paul, nor Stephen, all of whom were Jewish, includes himself among those responsible for the crucifixion. Had collective responsibility been intended, "the speakers would have been obliged to use the pronoun 'we' and to include themselves."[38]

Nostra Aetate states, "The Church regards with esteem also the Moslems," and lists some of the commonalities, but speaks of "the bond that spiritually ties the people of the New Covenant to Abraham's stock." The relationship with Judaism is of a different, unique nature. Cardinal Bea, in his book, explains that

> Christ is the link which enables the gentiles to be numbered among the inheritors of the promises....Faith creates so close a union between Christ and those who believe in him that they form one mystical person with him. It is in virtue of this union with Christ that like him they become the descendants of Abraham, and therefore sharers in the promises made to Abraham and his posterity.[39]

Cardinal Bea died in 1968; my father wrote in tribute to him,

> The rare combination of wisdom, learning, and saintliness of this very great man have made him one of the most outstanding sources of spiritual comfort in an age of so much darkness. He taught his contemporaries that we must understand the doctrines of faith in the context of love. His name will be cherished by the Jewish people as well as by all people of good will as an inspired architect of interreligious understanding and will remain a blessing forever.[40]

CONCLUSION

The ability to hold both Judaism and Christianity together, to look from the perspective of each, is perhaps the great achievement of *Nostra Aetate*. More important than changes in doctrine is the cultivation of a new relationship between the two great religions. *Nostra Aetate* sets forth a goal: to see the sacred in each other's religious faith. The text speaks of "mutual understanding and respect," but in the context of a conciliar document that phrase obviously refers not to social relations but to religious relations—indeed, the phrase calls into being a religious relationship of an entirely new order, composed not of theological supersessionism, but based on shared "spiritual patrimony."

What ultimately prevailed, however, were neither political manipulations, nor theological hairsplitting. Instead, the Second Vatican Council issued a short statement on the relationship of the Roman Catholic Church with Judaism and the Jewish people that inaugurated a new and extraordinary relationship that also set a tone for broader efforts at interreligious dialogue in a range of contexts.

Father Pawlikowski knows, better than most, how difficult it is to reinforce the teachings of *Nostra Aetate* and translate them into the words of sermons and catechisms. Pope Paul II visited a synagogue in Rome on April 13, 1986, and spoke of the unique bond between Catholics and Jews:

> The Jewish religion is not "extrinsic" to us, but in a certain way "intrinsic" to our own religion. With Judaism, therefore, we have a relationship which we do not have with any other religion. You are clearly beloved brothers and, in a certain way, it could be said that you are our elder brothers.[41]

At the same time, efforts have also been made over the decades to return to pre–Vatican II teachings of deicide and supersessionism, and Fr. Pawlikowski has been at the forefront of guiding such efforts in more positive directions, even as he has also reminded Jews of their responsibility to respond to *Nostra Aetate* by correcting negative Jewish attitudes toward Christianity. Over the years, he has become, we might say, the conscience of *Nostra Aetate*.

Notes

1. John Pawlikowski, "Rethinking Christianity: A Challenge to Jewish Attitudes," *Moment: Independent Journalism from a Jewish Perspective* 15, no. 4 (August 1, 1990): 36. His exact words are this: "Then, too, the bitter history of Christian persecution of Jews throughout the centuries...has left a deep scar on Jewish consciousness."

2. John Pawlikowski, "Towards a Renewed Theology of Christianity's Bond with Judaism," address to the International Council of Christians and Jews, Buenos Aires, Argentina, August 2014, http://www.jcrelations.net/Towards_a_Renewed_Theology_of_Christianity_s_Bond_with_Judaism.4948.0.html?&pdf=1.

3. John Connelly, *From Enemy to Brother: The Revolution in Catholic Teaching on the Jews 1933–1965* (Cambridge, MA: Harvard University Press, 2012).

4. Joshua Furnal, "Abraham Joshua Heschel and *Nostra Aetate*: Shaping the Catholic Reconsideration of Judaism during Vatican II," *Religions* 7, no. 70 (2016): 5.

5. Avery Dulles, "Covenant and Mission," *America* (October 21, 2002): http://www.americamagazine.org/issue/408/article/covenant-and-mission.

6. Furnal mentions Massimo Fagioli and Gavin D'Costa. John Connelly includes the role played by Ehrlich, but barely mentions Heschel,

taking his lead from Edward Kaplan's highly polemical and even nasty diatribe against Heschel's ecumenical work in his book *Spiritual Radical: Abraham Joshua Heschel in America, 1940–1972* (New Haven, CT: Yale University Press, 2007). Within the Orthodox Jewish world, there has been a long tradition of assuming that Rabbi Joseph Soloveitchik, the leader of modern Orthodox Judaism in the United States, opposed Jewish engagement in Vatican II. That understanding was based on an article published by Soloveitchik, "Confrontation," in *Tradition: A Journal of Orthodox Thought* 6 (2): 5–29. However, a recent article by Reuven Kimelman argues that Soloveitchik's article set forth goals for the church that were identical to those proposed by Heschel. Nonetheless, many Orthodox Jews today believe that Soloveitchik prohibited Jewish-Christian dialogue. Reuven Kimelman, "Rabbis Joseph B. Soloveitchik and Abraham Joshua Heschel on Jewish-Christian Relations," *The Edah Journal* 4, no. 2 (2004): 2–21.

7. Jerome-Michael Vereb, *"Because He Was a German!" Cardinal Bea and the Origins of Roman Catholic Engagement in the Ecumenical Movement* (Grand Rapids, MI: W.B. Eerdmans Pub. Co., 2006).

8. *John XXIII: Pope Paul on His Predecessor and a Documentation by the Editors of Herder Correspondence* (New York: Herder and Herder, 1965), 51.

9. Stjepan Schmidt, *Augustin Bea: The Cardinal of Unity*, trans. Leslie Wearne (New York: New City Press, 1992), 109.

10. Schmidt, *Augustin Bea*, 192–93.

11. The comment is frequently attributed to Raymond Brown, but I have not found a publication by him with that statement. The encyclical *Divino Afflante Spiritu* followed a prior encyclical, issued by Pope Leo XIII in 1893, that granted permission for some degree of critical study of Scripture, while polemicizing against rationalism and against claims that only some sections of the Bible were inerrant, while others are fallible.

12. James Tunstead Burtchaell, *Catholic Theories of Biblical Inspiration since 1810: A Review and Critique* (Cambridge: Cambridge University Press, 1969), 216.

13. Burtchaell, *Catholic Theories of Biblical Inspiration since 1810*, 217.

14. Schmidt, *Augustin Bea*, 190.

15. Augustin Cardinal Bea, *The Study of the Synoptic Gospels* (New York: Harper and Row, 1965), 17; cited by Schmidt, *Augustin Bea*, 193.

16. Benjamin Sommer, *Revelation and Authority: Sinai in Scripture and Tradition* (New Haven, CT: Yale University Press, 2015), 206.

17. Sommer, *Revelation and Authority*, 204–5.

18. Abraham Joshua Heschel, *God in Search of Man* (New York: Farrar, Straus and Cuddahy, 1955), 259–60; see also Heschel, *The Prophets* (New York: Harper and Row, 1963), 624–25.

19. Augustin Cardinal Bea, "Die Instrumentalitätsidee in der Inspirationslehre," *Studia Anselmiana* 27–28 (1951): 47–65.

20. Bea studied with Eduard Meyer, Jakob Barth, Hermann Strack, and Eugen Mittwoch.

21. See n. 5 above.

22. Norman Lamm, "The Jews and the Ecumenical Council: How Ought Jews React?" *Jewish Life* 1963, 6–12. See also http://brussels.mc .yu.edu/gsdl/collect/lammserm/index/assoc/HASH015c/cad0f88b .dir/doc.pdf (accessed July 17, 2017).

23. The final sentence is taken from the *Te Deum*. The memorandum from Cardinal Bea to Pope John XXIII is cited by John M. Oesterreicher, *The New Encounter: Between Christians and Jews* (New York: Philosophical Library, 1986), 164; see also John Connelly, *From Enemy to Brother*, 249.

24. Schmidt, *Augustin Bea*, 425.

25. Schmidt, *Augustin Bea*, 425.

26. Schmidt, *Augustin Bea*, 427.

27. Among those attending: Rabbi Finklestein, Rabbi Joseph Lookstein, Rabbi Albert Minda (Central Conference of American Rabbis, Minneapolis), and Rabbi Julius Mark (Emanuel, New York City).

28. Telegram sent by Rabbi Abraham Joshua Heschel to President John F. Kennedy, White House, on June 16, 1963; reprinted in *Moral Grandeur and Spiritual Audacity: Essays of Abraham Joshua Heschel*, ed. Susannah Heschel (New York: Farrar, Straus, Giroux, 1996), vii.

29. Francesco Gioia, *Interreligious Dialogue: The Official Teaching of the Catholic Church, 1963–1995* (Boston: Pauline Books, 1997), 78–79. See also Pope Paul VI, *Ecclesiam Suam* 107, August 6, 1964, http://w2 .vatican.va/content/paul-vi/en/encyclicals/documents/hf_p-vi_enc _06081964_ecclesiam.html.

30. Marc H. Tanenbaum, "Jewish-Christian Relations—Heschel and Vatican Council II," lecture at the Memorial Symposium in Honor of Rabbi Abraham Joshua Heschel Sponsored by the Department of Jewish Philosophy of the Jewish Theological Seminary, February 21, 1983. See

page 17 at http://www.ajcarchives.org/AJC_DATA/Files/Z582.CV01 .pdf (accessed May 13, 2018).

31. Xavier Rynne, *Vatican Council II* (New York: Farrar, Straus and Giroux, 1964), 305.

32. Rynne, *Vatican Council II*, 305.

33. Schmidt, *Augustin Bea*, 514.

34. Rynne, *Vatican Council II*, 518.

35. Rynne, *Vatican Council II*, 529.

36. Schmidt, *Augustin Bea*, 522.

37. Abraham Joshua Heschel, "From Mission to Dialogue," *Conservative Judaism* 21, no. 3 (Spring 1967): 10.

38. Augustin Cardinal Bea, *The Church and the Jewish People*, trans. Philip Loretz (London: Geoffrey Chaplan, 1966), 77.

39. Bea, *The Church and the Jewish People*, 56; he is here citing Galatians 3:26–29.

40. Schmidt, *Augustin Bea*, 707.

41. Eugene J. Fisher and Leon Klenicki, eds., *Spiritual Pilgrimage: Texts on Jews and Judaism* (New York: Crossroad, 1996), xxiii.

CHAPTER FOURTEEN

NOSTRA AETATE, OMNIA MUTANTUR
*The Times They Are a-Changing**

—⁓—

Amy-Jill Levine

For the fortieth anniversary of *Nostra Aetate*, October 2005, I was invited to deliver a paper in Rome. This was also the weekend of my only nephew's becoming a bar mitzvah. I had a choice: a church in Rome or a synagogue in Connecticut. My mother-in-law made the choice for me, and for the sake of *shalom bayit*, I went to Connecticut. For the fiftieth anniversary in October 2015, the Catholic Biblical Association (CBA) invited me to the annual meeting in Santa Clara to speak on *Nostra Aetate* and biblical studies. This time, my mother-in-law had no objections.

For that talk, and for this revision of it in honor of John Pawlikowski, I have no desire to kvetch about the shortcomings of *Nostra Aetate*, or any other document on Jewish-Catholic relations. Rather, this paper briefly summarizes the progress that has been made since 1965, and then it moves to what biblical scholars could and should do to advance Jewish-Catholic relations in our discipline. Both topics seek to complement Fr. Pawlikowski's substantial contributions in the fields of social ethics and theology. For the priest at the altar, the religious educator in the Sunday school, the worshiper in the pew, and the student in the classroom, Fr. Pawlikowski's theoretical discussions of soteriology, the role of the Trinity in Jewish-Catholic dialogue, and the impact of the Shoah on Catholic ethical

---

* Selections from this paper were presented as part of a talk for the annual meeting of the Catholic Biblical Association (Santa Clara, CA, August 9, 2016).

teaching must be complemented by equally rigorous attention to how the Bible, proclaimed in the Mass and read by the faithful, should be understood.

THE PROGRESS

Nostra Aetate 4 states, "Jews should not be presented as rejected or accursed by God....The Church, mindful of the patrimony she shares with the Jews and moved not by political reasons but by the Gospel's spiritual love, decries hatred, persecutions, displays of anti-Semitism, directed against Jews at any time and by anyone."

Sonya Cronin notes,

> Until the mid-1960s, while most interpreters of the Gospel of John were aware of a polemic against the Jews, they did not discuss it as an ethical issue of potential anti-Judaism, nor did they relate it to a concern for the modern day. However, a shift in focus in Johannine scholarship is noticeable beginning in the mid-1960s and 1970s and continuing to the present.[1]

Tracking Raymond Brown's scholarship on the Gospel of John, Cronin notes,

> In 1960, Brown displayed no awareness of potential anti-Judaism. By 1966...Brown defended the Gospel of John against charges of potential anti-Judaism. In 1998, at the end of his writing career and the year of his death, Brown issued an apology on behalf of the writer of John for the harsh statements made against "the Jews."[2]

Cronin's recognition of the change in tone and the topics to be addressed from the 1960s to the 1990s fits with my own impression of how the Synoptics have been interpreted.

As far as I can tell, greater awareness of the presentation of Jews and Judaism in (non-Jewish) religious studies began in the 1970s.

Such changes were not only, or even primarily, due to *Nostra Aetate*, but prompted also by changes in religious education. In the 1970s, campus religion departments started to separate from philosophy, and that move opened biblical studies to various humanities and social sciences approaches (cognitive and neuro-scientific approaches would follow in the ensuing decades). Concurrently, numerous biblical studies PhD programs increasingly ceased to presume a religious orientation on the part of either students or faculty. Jews and other non-Christians started to enroll in biblical studies courses not because of requirements but because of interest; in these classes, they were generally welcomed rather than catechized. In the secular world, schools, clubs, and politics became more religiously diversified. Changes in Catholic biblical scholarship, teaching, and preaching regarding Jews also came about because of other ecclesial pronouncements, not directly related to Jewish-Christian relations, that offered new exegetical possibilities, such as the Second Vatican Council document *Dei Verbum*, Dogmatic Constitution on Divine Revelation. Finally, it took until the 1980s before the impact of the Shoah began to be recognized in theological education, religious studies, preaching, and catechesis.

By the 1990s, Jewish-Catholic relations became not only corrective but constructive. For example, beginning in 1995, numerous Catholic high school faculty have taught "Bearing Witness," a curriculum created by, inter alia, the Anti-Defamation League (ADL), the National Catholic Educational Association, the U.S. Conference of Catholic Bishops, and the United States Holocaust Memorial Museum. It is "designed to provide Catholic school educators with the training and resources necessary to teach their students about the historical relationship between Jewish and Catholic communities and the impact of that relationship on Catholic teaching, catechesis and liturgy."[3] The curriculum appears sporadically across the U.S. Catholic parochial school system; mainstreaming it throughout—something perhaps the USCCB could recommend—would be ideal. The ADL is currently (2017) developing an education program on the Shoah for Catholic School teachers, and this too should be used nationally.

There is no comparable, institutionally supported program on introducing Christianity or discussing Jewish-Christian relations designed for Jewish day schools or Hebrew schools; there is no formal mechanism for Jewish children to receive instruction, from a position of respect, on the relationship between synagogue and church. I put into the search engines for the Schechter Day School Network[4] the terms *Christian, Christianity, Christmas, Jesus, Vatican II,* and *church.* The searches came up empty, save for generalizing comments about multiple religions in the United States. I thought I would find something substantive with *New Testament,* but the result was the word *new* in one sentence and *testament* in another. My own children are graduates of a Jewish community primary school; interreligious instruction was not part of the curriculum. Ignorance is often a two-way street, and better dialogical programs are needed in Jewish secondary school education.

On the doctrinal and catechetical levels, four major statements since *Nostra Aetate* have advanced Jewish-Catholic relations. "Notes on the Correct Way to Present the Jews and Judaism in Preaching and Catechesis in the Roman Catholic Church" (1985) from the Vatican Commission for Religious Relations with the Jews and "God's Mercy Endures Forever: Guidelines on the Presentation of Jews and Judaism in Catholic Preaching" (1988) from the National Conference of Catholic Bishops recognize how certain biblical depictions of Jews, when coupled with uninformed preaching, can inculcate or reinforce bigotry. The third statement is the Pontifical Biblical Commission's 2001 "The Jewish People and Their Sacred Scriptures in the Christian Bible." The document acknowledges that Jewish interpretations of the Scriptures are legitimate, even if they do not conform to Christian claims; it insists that supersessionist readings are illegitimate; and it recognizes that christological interpretations of the Old Testament are made retrospectively and therefore Jews should not be expected to find Jesus in Genesis or Isaiah.[5]

The fourth text, published December 10, 2015, is a twenty-five-page document from the Vatican's Commission for Religious Relations with the Jews, "The Gifts and the Calling of God Are Irrevocable: A Reflection on the Theological Questions Pertaining to Catholic-Jewish Relations."[6] The text states it is not a magisterial document, but it models how such statements should be written in that the Commission worked with two Jewish consultants (neither a biblical specialist). If one religious body is to offer reflections on another, it is wise to ask members of the other group if they can see themselves in the descriptions offered. "Gifts and Calling" 14 affirms, "Jesus was a Jew, was at home in the Jewish tradition of his time, and was decisively shaped by this religious milieu (cf. *Ecclesia in Medio Oriente* 20). His first disciples gathered around him had the same heritage and were defined by the same Jewish tradition." It continues,

> Jesus' central message on the Kingdom of God is in accordance with some Jewish thinking of his day. One cannot understand Jesus' teaching or that of his disciples without situating it within the Jewish horizon in the context of the living tradition of Israel; one would understand his teachings even less so if they were seen in opposition to this tradition.

It proclaims that Jesus is "fully and completely human, a Jew of his time, descendant of Abraham, son of David, shaped by the whole tradition of Israel, heir of the prophets, Jesus stands in continuity with his people and its history." Finally, perhaps belaboring the point, "Gifts and Calling" 15 notes,

> The soil that nurtured both Jews and Christians is the Judaism of Jesus' time, which not only brought forth Christianity but also, after the destruction of the temple in the year 70, post-biblical rabbinical Judaism....Thus Jews and Christians have the same mother and can be seen, as it were, as two siblings who—as is the normal course of events for siblings...developed in different directions.

The Jewish community has no hierarchical structure that would sponsor similar initiatives. However, there are regular meetings between the Vatican as well as the USCCB and (self-appointed) representatives of the Jewish community, from the Anti-Defamation League[7] to members of the International Jewish Committee for Interreligious Consultations (IJCIC)[8] to the American Jewish Committee.[9] The USCCB, in turn, had a Secretariat for Catholic-Jewish Relations (the position held so brilliantly by Eugene Fisher); the office has subsequently merged into the Secretariat for Ecumenical and Interreligious Affairs.[10] Since Fisher's time, dialogue with the Jewish community has, as least as far as I can tell, held a comparatively lower profile. Conversely, there may be terrific conversations happening, but no information has flowed from the conference tables in New York or Washington, DC, to synagogues or Jewish Community Centers in Middle Tennessee.

There are two major documents on Christianity produced by rabbis and Jewish scholars. The first, the 2000 statement *Dabru Emet*, "Speak Truth," endorsed at the time by over two hundred rabbis and Jewish scholars, proclaimed, inter alia, that Jews and Christians worship the same God, that National Socialism was not a Christian phenomenon,[11] and that "the controversy between Jews and Christians will not be settled until God redeems the entire world as promised in scripture and no-one should be pressed into believing another's belief."[12]

More recent is the December 3, 2015, statement signed by twenty-five Orthodox rabbis, "To Do the Will of Our Father in Heaven: Toward a Partnership between Jews and Christians."[13] Since its publication, over twice that number of Orthodox rabbis have added their endorsement. Among its striking proclamations are the following. First, it states, "As did Maimonides and Yehudah Halevi, we acknowledge that the emergence of Christianity in human history is neither an accident nor an error, but the willed divine outcome and gift to the nations." Second, it recognizes that we Jews could not engage in Jewish-Catholic dialogue were it not for the initial efforts of the Catholic Church. Because of those efforts, the rabbis stated, "Now that the Catholic Church has acknowledged the eternal Covenant between God and Israel, we Jews can acknowledge the ongoing constructive validity of Christianity as our partner in world redemption, without any fear that this will be exploited for missionary purposes."

Of course, not all Jews agreed.[14] Since this second statement is premised on theology rather than on the primarily historical claims of *Dabru Emet*, I am quite willing to cede commentary to those, such as Fr. Pawlikowski, who have expertise in theological studies. I am simply a student of the Bible; determining "divine will" is above my pay grade.

Despite the critiques of the various documents, Jewish-Catholic relations are moving forward. Now, *quo vadis*, where do we—that is, we biblical scholars who are also interested in Jewish-Catholic relations—go from here? There is still more work to be done. I focus on education because the real work has to be done in the classroom, in the pulpit, and in the pews.

WHAT HAVE WE LEARNED?

Popular biblical readings remain mired in negative stereotypes. Here are three examples, from the 1980s, 2000s, and summer 2016. The first is classic; the second is funny; and the third epitomizes the problem.

First, Elisabeth Fiorenza's *In Memory of Her*, published in 1983, neatly captured how little official teaching had made it from the classroom to the pulpit to the pew. Fiorenza writes,

> One of my friends spoke about Jesus, the Jew, to an adult education class in her parish. She encountered vehement objections to such a notion. Finally, after a lengthy discussion a participant expressed the religious sentiment underlying it: "If you are so insistent that Jesus was Jewish, then you are probably right. But the Blessed Mother for sure is not."[15]

For this parishioner, Judaism, however defined, is incompatible with the "Christian" Mary.

Second, when I was the CBA's visiting scholar to the Philippines in 2004, I had the privilege of addressing several congregations. At one church, I asked if any of the members had ever seen a Jew aside from me. One fellow did call out, "Jerry Seinfeld." That's a start. But when the rest of the congregation said no, I turned, pointed to the crucifix behind me, and noted that they had been looking at a Jew their whole lives.

Third, in summer 2016 in Melbourne, at the CASPA conference, a gathering of Catholic secondary school principals working in Australia, Tasmania, and New Zealand, a Dominican sister, known for her splendid work in the cause of social justice, gave one of the keynotes. She summarized the popular view of Jesus. He was

> challenging a highly stratified, hierarchical and gender biased society....He spoke to the exploited peasantry polarized by gender and patriarchal values, highly regulated by Jewish purity laws that legitimated the social hierarchies.... The Israelite masses were held hostage in poverty by the triple-tax system: tribute to the Roman Emperor, to the local Jewish client-king (Herod) through whom Rome ruled by proxy, and to the Temple and its priesthood in Jerusalem.

She continued, "Christ by his way of being in communion with others, created a confrontational lifestyle by enjoying table fellowship with outcasts (eschewing the purity rituals over relationships), having close women friends, embracing and healing the sick, engaging with so-called sinners and the outcasts of society." Jesus, we were told, "readily offered friendship to tax collectors" and "treated slaves as equals." The first section of the talk concluded, "These practices were in fundamental opposition to the dominant religious, cultural, political and economic hierarchies of the time, challenging the very foundation of the social order. No wonder he was killed!"[16]

Otherwise put, or at least the conclusion I drew from this litany, Jesus was killed because he was nice to women, eschewed purity, dined with tax collectors, condemned slavery, and offered free medical care.[17] Missing is any recognition of women's roles in first-century Jewish life, including teaching and patronage; ignored is the listing of only twelve male apostles. Missing is the fact that Jesus *restores people to ritual purity* rather than abrogates purity laws; overlooked also is how purity works, much as does multiculturalism today, by helping groups to maintain their identity against assimilationist and acculturationist pressures. Missing is why tax collectors were socially problematic. Ignored is the fact that Jesus never condemns slavery but rather appears to find it normal. Ignored as well is how the majority of the Jewish population continued to worship at the temple, including Jesus' own followers. I agree, however, on the free medical care.

These stereotypes are not themselves indications of anti-Jewish or antisemitic feelings. They are not based in hatred but are, rather, primarily indicators of educational failures. They are also a replay of early liberation theology, in which Jesus speaks truth to power, stands up for the outcast and the marginalized, and otherwise sets the social justice agenda for the twenty-first century. Problems occur when the model is based on constructing a negative image of Judaism over against which Jesus stands. The model is not based in history, and its ends, human liberation, do not justify its means, bearing false witness against Jews and Judaism.

Catholic theology and ethics, detached from their biblical and historical grounding, are likely to go astray, just as biblical studies that do not attend any good news or necessary challenge risk ossification and irrelevance.

FOR THE BIBLE TELLS ME SO

Lack of education creates problems; so does vague or incorrect education. Annotated Bibles can be very helpful, or very dangerous. On this matter, I turned to the annotated Bible featured on the homepage of the U.S. Conference of Catholic Bishops.[18] The NABRE (New American Bible, Revised Edition), released on March 9, 2011, "is the culmination of nearly 20 years of work by a group of nearly 100 scholars and theologians, including bishops, revisers and editors."[19] The translation on the whole is pleasing; the notes, however—despite their attention to *Nostra Aetate*—threaten to inculcate or reinforce rather than correct anti-Jewish stereotypes. The following are a few of the numerous examples where problems may surface.

Several times, the NABRE's notes are either incorrect or misleading. For example, for Matthew 7:6 ("Do not give what is holy to dogs, or throw your pearls before swine, lest they trample them underfoot, and turn and tear you to pieces") the NABRE notes incorrectly state,

"**Dogs** and **swine** were Jewish terms of contempt for Gentiles," and concludes,

> This saying may originally have derived from a Jewish Christian community opposed to preaching the gospel (**what is holy, pearls**) to Gentiles. In the light of Mt 28:19 that can hardly be Matthew's meaning. He may have taken the saying as applying to a Christian dealing with an obstinately impenitent fellow Christian (Mt 18:17). [Bold emphases are original in all quotations of the commentary.]

The problems here are manifold. First, the epithets are cross-cultural insults rather than Jewish-determined ethnic slurs. The Cynics, so-named because they, like dogs, cared nothing for social convention, did not take their name from Jewish-identified slurs. Second, the note seeks to protect both Jesus and the (predominantly Gentile) church from a negative statement: by assigning the verse to a *Jewish*-Christian source, the notes exculpate both Jesus and the (Gentile) church.

This same move to assign negative comments to hypothetical Jewish-Christian sources and so to protect both Jesus and the Evangelists from problematic comments surfaces in the notes to Matthew 18:17:

> **Treat him...a Gentile or a tax collector**: just as the observant Jew avoided the company of Gentiles and tax collectors, so must the congregation of Christian disciples separate itself from the arrogantly sinful member who refuses to repent even when convicted of his sin by the whole **church**. Such a one is to be set outside the fellowship of the community. The harsh language about **Gentile** and **tax collector** probably reflects a stage of the Matthean **church** when it was principally composed of Jewish Christians. That time had long since passed, but the principle of exclusion for such a sinner remained. Paul makes a similar demand for excommunication in 1Cor 5:1–13.

The notes miss the extensive communications between Jews and Gentiles, including the "Court of the Gentiles" in the Jerusalem Temple where "observant Jews" and Gentiles necessarily mingled—the "god-fearers" who affiliated with Jews in synagogues, the Gentiles who built synagogues for Jews (see Luke 7:1–10), and the Gentiles among whom Jews in the Diaspora lived (Philo and Josephus are only two of the numerous examples). Observant Jews need not and generally did not avoid contact with Gentiles. (One does wonder what the Catholic of these notes would think upon encountering such an observant Jew today.) For Matthew, the "Gentiles" and the "tax collectors" are precisely the groups to be evangelized; the issue for the Gospel is not Jewish observance but ecclesial outreach.

Concerning the comment Matthew ascribes to Jesus, "Woe to you, scribes and Pharisees, you hypocrites. You traverse sea and land to make one convert, and when that happens you make him a child of Gehenna twice as much as yourselves" (Matt 23:15), the notes read, "In the first century A.D. until the First Jewish Revolt against Rome (A.D. 66–70), many Pharisees conducted a vigorous missionary campaign among Gentiles." There is no primary evidence supporting this claim, and if there were, the note insisting that "the observant Jew avoided the company of Gentiles and tax collectors" would make even less sense. The observant Jew (e.g., a Pharisee) cannot be both an evangelist to the Gentiles and avoid those Gentiles at the same time. Pharisees were interested in teaching fellow Jews, not in converting Gentiles.

Matters become increasingly convoluted with the notes to Matthew 27:25, the infamous "blood cry," although here the annotators do invoke *Nostra Aetate*. The verse reads, "And the whole people said in reply, 'His blood be upon us and upon our children.'" The notes read,

> Matthew sees in those who speak these words **the** entire **people** (Greek *laos*) of Israel. **His blood…and upon our children**: cf. Jer 26:15. The responsibility for Jesus' death is accepted by the nation that was God's special possession (Ex 19:5), his own **people** (Hos 2:25), and they thereby lose that high privilege; see Mt 21:43 and the note on that

verse. The controversy between Matthew's church and Pharisaic Judaism about which was the true people of God is reflected here. As the Second Vatican Council has pointed out, guilt for Jesus' death is not attributable to all the Jews of his time or to any Jews of later times.

Although the annotators elsewhere ascribe verses to Matthew's (hypothetical) Jewish-Christian source and so, by implication, question their historicity, here they presume historical accuracy, despite how bizarre such a comment from "all the people" would have been. Next, claiming that Jews lose the privilege of being the chosen people of God runs counter to the very Council just cited. *Nostra Aetate* 4 states,

> The Church, therefore, cannot forget that she received the revelation of the Old Testament through the people with whom God in His inexpressible mercy concluded the Ancient Covenant. Nor can she forget that she draws sustenance from the root of that well-cultivated olive tree onto which have been grafted the wild shoots, the Gentiles.(7) Indeed, the Church believes that by His cross Christ, Our Peace, reconciled Jews and Gentiles, making both one in Himself.(8)
>
> The Church keeps ever in mind the words of the Apostle about his kinsmen: "theirs is the sonship and the glory and the covenants and the law and the worship and the promises; theirs are the fathers and from them is the Christ according to the flesh" (Rom. 9:4–5), the Son of the Virgin Mary. She also recalls that the Apostles, the Church's main-stay and pillars, as well as most of the early disciples who proclaimed Christ's Gospel to the world, sprang from the Jewish people.

Since Paul insists that Jews retain "the glory…and the promises" and since *Nostra Aetate* affirms Paul's locating the Jews still in their role, it is inappropriate (at best) for the annotators to strip this role from the Jewish community. The better annotation would have been something along the lines of, "with Matthew's Great Commission

(28:16–20), the (Gentile) nations are elevated to the sharing of the covenants with Israel."

Elsewhere, the NABRE repeats the common stereotype of Jewish misogyny. For example, the notes to Luke 8:1–3 read,

> Luke presents Jesus as an itinerant preacher traveling in the company of the Twelve and of the Galilean women who are sustaining them out of their means....The association of women with the ministry of Jesus is most unusual in the light of the attitude of first-century Palestinian Judaism toward women. The more common attitude is expressed in Jn 4:27, and early rabbinic documents caution against speaking with women in public.

Such comments are common in many Bible studies; they are also uninformed. First, women serving in patronage capacities traverse both Jewish and Roman culture. Women served as patrons of Pharisees;[20] women accompanied Simon bar Gioras as he attempted to wrest the land of Israel from Rome.[21] Next, to cite unamed "early rabbinic documents" is to disregard issues of dating these sources, to ignore positive rabbinic comments on the same subject, and disregard history by making select rabbinic comment normative for the Second Temple period. It would be equally illegitimate for me to cite a church father (e.g., Tertullian's *On the Apparel of Women*) as normative for Jesus and his followers, and then refer to rabbinic statements about Beruriah, who according to *b. Pesach.* 62b, learned "three hundred laws from three hundred teachers in one day," as indicating how much better Judaism is than Christianity. Finally, John 4 concerns not just any woman but a "Samaritan," for, as John states, "Jews do not share things in common with Samaritans." One could equally read the disciples' surprise at finding Jesus in conversation with the woman as indicating that, to this point, Jesus fully eschewed women's company, but such a reading would be equally ungenerous as those that declare early Judaism as the epitome of misogyny and Jesus as the inventor of feminism.[22]

Matters are little better when we come to John 9:22, the first "expulsion from the synagogue" reference: "the Jews had already agreed that if anyone acknowledged [Jesus] as the Messiah, he would be expelled from the synagogue." The notes affirm,

> This comment of the evangelist (in terms used again in Jn 12:42; Jn 16:2) envisages a situation after Jesus' ministry. Rejection/excommunication from the synagogue of Jews who confessed Jesus as Messiah seems to have begun ca. A.D. 85, when the curse against the *minim* or heretics was introduced into the "Eighteen Benedictions."

Among the many problems here, I note five. First, lay readers will have no clue what *minim* or "Eighteen Benedictions" means. Second, readers may wonder if Jews today are cursing Christians in synagogues (N.B., we are not). Third, we have no evidence that Jews were expelling Christ confessors from their assemblies; to the contrary, Paul spoke of internal synagogue discipline (Phil 3), which indicates that Jesus' followers were still synagogue affiliates. Fourth, nothing in the "Eighteen Benedictions" prompts "expulsion."[23] Finally, there was no authority over all synagogues in approximately 85 CE, and the rabbis themselves are not based in synagogues but in study halls.

Nor does the note address why a synagogue might seek to expel Jesus followers. Readers will be left supposing that Jewish antipathy to Jesus, an antipathy whose explanations the annotators fail to give, was the problem. The notes might have remarked, for example, on how proselytizing Gentiles in the Diaspora would have endangered Jewish populations. To advise Gentiles that they should reject the gods of their family and country and turn to the God of Israel would be to put the people of Israel in danger. They might have considered how the pronouncement that only Jesus grants salvation (John 14:6, "I am the way and the truth and the life. No one comes to the Father except through me") or that Torah is secondary to Jesus, would have sounded to faithful Jews.

The notes for Revelation similarly miss opportunities. In describing the Letter to Smyrna (Rev 2:8–11), with its enigmatic comment, "I know the slander of those who claim to be Jews and are not, but rather are members of the assembly of Satan," the annotations offer, "The letter to Smyrna...calls those Jews who are slandering them members of the assembly of Satan." The annotation ignores what John says: these slanderers are *not* Jews but only claim to be so; likely they are Gentiles who have adopted some Jewish trappings along with the worship of Jesus.[24] Exacerbating the problem, the notes continue, "**Smyrna**...also had a large Jewish community very hostile toward Christians" and that "accusations made by Jewish brethren there occasioned the persecution of Christians; cf. Acts 14:2, 19; 17:5, 13." Acts 14:2 is set in Iconium; Acts 14:19 is set in Lystra; Acts 17:5 is set in Thessalonica; and Acts 17:13 is set in Beroea. The Book of Acts, likely written in the early second century and with its own agenda regarding the (il)legitimacy of synagogues as correct transmitters of Israel's Scriptures, never mentions "Smyrna." Missing also, as it is in the notes to John 9, is what would have prompted any persecution.

Given *Nostra Aetate*'s concern to avoid demonization, I had some optimism that readers of the infamous John 8:44, wherein Jesus refers to "the Jews" as belonging "to your father the devil," would receive at least a warning. I also anticipated a note on John 20:19, where the disciples hide "for fear of the Jews." The annotators chose not to comment on these verses, although the introduction to the Gospel offers this:

> The polemic between synagogue and church produced bitter and harsh invective, especially regarding the hostility toward Jesus of the authorities—Pharisees and Sadducees— who are combined and referred to frequently as "the Jews" (see note on Jn 1:19). These opponents are even described in Jn 8:44 as springing from their father the devil, whose conduct they imitate in opposing God by rejecting Jesus, whom God has sent. On the other hand, the author of this gospel seems to take pains to show that women are not inferior to men in the Christian community: the woman at the well in Samaria (Jn 4) is presented as a prototype of a missionary (Jn 4:4–42), and the first witness of the resurrection is a woman (Jn 20:11–18).

The introduction notes the problematic language, but it leaves readers no guidance on how to address it. The attached claims regarding women are irrelevant to the use of *Ioudaios* ("the Jews") language, and in context they can suggest that *unlike the Jews who hold women are inferior*, Jesus (again) invents feminism.

The note to John 1:19 is more helpful:

> **The Jews**: throughout most of the gospel, the "Jews" does not refer to the Jewish people as such but to the hostile authorities, both Pharisees and Sadducees, particularly in Jerusalem, who refuse to believe in Jesus. The usage reflects the atmosphere, at the end of the first century, of polemics between church and synagogue, or possibly it refers to Jews as representative of a hostile world.

If the *Ioudaioi* for the Fourth Gospel do represent "a hostile world," then a nod to *Nostra Aetate* would have been helpful. Debates will continue on what the evangelist intimates with the seven (or seventy-one) uses of *Ioudaioi*, and I do not find the argument that the definition can be limited to a sector of the Jerusalem Temple authorities ultimately helpful.

Then there are the Pharisees. For Mark 2:17, Jesus' comment, "Those who are well do not need a physician, but the sick do. I did not come to call the righteous but sinners," the annotators announce, without a hint of caution, "Because the scribes and Pharisees were self-righteous, they were not capable of responding to Jesus' call to repentance and faith in the gospel." For Mark 2:27, "The sabbath was made for man" (the question of inclusive language is left for another article), the annotators find "a reaffirmation of the divine intent of the sabbath to benefit Israel as contrasted with the restrictive Pharisaic tradition added to the law." By Mark 3:4, on Jesus' question, "Is it lawful to do good on the Sabbath...?" the "restrictive tradition" degenerates with the annotation describing how Jesus' question "places the matter in the broader theological context outside the casuistry of the scribes." Mark 7 is, for the annotators, designed to function "against the Pharisees' narrow, legalistic, and external practices of piety in matters of purification (Mk 7:2–5), external worship (Mk 7:6–7), and observance of commandments." The notes repeat classic anti-Jewish constructions, even as they (unintentionally) echo early Protestant charges against the Catholic Church.

Finally—because I can only record so much before weeping over the lost opportunities—from Mark 10:23–27, the "camel/needle," saying, we read, "In the Old Testament wealth and material goods are considered a sign of God's favor (Jb 1:10; Ps 128:1–2; Is 3:10). The words of Jesus in Mk 10:23–25 provoke astonishment among the disciples because of their apparent contradiction of the Old Testament concept (Mk 10:24, 26)." Apparently, these disciples, as well as the annotators, missed all of wisdom literature, the vast majority of prophetic literature that condemns the rich, the Old Testament's particular concern for the poor, the widow, the orphan and the stranger, and rabbinic literature's extensive concerns for social justice. Readers are left with the negative stereotype of the Jew who worships money.

Despite some good moves in the introductions to each book, the notes are where readers will turn for authoritative Catholic teaching. The notes do damage. Surely fifty years after *Nostra Aetate*, in a 2011 publication, Catholic biblical studies should not be so tone-deaf to the impact of words on readers.

THE USCCB WEBSITE

After looking at the notes to the Bible published on the USCCB website, I did a general search on the site for material on Jews and Judaism. Along with the various pronouncements and notes on committee meetings, I found material that looked promising, but was not immediately accessible. The site advertises a three-minute video segment by Fr. John Crossin, OSFS (USCCB executive director, Secretariat for Ecumenical and Interreligous Affairs), on "the Jewish background of Jesus," but the link is broken (it did, however, direct me to a number of other videos).[25] I found an essay by Fr. Crossin, "Ecumenical and Interreligious Sensitivity in Preaching,"[26] which makes helpful general points, such as, "When preaching, avoid using antiquated, biased or casual terms to describe Jews, as these give offense as words with a troubled historical past whose meanings are often connected to the denigration of Jews." Because the essay gives no examples of what such terms would be (for examples see the commentary on Mark 7 previously discussed), the homilist or teacher will not know how to implement the guideline. Father Crossin helpfully notes, "Preach about Judaism and its members mindful of the fact that Jesus was born, lived and died a Jew, who brought forward in himself all that God promised from Abraham's day." Again, however, no examples are given. If homilists are not educated about first-century Judaism—or if they take their cues from the USCCB online Bible annotations—the guidelines either go nowhere or will backfire.

For resources, the essay recommends, among others, the website for Cadeio (the Catholic Association of Diocesan Ecumenical and Interreligious Officers). I followed the advice to "Check out their website: www.cadeio.org." A search for "Judaism" on the site yielded nothing. For "Jews," there were three links: one to the pope's message for "the World Day of Prayer for the Care of Creation," one for "Cadeio Institutes for Continuing Formation," and one for the *Nostra Aetate* Conference held at Catholic University, May 19–21, 2015.[27] Under "Jewish" I found a bibliography for "Jewish/Christian relations"; most of the sources listed are from the 1980s, and the most recent publication is from 1996.[28] Then again, nothing turned up in the search engine when I put in "Jesus," so likely there are more resources to be found. The problem is that the seeker, especially the impatient one, will find nothing of help on this site.

I also found a six-page book entitled *Jesus and the Jews*, with a list price of twelve dollars. I did not purchase the volume; two dollars per page is also above my pay grade.[29]

WHAT CAN BIBLICISTS DO?

On May 4, 2001, the International Catholic-Jewish Liaison Committee's 17th Meeting published "Recommendation on Education in Catholic and Jewish Seminaries and Schools of Theology." After seventeen meetings, practical suggestions are warranted. The committee insisted, "Courses dealing with the biblical, historical and theological aspects of relations between Jews and Christians should be an *integral* part of the seminary and theological curriculum, and not

243

merely electives," and "All who graduate from Catholic seminaries and theology schools should have studied the revolution in Catholic teaching on Jews and Judaism from *Nostra Aetate* through to the prayer of Pope John Paul II at the Western Wall on March 26, 2000."[30]

In summer 2016, I did an Internet search for biblical studies syllabi taught at Catholic seminaries—I did not find many, and the few that I found did not mention anything about Jews and Judaism, save for an occasional bibliographical reference with "Jew" in the title. This situation is easily improved. For example, bibliographies and sample syllabi could be posted on the CBA website.

The Commission for Religious Relations with the Jews' "Notes on the Correct Way to Present Jews and Judaism in Preaching and Catechesis in the Roman Catholic Church" mandates that such presentation depict "Jews and Judaism, not only in an honest and objective manner, free from prejudices and without any offences, but also with full awareness of the heritage common" to Jews and Christians.[31] This good text could be updated with examples: guidelines tend to gain more traction when they enhance the "what" that should be done with the "how." We are told, "Jews and Judaism should not occupy an occasional and marginal place in catechesis: their presence there is essential and should be organically integrated."[32] Needed are specific exegetical examples. The biblical verses "Notes" cites are offered without historical-critical or literary-contextual exegesis, and they serve primarily to reinforce Catholic theology. They appear not in the context of biblical exegesis narrowly defined but in order to reject Marcionism and describe the relationship between the Old Testament and the New (e.g., Gen 12:1–3 [the only OT citation]; Mark 12:29–31; John 10:16; 14:6; 17:33; Rom 4:11–12; 8:19–23; 9—11; 1 Cor 5:6–8; 10:4, 11; 11:1–11; 15:28; Eph 4:12–19; Heb 4:1–11; 5:1–10; 6:13–18; 10:1). We are told that typology "makes many people uneasy and is perhaps a sign of a problem unresolved."[33] We need guidance on ways forward.

Under the heading "Jewish Roots of Christianity," we learn, correctly, that Jesus "is fully a man of his time, and of his environment."[34] We do not however learn what constitutes that environment, save that it is "Jewish Palestinian." The term *Palestinian* is anachronistic. Rome popularized the term, following the Bar Cochba Revolt

(132–35 CE), to eliminate the name *Judea*. To speak of Jesus historically means to speak not about "Palestinian Judaism" but about "Judean and Galilean as well as Diaspora Judaism." We learn that Jesus "showed great liberty toward [biblical law] (cf. the 'antitheses' of the sermon on the Mount: Mt 5.21–48, bearing in mind the exegetical difficulties; his attitude to rigorous observance of the Sabbath: Mk 3.1–6, etc.)."[35] The problem here: Jesus shows no more, and no less "liberty" than did other Jews, who themselves needed to determine what constituted "work" on the Sabbath as well as asserted that life always trumps Sabbath practice. The so-called antitheses are not antithetical at all; they are, rather, intensifications. The law forbids murder, and Jesus forbids hatred; the law forbids adultery, and Jesus forbids lust. Jesus engages in miracle working on the Sabbath, and the congregations give glory to God rather than reject his views (thus proving both that people appreciate free health care, and that free health care is a miracle). Correctly, the statement notes that Jesus' "relations with the Pharisees were not always or wholly polemical."[36] The examples are not, however, fleshed out. The document then cites Jesus' praise of a Pharisee, "the scribe" of Mark 12:34. The problem here: this scribe is never identified as a Pharisee.

We can also do more with education for clergy, Sunday school teachers, parochial school religion teachers, and others in a position of education. In summer 2014, I worked with the faculty and staff of forty-nine Catholic colleges (about 4,750 people) in Australia as well as conducted workshops on Jesus' Jewish context for priests in Ballarat, Sale, and Melbourne. I shall be doing similar programs for Catholic priests, religious educators, and parochial school teachers this coming summer (2017) in Queensland and South Australia. It would be splendid were the USCCB to do what the bishops in Victoria did: arrange programs on preventing anti-Jewish teaching. I do such programs in the United States almost every other week, but in the United States, Catholic clergy and religious educators generally do not come, whereas liberal Protestants, Episcopalians, and increasing numbers of Evangelicals and Mormons do.

We can set up a list of trigger warnings on where sermons are likely to go wrong because of stereotypes—this would be the one form of prophylaxis on which, perhaps, the USCCB would sign off.

Such prophylaxis would also give us a safer (*sefer*) Torah. The list of misperceptions at the back of the *Jewish Annotated New Testament* is a good start.

We can set up, on the CBA website, if not on the USCCB portal, guidelines on how to preach the passion (the erstwhile Jewish-Christian relations group of the CBA did develop a version of this, but it needs to be readdressed); we also need to include attempts that do not work. We can post information on how to talk about the "Jews" in the Gospel of John, or on how to talk about soteriology (always an issue). Those of us who preach might upload homilies on difficult passages.

Next, we can, in our Tanakh/Old Testament courses, make sure to include Jewish readings when we look at tradition history. I prefer to use the term *Tanakh/Old Testament* in reference to the first part of the Christian canon; *Hebrew Bible*—a term of Protestant hegemony (given that the Catholic Old Testament has Greek material in it and the Eastern Churches are using the LXX)—erases the canonical distinctions between church and synagogue and leaves us with a Protestant default. For example, we might introduce our students to Jewish commentaries on *Parasha Shoftim*, Deuteronomy's "wipe out the Canaanites" passage (Deut 16:18—21:9): this was my son's bar mitzvah *parashah*, and it was salutary to see not only Alexander wrestle with these verses, but also to see how much wrestling there is in the Jewish tradition.

And we should in our New Testament classroom bring in Jewish readings on related subjects. For example, on the so-called antitheses (Matt 5:38–39), not only do we lack examples of the *lex talionis* (Exod 21:24–25) ever being carried out, we might note that rabbinic Judaism does not seek an "eye for an eye" but rather promotes monetary compensation, based on pain, medical expenses, loss of work due to injury, and embarrassment/emotional toil, in case of the loss of a limb (*b. Bava Kamma* 83b–84a). Similarly, it would be good for classes and congregations to know that when Jesus says, "The sabbath was made for man, not man for the sabbath" (Mark 2:27), that the Talmud, *Yoma* 65b, says exactly the same thing: "The Sabbath was made for you; you were not made for it."

CELEBRATION AND HOPE

The work that Fr. John Pawlikowski continues to shepherd is not yet done. As *Pirke Avot* states, "It is not your duty to complete the task, but neither are you free to desist from it." In ethics, theology, liturgics, and historical approaches to the Shoah, Fr. Pawlikowski has been in the vanguard. We in biblical studies have much to learn from his sensitivity to language, from his tenacity in assuring that facile comments about Jews and Judaism be corrected, and from his insistence that avoiding anti-Jewish preaching and teaching can, with continual education, be corrected.

In the spirit of joy for all that has been accomplished, both by Fr. Pawlikowski specifically and by those engaged in Catholic-Jewish relations in general, perhaps a new song is an appropriate form of celebration. We start with the old way of seeing things, and then we change the words. With apologies to Irving Berlin and anyone who has ever appeared in a production of "Annie Get Your Gun":[37]

The Old Verses

Anything Jews can do
Christ can do better.
Says the Creator,
"We're greater than you."
Jews are so legal,
They just have no feelings
Jesus does healings
On Sabbath days, too.
Jesus loves everyone,
Jews are so tribal.
So says our Bible,
We're better than you.
Jews hate their women
While Jesus protects them.
He resurrects them;
He's better than you.

247

The New Song:

Most of what Jesus said,
Jesus said Jewish.
Not everything's newish
In what Jesus spoke to.
Let's look at Jesus
Within his own context
To ignore it is sinful.
Thank you, Vatican II.

Notes

1. Sonya Cronin, "Raymond Browm [*sic*], 'The Jews,' and the Gospel of John" (PhD diss., Florida State University College of Arts and Sciences, 2009), v; https://fsu.digital.flvc.org/islandora/object/fsu:181218/datastream/PDF/view. Cronin cites Fr. Pawlikowski (*Catech. Prej.*) along with Rosemary Reuther as among writers in the "early 1970s" who "began to raise awareness of the hostility towards the Jews in the biblical text" (p. 1). See now the published version of the dissertation, Sonya Shetty Cronin, *Raymond Brown, "The Jews", and the Gospel of John: From Apologia to Apology*, Library of New Testament Studies (London: Bloomsbury T&T Clark, 2015).

2. Cronin, *"The Jews", and the Gospel of John*, 2. Cronin's introduction offers a helpful sketch of the major biblical studies publications from the 1970s to the 1990s.

3. Bearing Witness, accessed August 3, 2017, http://www.adl.org/education-outreach/holocaust-education/c/bearing-witness-program.html.

4. http://schechternetwork.org (accessed August 3, 2017).

5. See Amy-Jill Levine, "Roland Murphy, The Pontifical Biblical Commission, Jews, and the Bible," *Biblical Theology Bulletin* 33, no. 3 (fall 2003): 104–13, and Levine, "The Jewish People and Their Sacred Scriptures in the Christian Bible: A Jewish Reading of the Document," *The Bible Today* (May/June 2003): 167–72. For additional commentary, from a Jewish perspective, on the PBC document, see Jon D. Levenson, "Can Roman Catholicism Validate Jewish Biblical Interpretation?" *Studies in Christian-Jewish Relations* 1 (2005–06): 170–85. See also Joan E.

Cook, "The New PBC Document: Continuity, Discontinuity, and Progression Revisited," accessed August 3, 2017, https://www.bc.edu/content/dam/files/research_sites/cjl/texts/cjrelations/resources/articles/cook.htm, which offers a summary of scholarship on the PBC, including commentary by Fr. Pawlikowski.

6. http://www.vatican.va/roman_curia/pontifical_councils/chrstuni/relations-jews-docs/rc_pc_chrstuni_doc_20151210_ebraismo-nostra-aetate_en.html (accessed August 3, 2017).

7. The ADL website has a separate archive on ADL/Vatican relations (http://archive.adl.org/presrele/vaticanjewish_96/default.html [accessed August 3, 2017]), although the site has not been updated since 2012. The website has numerous data on Jewish-Catholic relations, from meetings with the Vatican, with USCCB representatives, and with local Catholic clergy.

8. "The International Jewish Committee on Interreligious Consultations (IJCIC) serves on behalf of, and as an instrument of, its constituent member organizations to maintain and develop relations with the Vatican's Commission on Religious Relations with the Jews, the Orthodox Christian Church, the World Council of Churches, and other international religious bodies" (http://ijcic.org [accessed August 3, 2017]).

9. E.g., "AJC Meets Pope Francis, Addresses Vatican Conclave on Nostra Aetate Jubilee" (https://www.ajc.org/news/ajc-meets-pope-francis-addresses-vatican-conclave-on-nostra-aetate-jubilee [accessed August 3, 2017]).

10. "The dialogue with the National Council of Synagogues continues today under the direction of Rabbi Gil Rosenthal, Executive Director of the National Council of Synagogues and the Most Rev. Wilton Gregory, Archbishop of Atlanta. A dialogue with the Orthodox Union continues under the chairmanship of Rabbi Fabian Schonfeld, former President of the Orthodox Union, and Bishop William Murphy of the Diocese of Rockville Center, New York" (http://www.usccb.org/beliefs-and-teachings/ecumenical-and-interreligious/jewish/ [accessed December 14, 2016]).

11. Personally, I believe one judges a tradition on the best it offers, rather than on the worst; thus for Roman Catholicism mid-twentieth-century, I look to Angelo Roncalli rather than to Adolph Hitler.

12. http://www.jcrelations.net/Dabru_Emet_-_A_Jewish_Statement_on_Christians_and_Christianity.2395.0.html (accessed August 3, 2017). The text is not without its problems, as noted, inter alia, by David Berger,

"Dabru Emet: Some Reservations about a Jewish Statement on Christians and Christianity," *Dialogika* (October 28, 2002), http://www.ccjr.us/dialogika-resources/documents-and-statements/analysis/286-dabru-emet-berger; Jon D. Levenson and David Rosen, "'Dabru Emet': Its Significance for the Jewish-Christian Dialogue," an address given at the twentieth-anniversary celebration of the Dutch Council of Christians and Jews (OJEC) at Tilburg, The Netherlands, November 6, 2001, https://www.rabbidavidrosen.net/wp-content/uploads/2016/02/Dabru-Emet-Its-Significance-for-Jewish-Christian-Dialog.pdf; and Jon D. Levenson, "How Not to Conduct Jewish-Christian Dialogue," *Commentary* (December 1, 2001), https://www.commentarymagazine.com/articles/how-not-to-conduct-jewish-christian-dialogue/. I signed the document, but only after (a) numerous emails with David Sandmel, who shepherded the project under the auspices of the Baltimore Institute for Christian-Jewish Studies (now the Institute for Islamic-Christian-Jewish Studies), and (b) concluding that the benefits of the text outweighed the problems.

13. Sponsored by the Center for Jewish-Christian Understanding and Cooperation (CJCUC) in Efrat, Israel (http://cjcuc.com/site/2015/12/03/orthodox-rabbinic-statement-on-christianity/ [accessed August 3, 2017]).

14. See, e.g., Yair Hoffman, "New 'Orthodox' Rabbinic Statement on Christianity—An Analysis," *The Yeshiva World* (December 20, 2015), http://www.theyeshivaworld.com/news/headlines-breaking-stories/371619/the-new-orthodox-rabbinic-statement-on-christianity---an-analysis.html.

15. Elisabeth Schüssler Fiorenza, *In Memory of Her* (New York: Crossroad, 1983), 106.

16. Sr. Sheila Flynn, "Dismantling Privilege," CaSPA (Catholic Secondary Principals Australia, 2016 National Conference Melbourne), accessed May 16, 2018, http://www.pavcss.org.au/members/files/sept2016/Flynn%20Dismantling%20Privilege%20Talk%20Final%20July%2016.pdf. The only footnote to any of these quotes is *Truly Our Sister* by Elizabeth Johnson, CSJ. This volume's full title is *Truly Our Sister: A Theology of Mary in the Communion of Saints* (London: Continuum, 2009). Johnson goes out of her way to avoid setting up Jewish culture as the negative contrast to Jesus; see especially, "A Pernicious Contrast," 185–90.

17. The problems have been documented by numerous scholars. For one eloquent example, see Elena Procario-Foley, "Liberating Jesus: Christian Feminism and Anti-Judaism," in *Frontiers in Catholic Feminist Theology: Shoulder to Shoulder*, ed. Susan Abraham and Elena Procario-Foley (Minneapolis: Fortress Press, 2009), 97–118.

18. http://www.usccb.org/bible/ (accessed August 3, 2017). Note all quotations of notes or biblical verses in this section of the chapter are taken from this website.

19. http://www.usccb.org/bible/.

20. Josephus, *Ant.* 17.41 (17.2.4), "For there was a certain sect of men that were Jews, who valued themselves highly upon the exact skill they had in the law of their fathers, and made men believe they were highly favored by God, by whom this set of women were inveigled. These are those that are called the sect of the Pharisees, who were in a capacity of greatly opposing kings." See also *Ant.* 17.42–43 on women's financial support for Pharisees at the time of Herod.

21. Josephus, *War* 4.505 (4.9.3), "At first they suspected him, and only permitted him to come with the women he brought with him into the lower part of the fortress, while they dwelt in the upper part of it themselves."

22. For a succinct, well-documented treatment of gender roles among Jews at the time of Jesus, see Tal Ilan, "Gender," in *The Jewish Annotated New Testament*, ed. Amy-Jill Levine and Marc Z. Brettler, 2nd ed. (New York, Oxford University Press, 2017), 611–14.

23. Ruth Langer, *Cursing the Christians? A History of the Birkat Ha-Minim* (New York: Oxford University Press, 2012); for a summary of these arguments, see Ruth Langer, "Cursing the Christians? History of the *Birkat HaMinim*," BibleInterp.Com (Jan 2012), http://www.bibleinterp .com/articles/lan368024.shtml; and, Ruth Langer, "*Birkat ha-Minim*: A Jewish Curse of Christians?" in Levine and Brettler, *Jewish Annotated New Testament*, 653–54.

24. See, inter alia, E. Leigh Gibson, "The Jews and Christians in the Martyrdom of Polycarp," in *The Ways That Never Parted: Jews and Christians in Late Antiquity and the Early Middle Ages*, ed. A.H. Becker and A. Yoshiko Reed (Minneapolis: Fortress Press, 2007), 145–58; David Frankfurter, "Jews or Not? Re-constructing the 'Other' in Rev 2:9 and 3:9," *Harvard Theological Review* 94 (2001): 403–25; Frankfurter, "So-Called Jews and Their Synagogue of Satan," in *The Jewish Annotated New*

Testament, 2nd ed., ed. Amy-Jill Levine and Marc Z. Brettler (New York: Oxford University Press, 2017), 543.

25. http://www.usccb.org/beliefs-and-teachings/ecumenical-and -interreligious/jewish/ (accessed November 27, 2016).

26. http://www.usccb.org/beliefs-and-teachings/ecumenical-and -interreligious/upload/Ecumenical-and-Interreligious-Sensitivity-in -Preaching-Father-John-Crossin.pdf (accessed November 27, 2016).

27. http://cadeio.org/blog/?s=jews (accessed November 27, 2016).

28. http://cadeio.org/blog/wp-content/uploads/2013/01/ DBibliographyJewishOrth.pdf (accessed November 27, 2016).

29. http://store.usccb.org/jesus-and-the-jews-p/7-011.htm (accessed November 27, 2016).

30. International Catholic-Jewish Liaison Committee, "Recommendation on Education in Catholic and Jewish Seminaries and Schools of Theology," May 4, 2001, https://www.bc.edu/content/dam/files/ research_sites/cjl/texts/cjrelations/resources/documents/ interreligious/education.htm.

31. Commission for Religious Relations with Jews, "Notes on the Correct Way to Present the Jews and Judaism in Preaching and Catechesis in the Roman Catholic Church," 1985, http://www.vatican.va/ roman_curia/pontifical_councils/chrstuni/relations-jews-docs/rc_pc _chrstuni_doc_19820306_jews-judaism_en.html. See "Preliminary Considerations," accessed August 3, 2017.

32. "Notes on the Correct Way to Present the Jews," §I.2.

33. "Notes on the Correct Way to Present the Jews," §II.3.

34. "Notes on the Correct Way to Present the Jews," §III, 1.

35. "Notes on the Correct Way to Present the Jews," §III, 2.

36. "Notes on the Correct Way to Present the Jews," §III, 5.

37. With my gratitude to Scott Gilbert for compositional genius.

CHAPTER FIFTEEN

PROPHETIC UNIVERSALISM AND PARTICULARISM IN JEWISH LITURGY

—m—

Ruth Langer

Over the years that I have been involved in Christian-Jewish dialogue, it has been an enormous honor to have had many opportunities to think together with Fr. John Pawlikowski, to be challenged by his wisdom, and, on occasion, to challenge him in return. With great humility, I offer this essay for his Festschrift.

In December 2015, for the fiftieth anniversary of *Nostra Aetate*, the Commission for Religious Relations with the Jews issued a lengthy reflection, reviewing the progress of the previous half-century of dialogue and discussing major challenges that still needed to be addressed, including understanding better each other's concepts of covenant. In the course of this discussion, it wrote,

> Christians are...convinced that through the New Covenant the Abrahamic covenant has obtained that universality for all peoples which was originally intended in the call of Abram (cf. Gen 12:1–3). This recourse to the Abrahamic covenant is so essentially constitutive of the Christian faith that the Church without Israel would be in danger of losing its locus in the history of salvation. By the same token, *Jews could with regard to the Abrahamic covenant arrive at the insight that Israel without the Church would be in danger of remaining too particularist and of failing to grasp the universality of its experience of God. In*

this fundamental sense Israel and the Church remain bound to each other according to the covenant and are interdependent.[1]

This echoes statements about Jewish particularism made in recent years by Cardinals Walter Kasper and Kurt Koch, the presidents of the commission,[2] critiqued in response by Adam Gregerman.[3] As a further step toward dialogue on this point, this essay addresses this challenge by exploring the tension between universalism and particularism as expressed in one aspect of Jewish liturgy: its readings from the Prophets.[4] In this, I apply to Judaism the Christian maxim *lex orandi, lex credendi* (literally, the law of praying is the law of believing, but less literally, prayer shapes theology), to understand how this liturgy shapes a lived theology. What we discover is that while Jewish liturgy contains universalist voices, particularist voices indeed are more characteristic and shape the overall message. The historical intersection with Christianity, if anything, has contributed to the tendency to a particularism that reflects most deeply on God's specific covenant with Israel and not on its more universal predecessors, the Noahide and Abrahamic covenants.

Overwhelmingly, the presence of non-Jews in the liturgy is negative and oppositional, reflecting the experience of Jews throughout most of their history.[5] Most of the Torah's narrative concerns either Israel's escape from the Egyptians or anticipation of its life in a homeland surrounded by often malevolent outsiders. The universally oriented prologue of Genesis does not stand alone in Jewish understanding, but is the narrative context from which the text's and God's focus narrows to God's covenant with the nation of Israel at Sinai. Non-Israelites belong to the *other* nations, or when living among the Israelites, are local "strangers" (*gerim*). In the rabbinic transformation of this narrative's emphases, naturalized *gerim* are converts, joining Israel's covenantal particularity.[6] If it is a theological universalism to share one's message with the world, then this fits the cardinals' challenge. However, it is more accurate to understand this as an exclusivism that teaches that participation in God's blessing or salvation is only possible through one's own path.

Before proceeding, it is important to understand how the terms *universalism* and *particularism* are being used here. The cardinals could be read as modifying two of four categories common among philosophers of religion to describe one religion's attitude to others. *Universalism* usually is a claim that God has revealed truth to all humanity. Religious universalists seek to discern how this one truth finds expression in other religions as well as their own. *Particularism* is apparently a variation on the philosophical category of "exclusivism," an understanding that one's own path is the only correct one and all others are false.[7] However, the cardinals' use of the terms is fully the opposite. *Universalism* here reflects instead a welcome to all to join in one's own understanding of the truth, or from the Christian perspective, to achieve the salvation offered to all through the Christian path. This is a philosophical exclusivism. *Particularism* coheres more with a closed-door nationalism, something that has characterized Judaism at many points in its history because conversion to Judaism was forbidden by Christian and Islamic governing powers, endangering the convert. It is less common today. Indeed, although there is a vast range of understandings of other religions among Jewish thinkers, Judaism has frequently been open to the possibility of the philosophical and theological legitimacy of other religions for their adherents, not requiring their conversion for their salvation.[8] In this sense, Judaism is more theologically universalist than Christianity, even as it is a sociologically more particularist community.

How does this play out in Jewish liturgy? Rabbinic liturgy took shape after the Roman destruction of the Temple in 70 CE and in response to the renewed exile caused by that tragedy; it remains normative today.[9] If one were to distill its message, flattening most of its richness, the overriding theme would be the hope for the eschatological redemption of Israel from this state of exile.[10] This in itself is an inherently particularist narrative; God's salvation consists of the restoration of Israel's proper national existence, here on earth.[11] However, Judaism also asks the universal question: What happens to the other nations at this point? Do they participate in Israel's salvation, and if so, do they do so in their own particularities, or only if they join

Israel? Liturgical answers to this question build on the prophetic visions, maintaining some of the ambiguity inherent in those.

This liturgy is intensely but selectively biblical, lifting up certain elements and ignoring others, reshaping the canon and its emphases. An analogous process happened among Christians, resulting in two overlapping but different Bibles. Thus, the Torah (Pentateuch) came to be read word for word in order over the weeks of each year,[12] with additional pericopes selected for holy days. On Sabbaths and festivals, shorter selections accompany this reading from the Prophets, chosen because of some connection to the Torah reading or the day. Although the entire Bible appears on Jewish curricula of study, many Jews encounter only those prophetic pericopes selected for liturgical use and today printed along with the relevant Torah reading in pew Bibles or festival prayer books (i.e., without their larger original contexts). This reading is called the *haftarah* (pl. *haftarot*), derived from the verb "to dismiss," indicating its original placement at the end of the service.[13] The connection between the *haftarah* and the Torah or the season is most often in its opening verse(s) and not necessarily characteristic of the entire passage.[14] However, as we shall see, there were other theological concerns embedded in the choice of particular prophetic portions.

Although the Sabbath morning and holy day reading from the Prophets is mentioned in the earliest rabbinic literature,[15] nothing there contradicts the image from Luke 4 of the reader freely choosing his own passage. The earliest evidence for more established readings emerges from the sixth century and onward, in collections of sermonic material and poetic substitutions for the statutory prayers on Sabbaths and holy days from the Land of Israel and from a Babylonian talmudic discussion of readings for specially marked days. We know from these, and from preserved lists of readings from approximately five hundred years later, that there was great variation in the choices of prophetic readings between these two centers of rabbinic Jewish life (and others). While both looked for some verbal connection to the Torah reading on regular Sabbaths and some thematic connection on holidays, the choices in the Land of Israel placed more emphasis on eschatological themes. Almost half of this cycle's readings come from Isaiah, and two-thirds of those from Deutero-Isaiah, emphasizing the national return to the Land of Israel.[16] This parallels the tendency of sermonic material from that center to conclude with messianic "words of comfort," suggesting a cultural norm. This cycle disappeared fully after the devastation wreaked by the Crusaders in the Holy Land. All Jews since follow some version of the Babylonian cycle, which markedly avoids these eschatological themes, focusing instead more on historically oriented readings.[17] The result is that t he now-common cycle draws from a much broader list of prophetic books and genres of literature within them, while excluding many of the texts most likely to express universalist visions. Overtly universal visions, like Isaiah 2:2–3 (cf. Mic 4:1–2), appeared in neither cycle.[18]

The exceptions are mostly readings that had their origins in the Land of Israel, most notably those for the ten-week season beginning mid-summer around the anniversary of the Temples' destructions in 586 BCE and 70 CE on the Ninth of Av. In the "triennial" cycle of the Land of Israel, they were not tied to particular Torah readings; in the Babylonian annual cycle, they accompany the conclusion of Numbers and most of Deuteronomy. On the three Sabbaths preceding the Ninth of Av, the *haftarot* are prophetic rebukes chosen to anticipate the tragedies and generate liturgical memory of them, drawing later generations into the communal mourning. The *haftarot* of the seven weeks following are dedicated to assuaging this pain, to consoling those hearing them and looking to the future redemption. All seven readings come from Deutero-Isaiah, but as Elsie Stern has argued, the rabbinic choice of passages and their ordering constructs a new, postprophetic narrative. This was necessitated by the rabbis' own historical location: while these late Isaianic texts were responding joyfully to the return from the Babylonian exile, the rabbis employed these as *haftarot* in a world still awaiting God's redemption.[19] In addition, Christianity's oppositional presence arguably shaped elements of this cycle.

If we experience these seven *haftarot* of consolation in their order, what messages do we hear about universalism and particularism? We will consider the texts, their biblical contexts, and relevant commentaries on the liturgical texts.[20] The first, Isaiah 40:1–26, opens, "Comfort, oh comfort My people, says your God. Speak tenderly to Jerusalem and declare to her that her term of service is over"

(vv. 1–2a).[21] In the continuation, God's advent is announced locally, to Judah and Zion (v. 9). However, God is also the universe's Creator (vv. 12, 18–26), and in this context, "all nations are as naught in His sight" (v. 17), presumably not including Israel, for whom God is "like a shepherd [who] pastures his flock" (v. 11). When God appears, though, in grand procession, "all flesh, as one, shall behold, for the Lord Himself has spoken" (v. 5). Thus, the status of the Gentile nations is ambiguous; they cannot help but recognize God, but only because of God's special relationship with Israel. God has no particular regard for them.

In the second *haftarah*, Isaiah 49:14—51:3, God continues to try to comfort a doubting Israel. One sign that God's redemption is genuine is that the nations will become Israel's servants, bowing to her, licking the dust of her feet (vv. 22–23). With this reversal of fortunes, all will know that God is Israel's Savior (v. 26). Thus, the voice of the *haftarah* is particularistic and triumphalist. This contrasts starkly with its larger context in Isaiah, suggesting a deliberate editorial choice. It begins after 49:6b, "I will also make you a light of nations, that My salvation may reach the ends of the earth" and ends before 51:4–5, which similarly suggests God's salvific concern for all humanity.[22] Some commentators on the *haftarot* seek to explain this editing. Mendel Hirsch, son of the leading nineteenth-century German rabbi Samson Raphael Hirsch, wrote,

> The opening words of the Haphtora takes us into the middle of one of the speeches of God. In the preceding verse, the importance and world-historic meaning of Israel's mission had been specified in the world of its greatness, how it was sent into the world to bring light and freedom to the nations, to prepare the way for the universal brotherhood of all peoples, and to found the Kingdom of God on earth.[23]

Where Hirsch essentially apologized for the omission of the universalist passages, Nosson Scherman's Stone *Chumash*, widely used in American orthodox synagogues today, argues that Jews fell from "their spiritual pinnacle" that made them "a light to the nations" and were exiled, making this universalist verse no longer relevant. Therefore, the *haftarah* begins with Israel's response to its current sense of abandonment and contains only God's assurances of constant presence.[24]

The third *haftarah*, Isaiah 54:11—55:5, has been extracted fully from its biblical context. The chapter's beginning will be read in another two weeks. It is almost fully inward-looking, describing the reversal of Israel's misfortunes enumerated in Lamentations, the primary text of the Ninth of Av. It is possible to read 55:1–2 as a more universal call, "Ho, all who are thirsty, come for water"[25]; however, the continuation suggests that it is Israel's restored glory that will entice the nations to join her in service to God. Joseph Hertz suggests that this is a "description of the unconscious influence which Israel's loyalty to his Divinely-appointed mission is sure to effect."[26] Thus, this glance at the nations does not really reflect universalist concerns.

The fourth *haftarah* returns to Isaiah 51, skipping nine verses from the end of the second *haftarah* to read 51:12—53:12. As discussed there, among these skipped verses, 51:4–5 express overtly universal themes.[27] This fourth *haftarah* focuses almost entirely on comforting Israel. Zion is God's people (51:16). God will turn the divine wrath from Israel to Israel's tormenters (51:22–23); the uncircumcised and unclean shall never enter Jerusalem again (52:1), but they will witness the victory of God (52:10). This would seem to be an entirely negative characterization of non-Jews (and one that is contradicted in *haftarot* taken from later in Isaiah; see further). Again we find modern commentators seeking to mitigate this particularist focus. For instance, Hertz comments that God's laying the foundations of the earth (51:16, JPS 1917 translation) points not to creation but instead is to be read allegorically. It means "to teach mankind what are the true foundations of human society: not 'blood and iron' but Truth, Justice, Peace—ideals which the Servant of the Lord was to teach the children of men."[28] Fishbane universalizes 52:6, "My people shall learn My name," writing, "The expression is thus a variant of 'and *all mankind* shall know that I the Lord am your Savior' (Isa 49:26)."[29]

The fifth *haftarah* offers further reassurance to Zion, returning to the opening verses of Isaiah 54. Here again, Isaiah sounds a triumphalist note, "For you shall spread out to the right and the left; your offspring shall dispossess nations and shall people the desolate towns" (54:3). This sounds like an expansionist Israel, victorious over the world. However, Fishbane states explicitly that these nations are "the foreigners who had occupied regions from which Israelites had been exiled."[30] In other words, this only describes what is necessary for Israel to return home. The *Etz Hayim* pew Bible of the Conservative Movement, which selects its limited comments on the *haftarot* from Fishbane, omits this comment entirely.[31] While Fishbane and Hertz probably sought here to explain Isaiah's intent historically, liturgy also constructs an active memory with its messages applied to the present as well. In the context of today's questions of Israeli-Palestinian relations, this has the potential of being a "difficult" text.[32] It is important to note, as well, that this *haftarah*, along with the second half of the chapter, is also the reading accompanying the Noah narratives from Genesis. Thus, it transforms their more universal focus into one where Israel is at the center.[33]

The series now jumps to Isaiah 60,[34] and its beautiful imagery of Israel's glorious redemption—which it contrasts with the denigration of the nations. Thick clouds will cover other peoples, but God will shine on Israel (v. 2), to the point that other nations will walk by Israel's light (v. 3). The riches of the nations will flow to Israel (v. 5), welcome as offerings in the Temple (v. 7). Those who destroyed the land shall rebuild it, "their kings shall wait upon you" (v. 10), and those who do not serve Israel shall perish (v. 12). Consistent with what we have seen already, this text's statement about Israel's relationship to the nations remains triumphal, even in the eyes of modern commentators. Hertz writes that this *haftarah* "gives the highest spiritual interpretation of" God's promise to make Israel "high above all nations." The nations will not be walking by Israel's light, but toward it, "from the outer darkness, to share the Divine light with Israel." Upon their arrival, "the nations will gladly and humbly build Jerusalem."[35]

Finally, the series concludes with Isaiah 61:10—63:9. Israel is comforted; God reassures her that her troubles will not recur, uttering messianic promises. Skipped between the fourth and fifth weeks had been the entirety of Isaiah's suffering servant song (52:13—53:12), so important to Christian self-understanding. Indeed, Isaiah's servant language and most language that reflects directly on the person of the messiah is almost entirely absent from the Babylonian tradition of *haftarot*. The opening of this *haftarah* reinforces a sense that this was deliberate, as it also skips verses important to Christians, here those that Jesus read in the Nazareth synagogue (Luke 4:18–19). If this is the case, the conclusion of this *haftarah* is likely also not coincidental. It, and consequently the entire series, concludes on a strikingly anti-Christian note. Isaiah 63 predicts God's bloody trampling of Edom. As is well-known, and as Fishbane reminds his readers most explicitly, "in rabbinic tradition, Edom is a symbol for Rome and Christendom (see Ibn Ezra). This identification gave the haftarah ongoing relevance in late antiquity and the Middle Ages."[36] Other commentators are only slightly more circumspect, similarly restricting this association to the past.[37] That past, though, was the point at which this series of readings crystallized as among the earliest documented *haftarot*, the subject of homiletical materials compiled probably in the fifth to sixth centuries in the *Pesiqta D'Rav Kahana*, when the Land of Israel, its place of composition, was under Byzantine (i.e., Christian) Roman control.[38]

Thus, this series of *haftarot*, drawn in its entirety from the largest source of universalistic passages in the prophetic corpus, constructs a message that is deeply particularistic and triumphalistic.[39] Where the nations are included, they are on the periphery, recognizing God and occasionally even bringing tribute, after witnessing what God has done for Israel. There is no indication that they are included in this divine salvation or even invited to join Israel. Not free to change these inherited readings, some but not all modern commentators offer apologies for this situation.

This is not the situation in all the prophetic passages chosen for synagogue use. Two *haftarot* from Deutero-Isaiah, both read more frequently, offer a somewhat different picture. Their conclusions are, both in the postexilic prophetic corpus and among the *haftarot*, uniquely inclusive of Gentiles. Isaiah 55:6—56:8, read in the afternoon of every fast day (except Yom Kippur), speaks of God's invitation to foreigners to "attach themselves" to him and even to serve in the reconstituted Temple, on condition that they take on covenantal practices. Under these circumstances, God's house will be called "a house of prayer for all peoples." However, as Hertz points out, this apparently requires that the Gentiles convert to Judaism. A similar if more apocalyptically couched theme emerges in the final chapter of Isaiah, read whenever the new month begins on the Sabbath. It prophesies that those accompanying the Israelites on their return will be allowed to serve as priests and Levites in the Temple. Its penultimate verse, repeated to conclude the reading, proclaims, "And new moon after new moon, and sabbath after sabbath, all flesh shall come to worship me, said the Lord" (66:23). As Fishbane indicates, while some other prophetic passages like Zechariah 14:16–19 (read on the first day of Sukkot) and 1 Kings 8:27 speak of the nations' coming to worship God, that worship seems to be just prayer and prostration, not sacrifice, as these two readings indicate.[40] Therefore, there may be a fuller inclusion of non-Jews in the salvation described in these chapters.

That is certainly the case in the Book of Jonah, read in its entirety as the *haftarah* on Yom Kippur afternoon. God has sent Jonah to decree the destruction of the non-Jewish city Nineveh because of its evil ways. When all the city repented and God reversed his decree, Jonah is deeply upset. The book concludes with God's affirmation that the Gentile city is also a divine creation, one about which God cares and deserving of divine forgiveness. The *haftarah* itself concludes by bringing this message that God is a forgiving deity back to Israel with the addition of Micah 7:18–20. However, this diminishes neither the impact of the universal message of Jonah itself, nor its expression of the tension we have seen throughout between universalism and particularism.

Let us return to the challenge raised by the cardinals. They understand that the essential element of God's covenantal blessing to Abraham is its universal one, to be a blessing to the world. This, they say, Christians actualize through their mission to bring all to God's salvation, as made available by baptism. This is actually a theological exclusivism, a recognition that only the Christian path represents divine truth. This is what Michael Walzer calls the "first universalism" or "covering law universalism" in which "there is one God, so there is one law, one justice, one correct understanding of the good life or good society or the good regime, one salvation, one messiah, one millennium for all humanity." Consequently, it makes no space for particularity or nationhood. This idea has its roots in the Prophets, especially in the idea that Israel should be a light of the nations,[41] but as we have seen, the *haftarot* mostly dodge these passages.[42] Indeed, there is no question that they speak of the world's nations very much from within Israel's own particularity as a nation.

The *haftarot* represent better Walzer's "second universalism" or "reiterative universalism," where the horizon is also universal human-ity but with a recognition that within this there is multiplicity, special concern for our own, and defining of boundaries. This is actually closer to a theological universalism that recognizes that other peoples also know the truth. Walzer finds sources for this in the Prophets as well: Amos 9:7 speaks of God's saving different nations separately (read liturgically with Lev 16:1 or 19:1—20:15 by Ashkenazim); Micah 4:5 includes a verse not found in its contemporaneous Isaiah 2,[43] when all the nations are going up to Jerusalem: "Though all the peoples walk each in the names of its gods, we will walk in the name of the Lord our God forever and ever." There is thus space for multi-ple particularities without abandoning universalism.[44]

Within this, Israel is in covenant with God not simply through the primitive Abrahamic covenant, but through the detailed Sinai covenant made only with her. Jewish theologians are only beginning to grapple, often unsuccessfully, with the Christian self-understanding of being included in this relationship.[45] Walzer's theory enables a theological understanding of Christianity (and other world religions) as being in a saving relationship with God, but not in a way identical to Judaism's. While this does not find much expression in the *haftarot* themselves, it does find substantial expression in the contemporary comment on them, in their modern reinterpretations. This reitera-tive, nonexclusivist universalism, grounded in a particularity that rec-ognizes the legitimacy of other particularities, offers an answer to the cardinals' challenge that Israel retrieve its universalist heritage and not "remain *too* particularist" (emphasis mine). God is universal; God's specific relationships with and expectations of different human communities are particular. This is more consistent with the voice of the Prophets, as reshaped by the liturgical tradition of *haftarah* readings, than Walzer's "first universalism," the meaning conventionally given to the term within Christian theology.

Notes

1. Commission for Religious Relations with the Jews, "'The Gifts and the Calling of God Are Irrevocable' (Rom 11:29): A Reflection on Theological Questions Pertaining to Catholic-Jewish Relations on the Occasion of the 50th Anniversary of *Nostra Aetate* (No. 4)," December 10, 2015, §33, http://www.ccjr.us/dialogika-resources/documents-and -statements/roman-catholic/vatican-curia/1357-crrj-2015dec10. Emphasis mine. Compare §13: "Without her Jewish roots the Church would be in danger of losing its soteriological anchoring in salvation history and would slide into an ultimately unhistorical Gnosis."

2. See the footnotes to §13 in Philip A. Cunningham, "The Sources behind 'The Gifts and the Calling of God Are Irrevocable' (Rom 11:29): A Reflection on Theological Questions Pertaining to Catholic-Jewish Relations on the Occasion of the 50th Anniversary of *Nostra Aetate* (No. 4)," *Studies in Christian-Jewish Relations* 12 (2017): 8, doi.org/10 .6017/scjr.v12i1.9792. Cunningham has annotated the document to provide a guide to sources that stand behind the text.

3. Adam Gregerman, "Response: Jewish Theology and Limits on Reciprocity in Catholic-Jewish Dialogue," *Studies in Christian-Jewish Relations* 7 (2012): 4–7, doi.org/10.6017/scjr.v7i1.2074.

4. I have addressed some aspects of the larger liturgical question in an earlier article, "Jewish Liturgical Memory and the Non-Jew: Past Realities and Future Possibilities," in *Jewish Theology and World Religions*, ed. Alon Goshen-Gottstein and Eugene Korn (Oxford: Littman Library of Jewish Civilization, 2012), 167–86. There is more to be done.

5. On this, and on attempts to mitigate this in modern liberal Jewish liturgies, see my "Theologies of Self and Other in American Jewish Liturgies," *CCAR Journal: A Reform Jewish Quarterly* (Winter 2005): 3–41.

6. Alon Goshen-Gottstein, "Judaism: The Battle for Survival, the Struggle for Compassion," in *The Religious Other: Hostility, Hospitality, and the Hope of Human Flourishing*, ed. Alon Goshen-Gottstein (Lanham,

MD: Lexington Books, 2014), 30–31. The final section of this essay contains a proposal for a contemporary reversal of this situation.

7. For a summary of the four positions in their conventional understandings and in dialogue between Jewish and Christian applications of them, see Alan Brill, *Judaism and Other Religions: Models of Understanding* (New York: Palgrave Macmillan, 2010), 15–21.

8. Brill's volume surveys these possibilities.

9. This normativity applies to the traditional end of today's Jewish spectrum. The liberal end understands itself free to rewrite or reject certain prayers, or to introduce new ones. Nonetheless, the basic liturgical structure and calendar are shared. My focus here is the traditional expression. How quickly individual prayers took form or were accepted outside of rabbinic circles is a matter of debate.

10. See, for instance, Reuven Kimelman, "The Literary Structure of the Amidah and the Rhetoric of Redemption," in *The Echoes of Many Texts: Reflection on Jewish and Christian Traditions; Essays in Honor of Lou H. Silberman*, ed. William G. Dever and J. Edward Wright (Atlanta: Scholars Press, 1997), 171–218.

11. There is no single authoritative expression of this vision. Traditionally it involves ingathering of the exiles, including the resurrected dead, the establishment of just Davidic rule (the messiah), the rebuilding of the Jerusalem Temple, and the reestablishment of its Torah-decreed cult. Jews at the religiously liberal end of the spectrum emphasize the hope for a "messianic age" of peace and justice and generally reject any hopes for the reestablishment of Davidic rule or the Temple and its cult. Secular Zionists emphasize the ingathering of the exiles. Essentially all Jews would agree that today's secular state of Israel, though meeting some elements of this vision, does not represent its fulfillment. For a summary of the evolution of Jewish views of the messiah, see Harold Louis Ginsberg, et al. "Messiah," in *Encyclopaedia Judaica*, ed. Michael Berenbaum and Fred Skolnik, 2nd ed. (Detroit: Macmillan Reference USA, 2007), 14:110–15.

12. An alternative cycle was common in the first millennium in the Land of Israel, in which the entire Torah was read over about three and a half years. This annual cycle, that of Babylonian rabbis, gradually became universally dominant over the last centuries of the first millennium.

13. Subsequently, other prayers were added following it. On most days that a *haftarah* is read, it became customary to recite the day's

"additional service" (*musaf*) in conjunction with the morning service after its reading of Scripture.

14. *B. Megillah* 23a–b teaches that the prophetic reading should have at least twenty-one verses. Not all do.

15. *M. Megillah* 4:2 restricts the reading to these times.

16. For a list of these readings, see Ben Zion Wacholder, "Prolegomenon," in *The Bible as Read and Preached in the Old Synagogue*, by Jacob Mann, vol. 1 (New York: Ktav, 1971), LI–LXVII (Appendix I). Unfortunately, only the opening verses of the readings can be determined.

17. See Michael Fishbane, *The JPS Bible Commentary: Haftarot* (Philadelphia: Jewish Publication Society, 2002), "Introduction," esp. xxiii–xxx. This volume, and any standard Jewish Bible, will provide a list of the *haftarah* readings for today's most dominant rites, those of Ashkenaz (medieval Germany) and Sefarad (medieval Spain). For an accessible fuller list in English, see "Haftarah," *Wikipedia*, accessed August 2017, https://en.wikipedia.org/wiki/Haftarah, under "List of *Haftarot*." The *JPS* has not produced a one-volume pew Bible, although its Bible commentary series is only on books used liturgically.

18. Wacholder, "Prolegomenon," LXVII, lists Isa 2:4 as the incipit of the *haftarah* for Deut 21:10, but he indicates that the *haftarah*'s source is unknown, and a reading beginning at this point only appears in one source.

19. For a detailed analysis of these *haftarot* and their strategies, see Elsie R. Stern, *From Rebuke to Consolation: Exegesis and Theology in the Liturgical Anthology of the Ninth of Av Season* (Providence, RI: Brown Judaic Studies, 2004). For a brief summary, see her "Concepts of Scripture in the Synagogue Service," in *Jewish Concepts of Scripture: A Comparative Introduction*, ed. Benjamin D. Sommer (New York: New York University Press, 2012), 18–20, 24–26.

20. And not biblical commentaries per se. Commentaries on the *haftarot* in "pew Bibles" tend to be brief or nonexistent. I have consulted those most influential in the English-speaking world.

21. Translations follow the New Jewish Publication Society version, as in Fishbane, unless otherwise indicated.

22. These passages, however, may well have been read at other times in the Land of Israel, perhaps with Exod 22:24 (beginning with Isa 48:10) and certainly with Gen 24:1 (beginning Isa 51:1 or 2).

23. Mendel Hirsch, *The Haftoroth*, trans. Isaac Levy (Brooklyn, NY: Judaica Press, 1989), 410. This volume accompanies the five-volume translation of Samson Raphael Hirsch's Torah commentary, but its contents do not appear in the pew Bible version.

24. Nosson Scherman, *The Chumash*, Stone ed. (Brooklyn, NY: Mesorah Publications, 1993), 1197.

25. Fishbane, *JPS Bible Commentary*, on 55:1, 293–94, citing Ibn Ezra.

26. J. H. Hertz, *The Pentateuch and Haftorahs: Hebrew Text, English Translation and Commentary*, 2nd ed. (London: Soncino Press, 1963), 819, on 55:5. The first edition of this commentary was published in individual volumes 1929–36. It is still used as a pew Bible in many English-speaking synagogues.

27. These were likely included in the triennial cycle *haftarah* for Gen 24:1–2 that began with Isa 51:1 (or 2), with these first verses being the reason for the association. Another, for Gen 2:4, began only with 51:6.

28. Hertz, *The Pentateuch and Haftorahs*, 836.

29. Fishbane, *JPS Bible Commentary*, 300. Emphasis mine.

30. Fishbane, *JPS Bible Commentary*, 303. Compare Hertz, *The Pentateuch and Haftorahs*, 857.

31. David L. Lieber et al., eds., *Etz Hayim: Torah and commentary* (New York: Rabbinical Assembly, United Synagogue of Conservative Judaism, 2005), 1138. This volume adapts the *JPS Bible Commentary* into a pew Bible for the Conservative Movement.

32. I write this on the day after the Israeli Knesset approved a bill legalizing existing Jewish homes illegally built on private Palestinian lands. It is expected that the Israeli courts will block the bill. See "In Historic First, Israel Legalizes West Bank Outposts with Sweeping New Legislation," *Times of Israel*, February 6, 2017, http://www.timesofisrael.com/in -historic-first-israel-legalizes-west-bank-outposts-with-sweeping-new -legislation/.

33. This echoes Elsie Stern's observation in her *From Rebuke to Consolation*, 19, that the choice of a *haftarah* from Isa 42:5—43:11 with its emphasis on God's special relationship with Israel "adds a particularist valence to the relatively universalist primeval history of Gen 1—6."

34. Some of the intervening pericopes are read at other times, Isa 55:6—56:8 on the afternoon of every fast day, i.e., multiple times during the year; and Isa 57:14—58:14 on the Day of Atonement, also a fast day.

35. Hertz, *The Pentateuch and Haftorahs*, 874–75, introduction, on v. 3, and vv. 10–14. Scherman, *The Chumash*, 1201, seems unconcerned about the status of the nations at the final redemption except that they recognize Israel/Jerusalem and "pay homage to her." Compare Hirsch, *The Haftoroth*, 437–38, though, who reads this as echoing Isa 2:2–3's universal participation in Israel's redemption.

36. Fishbane, *JPS Bible Commentary*, 315.

37. Hertz, *The Pentateuch and Haftorahs*, 885, perhaps reflecting on the rise of Hitler, comes closest to contemporizing this passage, characterizing Edom "as the type of enemies who knew neither righteousness nor pity in their dealings with Israel." Scherman, *The Chumash*, 1203, merely identifies Edom as "the offspring of Esau, ancestor of the Roman Empire, which brought about the current exile."

38. See Michael Hilton, "Christian Influences on the Reading of the Prophets," in *Renewing the Vision: Rabbis Speak Out on Modern Jewish Issues; Essays Marking the Fortieth Anniversary of the Leo Baeck College*, ed. Jonathan A. Romain (London: SCM Press, 1996), 149–50. He correctly critiques scholars (like Eric Werner, *The Sacred Bridge: The Interdependence of Liturgy and Music in Synagogue and Church during the First Millennium* [New York: Dennis Dobson/Columbia University Press, 1959], 77–88) who have suggested that much more of the series of *haftarot* developed in response to Christianity. All base their conclusions on Ludwig Venetianer, "Ursprung und Bedeutung der Propheten-Lektionen," *Zeitschrift der Deutschen Morgenländischen Gesellschaft* 63 (1909): 103–70. However, Venetianer's study compares the *haftarot* as documented in Byzantine-era midrash to church lectionaries from the early modern period and later. We know today that these Tridentine lectionaries bear little similarity to those of the earlier church, where readings were often not standardized at all and what standardization existed was very local. See M. S. Driscoll, "Lectionaries, I: Historical," in *New Catholic Encyclopedia*, 2nd ed. (Detroit: Gale, 2003), 8:434–38. However, it is important to note that this victory over Edom appears in other *haftarot* as well, especially paired with the Genesis narratives about Esau: Mal 1:1—2:7 (Gen 25:19—28:9); Obad 1:1–19 (Gen 32:4—36:43, Sephardim), but also Amos 9:7–15 (Lev 16:1 or 19:1—20:27).

39. Examples of other *haftarot* offering a similar picture include Isa 27:6—29:23 (for Exod 1:1—6:1); Isa 40:27—41:16 (for Gen 12:1—17:27); Isa 42:5—43:11 (for Gen 1:1—6:8). Fishbane, *JPS Bible*

Commentary, 6, cites medieval debates over whether "light of the nations" (42:6) refers to the prophet and the tribes of Israel, or Israel and the nations of the world. Note that this is the only instance where a *haftarah* includes this phrase.

40. Fishbane, *JPS Bible Commentary*, 460, 463–64, 326–27, 330–31; Hertz, *The Pentateuch and Haftorahs*, 1037.

41. Michael Walzer, "Nation and Universe," in *Thinking Politically: Essays in Political Theory*, ed. David Miller (New Haven, CT: Yale University Press, 2007; original publication in *The Tanner Lectures on Human Values*, ed. Grethe B. Peterson, vol. 11, 507–56 [Salt Lake City: University of Utah Press, 1990]), 184. My thanks to Shira Wolosky for pointing me to this essay.

42. The one exception is unavoidable, as the *haftarah* for the beginning of Genesis parallels Isa 42:5, and the phrase occurs in 42:6.

43. Dating according to Fishbane, *JPS Bible Commentary*, 534.

44. Walzer, "Nation and Universe," 188–99. He also invokes Jer 18:7–10, p. 188.

45. See, for instance, Eugene Korn, "Covenantal Possibilities in a Post-Polemical Age: A Jewish View," *Studies in Christian-Jewish Relations* 6 (2011): 1–13, doi.org/10.6017/scjr.v6i1.1911.

CHAPTER SIXTEEN

PUERTO RICAN COMINGS AND GOINGS

Jewish Identities and the Complications of Diaspora

—ɷ—

Carmen M. Nanko-Fernández
and Jean-Pierre M. Ruiz

INTRODUCTION

The notion of diaspora has resonances as old as the Septuagint, where that word is used to describe the Jewish people outside the Land of Israel, with particular reference to the Babylonian exile of 587 BCE and subsequently to the dispersion that was the result of the destruction of the second Temple by the Romans in 70 CE.[1] This chapter focuses on Puerto Rico and the ways in which the comings and goings to and from the island have shaped and reshaped Jewish identities on the island and on the U.S. mainland for more than five centuries.

We start with a sketch of the Jewish presence in Puerto Rico, beginning with the present and then looking back to the Spanish colonial era, and then pointing to the promising signs of Christian-Jewish *convivencia* in present-day Puerto Rico. We then turn to the reality of the Puerto Rican diaspora and of *el vaivén*, the historical pattern of frequent comings and goings between the island and the U.S. mainland, focusing specifically on what we can learn from Aurora Levins Morales about the complex construction of Jewish identity and on the sort of multiple belonging that the back-and-forth of the *vaivén* makes possible.

We want to thank John Pawlikowski, at whose invitation this essay first began to take shape as presentations for the Christianity and Judaism Consultation at the June 2016 Convention of the Catholic Theological Society of America in San Juan, Puerto Rico. Our debt of gratitude extends well beyond the invitation that led to this essay. Not only do we applaud John's distinguished record of advancing Catholic-Jewish understanding; we also acknowledge his commitment to the growth in understanding and mutual respect between U.S. Latino/a Catholics and Jews. It was with his support and leadership that the Bernardin Center for Theology and Ministry of the Catholic Theological Union and the American Jewish Committee cosponsored *Comunidades y Convivencia.* That summer 2007 event in Chicago brought together Latina/o Catholic scholars and pastoral ministers from across the United States with leading members of the Jewish community over a period of several memorable days of study and fellowship. That gathering demonstrated convincingly that "it is the sharing of lived daily experience by Latino/a Christians and Jews that will build a solid foundation for growth in understanding and for shared commitment to stand together in solidarity to work for *tikkun olam,* the healing of the world."[2]

As Latina/o theologians, we are inclined to pay attention to particularity, and this question of Latino/a-Jewish relations is an ongoing one. Complex and multifaceted histories and experiences serve as points of departure for considering anew the ways dialogue can move forward, and in critically reflecting on our not-so-innocent histories.[3] By focusing on the history and present reality of Puerto Rico, this essay takes a deliberate step in that direction.[4]

CONTEMPORARY JUDAISM ISLAND-STYLE

In investigating the Puerto Rican–Jewish connection, one gets the sense of a story framed by two colonizations with not much in between, a centuries-old presence at best, and then a contemporary reality born (after 1898) of U.S. occupation, economic opportunity, and diaspora—from Nazi-occupied Europe and then Cuba. Puerto

Rico, home to the largest Jewish population in the region, is the only Caribbean island with a Conservative synagogue (in Miramar), a Reform congregation (in Condado), and the orthodox Chabad Lubavitch of Puerto Rico with a center in Isla Verde and a storefront in Old San Juan.[5]

Shaare Zedek and the Jewish Community Center (JCC) date back to 1935 with the gathering of twenty-six families in spaces that included the San Juan Casino and El San Juan Hotel.[6] By 1953, the community had purchased and remodeled a mansion and established a presence that consisted of the JCC and the synagogue, "Ashkenazi-Conservative, and an affiliate of the United Synagogues of America."[7] The 1950s saw an increase in the Jewish population from the United States during the industrialization of the island under Operation Bootstrap. The diaspora of Cuban Jews in the years following the Cuban Revolution, and of Argentinian Jews during the "Dirty War," shifted demographics from an English-speaking congregation to a more Spanish-speaking one with an Argentinian rabbi and JCC director. Tensions in colonized spaces shaped by multiple diasporas remain evident in the mundane. "Language is a problem," explains JCC director Diego Mendelbaum. "Some of our members don't speak English and some don't speak Spanish. If we give talks in Spanish, there's a group of English-speakers who won't come, and vice-versa."[8]

Temple Beth Shalom was established in 1967, born out of conversations expressing dissatisfaction "with the drift to the extreme right of conservatism at Shaare Tzedek."[9] The congregation's early years were spent in borrowed Christian spaces. What began as a small English-speaking congregation now identifies as "as a diverse, multigenerational, multicultural, inclusive community with an emphasis on social justice, education and dynamic experiences in Judaism."[10] The congregation includes "snowbirds" fleeing East Coast winters and Puerto Rican-born converts, many claiming converso heritage.[11] This local population of "Spanish-speaking Jews-by-Choice" have impacted not only the languages of service but the style of worship. Their website notes, "With the influx of Spanish-speaking members we have become a very musical place of worship. Our services often have musical accompaniments by different combinations of guitar, piano, bongos, violins, cello, clarinet, and voices. We are fortunate to have so many members who add musical inspiration to our prayers."[12]

Congregation Shaarei Torah was founded in 1999 and through its synagogue and education center serves tourists, business travelers, and Jewish residents, including those on ten other Caribbean islands.[13] In late 2013, the congregation broke ground for new facilities to accommodate a synagogue, school, and the first and only mikveh in Puerto Rico.[14] At the groundbreaking ceremony for the first ever synagogue to be built on the island, founding Rabbi Mendel Zarchi noted, "This is a great testament to the tolerance and acceptance of the people of Puerto Rico of all people from all of races, and their great affinity for the Jewish people."[15]

JEWS IN PUERTO RICO: HISTORY AND ITS MYSTERIES

In the Americas, in the beginning was *not* the word, but a translator. In his diary entry for November 2, 1492, Cristóbal Colón wrote of sending a small party of men, two Spaniards and two Indios, into Cuba in search of the cacique, the indigenous leader. One of the Spaniards was Luys de Torres "que...avía sido judío y sabía dizque ebrayco y caldeo y aun algo arávigo."[16] Luis de Torres "who had been a Jew," was a translator who could speak Hebrew, Aramaic, and some Arabic, languages that could prove useful in encounters with people in Asia, possibly Jewish traders or descendants of the lost tribes of Israel. Luis de Torres is credited as being the first known Jewish settler in the Americas, a recent converso who did not return to Spain but remained behind, though where seems to be a matter of dispute. Some claim de Torres was part of the settlement on Hispaniola that Colón found destroyed on his second voyage a year later. The location of that fort, built from the lumber and furnishings of the shipwrecked *Santa María*, is thought to be in Haiti. Other sources, allegedly confusing him with a later explorer, suggest that de Torres settled in Cuba with gifts from a cacique "not merely lands but also slaves—five adults and a child," and a yearly allowance from the Spanish crown.[17]

Jews are woven deeply into the fabric of the age of *encontronazos* and *encuentros*, of violent collisions and less than innocent encounters. In the prologue to his 1492 log, Colón observed that the expulsion of the Jews was coextensive with his command to head to the Indies.[18] The navigational and astronomical science of Portuguese Jews guided and informed his endeavors.[19] The financing of his four journeys, especially the second that secured Puerto Rico in the constellation of conquest, was funded by loans from well-placed conversos, and, sadly, by wealth gained from properties and valuables seized from those Jews forced into diaspora.[20] Among the twelve hundred men, and seventeen well-stocked ships in the 1493 voyage, and in others to come, there were Sephardim, conversos, and crypto-Jews in search of new places to land. Since the Inquisition followed the flag, there could be no public displays of Judaism, and for survival the descendants of diaspora had to go to ground, and on an island, move inland. Ever suspect, so-called New Christians had to find alternate ways to tradition their Judaism in domestic spaces, seeding family practices and names with clues mysterious to later generations in search of their roots.

Among the mysteries is the contested question of Colón's own origins. In late 1898, Spanish scholar Celso García de la Riega challenged the Genovese origin story and proposed that Colón was from a Jewish family in Pontevedra, Galicia, in northwest Spain.[21] His hypothesis was propagated by a few others, notably Constantino de Horta y Pardo, whose defense of Colón's Galician roots was published in 1911.[22] The hypothesis persists to this day, supported in part by documentation tracing Colón's matrilineal and patrilineal names to Pontevedra and to the Inquisition, and to curious connections between the naming of his discoveries with familiar places in Galicia.[23]

A 2009 study by linguistics professor Estelle Irizarry looked at Colón's use of language and syntax. Employing the technological tools of digital humanities, she examined his writings[24] and determined that Colón was a native Catalan-speaker and Jewish.[25] Irizarry cited, among other evidence, distinctly Catalonian and Ladino characteristics in his writing and punctuation, particularly his use of *vírgulas*. This research joins other recent scholarship positing Colón's origins as a converso or crypto-Jew from Catalan or the Balearic Islands.[26]

In the words of Aurora Levins Morales,

> The colony of Puerto Rico is an island haunted, in its early years, by memories of fire and smoke. The treasurer Blas de Villasante is a grandson of Medina the Jew, burned in Sevilla. Bailiff Miguel Díaz is the son of conversos from Aragon. Bartolomé de las Casas may be related to those other Casas and Cases whose names are inscribed in the rolls of the inquisition. The island is full of next of kin.[27]

The definitive determination of Colón's heritage is beyond the ambitions of this study, yet more than a century of controversy raises intriguing questions, among them the following: Why have historians been so quick to read Colón's story through exclusively Christian lenses? What assumptions would shift if Colón's millennial apocalypticism is examined from the perspective of a converso influenced by Joachim de Fiore and Franciscan apocalypticism as well as Jewish apocalypticism fueled by the expulsion and the Inquisition? What does living Judaism look like in diaspora, when one is forced into complicated and risky multiple belongings? Was Judaism absent from the island because there was no public presence, or did it live in domestic and popular religious practices that we have not yet begun to explore in their layers of complexity? Was Judaism traditioned, encoded, and even hidden in plain sight like the religious practices of West Africa? Hints of diasporas ignored or forgotten are coded into DNA and names, into hybrid languages and daily practices— strategies resisting erasure, concealed beneath layers of accretion, memories planted by ancestors to insure survival. Where might these complicated stories of embodied interreligious multiple belongings and multiple yearnings take us and what are implications in concrete terms, for example, as Spain navigates its newly legislated right of return for the descendants of the Sephardim?

SIGNS OF
CONVIVENCIA TODAY

Lived Judaism in Puerto Rico is the result of multiple diasporas and ongoing movements that lead people *to* and not only *away from* the island: exiles, refugees, snowbirds, retirees, former soldiers and sailors, and descendants of conversos and crypto-Jews. The Jewish presence in Puerto Rico emerges from the consequences of two colonial aggressions four hundred years apart. The majority are visible, self-identified, practitioners of Judaism in its rich variety rooted in twentieth-century migrations to a U.S. colony. A minority are local converts, some claiming to be descended from conversos and crypto-Jews. An unknown (and possibly unknowable) historic minority traces itself back to Sephardic ancestors forced to live on the down-low in a Catholic colony. In such circumstances, *convivencia* as public, intentional, and committed living together draws not so much from the past but finds expression in concrete and symbolic actions in the lived present. Characterized by commitments to share struggles, to remember together, and to move forward together, two examples from this Puerto Rican context are particularly instructive.

In August 2006, the Puerto Rican Legislature declared that May 30 be commemorated annually as "Lod Massacre Memorial Day" in remembrance of that date in 1972 when sixteen Puerto Rican pilgrims to the Holy Land were among the twenty-six people killed in a terrorist attack at Lod Airport.[28] The legislation frames both collective remembrance of those who suffered—the dead and the survivors—and the necessary reflection on the horrific event as moral and patriotic imperatives with implications for the future. Those affected by the violence are described as victims of "fanaticism that made use of anti-Semitic discourse."[29] The act condemns violence against innocent people as "morally loathsome and radically incompatible with the claims of vindication," particularly when there are legitimate alternatives.[30] Collective and public remembrance in this case is an annual call for awareness with the hopes of creating a better future, a renewable teachable moment on *convivencia* with its obligations "that we should be supportive towards those who suffer aggressions and persecutions, but never to tolerate actions against innocent people, or the attempt to instill hate for ethnical, religious, or cultural reasons."[31]

On December 13, 2015, the eighth day of Hanukkah coincided with the first Sunday of the Jubilee Year of Mercy decreed by Pope Francis. San Juan Archbishop Roberto González Nieves invited leaders of the Puerto Rican Jewish community to the cathedral. Delegations from the Conservative and the Reform congregations participated in an interreligious service following Mass, with remarks by their leaders recalling the significance of *Nostra Aetate* on its fiftieth anniversary. In that spirit, Rabbi Norman Patz of Temple Beth Shalom reminded all present that "neither church nor synagogue nor mosque can afford to be prisoners of the past, rendered unable to face the present, let alone the future."[32] His bilingual appeal in the words of the prophet Malachi drew "loud, spontaneous applause that echoed in the huge sanctuary": "'Have we not all one Father? Has not one God created us?' No tenemos todos un mismo padre? No nos ha creado un mismo dios?"[33] For Patz as for the prophet, this shared reality challenges all of us to question, "Why do we break faith with one another, profaning the covenant of our ancestors?"[34] That final night of the festival of lights, commemorating "the first fight in history for religious freedom," invites everyone to respond with renewed dedication to the goals of *Nostra Aetate.*

Five hundred and twenty-three years after expulsion from Spain and forced conversion, the words of one Temple Beth Shalom participant are eloquent testimony to how far things have come and how much remains to be done:

> After the conclusion of the ceremony, hundreds of people came forward to hug and kiss the Jewish participants, to say *shalom* (or *paz*), in a few cases to proudly tell us that they knew some Hebrew or had traveled to Israel, or had participated in the church production of *Fiddler on the Roof*, and to photograph—or be photographed with—the hanukkiah in the cathedral. It was truly extraordinary.[35]

JUAN EPSTEIN AND
THE SOCIALIZATION OF PUERTO RICAN
JEWS IN THE DIASPORA

In the 1970s, Puerto Ricans constituted the largest segment of the Latina/o population of New York City.[36] The WABC television sitcom of that era, *Welcome Back, Kotter*, presented the escapades of a onetime misfit-turned-teacher who returned to his alma mater, (the fictitious) James Buchanan High School in the Bensonhurst section of Brooklyn, to take over the homeroom of the Sweathogs, a remedial class of colorful misfits, one of whom happened to be named Juan Epstein. Played by Robert Hegyes, the Epstein character was a Puerto Rican Jew. In the pilot episode, he is introduced to Mr. Gabe Kotter (played by Gabriel Kaplan) by Vinny Barbarino (played by John Travolta) as "the toughest kid in school, voted most likely to take a life." Kotter turns toward him and says, "Epstein, huh?" Epstein stands and proudly identifies himself as "Juan Luis Pedro Felipo [*sic*] de Huevos Epstein, from San Juan." Kotter inquires, "Your mother's Puerto Rican?" Epstein replies, "No, my father. My mother's name is Bibberman." Kotter adds, "I didn't know, you know, that there were Epsteins in Puerto Rico," so Epstein explains, "Oh there weren't, until the winter of '38, when a boat carrying a shivering Lou Epstein from Odessa to the Bronx stopped in San Juan. 'Oy,' my grandfather said! 'Look at the palm trees! Feel this heat! Look at this tan! Hey, who needs Miami!' From that day on, there were Epsteins in San Juan!" Kotter has just one more question for the tough guy among the Sweathogs, whose curly hair is styled tall, and who sports blue jeans and a sleeveless denim jacket with a small Puerto Rican flag patch sewn onto the back. "That's very interesting Epstein. What's your favorite subject?" "Assault," says Epstein, flashing a broad smile.[37] Yet later in the same episode, when the curmudgeonly vice principal enters the classroom to check up on the newly hired teacher he still remembers from Kotter's days as one of the original Sweathogs, Epstein leaps to his defense by volunteering, "Hey Mr. Kotter, I'm gonna do a report on the implications of the socializations of Puerto Rican Jews."

The 1970s were marked not only by four seasons of "Welcome Back, Kotter," but also by the bombing of Fraunces Tavern on January 24, 1975, the Manhattan site of George Washington's 1783 farewell address to his officers. In a typewritten note found in a nearby phone booth, a Puerto Rican nationalist group that called itself the Fuerzas Armadas de Liberación Nacional Puertorriqueña (FALN, the Armed Forces of Puerto Rican National Liberation) claimed responsibility for the attack that left three dead and eleven injured.[38] The note made it clear that their choice of Fraunces Tavern as the target was intended to link the Puerto Rican struggle for self-determination with the American War of Independence against Great Britain: "The Yanki government is trying to terrorize and kill our people to intimidate us from seeking our rightful independence from colonialism."[39]

A little more than three years later, on July 12, 1978, a pipe bomb that was being constructed by William Morales accidentally detonated in his apartment.[40] Although no one was ever tried for the Fraunces Tavern bombing, Morales was convicted for his possession of explosives, but escaped from Bellevue Hospital's prison ward despite his serious injuries. During the 1980s, sixteen other FALN members were convicted of seditious conspiracy and sentenced to lengthy prison terms. In 1999, President Clinton granted them clemency, an offer that was refused by Oscar López Rivera, whose sentence was eventually commuted by President Barack Obama during the waning days of his administration.[41]

Being Puerto Rican in New York, the capital city of the Puerto Rican diaspora, was very rarely a laughing matter. Even the characterization of Juan Epstein, whose favorite subject was assault and who was voted "most likely to take a life," pins its fabricated laugh track to lingering *West Side Story* stereotypes of Puerto Rican New Yorkers as violent lowlifes and gang members.[42] The complexities of the Puerto Rican diaspora—with its implications for the construction of diasporic identities—deserves close and careful attention.

DIASPORICANS

Unlike Cuban Americans, and unlike unauthorized resident Mexican Americans for whom voluntary return to their homeland under present circumstances is risky at best, Puerto Ricans living on the U.S. mainland do not refer to ourselves as Puerto Rican Americans.[43] This is, on the one hand, a matter of the geopolitics of colonialism. Whereas Cuba gained its independence from the United States on May 20, 1902, fewer than four years after the Treaty of Paris brought the Spanish-American War to an end, to this day Puerto Rico continues to be an unincorporated territory of the United States, with its inhabitants granted U.S. citizenship under the provisions of the Jones-Shafroth Act of 1917.[44] Puerto Rico's neocolonial status is a distinctly mixed blessing, inasmuch as Puerto Ricans can come and go to and from the U.S. mainland as they wish, and, more often than not, as economic need pushes them from the island to the mainland.[45] We speak about this back-and-forth movement between the mainland and the island as *el vaivén*. As Jorge Duany explains, "This culturally dense word refers to the constant comings and goings in which large numbers of Puerto Ricans are involved....It suggests that those who are here today may be gone tomorrow, and vice versa. More ominously *vaivén* also connotes unsteadiness, inconstancy, and oscillation."[46] In 1993, *el vaivén* made it to the big screen in Luis Molina Casanova's film, *La guagua aérea* (The flying bus), an adaptation of Luis Rafael Sanchez's 1984 essay about the so-called Great Migration from Puerto Rico to the U.S. mainland from the 1940s into the 1960s.[47] Advertised as "Un drama para reir, una comedia para pensar," "a drama for laughs, a comedy to think about," the bus with wings of the title is Transcaribbean Airlines' midnight flight from San Juan to New York during the 1960 Christmas season, and the film tells the story of the varied group of Puerto Rican passengers who make the trip.[48] With steamships that provided passage between the island and the U.S. mainland in the first four decades of the twentieth century giving way to today's relatively inexpensive airfares, the *vaivén* continues unabated. In fact, with the increase of migration from Puerto Rico to Florida, the population of the Puerto Rican diaspora on the U.S. mainland (5.1 million) now outnumbers the Puerto Rican population on the island (3.5 million).[49] Yet Duany also notes, "Among all recent Latino migrants to the United States (including Mexicans, Cubans, and Dominicans, only Puerto Ricans insist on calling themselves simply Puerto Ricans, rather than Puerto Rican—Americans, which speaks volumes about their persistent stress on national origin and their adamant rejection of a hyphenated ethnicity."[50]

Luis N. Rivera-Pagán writes that "Puerto Rican culture cannot be genuinely studied or assessed if the creativity of the diaspora community is neglected or its significance diminished." He adds, "Diaspora entails a dislocation, a painful process of forging new strategies to articulate cultural differences and identifications. The émigré exists in ambivalent tension, especially in the Western cosmopolis with its heterogeneous and frequently conflicting ethnocultural minorities that belie the mythical *e pluribus unum*."[51]

"Diasporic existence," says Rivera-Pagán, "questions fixed and static notions of cultural and community identity. Identity is not conceived any more as a pure essence to be nostalgically preserved, but as an emancipatory project to be fashioned, in an alien territory, in a foreign language, as a polyphonic process of creative imagination."[52] The displacement associated with living in a diasporic condition— whether short-term or long-term—resituates and reorients those who are involved vis-à-vis imagined, constructed, and imposed mappings of centers and peripheries. Far from home, "the émigré's cultural differences produce subaltern significations that resist the cultural cannibalism of the melting pot."[53]

The Puerto Rican diaspora in the United States has long been fertile soil for the development and expression of Puerto Rican nationalism. Prior to the U.S. invasion of Puerto Rico in 1898, New York provided both a safe haven for Puerto Rican nationalists and Cuban revolutionaries alike, and a setting in which they could engage in the construction of a distinctive identity.[54] For example, in 1895 it was in New York that the flag of Puerto Rico was first presented, a flag that was deliberately modeled after that of Cuba but with its colors inverted.[55] While that flag was eventually adopted by the Estado Libre Asociado in 1952, prior to that it was illegal to display the Puerto Rican flag in Puerto Rico, because it was recognized (and rightly so) as a powerful symbolic affirmation of political nationalist identity over against the imposed colonial condition.[56] As Nelson A. Denis writes, "The flag of Puerto Rico has a turbulent and politically charged history....In 1948, Public Law 53 made ownership of this flag—no matter how small and even if kept in a closet, box, attic, or basement—punishable by several years' imprisonment. Puerto Rican homes were searched and people were jailed."[57]

Drawing on the distinction between political nationalism and cultural nationalism as developed by Duany, Ramón E. Soto-Crespo writes,

> If cultural nationalism permits the easy export of a cultural affiliation abroad, these particularities acquired a political dimension in the Puerto Rican [*U.S. mainland*] barrios. For instance, where a song in Puerto Rico may be an expression of its culture, in the mainland barrios it becomes a political statement attesting to a national identity.[58]

The song to which Soto-Crespo refers is "Lamento Borincano," a bolero composed in 1929 by Rafael Hernández.[59] This is an instance in which, as Rivera-Pagán suggests, the dislocation of diaspora offered a space for articulating cultural differences (Puerto Rican culture over against U.S. culture) and identifications, for asserting a distinctive identity.

MULTIPLE BELONGING: AURORA LEVINS MORALES AND THE "ALMOST UNBEARABLE DENSITY OF STORIES"

Identities shaped in the Puerto Rican *vaivén* are as complicated as they are distinctive. Consider, for example, the case of Aurora Levins Morales. Born in 1954 in Indiera Baja, Maricao, Puerto Rico, she explains,

> My mother was born in New York in 1930, raised in Spanish Harlem and the Bronx. I represent the generation of

return. I was born deep in the countryside of Puerto Rico, and except for four years when I was very young, lived there until I was 13....For my mother, the Barrio is safety, warmth. For me, it's the fear of racist violence that clipped her tongue of all its open vowels, into crisp imitation British....Where I grew up, I fought battles to prove that I was Puerto Rican with the kids who called me "Americanita," but I stayed on the safe side of that line: Caribbean island, not Portah Ricah; exotic tropical blossom, not spic—living halfway in the skin and separating myself from the dark bad city kids in Nueva York.[60]

As though that were not complicated enough, Levins Morales explains,

I came from an almost unbearable density of stories, thick as the red clay of my barrio. People ask me my name and I say my great-grandmother's grandmother was a rebel and a rabbi's wife. I say my great-grandfather seduced a servant and his wife cast her out. They ask where I'm from and I say slaveholders and slaves. I open my mouth and spill stories. My mother says the mix was outside her, in the streets and apartment buildings. I say the mix is in my body. I am the mix.[61]

The traditional practice of using both her father's surname (Levins) and her mother's surname (Morales) underscores one of the many intricacies of Puerto Ricanness, the mix in her own body of Eastern European Jewish and Puerto Rican identity. Her father, Richard Levins, was a Brooklyn-born descendant of Ukrainian Jews. A distinguished academic and a left wing political activist, Levins himself was caught up in the Puerto Rican *vaivén*. He writes,

In the summer of 1949 I met Rosario Morales. Our courtship was also my introduction to the South Bronx and to Puerto Rico. I frequented the *mavi* stand near the 163rd street elevated station and learned to fry *tostones*. I started to learn Spanish from a few pamphlets about *El Grito de Lares* (the rebellion of 1868 against Spain) and the sugar strike of the 1940s.[62]

A self-described "third generation Red," Richard Levins "grew up in a home where political ideas were part of everyday conversation and somebody was always involved in anti-fascist, anti-racist and pro-labor activities," and on that basis he admits, "I was ready on general principles to support the Puerto Rican struggle for independence before I met Puerto Rico."[63] He and Rosario moved to Puerto Rico in 1951, where both became actively involved with the Puerto Rican Communist Party and with the nationalist movement. In 1956, they returned to the mainland United States, only to make their way back to Puerto Rico four years later. Levins accepted a position as an ecologist on the faculty of the University of Puerto Rico from 1961 to 1967, but was denied tenure there on the basis of his political activism. So in 1967, he and his family returned to the U.S. mainland, where he accepted a position at the University of Chicago. Richard Levins ended his academic career at Harvard University's T. H. Chan School of Public Health, and died in January 2016.[64]

His daughter Aurora speaks of her own multiple belonging by identifying herself as a "child of two cultures of resistance." She writes,

> I grew up among *jíbaras*, a multilayered name for country people, which is used on the one hand to romanticize the imaginary "simple but honest" noble peasants or country workers of yesteryear and on the other is a common put-down implying stupidity and lack of sophistication, like "hick." But which originally meant, in the language of the Arawak people, "she who runs away to be free," referring to the mixed-blood settlements of escaped slaves, fugitive Indians, and European peasants who took to the mountains to escape state control....I am also the daughter of an urbanized descendant of the impoverished island elite. My mother came from small-town *hacendados* fallen on hard times and grew up in the collective working-class immigrant culture of New York

City in the 1930s and 40s with an inheritance of practicality, of pride in work well done, of adaptability to the shifting currents of history. She became a communist in the late forties, a feminist before there was a movement to back her, and when any piece of politics makes her queasy, she trusts her own gut feeling over anyone else's credentials.

And I grew up as the tropical branch of a tribe of working-class Jewish thinkers who were critiquing the canons of their day from the shtetls of Eastern Europe, arguing about identity politics and coalitions, assimilation and solidarity way back into the last century. My father's great-great-grandmother, a rabbi's wife in 1860s Ukraine, challenged the patriarchal rules of Judaism by standing up and calling out, "Your God is a man!" His grandmother Leah Shevelev, an immigrant to New York at the turn of the century, was an organizer of garment workers and unemployed workers and worked as a birth control educator with Margaret Sanger. His father helped found the Communist Youth Movements. In the extended family over which my great-grandmother Leah ruled, my father grew up an internationalist, profeminist man and an original, creative thinker who loved intellectual work and was unimpressed by the rituals and self-importance of academic institutions.[65]

Thus, Levins Morales can declare, "How I think and what I think about grows from my identity as a *jíbara* shtetl intellectual and organizer."[66] She often writes of the complexity of her multiple belonging. "Born at the crossroads," a phrase she uses to describe herself in *Getting Home Alive*, a book she coauthored with her mother Rosario Morales, aptly describes the multiple belonging that Levins Morales actively embraces.[67] Far from being a matter of confusion or fragmentation, for Rosario Morales and her daughter, multiple belonging is a matter of living with the nourishment of many deep and intertwining roots.

Of Levins Morales and her mother, Lourdes Rojas writes,

Both authors are equally proud of their historical past and cultural present. They are aware of being a product of many diasporas, drawing strength equally from all of their roots and they also are cognizant of, and committed to, their historical present....Together, they are new entities like their texts, culturally and socially, rooted in an integrated plurality.[68]

For Aurora, her father's Jewish heritage adds yet another element to the complex density of her own story. She writes,

I am what I am, I am Boricua as Boricuas come from the isle of Manhattan, and I croon sentimental tangos in my sleep and AfroCuban beats in my blood....I mean there it was yiddish and spanish and fine refined college educated english and irish which I mainly keep in my prayers.[69]

As for her prayers, in *Getting Home Alive*, she writes, "I was scared when I'd done it, crossed myself in the name of the Father and the Son and the Holy Ghost in front of the Synagogue that I passed almost every day on the way to school, to the supermarket, the subway."[70]

It is to Yiddish that Levins Morales turns for the title of a memoir she includes in the second book on which she and her mother collaborated.[71] For that memoir, she borrows from the words of David Edelstadt (1866–92), a Russian Jewish emigrant to the United States. The memoir is entitled *Tsu Got Vel Ikh Veynen*, "To God I cry out," and it begins by quoting the Yiddish text of Edelstadt's text, followed by an English translation:

Tsu got del [*sic*] ikh veynen
Mit a groys geveyn
Tsu vos bin ikh geboyren
A neyterin tsu zein?

To God I cry out
with a great cry

Why was I born
To be a seamstress?[72]

The memoir tells the story of Levins Morales's maternal grandmother Lola Morales, who migrated from the island to the U.S. mainland in the 1950s and found employment doing "Garment work, piece work, at the minimum wage." As part of the Great Migration,

> thousands of women who had been doing piecework in their wooden houses in the countryside of the island poured into the sweatshops of the New York garment industry. They sat at rows of noisy machines, doing the same thing over and over, needle points flashing a fraction of an inch from their fingers.[73]

Through the words of Edelstadt's poem, the life of Levins Morales's Puerto Rican maternal grandmother intersects with the lives of her paternal great-grandmother Leah Shevelev and her younger sister Betty ("once Rivieka").

This is a memoir of working-class struggles shared across the decades of the twentieth century by women who never even knew each other. Yet, bound together by the blood-soaked threads of the New York sweatshops where they toiled, the Puerto Rican and Ukrainian foremothers whose tale Levins Morales weaves are a vital part of the almost unbearable density of stories that intersect in her own body. These are stories that are taken up in her family's *vaivén*, their comings and goings between Puerto Rico and the U.S. mainland, a movement in which her father's family also took part through their emigration from Ukraine to New York and through her father's own *vaivén* to and from Puerto Rico.

Levins Morales put the finishing touches on the coauthored collection *Cosecha and Other Stories* after her mother's death in 2011. When her father died on January 19, 2016, she wrote that because her father was an atheist, she could not bring herself to pray the traditional mourner's kaddish for him, but because he "did believe in forces greater than himself," she composed a kaddish of her own,

287

"celebrating his faith in their endurance and hopefulness." It reads, in part,

> Joyously celebrated be the infinite complexity and beauty of the universe, its endless dialectic, its loops of positive and negative feedback, equilibrium and change, its constant evolution; and celebrated be human creativity and solidarity and courage. May they establish liberation in our lifetimes and in our days and in the lives of all peoples everywhere, speedily and soon, and let us say, ¡Que viva!

It is not Aramaic "amens" or even the Yiddish of her father's immigrant grandparents that punctuate this kaddish, but the Spanish acclamation *¡Que viva!* This phrase from Levins Morales's Puerto Rican mother's tongue punctuates this barely secular prayer that eloquently honors the values to which Richard Levins devoted his life, and yet it is deeply imbued with the spirit of the traditional prayer.

Thus, for Levins Morales, who comes "from an almost unbearable density of stories," the mix—the multiple belonging—that finds expression in stories spun in English and Spanish and Yiddish ("I open my mouth and spill stories"), comes from within, for, as she tells us "the mix is in my body. I am the mix."[74]

CONCLUSION: INTERSECTIONS AND THEIR COMPLICATIONS

Multiple belonging is complicated, as complicated as the centuries-old *vaivén* of Jews to and from Puerto Rico, and of Puerto Ricans to and from the U.S. mainland. As Latino/a theologians, we come to this particular study as implicated and embedded in the weave of diasporas with our own "density of stories" that intersect in the complex latinidad that characterizes New York City. DiaspoRican Jean-Pierre Ruiz's father Pedro Ruiz was one of the many thousands of Puerto Ricans who migrated from the island to the U.S. mainland during the so-called Great Migration of the 1950s. Pedro Ruiz found work as a cook at the Laurel kosher deli on Main Street in Flushing,

Queens, so that matzoh ball soup and pastrami were as familiar to his family as the asopaos and perníl that are among the cherished comfort foods of Puerto Rican *comida criolla*. In 1923, Carmen Nanko-Fernandez's grandparents, Emilio and Carmen Fernández, arrived in New York City from Galicia, but only after a sojourn in Cuba. They became part of the city's complex diasporic pan-Hispanic presence from Latin America, the Iberian Peninsula, and the Sephardic diaspora. Multiple belonging can be found at intersections like those we reflect on in this essay, as well as the intersections chronicled by the early twentieth-century Puerto Rican migrant Bernardo Vega in a memory from his first visit to Harlem, at the time an economically struggling neighborhood of immigrants including Jews, Cubans, and Puerto Ricans. His journey took him to the local open-air market and a Sephardic restaurant called La Luz, located in the area later known as El Barrio. Intrigued by this polysensual, multilingual experience that was both familiar and unfamiliar, Vega came to recognize "New York City was really a modern Babylon, the meeting point of people from all over the world."[75]

In the retrieval of so many stories and relationships that are too often ignored, and in the critical, constructive attention focused on the complex particularities of daily living, Latino/a theologies map out promising (though sometimes circuitous) alternate routes in the ongoing and urgently necessary tasks of furthering interreligious dialogue and of building the sort of *convivencia* that is nourished by mutual understanding and respect.

Notes

1. See Robin Cohen, *Global Diasporas: An Introduction*, 2nd ed. (New York: Routledge, 2008), esp. 21–36: "Classical Notions of Diaspora: Transcending the Jewish Tradition." Also see Kevin Kenny, *Diaspora: A Very Short Introduction* (New York: Oxford University Press, 2013); Shaye D. Cohen and Ernest S. Frerichs, eds., *Diasporas in Antiquity*, Brown Judaic Studies 288 (Atlanta: Scholars Press, 1993); Ernest S. Gruen, *Diaspora: Jews amidst Greeks and Romans* (Cambridge, MA: Harvard University Press, 2002).

2. Jean-Pierre Ruiz, "Beginning a Conversation: Unlikely Hermanos; Jews and Latinos/as in the United States," *Apuntes* 29, no. 2 (Summer 2009): 55. Also see Carmen M. Nanko-Fernández, "Locating the Daily: Lo Cotidiano as a Locus for Exploring Christian—Jewish Relations latinamente," *Apuntes* 29, no. 2 (Summer 2009): 56–71.

3. See Ruiz, "Beginning a Conversation," 53: "What, then, is the history and present experience of Jews and Latinos/as in the United States? That complex and multifaceted history and that experience are the point of departure for considering the ways in which the dialogue can move forward."

4. The history of Jewish-Christian relations on the Iberian Peninsula prior to 1492 is another important dimension of this history that fascinates us. See Jean-Pierre M. Ruiz and Carmen M. Nanko-Fernández, "Dialogues in the Margins: The *Biblia de Alba* and the Future of Catholic-Jewish Understanding," in *Toward the Future: Essays on Catholic-Jewish Relations in Memory of Rabbi León Klenicki*, ed. Celia M. Deutsch, Eugene J. Fisher, and James Rudin (Mahwah, NJ: Paulist Press, 2013), 35–51. Also see Jean-Pierre Ruiz, "From Disputation to Dialogue: Jews and Latinos/as toward a New Convivencia," *New Theology Review* 22, no. 2 (2009): 36–47.

5. Rahel Musleah, "The Jewish Traveler: Puerto Rico," *Hadassah Magazine*, December/January 2013, http://www.hadassahmagazine .org/2013/12/10/jewish-traveler-puerto-rico/; Larry Luxner, "Puerto Rico's Jews Planting Roots on an Island with Little Jewish History," *Luxner News Inc.*, August 3, 2004, http://www.luxner.com/cgi-bin/ view_article.cgi?articleID=1237.

6. Musleah, "Jewish Traveler"; Eli Ross, "Puerto Rico," AJC Archives, 1970, 365–68, http://www.ajcarchives.org/ajc_data/files/ 1970_8_latamerica.pdf, identifies 1937 as the founding year.

7. Ross, "Puerto Rico," 366–67.

8. Luxner, "Puerto Rico's Jews." In 2004, it was estimated that 90 percent of the 255 families in Shaare Zedek had roots in Cuba.

9. Temple Beth Shalom, "History of Our Temple," accessed May 21, 2017, http://www.tbspr.org/about/history.

10. Shula Feldkran, president, Temple Beth Shalom, "Shalom, Welcome and Bienvenidos," Temple Beth Shalom Puerto Rico, accessed May 24, 2017, http://www.tbspr.org/about/presidentmessage. See too Judy Maltz, "Where Cubans and Americans Break Challah Together,"

Haaretz, June 10, 2015, http://www.haaretz.com/jewish/features/
.premium-1.660512. Please note that the access dates for notes 10 and 12
are important because they are prior to Hurricane Maria. The section of
this chapter on contemporary Puerto Rico was written prior to the
hurricane which has now so completely altered life on the island.

11. Musleah, "Jewish Traveler."

12. Feldkran, "Shalom, Welcome and Bienvenidos."

13. Maltz estimates that half of the Puerto Rican Jewish population is
from Cuba.

14. Karen Schwartz, "Groundbreaking Unearths Jewish 'Firsts' for
Puerto Rico," *Chabad.org News*, December 12, 2013, http://www
.chabad.org/news/article_cdo/aid/2425825/jewish/Groundbreaking
-Unearths-Jewish-Firsts-for-Puerto-Rico.htm.

15. Schwartz, "Groundbreaking Unearths Jewish 'Firsts' for Puerto
Rico."

16. For an English translation of the diary of Christopher Columbus,
see http://www.americanjourneys.org/pdf/AJ-062.pdf (accessed May
21, 2017). In Spanish, see *Diario of 1492 Christopher Columbus*, Viernes
2 de noviembre, Kings College London, accessed May 21, 2017, http://
www.ems.kcl.ac.uk/content/etext/e019.html.

Colón's 1492 journal was recopied on the initiative of Queen Isabela,
and both the original and early copies were subsequently lost. The version
of the log that survives was copied and annotated by Bartolomé de las
Casas and appears in his multivolume *Historia de las Indias*. A digital copy
is available at Biblioteca Virtual Miguel de Cervantes, Fray Bartolomé de
las Casas, *Historia de las Indias: Tomo 1* (Madrid: Impr. de M. Ginesta,
1875), http://www.cervantesvirtual.com/obra-visor/historia-de-las
-indias-tomo-1--0/html; *Historia de las Indias: Tomo 2*, http://www
.cervantesvirtual.com/obra-visor/historia-de-las-indias-tomo-2--0/
html/; *Historia de las Indias: Tomo 3*, http://www.cervantesvirtual.com/
obra-visor/historia-de-las-indias-tomo-3--0/html/.

For a discussion of las Casas and the log of Colón's first journey, see
Lawrence A. Clayton, *Bartolomé de las Casas: A Biography* (Cambridge:
Cambridge University Press, 2012), 397–99.

17. M. Kayserling, *Christopher Columbus and the Participation of the
Jews in the Spanish and Portuguese Discoveries*, trans. Charles Gross (New
York: Longmans, Green, 1894), 90–95, https://archive.org/stream/
chriscolpartjews00kaysrich#page/n5/mode/2up.

18. Prologue to the diario, accessed May 21, 2017, http://www.ems
.kcl.ac.uk/content/etext/e019.html#d0e57: "Así que después de aver
echado fuera todos los judíos de todos vuestros reynos y señoríos, en el
mismo mes de enero, mandaron Vuestras Altezas a mí que con armada
suffiçiente me fuese a las dichas partidas de Yndia."

19. See Howard M. Sachar, *Farewell España: The World of the
Sephardim Remembered* (New York: Alfred A. Knopf, 1994), 334.

20. Kayserling, *Christopher Columbus and the Participation of the
Jews*, 103–10; appendices X–XVII, 157–69. Finance minister Luis
Santángel and treasurer Gabriel Sánchez were conversos.

21. *Cristobal Colón ¿Español?* Conferencia por Celso García de la
Riega por la Sociedad Geográfica de Madrid, 20 Diciembre 1898 (Madrid:
Establecimiento Tipográfico de Fortanet, 1899), https://ia600205.us
.archive.org/23/items/cristobalcolbon00garcrich/
cristobalcolbon00garcrich.pdf. Days before his death in 1914 García de la
Riega's book *Colón Español, Origen y Patria* was published in Madrid.

22. Constantino de Horta y Pardo, *La verdadera cuna de Cristóbal
Colón* (New York: J. B. Jonathan, 1911). Alicante: Biblioteca Virtual
Miguel de Cervantes, 2007, http://www.cervantesvirtual.com/nd/ark:/
59851/bmcd50j2.

23. "Podría Ser Cristóbal Colón Judío o de Etnia?" Posted to the
blog *Celso García de la Riega*, February 8, 2014, accessed May 21, 2017,
https://celsogarciadelariega.wordpress.com/2014/02/08/1165/.

24. Amy Earhart, "Estelle Irizarry and Linguistic Analysis of Hispanic
Poets," accessed May 21, 2017, http://dhhistory.blogspot.com/2015/
04/estelle-irizarry-and-linguistic.html.

25. Estelle Irizarry, *Christopher Columbus: The DNA of His Writings*
(San Juan, PR: Ediciones Puerto, 2009).

26. See, e.g., Charles J. Merrill, *Colom of Catalonia: Origins of
Christopher Columbus Revealed* (Spokane, WA: Demers Books, 2008);
Nito Verdera, *Cristóbal Colón, Originario De Ibiza Y Criptojudío:
Cartografía Antigua Y La Conexión Judía, Claves Del "descubrimiento"
De América; Las Bulas De Alejandro VI Excluyeron a Portugal De La
Conquista Del Nuevo Mundo* (Eivissa: Consell Insular d'Eivissa i
Formentera, Conselleria de Cultura, 1999); Nito Verdera, *De Ibiza Y
Formentera Al Caribe: Cristóbal Colón Y La Toponimia* (Spain: N. Verdera,
2000).

27. Aurora Levins Morales, *Remedios: Stories of Earth and Iron from the History of Puertorriqueñas* (Cambridge, MA: South End Press, 1998), 100.

28. Act No. 144 (S.B. 1535) (certified English translation), approved August 2, 2006, accessed May 21, 2017, http://www.oslpr.org/download/en/2006/A-0144-2006.pdf.

29. Act No. 144 (S.B. 1535).

30. Act No. 144 (S.B. 1535).

31. Act No. 144 (S.B. 1535).

32. Remarks of Rabbi Norman Patz in "A Historic Act of Reconciliation: *Nostra Aetate* at the Cathedral of Old San Juan," *Temple Beth Shalom*, accessed May 16, 2018, https://www.sholom.net/2016/01/04/a-historic-act-of-reconciliation-nostra-aetate-at-the-cathedral-of-old-san-juan/.

33. Patz in "A Historic Act of Reconciliation."

34. Patz in "A Historic Act of Reconciliation."

35. Patz in "A Historic Act of Reconciliation."

36. According to a study published by Laird W. Bergad under the auspices of the Center for Latin American, Caribbean and Latino Studies of the City University of New York's Graduate Center, "Have Dominicans Surpassed Puerto Ricans to Become New York City's Largest Latino Nationality? An Analysis of Latino Population Data from the 2013 American Community Survey for New York City and the Metropolitan Area," in 2013 the Dominican population of the New York metropolitan area surpassed Puerto Ricans, who had up until then constituted the largest Latino group in the New York metropolitan area. The Mexican population is the third most numerous Latino national group. http://clacls .gc.cuny.edu/files/2014/11/AreDominicansLargestLatinoNationality.pdf (accessed May 21, 2017). Also see Carlos Vargas-Ramos and Juan C. García-Ellín, "Demographic Transitions: Settlement and Distribution of the Puerto Rican Population in the United States," in *The State of Puerto Ricans 2013*, ed. Edwin Meléndez and Carlos Vargas-Ramos (New York: City University of New York Hunter College Center for Puerto Rican Studies, 2013), 23–25.

37. https://youtu.be/Z8O5JZ8vlI0 (accessed May 21, 2017).

38. "We, FALN, the Armed Forces of the Puerto Rican Nation take full responsibility for the especially detonated [*sic*] bomb that exploded today at Fraunces Tavern, with reactionary corporate executives inside."

http://www.latinamericanstudies.org/puertorico/FALN-3.pdf (accessed May 21, 2017).

39. Ample evidence of organized and widespread U.S. government-sponsored violence aimed at suppressing anticolonial nationalist activism in Puerto Rico can be found in Nelson Denis, *War against All Puerto Ricans: Revolution and Terror in America's Colony* (New York: Nation Books, 2015).

40. See Mara Bovsun, "FALN Bomb Kills 4 at Fraunces Tavern, Where George Washington Said Farewell to Troops," *New York Daily News*, January 21, 2012, http://www.nydailynews.com/new-york/justice-story-faln-bomb-kills-4-fraunces-tavern-george-washington-farewell-troops-article-1.1008711.

41. See Shane Bauer, "This Man Is Serving 75 Years for 'Seditious Conspiracy.' Is He a Danger to Society?" *Mother Jones*, May 29, 2014, http://www.motherjones.com/politics/2014/05/oscar-lopez-rivera-75-years-seditious-conspiracy.

42. See Larry Luxner, "Puerto Rican Jews Plant Roots," *Jewish Telegraphic Agency*, September 7, 2004, http://www.jta.org/2004/09/07/life-religion/features/puerto-rican-jews-plant-roots. On the other hand, see Robert M. Levine, *Tropical Diaspora: The Jewish Experience in Cuba* (Gainesville: University Press of Florida, 1993); also see Caroline Bettinger-López, *Cuban-Jewish Journeys: Search for Identity, Home, and History in Miami* (Knoxville: University of Tennessee Press, 2000).

43. Many of those who fled Cuba after Fidel Castro came to power in the 1959 Revolution understood their experience as *el exilio*, the exile. Many in the first generation of Cuban exiles understood their condition not as a temporary predicament, for the reality of the Cold War chill between the communist regime of their native land and the land of their exile made it unrealistic to imagine that they could return anytime soon. See Gustavo Pérez Firmat, *Life on the Hyphen: The Cuban-American Way*, 2nd ed. (Austin: University of Texas Press, 2012).

44. http://www.legisworks.org/congress/64/publaw-368.pdf (accessed August 2, 2017).

45. See Duany, "The Puerto Rican Diaspora to the United States: A Postcolonial Migration?" February 13, 2009, http://centropr.hunter.cuny.edu/sites/default/files/past_events/Jorge_Duany_Puerto_Rican_Diaspora.pdf. Also see Kurt Birson, "Puerto Rican Migration in the 21st

Century: Is There a Brain Drain?" in Meléndez and Vargas-Ramos, *The State of Puerto Ricans 2013*, 27–31.

46. Jorge Duany, *The Puerto Rican Nation on the Move: Identities on the Island and in the United States* (Chapel Hill: University of North Carolina Press, 2003), 2–3.

47. Luis Rafael Sánchez, *La guagua aérea* (San Juan, PR: Editorial Cultural, 2000); Luis Rafael Sánchez, "The Flying Bus," translated by Elpidio Laguna-Diaz, in *Herencia*, ed. Nicolas Kanellos (New York: Oxford University Press, 2003), 631–38.

48. http://diasporapuertorriquena.weebly.com/blog/la-guagua-area (accessed August 2, 2017). Also see Gabriel Ignacio Barreneche, Jane Lombardi and Héctor Ramos-Flores, "A New Destination for 'The Flying Bus'? The Implications of Orlando-Rican Migration for Luis Rafael Sânchez's 'La guagua aérea,'" *Hispania* 95, no. 1 (March 2012): 14–23.

49. Jens Manuel Krogstad, "Puerto Ricans Leave in Record Numbers for Mainland U.S.," *Pew Research Center*, October 14, 2015, http://www.pewresearch.org/fact-tank/2015/10/14/puerto-ricans-leave-in-record-numbers-for-mainland-u-s/.

50. Duany, *The Puerto Rican Nation on the Move*, 283. On Puerto Ricanness within the Puerto Rican diaspora in Orlando, see Luis Sánchez, *The New Puerto Rico: Identity, Hybridity and Transnationalism within the Puerto Rican Community in Orlando, Florida* (Saarbrücken, Germany: VDM Verlag Dr. Müller, 2009), 65–85. Also see Bernarda Albertha Maria Kerkhof, "Contested Belonging: Circular Migration and Puerto Rican Identity" (PhD diss., University of Utrecht, Netherlands, 2000); also Jorge Duany, *Blurred Borders: Transnational Migration between the Hispanic Caribbean and the United States* (Chapel Hill: University of North Carolina Press, 2011), 105–33: "The Orlando Ricans: Overlapping Identity Discourses among Middle-Class Puerto Rican Immigrants."

51. Luis N. Rivera-Pagán, *Essays from the Diaspora* (México, DF: El Faro, 2002), 4, 5.

52. Rivera-Pagán, *Essays from the Diaspora*, 5–6.

53. Rivera-Pagán, *Essays from the Diaspora*, 6.

54. Jorge Duany writes that "between 1868 and 1895 the United States admitted only 690 Puerto Ricans....This small group of exiles has been called 'the Pilgrims of Freedom' because they supported the island's independence from Spain....Among them were prominent intellectuals such as Eugenio María de Hostos, Ramón Emeterio Betances, Segundo

Ruiz Belvis, Lola Rodríguez de Tió, Sotero Figueroa, and Arturo Alfonso Schomburg." In Duany, *Blurred Borders*, 48.

55. See United States District Court for the District of Puerto Rico, "The Flag of Puerto Rico," accessed May 21, 2017, http://www.prd .uscourts.gov/?q=node/243.

56. See Malavet, *America's Colony*, 93.

57. Nelson A. Denis, *War against All Puerto Ricans*, 299n34.

58. Ramón E. Soto-Crespo, *Mainland Passage: The Cultural Anomaly of Puerto Rico* (Minneapolis: University of Minnesota Press, 2009), 12. See Duany, *The Puerto Rican Nation on the Move*.

59. See José Luis González, *Puerto Rico: The Four-Storeyed Country and Other Essays*, trans. Gerald Guinness (New York: Markus Wiener, 1993), 85–90: "The 'Lamento Borincano': A Sociological Interpretation." Also see Flores, *The Diaspora Strikes Back: Caribeño Tales of Learning and Turning* (New York: Routledge, 2009), 57.

60. Aurora Levins Morales, "…And Even Castro Can't Change That!" in *This Bridge Called My Back: Writings by Radical Women of Color*, ed. Cherrie Moraga and Gloria Anzaldúa, 4th ed. (Albany: State University of New York Press, 2015), 48.

61. Levins Morales, *Remedios*, 196.

62. Richard Levins, "A Permanent and Personal Commitment," accessed May 21, 2017, http://www.peacehost.net/WhiteStar/Voices/ eng-levins.html.

63. Levins, "A Permanent and Personal Commitment."

64. "In Memoriam: Richard Levins, Ecologist, Biomathematician, and Philosopher of Science," Harvard T. J. Chan School of Public Health News, January 22, 2016, http://www.hsph.harvard.edu/news/features/ in-memoriam-richard-levins-ecologist-biomathematician-and -philosopher-of-science/.

65. Aurora Levins Morales, "Certified Organic Intellectual," in *Telling to Live: Latina Feminist Testimonials*, ed. the Latino Feminist Group (Luz del Alba Acevedo et al.) (Durham, NC: Duke University Press, 2001), 28.

66. Morales, "Certified Organic Intellectual," 28.

67. Aurora Levins Morales, "Child of the Américas," in *Getting Home Alive*, by Rosario Morales and Aurora Levins Morales (New York: Firebrand Books, 1986), 50.

68. Lourdes Rojas, "Latinas at the Crossroads: An Affirmation of Life in Rosario Morales and Aurora Levins Morales' *Getting Home Alive*," in *Breaking Boundaries: Latina Writing and Critical Readings*, ed. Asunción Horno Delgado (Amherst: University of Massachusetts Press, 1989), 175.

69. Levins Morales, *Getting Home Alive*, 138.

70. Morales, *Getting Home Alive*, 112.

71. Levins Morales writes, "After thirteen I grew up Jewish. Well, *one* of my worlds was Jewish, 100 percent Jewish, except for me. No, including me, because that was my place to become Jewish. I asked Lorna to teach me Yiddish, and I can still write *tish* for table—*tish, tishel, tishele*—a little table, holding only those few letters and the one song, so that I sit like all the other young ones born in this country—the amerikaner—sit smiling a silly uncomprehending smile at the joke in Yiddish while the others shout their laughter so that she turns to us and starts the story over again in English, 'A Jew and a Gentile went to heaven…,'" in Morales, *Getting Home Alive*, 113.

72. Aurora Levins Morales, "Tsu Got Vel Ikh Veynen," in Rosario Morales and Aurora Levins Morales, *Cosecha and Other Stories* (Cambridge, MA: Palabrera Press, 2014), 11.

73. Levins Morales, "Tsu Got Vel Ikh Veynen," 12–13.

74. Levins Morales, *Remedios*, 196.

75. Bernardo Vega, "Memoirs of Bernardo Vega (excerpts)," in *Hispanic New York: A Sourcebook*, ed. Claudio Iván Remeseira (New York: Columbia University Press, 2010), 77.

CHAPTER SEVENTEEN

LEARNING FROM THE OTHER

The Nostra Aetate *Trajectory in Our Time*

———ɯ———

Mary C. Boys, SNJM

The ratification of *Nostra Aetate* on September 28, 1965, at the Second Vatican Council is often spoken of as a "watershed event" or as a "turning point" in the Catholic Church's relationship with the Jewish people. Gregory Baum has characterized the church's new understanding of its relations with Jews and Judaism as the "most radical change in the ordinary magisterium of the church that emerged from the Council."[1] Michael Barnes has aptly spoken of it as a "conversion to the providential mystery of otherness."[2] In 2002, Walter Cardinal Kasper called Judaism a "sacrament of every otherness that as such the Church must learn to discern, recognize and celebrate."[3] Alberto Melloni later built on Kasper's phrase:

> In the text and in life, in experience and in history, Judaism has become the paradigm not only of interreligious dialogue, but also the paradigm of every difference, the sacrament of all otherness, the *locus theologicus* where the Christians can show that every "other" alludes in its very alterity to the One who is totally other and yet is totally close to every woman and to every man.[4]

For the contributors to this book in honor of the eminent ethicist John Pawlikowski, the *Nostra Aetate* trajectory indeed has radical

298

implications, including how we might engage otherness. By "trajectory," I refer to the rich, complex commentary on *Nostra Aetate* since 1965 manifest in official texts and theological exchanges, as well as in various dialogues.[5] The Holy See has promulgated important declarations through its Commission on Religious Relations with the Jews and Pontifical Biblical Commission; papal speeches and activities, as well as statements from (or authorized by) episcopal conferences provide other official texts.[6] The past fifty years have seen an astonishing amount of theological analysis in an array of publications, including an online peer-reviewed journal (*Studies in Jewish-Christian Relations*), websites, and a copious library of books and articles—many authored by John Pawlikowski and far more reflecting his influence.

In my experience, however, particularly in the present U.S. Catholic Church, the radical nature of this trajectory is too little recognized. It is rare that I hear a sermon shaped by the body of the church's recent teaching on Jews and Judaism. Rather, I frequently hear "misplaced caricaturistic opposites: e.g.: legalism-faith; flesh-spirit; fear-love; doctrine-life; earth-heaven; cult-works; institutional sclerosis-prophetic élan; promise-realization."[7] Occasionally, passing references are made to *Nostra Aetate* 4, especially to the key assertion that "what happened in His passion cannot be blamed upon all the Jews then living, without distinction, nor upon the Jews of today." Little or no explanation, however, accompanies the reference, thereby obscuring its significance. To those mindful of John's passion narrative, in which "the Jews" shout, "Away with him! Away with him! Crucify him!" (John 19:15), the citation from *Nostra Aetate* 4 seems anomalous.

The reality is that weighty biblical and theological arguments undergird the *Nostra Aetate* trajectory, but the profundity of those arguments is obscured by lack of sufficient explanation, ambiguity, and the occasional contradiction.[8] It is misleading to think that the church can simply flip a theological switch, claiming in essence, "In the past we taught that the Jews were responsible for the death of Jesus, but now we teach that Jews as a people should not be blamed for the crucifixion." Radical change demands a substantive account.

If the church is to do justice to what *Nostra Aetate* inaugurated, it is requisite to acknowledge how formidable it is to live into the "providential mystery of otherness." As the tragic resurgence of nationalist and racist movements (including antisemitism) in our time reveals, encountering "otherness" is challenging. An aversion to difference and a reversion to tribalism are aspects of the human condition that impede the formation of just societies and maintain inequality. Social media compounds the problem by serving as a carrier for fake news, including outrageous and baseless accusations that blatantly disparage some "other" who differs religiously, ethnically, or by skin color. As an educator, I am deeply worried about the lack of critical thinking skills and media literacy apparent in the susceptibility to "truthiness," that is, the "quality of preferring concepts or facts one wishes to be true, rather than concepts or facts known to be true."[9] As a theologian I am concerned that religious leaders pay too little heed to Judaism as a "sacrament of otherness."

Because Jews have been the church's *quintessential other* for nearly two millennia, giving fresh resonance to the depth and breadth of the *Nostra Aetate* trajectory that transformed enmity into a sibling relationship may well serve as a vital object lesson in changing attitudes to the "other." How might the church tell this story in such a manner as to get people's attention and motivate them to think more deeply about relations between Christians and Jews? In the confines of this essay, I pose two possibilities: situating Vatican II in its historical and cultural context, and confessing to the church's painful history vis-à-vis Judaism while committing to fostering a more just relationship.

CONTEXT

Mere passing references to Vatican II will not suffice, particularly as more than fifty years have passed since its conclusion. The Council's story needs to be told, beginning with the bold decision of Pope John XXIII fifty-eight years ago (January 25, 1959) to convene a council in order to renew the church (*aggiornamento*). It is a dramatic story of a world church assembling from across the globe, theological experts briefing bishops in informal sessions, and the hierarchy conversing with official observers from Protestant and Orthodox churches.[10] It is also a story of political intrigue, conflict, and compromise. Of course, no one story of the Council is adequate to the ferocity with which its significance continues to be argued.[11] From my own perspective, John O'Malley's characterization of the way Vatican II affected the church's posture and tone is crucial to the story. It was movement

> from commands to invitations, from laws to ideals, from definition to mystery, from threats to persuasion, from coercion to conscience, from monologue to dialogue, from ruling to serving, from withdrawn to integrated, from vertical to horizontal, from exclusion to inclusions, from hostility to friendship, from rivalry to partnership, from suspicion to trust, from static to ongoing, from passive acceptance to active engagement, from fault-finding to appreciation, from prescriptive to principled, from behavior modification to inner appropriation.[12]

Historian John Connelly's book *From Enemy to Brother* provides a fascinating backstory to the theological evolution that eventuated in *Nostra Aetate*. His book testifies to the importance of perspectives brought by "the other," as converts to Catholicism played the crucial role: "Without converts to Catholicism, the Catholic Church would never have 'thought its way' out of the challenges of racist anti-Judaism."[13] Connelly exposes the lethal mix of racist and anti-Jewish theology that dominated Catholic life in Germany in the 1930s. He then traces the slow unfolding of new insights significantly shaped by encounter with the Jewish other. It is worth pausing here to look more closely at two figures who stand out in Connelly's telling, Johannes Oesterreicher and Karl Thieme. Their opposition to antisemitism and painstaking theological reflection provided the fundamental foundation for *Nostra Aetate*.

The first systematic critiques of antisemitism appeared in four Catholic journals in Vienna in 1937, including that of Johannes Oesterreicher, *Die Erfüllung*. Oesterreicher, a convert from Judaism who became a priest, countered the views of those who claimed that baptism did not erase "blood and race"—that Jewish converts were not equal to Aryans because of their foreign blood and hereditary sin. In 1940, Oesterreicher published *Racisme, antisémitisme, antichristianism: Documents et critique*.[14]

Oesterreicher's principal collaborator in those years was Karl Thieme, a former Lutheran who became a Catholic because he was appalled by the control the Nazis exerted over German Protestantism. In seeking admission to the Catholic Church, in October 1933 he wrote to Pope Pius XI that Jesus "loved his Jewish people, even if unbaptized, with burning heart, as we love our own."[15] Thieme denounced the Nuremberg racial laws as "outrageous and barbarous" denials of a person's intellectual and spiritual character. Having coauthored a forty-page memorandum against antisemitism that Oesterreicher had published in *Erfüllung* in 1937, Thieme wrote again to the pope in late 1938, requesting that his Christmas address "contain a word for the persecuted Jews." No such word was forthcoming, nor did the Vatican follow Thieme's lead and condemn the Nuremberg laws.

Oesterreicher, Thieme, and others who denounced antisemitism as racist were courageous, even audacious. Theirs was a lonely position to take, requiring them to oppose prominent Catholic scholars and church officials who viewed the Nazi racial laws as according with the divine will. Thieme, however, was one of the very few who had not converted from Judaism; thus, his consistent denunciation of antisemitism was unrelated to the need of the Jewish converts to argue that their Jewish origins had not made them lesser Christians.

Even with their courageous opposition to antisemitism, both he and Oesterreicher through the 1930s and 1940s maintained a traditional view of Jews as guilty of the death of Christ; they believed that Jewish suffering would endure until Jews recognized Jesus as the Messiah. Oesterreicher had founded the Viennese Mission to the Jews in 1934, and continued his missionary efforts through the 1940s after he immigrated to New York. In Thieme's 1945 book, *Kirche und Synagoge*, he argued that God was punishing two peoples: Germans and Jews. When Oesterreicher objected that Thieme had carried classic Lutheran disdain into Catholicism, Thieme responded, "God is an enemy to them only because they were hostile to him and are hostile to him and reject his witnesses as incorporated in Christians in the present day."[16]

By the 1950s, however, Thieme was speaking quite a different language. The postwar years afforded him an opportunity to converse with Jews, and he began to realize how much conversionary language offended them. Candid correspondence with Martin Buber ultimately convinced him that Jews were the "older brothers" of Christians—not the younger, prodigal son superseded by Christians. Rather, Jews were like the loyal son whose father declared, "You are always with me and everything that is mine is yours." Yet his conversations with Buber, Theodore Adorno, Jules Isaac, and others triggered theological disequilibrium. Thieme confessed to Adorno that he was walking on a "razor sharp ridge," and he feared falling into either anti-Judaism or heresy.

His theological breakthrough came via a fresh reading of Romans 11:23–27, particularly verses 25–26: "So that you may not claim to be wiser than you are, brothers and sisters, I want you to understanding this mystery: a hardening has come upon part of Israel, *until the full number of the Gentiles has come in. And so all Israel will be saved*" (emphasis added). Thieme read Paul as claiming that Israel's salvation would come only after the "full number of the Gentiles" had entered God's reign. Thus, he wrote to Buber that the final reconciliation of Jews and Christians could come only when "Christians of Pagan origin have given evidence for their faith through a practical life of love."[17]

Thieme referred to his changed understanding of Judaism as a conversion. He declared in a public letter of August 1950 that he was convinced that a "Jewish person, not only as an individual person, but also in a certain sense precisely as a '*Jew* can be pleasing to God.'" Thieme continued, "I am certain that if God's grace permits 'Israel according to the flesh' to continue to exist to the end of time, and *then* made recipient of very great compassion, then their character as chosen people has not been abolished, but only suspended in some of its effects."[18] Christians were called to follow the teachings of Christ. Evangelization should be by deed rather than word.

The postwar theological exchanges between Oesterreicher and Thieme and their Jewish interlocutors marked the first time since

Justin Martyr's *Dialogue with Trypho* that Jews and Christians had embarked on a serious theological exchange, other than the debate over Jesus' messianic status. Connelly observes,

> Once Christians began talking to Jews about theology— whether to the French thinkers Jules Isaac and Edmond Fleg, Swiss rabbis Eugen Messinger and Lothar Rothschild, or German-Jewish intellectuals such as Martin Buber or Schalom Ben Chorim—they began to realize how obscene much of their own teaching sounded when spoken in the shadow of the war's crimes.[19]

By 1954, Thieme had arrived at an important, if controversial formulation. He referred to Jews as "our separated 'elder brethren' of the stem of Abraham." With them, Christians hope "for the day of the Lord, which will surely come. But, in still irreconcilable contrast with them, we hope for that day to be the glorious enthronement of Him who began His kingship in the obscurity of His Cross and resurrection: the returning Jesus of Nazareth."[20] Although Jews and Christians differed in how they understood salvation, Thieme encouraged discerning exchange until the day came when there would be "one flock and one shepherd" (John 10:16) and when "all peoples would serve God shoulder to shoulder" (Zeph 3:9).

His former partner Oesterreicher objected to Thieme's language about Jews as "elder brothers." Yet over the course of the next decade, Oesterreicher rethought this criticism, due in large measure to his own conversations with Jewish interlocutors and then his participation in the subcommittee that drafted what was eventually ratified as *Nostra Aetate* 4. Thieme's influence on *Nostra Aetate* is evident, not only in the use of Romans 11, but also in the eschatological vision of Zephaniah. Although he did not live to witness *Nostra Aetate*, it reflects his thinking more than anyone else.

The work of Oesterreicher and Thieme hints at just how fraught the theological journey to *Nostre Aetate* was. Their perseverance in challenging how the church related to Jews is a model for those who advocate for a church that lives out the *Nostra Aetate* trajectory more fully.

CONFESSION AND RECOMMITMENT

The scandal of clergy sexual abuse in the Catholic Church has done untold damage. Among its evils is the failure of many church leaders, even at the highest levels, to confront and discipline perpetrators; in far too many cases, protecting institutional interests took precedence over care for victims. Analogously, church leaders have been reluctant to confess to the extent of the church's "tortured history" with Jews, which has the effect of hiding the radical change that Baum identified.[21] Certainly, a second, more candid edition of *We Remember: A Reflection on the Shoah* would be valuable. Official documents, however solid, need to be complemented with more accessible and memorable modes of communication, particularly images, stories, and symbols.

The story of the ghetto in Rome, where that city's Jews were confined in poverty and squalor from 1555 to 1870, encompasses both the tormented history and its transformation. In the papal bull *Cum Nimis Absurdum* of July 12, 1555, Pope Paul IV strikingly expressed his disdain for Jews:

> Since it is absurd and improper that Jews—whose own guilt has consigned them to perpetual servitude—under the pretext that Christian piety receives them and tolerates their presence should be ingrates to Christians, so that they attempt to exchange the servitude they owe to Christians for dominion over them; we—to whose notice it has lately come that these Jews, in our dear city and in some other cites, holdings, and territories of the Holy Roman Church, have erupted into insolence: they presume not only to dwell side by side with Christians and near their churches, with no distinct habit to separate them, but even to erect homes in the more noble sections and streets of the cities, holdings, and territories where they dwell, and to buy and possess fixed property, and to have nurses, housemaids, and other hired Christian servants, and to perpetrate many other things in ignominy and contempt of the Christian name—considering that the Roman Church tolerates the

Jews in testimony of the true Christian faith and to end that they, led by the piety and kindness of the Apostolic See, should at length recognize their errors, and make all haste to arrive at the true light of the Catholic faith, and thereby to agree that, as long as they persist in their errors, they should recognize through experience that they have been made slaves while Christians have been made free through Jesus Christ, God and our Lord, and that it is iniquitous that the children of the free woman should serve the children of the maid-servant.[22]

On July 26, 1555, all of Rome's Jews were rounded up and required to live in a seven-acre section of the city along the Tiber, which frequently flooded the ghetto. By separating and restricting Jews so that they lived in misery, Pope Paul IV hoped that such dire conditions would inspire them to convert.[23] Not only were they forbidden to own property and forced to wear distinctive clothing, but they were also compelled to stand outside the Church of San Gregorio della Divina Pietà on the Sabbath to listen to conversionary sermons. Apparently, many Jews inserted wax in their ears so as to dull the message. When San Gregorio was renovated in 1858, an inscription was put on the façade in Latin and in Hebrew:

I held out my hands all day long
   to a rebellious people,
who walk in a way that is not good,
   following their own devices;
a people who provoke me
   to my face continually. (Isa 65:2–3)

In the church's theology of the time, by refusing to convert, Jews were considered unfaithful to God—perfidious.

In 1870, in the wake of the unification of Italy and the end of the Papal States, the ghetto was demolished and Jews given citizenship. So the ghetto ended—though the inscription remains on the Church of San Gregorio as testimony to the derisive attitude toward Jews. Rome's magnificent Great Synagogue (Templo Maggione di

Roma) built between 1901 and 1904 on the site of the ghetto's synagogue sits just west of San Gregorio, bearing witness to the perseverance of Roman Jews.[24]

Today, in addition to the Great Synagogue, Rome's ghetto (or Jewish Quarter) is the site of numerous kosher restaurants, bakeries, and specialty shops. It is both a gathering spot for Rome's Jews and a major tourist site. While wandering there in 2014, I noticed a large photo of a smiling Pope Francis prominently displayed in a bakery close to the Great Synagogue—a symbol of the transformation of the ghetto.

Yet there is another ghetto, one much more difficult to dismantle. In many respects the church has confined Judaism to a "theological ghetto," by virtue of teachings that both distorted and denigrated Judaism. I first thought of this term while reading personal reflections by the French Jewish historian Jules Isaac regarding his momentous meeting with Pope John XXIII in June 1961. Isaac's notes reminisced on the task he had set for himself: to help John XXIII understand that the Catholic Church had enclosed "old Israel" not only in a physical ghetto but also in a spiritual ghetto. Isaac asked himself, "How to make someone understand, in a few minutes, what this spiritual ghetto has been in which the Church has progressively enclosed the old Israel—at the same time as the physical ghetto."[25]

The theological ghetto constricts Judaism insofar as it defines that tradition only from Catholic perspectives and within Catholic categories. In the past, virtually no effort was made to understand Judaism on its own terms or to explore its depth and breadth. Rather, Judaism became the principal other to Christianity. Held responsible as a people for having crucified Jesus Christ and, therefore liable to the charge of being "Christ killers," Jews were presented as unfaithful to God and blind to his ways. Their covenant superseded by Christianity's new covenant in Christ, Jews had no share in salvation. One classic formulation from the General Council of Florence (1442) asserts,

> [The Holy Roman church] firmly believes, professes and teaches that the legal [statutes] of the Old Testament or Mosaic Law, divided into ceremonies, holy sacrifices and

sacraments, were instituted to signify something to come, and therefore, although in that age they were fitting for divine worship, they have ceased with the advent of our Lord Jesus Christ, whom they signified....Therefore, she denounces as foreign to the faith of Christ all those who after that time observe circumcision, the Sabbath and other laws, and she asserts that they can in no way be sharers of eternal salvation, unless they sometime turn away from their errors.[26]

From the perspective of the theological ghetto, Jews had to undergo conversion to Christianity if they had hope of salvation. Even after *Nostra Aetate*, this understanding lingers. Consider, for example, the debate over the Good Friday Prayer for the Jews composed by then Pope Benedict XVI in 2007 with the subtitle "Pro Conversione Iudaeorum." A 2008 publication of the United States Conference of Catholic Bishops, *Doctrinal Elements of a Curriculum Framework for the Development of Catechetical Materials for Young People of High School Age*, lists bringing "all to Jesus Christ and to his Church" as one of four aims of dialogue with Jews.[27] In a 2012 issue of *Theological Studies*, Gavin D'Costa argued "mission to the Jews is theologically legitimate"; the magisterium teaches that "mission to the Jewish people and individuals is required if Catholics are to be faithful to the truth of the gospel."[28]

Responses by Edward Kessler and John Pawlikowski debate D'Costa's claims in that same issue.[29] Pawlikowski argues for the importance of integrating classical theological views with the actual experience of encounter with those of other traditions of faith, including Jews. He writes, "Yet dialogue, while it definitely must be pursued on a theological plane for genuine authenticity, is first and foremost a personal encounter....I may not have as yet an adequate new theology of interreligious relations, but I can no longer continue merely with the classical theological foundations."[30] For Pawlikowski, mission to the Jews must be "radically rethought within Christian theology."[31]

Fundamental to any rethinking of Christian theology in relationship to Jews is commitment to the imperative initially expressed in 1975 by the Vatican Commission for Religious Relations with the

Jews (and reiterated a decade later in a subsequent document): "On the practical level in particular, Christians must strive to acquire a better knowledge of Judaism: they must strive to learn by what essential traits the Jews define themselves in light of their own religious experience."[32] A host of resources is available, including *The Jewish Annotated New Testament* and *The Jewish Study Bible*; these texts should be in the library of every homilist.[33] The *Nostra Aetate* trajectory requires learning, which is best done in the presence of the Jewish other, preferably by one's side, but also through the medium of print or video.

Jews and Christians, in the words of Cardinal Kasper, share a "vocation to a common witness to the one God and his commandments":

> This includes the unmasking and prophetic criticism of the new false gods and idols of our time, and a shared commitment to human dignity, to justice and peace in the world, to the dignity and worth of the family, and to the integrity of creation. Not least, Jews and Christians can together give witness to the dialogue, cooperation, and reconciliation that are possible even after a difficult and complex history. Likewise, they can stand together for *teshuvah*, i.e., for repentance and reconciliation.[34]

In our time (*nostra aetate*), the false gods of nationalism and racism belie human dignity and subvert reconciliation. In our time, the idol of "truthiness" gives sanction to shallow and delusional thinking. In our time, cavalier denials of climate change put all creation at risk.

If ever there were a time when recommitment to the meaning of Vatican II's *Nostra Aetate* and its legacy is vital, it is now:

> Dialogue with Judaism may help Christians to divine the presence of God in other faith traditions than Judaism, or indeed in other groups of humanity who differ from us in any way, such as in terms of ethnicity, culture, or gender. Surely in a world plagued by interreligious conflict, this

potentiality must be earnestly pursued. Indeed, one wonders about the impact on the entire world if Christians and Jews are able to work through their history of hostility and were to indeed become "blessings for each other."[35]

Nostra Aetate launched a movement of reconciliation. It calls us in our time to engage with the other, so that we might be a sign of hope to a world in which peace is so elusive.

Notes

1. Gregory Baum, "The Social Context of American Catholic Theology," *Proceedings of the Catholic Theological Society of America* 41 (1986): 83–100, esp. 87. John Pawlikowski often cites Baum's statement.

2. Michael Barnes, *Theology and the Dialogue of Religions*, Cambridge Studies in Christian Doctrine (Cambridge: Cambridge University Press, 2002), 239.

3. Walter Cardinal Kasper, "Address on the 37th Anniversary of Nostra Aetate," Oct. 28, 2002, http://www.jcrelations.net/Judaism+as+%22Sacrament+of+Otherness%22.2816.0.html?L=3.

4. Alberto Melloni, "Nostra Aetate and the Discovery of the Sacrament of Otherness," in *The Catholic Church and the Jewish People: Recent Reflections from Rome*, ed. Philip A. Cunningham (New York: Fordham University Press, 2007), 151.

5. See my article "The Nostra Aetate Trajectory: Holding Our Theological Bow Differently," in *Never Revoked:* Nostra Aetate *as Ongoing Challenge for Jewish-Christian Dialogue*, Louvain Theological and Pastoral Monographs 40, ed. Maryanne Moyaert and Didier Pollefeyt (Leuven, Belgium: Peeters, 2009), 133–57.

6. For discussion of major documents up to 2000, see my *Has God Only One Blessing? Judaism as a Source of Christian Self-Understanding* (New York: Paulist Press, 2000), 252.

7. Belgian National Catholic Commission for Relations between Christians and Jews, "Eighteen Theological Theses" (1973), in *Stepping Stones to Further Jewish-Christian Relations*, ed. Helga Croner (New York: Stimulus Books, 1977), 58.

8. On the ambiguity and contradiction, see my "Does the Catholic Church Have a Mission 'with' Jews or 'to' Jews?" *Studies in Christian-*

Jewish Relations 3, no. 1 (2008): 1–19, http://escholarship.bc.edu/scjr/vol3.

9. Stephen Colbert originated the term; see http://www.cc.com/video-clips/63ite2/the-colbert-report-the-word---truthiness (accessed August 1, 2017). In 2005, the American Dialect Society, from which the definition is taken, named *truthiness* its word of the year, as did Merriam-Webster the following year. See https://www.merriam-webster.com/press-release/2006-word-of-the-year (accessed August 1, 2017).

10. Tragically, Catholic women played little role, as over the course of the Council's four sessions, only twenty-three women were invited, and then only as auditors. See Carmel McEnroy, *Guests in Their Own House: The Women of Vatican II* (New York: Crossroad, 1996).

11. See Massimo Faggioli, *Vatican II: The Battle for Meaning* (New York: Paulist Press, 2012); *50 Years On: Probing the Riches of Vatican II*, ed. David G. Schultenover (Collegeville, MN: Liturgical Press, 2015), 51.

12. John W. O'Malley, *What Happed at Vatican II?* (Cambridge, MA: Belknap Press, 2008), 307.

13. John Connelly, *From Enemy to Brother: The Revolution in Catholic Teaching on the Jews, 1933–1965* (Cambridge, MA: Harvard University Press, 2012), 287.

14. John Oesterreicher, *Racism,antisémitisme, antichristianisme, documents et critique* (New York: Éditions de la Maison française, 1943).

15. Cited in Connelly, *From Enemy to Brother*, 123.

16. Connelly, *From Enemy to Brother*, 195.

17. Connelly, *From Enemy to Brother*, 203.

18. Connelly, *From Enemy to Brother,* 204–5.

19. Connelly, *From Enemy to Brother*, 176.

20. Connelly, *From Enemy to Brother*, 227.

21. See the 1998 document, *We Remember: A Reflection on the Shoah*, by the Commission for Religious Relations with the Jews, chap. 3: "The history of relations between Jews and Christians is a tormented one," accessed August 1, 2017, http://www.vatican.va/roman_curia/pontifical_councils/chrstuni/documents/rc_pc_chrstuni_doc_16031998_shoah_en.html.

22. Cited in Kenneth Stow, *Catholic Thought and Papal Jewry Policy 1555–1593* (New York: The Jewish Theological Seminary of America, 1977), 294. In the pope's thinking, "guilt" for the crucifixion is the principal cause of their "perpetual servitude."

23. See Kenneth Stow, "The Proper Meaning of '*Cum Nimis Absurdum*," *The Jewish Quarterly Review* 4 (1981): 251–52. Preceding the Rome ghetto was the one in Venice, decreed in 1516; after the ghetto in Rome was established, other Italian ghettos were established. See Kenneth Stow, "Ghetto," in *A Dictionary of Jewish-Christian Relations*, ed. Edward Kessler and Neil Wenborn (Cambridge: Cambridge University Press, 2005), 166.

24. A number of short videos on the Jewish ghetto in Rome are available on YouTube; the following has scenes of both the Great Synagogue and of the Church of San Gregorio: https://www.youtube.com/watch?v=Wupt9lAEh8c (accessed August 1, 2017).

25. Jules Isaac, "Notes on a Week in Rome," *SIDIC* 3 (1968): 11; see http://www.notredamedesion.org/en/dialogue_docs.php?a=3b&id=690 (accessed August 1, 2017). (SIDIC is the acronym for Service International de Documentation Judeo-Chretienne, a project of the Sisters of Our Lady of Sion.) See also Norman C. Tobias, *Jewish Conscience of the Church: Jules Isaac and the Second Vatican Council* (New York: Palgrave Macmillan, 2017).

26. See *The Christian Faith in the Doctrinal Documents of the Catholic Church*, ed. Josef Neuner and Jacques Dupuis, rev. ed. (New York: Alba House, 1996), nn. 1003 and 1004. For analysis of the context, see Jacques Dupuis, *Toward a Christian Theology of Religious Pluralism* (Maryknoll, NY: Orbis Books, 1997), 84–109.

27. A later edition of *Doctrinal Elements*, found as an appendix in *Handbook on the Conformity Review Process* by the Sub-committee on the Catechism of the USCCB's Committee on Evangelization and Catechesis, modifies this fourth aim: "Deepen mutual understanding of the one God and his plan for the world" (211). No explanation for the change was given. See http://www.usccb.org/about/evangelization-and-catechesis/subcommittee-on-catechism/upload/Conformity-Review-full-text-FINAL-Sept.pdf (accessed August 1, 2017).

28. Gavin G. D'Costa, "What Does the Catholic Church Teach about Mission to the Jewish People?" *Theological Studies* 73, no. 3 (2012): 590–613.

29. Edward Kessler, "A Jewish Response to Gavin D'Costa," *Theological Studies* 73, no. 3 (2012): 614–28, and John T. Pawlikowski, "A Catholic Response to Gavin D'Costa," *Theological Studies* 73, no. 3 (2012): 629–40.

30. Pawlikowski, "A Catholic Response," 632.

31. Pawlikowski, "A Catholic Response," 638.

32. Commission on Religious Relations with the Jews, "Guidelines and Suggestions for Implementing the Conciliar Declaration *Nostra Aetate*" (1975), and "Notes on the Correct Way to Present the Jews and Judaism in Preaching and Catechesis in the Roman Catholic Church" (1985); texts available at http://www.ccjr.us/dialogika-resources/ documents-and-statements/roman-catholic/vatican-curia (accessed August 1, 2017).

33. See *The Jewish Annotated New Testament*, 2nd ed., ed. Amy-Jill Levine and Marc Z. Brettler (New York: Oxford University Press, 2017); *The Jewish Study Bible*, ed. Adele Berlin and Marc Z. Brettler, 2nd ed. (New York: Oxford University Press, 2014).

34. Walter Cardinal Kasper, "Foreword," in *Christ Jesus and the Jewish People Today: New Explorations of Theological Interrelationships*, ed. Philip A. Cunningham et al. (Grand Rapids, MI: Wm. B. Eerdmans, 2011), xvii.

35. Philip A. Cunningham, "Judaism as a Sacrament of Otherness," accessed August 1, 2017, http://www.jcrelations.net/Judaism+as+ %22Sacrament+of+Otherness%22.2816.0.html?L=3.

CHAPTER EIGHTEEN

PEDAGOGICAL/PASTORAL PERSPECTIVE: JOHN PAWLIKOWSKI, INTERFAITH LEADER

A Jewish Tribute

―⁂―

Yehezkel Landau

I have had the privilege of knowing Fr. John Pawlikowski and following his work for more than thirty-five years. As a public Catholic theologian, social ethicist, educator, and international interfaith leader,
John has been a role model for many others—myself, as a Jew,
included. He has raised the bar of excellence and integrity in all these
fields very high. His scholarly and more popular writings transcend
the boundaries that separate religious communities or academic disciplines. In sum, he has inspired at least two generations of students,
teachers, and interfaith activists who have greatly benefited from his
wisdom and who have been stretched in their thinking and their
actions by the challenges he has posed to us all.

John's first and primary audience has always been his fellow
Catholics. He has been relentless in trying to overcome the tragic
legacy of Catholic anti-Judaism. Like others in the interfaith arena
who are committed to healing the Christian-Jewish rift, John is aware
that this is a long-range effort, not a quick fix. In the case of the
Roman Catholic Church, papal declarations and gestures can help,[1]
but two millennia of supersessionism, forced conversions, blood
libels, and recurring violence cannot be repaired overnight, or even in
one generation. John's writings have celebrated the radical shift in

314

Catholicism's relations with Jews and Judaism reflected in *Nostra Aetate*, the historic declaration issued by the Second Vatican Council. But in the decades since its promulgation in 1965, he has frequently advocated for additional official Catholic statements and actions to promote Christian-Jewish reconciliation. Beyond that, he has insisted that the recent changes in Christian theology be reflected in new articulations of Christian identity, a new ecclesiology, and a new Christian understanding of religious pluralism.[2]

John's appeals and admonitions have not been restricted to fellow Christians. He has also urged Jews to change their attitudes and behavior toward other faith communities, especially Christians. Before the *Dabru Emet* statement was issued in 2000 by over 220 Jewish scholars and religious leaders, calling on fellow Jews to view Christianity more positively, John publicly challenged his Jewish interlocutors to demonstrate reciprocity for the changes in Catholic and Protestant teaching about Judaism. As a prophetic witness challenging both Christians and Jews, he is an exemplar of faithful, honest, and loving criticism, or what Jewish tradition would call a combination of *teshuvah* (repentance and reorientation), *tokhachah* (compassionate critique), and *tikkun* (moral rectification, or, in the language of this volume, "righting relations" that have been severely damaged over centuries).

I first met John when he came to Jerusalem in September 1981 and delivered a guest lecture for the Israel Interfaith Association, where I was then a staff member. As editor of the association's newsletter, *Interfaith Israel*, I included excerpts from John's remarks in the May 1982 edition. His presentation was entitled "Modern Christologies in Light of Recent Developments in Jewish-Christian Relations," and it prefigured his Stimulus Book published soon after by Paulist Press.[3] I recall being struck by John's analytical and rhetorical gifts, and by his personal courage, as he shared his thoughts with the large audience assembled to hear him. In reflecting on how historical events, including "the tenacious vitality of the people Israel despite events like the Nazi Holocaust," have colored his thinking and his faith orientation, John said, "Let me assert without qualification that unless a Christian is prepared to accept a developmental notion of revelation, I see little hope in overcoming the dominance of the messianic fulfillment Christology in the churches with the disastrous consequences it has had for the image of Jews and Judaism."[4]

John was affirming that ideas have consequences. And theological ideas, with their claims about ultimate reality and transcendent truth, have a unique potential for doing great harm as well as great good. This lesson has been an integral part of John's witness as a public theologian. Anyone engaged in theological reflection or teaching needs to heed John's words. Like a biblical prophet, his message includes both warning and hope, admonition as well as encouragement to do better.

As he examined ideas and their import, one of John's laudable traits became readily apparent: his capacity for judicious discernment. He is careful and measured in his criticism, avoiding polemics. For example, when addressing the impact of the liberation theologian Gustavo Gutierrez, he offered this analysis:

> With respect to the question of Christology and Judaism, the position of Gustavo Gutierrez can only be assessed as a mixed blessing. It is encouraging to find missing from his work some of the classic stereotypes of Judaism, such as those connected with responsibility for the death of Jesus. His attempt to link the Exodus and the Christ event has definite possibilities for further development, and his emphasis on history as the unfulfilled side of the promise will find a genuine resonance within Jewish religious tradition. While he has far from an adequate understanding of the Torah tradition in Judaism, he at least avoids framing his understanding of the liberation to be found in the Christ event around the notion of freedom from Jewish legalism in the way that Pannenberg, Moltmann and Küng do. Yet enough of the traditional outlook in the Church regarding the invalidity of Judaism after Christ has crept into *A Theology of Liberation* to merit severe criticism of Gutierrez on this score.[5]

Liberation through Christ, as experienced and celebrated by believing Christians, is a subject John also addressed in his 1981

Jerusalem lecture. Reflecting on how Christian-Jewish dialogue in our time has changed Christian thinking on this matter, he said,

> Too often the Christian sense of liberation to be found in Jesus is stated in too general a way. Liberation cannot become fully implemented in a society until it has been transformed into socio-cultural structures. This is what the process of Torah was all about. Jesus himself, as a son of the Pharisaic revolution, was certainly aware of the need for this. But later Christian thought too often forgot this fact, thereby abandoning the quest for justice, the struggle against social structural sin, that is central to any authentic Christology. The Jewish-Christian dialogue, by enabling Christians to truly understand the function of Torah, can help the church move away from more generalized statements about the freedom found in Christ Jesus to action that creates liberating structures in our society.[6]

In these remarks, we can see the different aspects of John's vocation coalescing in a powerful way: the theologian, the social ethicist, the public educator, and the pioneer in Christian-Jewish relations. We can also recognize a true interfaith leader, using his gifts of thought and speech to articulate the practical benefits of a new theological understanding. For John, paradigm shifts in thought have no practical meaning if they do not lead to greater moral awareness that can transform human relations. And, for John, it is the living laboratory of interfaith relations, especially between Christians and Jews, that remains the central crucible for innovative thinking and deepened ethical responsibility.

Indeed, responsibility is a key concept and essential virtue for John. He often uses that term, along with its adjectival and adverbial forms, when inviting others to aspire to loftier moral heights. It is worth citing some illustrations in a presentation he delivered at Florida Atlantic University in February 2007. That talk was entitled "Catholicism's New Outreach to Jews and Muslims." At the time, John was not only a professor of social ethics and director of the Catholic-Jewish Studies Program at Catholic Theological Union; he was also the president of the International Council of Christians and Jews, which includes an Abrahamic Forum bringing together all three major monotheistic faiths. Speaking five and a half years after the terrorist attacks on September 11, 2001, John focused part of his presentation on the need "for overcoming the association of religion and violence we witnessed on 9/11."[7] John argued that for any religious witness to be credible in this regard, it has to acknowledge honestly past instances when the speaker's faith community committed or condoned violence. He added that such an honest confession needs to demonstrate genuine contrition, as well.

In his Florida Atlantic University presentation, John offered some cautionary advice for those engaged in interfaith relations: representatives of "each religious tradition must be careful in not highlighting the views of people in the other faith communities who have little status among their fellow believers."[8] This guideline was meant to prevent situations in which a partisan advocate in one faith community, often with a self-aggrandizing rather than a self-critical motive, cites an outlier in another community—who may, in contrast, be very self-critical—to substantiate his or her judgmental position. John qualified his point:

> To be sure, there is a fine line here. We do not want to engage only official institutional types. Certainly, people who are willing to critique *responsibly* their own religious tradition with respect to its views of other faiths must be included [in interfaith dialogues]. But it is destructive of genuine conversation if one community promotes the views of a person in another faith community who is not merely a *responsible* critic but really stands on the very fringe of that tradition. Obviously no hard and fast guidelines can be put forward in this regard. What is required, however, is sensitivity and a willingness to consult with key people in the other tradition.[9]

John's insistence on responsibility, for individuals and for institutions like the Catholic Church, reflects his deep concern as an ethicist for moral accountability as an index of faithfulness to one's tradition, to one's community, and ultimately to God. He has developed the personal credibility to hold others to this standard of behavior because his own conduct, as an intellectual and as a social activist, is in accord with that standard. No one could accuse John of being a "fringe" critic of his own church, for he is greatly respected by fellow Catholics. And when he directs a moral challenge to Jews, he has their respect, too, since he has demonstrated self-criticism toward his own tradition and has been on the front lines defending Jews, Judaism, and the state of Israel against harsher, less compassionate, critics. This is a crucial point, since some other Christians adopt a self-proclaimed "prophetic" stance when criticizing certain mainstream Jewish policies and statements, especially regarding the security and welfare of Israel. Sadly, many of them express their opposition without any love or sympathy for Israelis. It is John's longstanding solidarity with Jews, rooted in his sensitivity to their post-Holocaust sense of vulnerability, that gives him the moral standing to direct his own criticisms of Israeli government policies, especially regarding the Palestinians.[10] He also upholds a single standard of justice, rather than the double standard reflected in too many declarations that single out the state of Israel for moral reproach.

"The Nazi Holocaust has always been in the forefront of my approach, as a social ethicist, to contemporary moral perspectives," John wrote in a 2011 essay for the journal *Peace and Change*.[11] In that essay John addressed the moral challenges presented by the Israeli-Palestinian conflict, with the Holocaust in the background as both an unprecedented catastrophe for the Jewish people and as a moral touchstone for all of humanity. He emphasized the dignity of every human being as "the guiding moral principle" for ethical judgments in the political sphere and as an essential counterweight to state power.[12] He went on to argue, "In such a perspective, authentic religious vision in global society must see the survival of all persons as integral to the survival of any particular religious or national community." Expounding further, John wrote,

> There is no way for any religious or political community to survive meaningfully if it allows the death or suffering of other people to become a byproduct of its efforts at self-

preservation, no matter how legitimate that effort at self-preservation might be. This certainly applies to the various religious and national communities in Israel/Palestine, all of whom see their situation as one of "survival." "Survival" that is not rooted in a deep sense of the fundamental human dignity of all becomes a hollow and even dangerous slogan. The quest for religious and/or national survival can never turn a blind eye to the plight of others in our midst. We can never say "I'm sorry for what is happening to the [other] group but our own survival takes precedence."

If there is a moral lesson to be drawn from the above analysis, it would be that we need to redefine our identities individually and as members of religious and nationalistic communities in a way that includes the outsider within our universe of moral obligation. As a Christian ethicist, I have always insisted on the centrality of human rights for authentic Christian leadership.[13]

In a time when most human rights advocates ground their activism in some form of secular humanism, John's witness as a religious ethicist is of critical importance. I share his hope that people of all religious affiliations will heed his cry—not only fellow Christians, but also Jews and Muslims. We are all called to combat the dehumanization that inevitably characterizes long-term conflicts, including the hundred-year war over Israel/Palestine. In waging this struggle on behalf of our common humanity, we must affirm, with John Pawlikowski, "the need to recognize the ultimate connection and even integration among people, even those who might be legitimately regarded as enemies….If we allow humanity to be sucked out of those with whom we stand in conflict, we all become degraded."[14]

Examining the moral challenges posed by religious nationalism in both Israeli and Palestinian societies, John concluded,

In its most basic meaning…that a Jewish homeland is central to authentic Jewish identity, Zionism is not inherently racist any more than Palestinian nationalism is inherently racist. Both need to be tested in the crucible of the ethical framework I have been presenting above. If either fails to honor the fundamental humanity, dignity, and equality of its minorities and does not translate that into concrete social structures in their state which guarantee such dignity and equality, then they deserve a severe critique. But I do not believe that either is inherently incapable of meeting these ethical criteria. And I see nothing wrong with linking either Zionism with certain biblical perspectives or Palestinian nationalism with certain Islamic perspectives so long as adding such religious perspectives does not undermine the basic ethical framework that needs to prevail.[15]

For close to half a century, John Pawlikowski has championed a "basic ethical framework" as the foundation for interfaith efforts to advance inclusive justice and reconciliation. Other interfaith scholars, educators, and peace activists have much to learn from, and to emulate, in John's writing, his teaching, and his diligent efforts to heal our conflicted world. His perspective on Israel/Palestine is applicable to other countries afflicted by social and political conflicts, including the United States. For, as ethnic and religious loyalties assert themselves in increasingly polarizing ways, all people of faith must join forces to safeguard human dignity and equality, the imperative that John rightfully insists remain central in our minds, hearts, and actions.

Notes

1. See Yehezkel Landau, "Pope John Paul II's Holy Land Pilgrimage: A Jewish Appraisal," in *John Paul II in the Holy Land: In His Own Words,* ed. Lawrence Boadt, CSP, and Kevin di Camillo (Mahwah, NJ: Paulist Press, 2005), 129–56.

2. See John T. Pawlikowski, "Vatican II's Theological About-Face on the Jews: Not Yet Fully Recognized," *The Ecumenist* 37, no. 1 (Winter 2000).

3. *Christ Light.*

4. Yehezkel Landau, ed., *Interfaith Israel,* May 1982, 13.

5. *Christ Light,* 63–64.

6. Landau, *Interfaith Israel,* 14.

7. John T. Pawlikowski, "Catholicism's New Outreach to Jews and Muslims," presentation delivered at Florida Atlantic University, Boca Raton, FL, February 12, 2007, 16. Personal copy of the speech provided to the author by Pawlikowski.

8. Pawlikowski, "Catholicism's New Outreach to Jews and Musims," 19.

9. Pawlikowski, "Catholicism's New Outreach to Jews and Muslims," 19. Emphasis added.

10. As early as 1984, John was urging Israeli officials and American Jewish leaders to resist the annexationist tendencies of right-wing nationalists in Israel. He wrote, "I still remain convinced of one fundamental reality from the standpoint of Christian-Jewish dialogue. Christians in overwhelming numbers will reject and protest any attempt by Israel to totally absorb the West Bank/Gaza whether the annexation be publicly proclaimed or de facto. Basic justice demands the recognition of meaningful Palestinian sovereignty on the West Bank. This sovereignty cannot ignore legitimate Israeli security needs, but neither can the latter totally dictate the shape of a lasting political agreement." John T. Pawlikowski, "The Evolution of the Christian-Jewish Dialogue," *The Ecumenist* 22, no. 5 (July–August 1984): 67.

11. John T. Pawlikowski, "Ethics in a Globalized World: Implications for the Israeli-Palestinian Conflict," *Peace and Change* 36, no. 4 (October 2011): 51.

12. In his earlier 2007 presentation in Florida, John had asserted the same criterion for theological and ethical authenticity: "If our religious traditions are to constructively engage contemporary society, we must make human dignity, not right belief, the foundation of our faith perspective." Pawlikowski, "Catholicism's New Outreach to Jews and Muslims," 18.

13. Pawlikowski, "Ethics in a Globalized World," 551–52.

14. Pawlikowski, "Ethics in a Globalized World," 552–53.

15. Pawlikowski, "Ethics in a Globalized World," 553–54.

AFTERWORD

—⁓—

James Carroll

The Hebrew word *Shoah* can be translated as *catastrophe*. In Greek, the word *catastrophe* was used by Aristotle, in his *Poetics*, to define the turning point of the tragic drama, when its hidden action is laid bare for all to see. The "catastrophe" of *Oedipus Rex* occurred when the king recognized that he himself was guilty of the crimes that had brought the plague down on Thebes. With the Shoah, in the heart of twentieth-century Europe, the real meaning of two thousand years of Christian contempt for Jews was laid bare—a plague indeed—and a turning point was reached. The church began to confront its most grievous failure. There is no redeeming the Holocaust, but it has nevertheless forced the start of the most important change in Christian theology ever to take place. This is a book of tributes to one who ushered in that change—tributes that are themselves precious instances of the reckoning. The depth of these presentations makes clear both the power of the grip this ancient bigotry has on the Western imagination, and the way in which its off-key chords are struck even now in the dissonance of contemporary life.

As one who has depended over the decades on the work of the scholars represented in this collection, I am honored to add a last word in appreciation of John Pawlikowski. He has had a transforming effect on my thinking and life ever since I first met him in Jerusalem forty-four years ago. If I make brief reference to that personal history here, it is only because I am typical of a vast multitude who gratefully count Fr. Pawlikowski as a personal prophet and a beloved teacher. No one has done more to right the relations of Jews and Christians than this good priest. Certainly, no Catholic Christian has done more to help his church confront the Holocaust's consequences for the faith. Across an astonishing career, John Pawlikowski has bravely faced the meaning of that catastrophe, and insisted upon its being reckoned with. This book amounts to an acknowledgment of his accomplishment.

When John and I became friends, *Nostra Aetate*, the milestone declaration of the Second Vatican Council, had been issued only eight years before. It was already clear, of course, that *Nostra Aetate* marked a revolutionary turn in the Christian story away from the religious anti-Judaism that had long been a pillar of racial antisemitism. The formal Catholic renunciation of the Christ-killer slander, and the nascent affirmation of the permanence of the covenant God has made with Israel, did indeed, as essays in this volume emphasize, represent a profound act of *Teshuva* (repentance), a historic theological correction prompted by the Holocaust. But as the work in this book also demonstrates, *Nostra Aetate* was the beginning of something, not the completion. John Pawlikowski was one of the first to see that, and has built his life around the project of fulfilling the declaration's promise, not only with his prolific theological writing, but with his crucial participation in the Christian-Jewish dialogue, and his advocacy within the Catholic Church for ongoing reform of teaching about Jews and Judaism.

But even John Pawlikowski's lifetime of church-changing work represents the beginning of something, not the completion. That assumption, too, undergirds much of the writing in this volume. The commitment of scholars to the fulfillment of the promise of *Nostra Aetate* remains impressive, and this book shows that. The formal structures of Catholic Church leadership, too, have been responsive to the witness of the Second Vatican Council, with a succession of popes dramatically reaching out to the Jewish community; with a resounding set of moral acknowledgments by various members of the hierarchy; and with a transformation in official church teachings about Jews and Judaism, from changes in the *Catechism* to a Vatican renunciation of the mandate to work for the conversion of Jews.

But, to repeat, all of this amounts to the start, not the finish. As a practicing Catholic who finds himself in the pews most weeks, I myself am frankly troubled by a broad and continuing complacency in the wider church, ecumenically defined, when it comes to Christian attitudes about Jews and Judaism. That is especially true when it comes to the way preachers typically elucidate the Scriptures, the conscious lessons that congregations inevitably draw from that preaching, and the unexamined assumptions about the meaning of Jesus Christ that continue to subtly undercut right relations between Jews and Christians. Something is wrong, still.

To illustrate what I mean, let me describe what happened in my town last year. On March 11, 2016, a Friday night, the basketball teams of two Boston-area high schools met for a high-stakes, semifinal championship game: Catholic Memorial versus Newton North—two superb and highly regarded high schools. Tensions were mounting as students from both schools packed the gym. That the Catholic Memorial student body is all boys incited some of the Newton North kids to chant an offensive taunt, "Where are your girls?" The apparently homophobic, off-color taunt "sausage fest" was thrown in for, let's call it, bad measure. Kids being kids. High spirits. Rude manners.

But that is when a startling thing happened. From the Catholic Memorial side of the gym came a rebuttal chant, involving, school officials later acknowledged, something like seventy-five students. And what was it? The Catholics loudly aimed a scathing accusation against the opposite throng of Newton North students: "You killed Jesus! You killed Jesus! You killed Jesus!" The rhythm took hold: "You killed Jesus! You killed Jesus!"

Newton is a middle-to-upper-middle-class suburb. Yes, some Jews live there. Newton North is a public high school. Apparently, to Catholic Memorial students, Jewishness is a main note of the school's identity. But what does it signal that, when confronted with an adolescent challenge from rivals, these Catholic young people—well on their way to an excellent eduction and already the products, in most cases, of extensive religious instruction in the spirit of Vatican II—had immediate and instinctive recourse to a lowest-drawer anti-Jewish slur? When had "You killed Jesus!" rung out more unexpectedly?

Catholic Memorial won the basketball game, heading for the metro championship game, but for days after the brouhaha, the city-wide conversation was dominated by shock at what the Catholic chanters had done.

As it happened, the day before, on March 10, Cardinal Sean O'Malley, the archbishop of Boston, had participated at Temple Emanuel in Newton in a fiftieth anniversary observance of *Nostra Aetate*. The cardinal proposed that we "build a civilization of love," and his heartfelt good will had edified those in attendance. But a day later, Boston could wonder what kind of civilization was actually being built. Where had that foul, anti-Jewish taunt come from—a full half-century after the deicide charge had been formally renounced by the Catholic Church?

On the following Monday, the administrators of Catholic Memorial announced that the school's student body would be punished for the antisemitic chant by being forbidden to attend the follow-up championship game. The administrators issued a statement that read, "There are no excuses for the actions of the student-spectators who took part in the chanting. Their behavior was appalling; their actions and words do not align with the teachings or the value system of our school or the Catholic Church."

But, despite *Nostra Aetate*, and all the progress accomplished by the Jewish-Christian dialogue, which in Boston has been exemplary; indeed, despite the work of many contributing to this volume, a Catholic must still ask, is that so? How deeply into the consciousness of the ordinary faithful has the transformation of Vatican II on this urgent question penetrated? To ask the question in a more pointed way: Does the reformed theology enshrined in a book like this actually outweigh the ongoing impact of troubling, anti-Jewish gospel texts that seem to contradict it? How has the reforming post–*Nostra Aetate* scholarship, even when paired with reconciling pronouncements of popes and bishops, actually influenced the attitudes of legions of Christian preachers, decisively, including Catholics, who routinely fail to measure those texts against the new theology that would force a change in how they are read and heard?

Exactly two weeks after the notorious basketball game in Boston, the Christian world celebrated Good Friday: "Let his blood be upon us and upon our children." The anti-Jewish texts of the passion narrative are reiterated with power every year. The boys and young men of Catholic Memorial High School may or may not have been taught about *Nostra Aetate*, but they have certainly, year in and year out, been present for the reading of the passion. Have they been enabled to hear that anti-Jewish narrative as if they themselves are Jews? Have they been helped to understand how those texts came to be written? And when? And by whom? Not by eyewitnesses reporting "facts" shortly after the death of Jesus, but by successor generations filtering memory through theology? Have the Catholic Memorial students been helped to understand that the polemical authors of that denigrating phrase "the Jews," which appears eighty-seven times in the Gospels, were themselves Jews? Have the Catholic young people, in sum, been provided with the critical mindset necessary to hear the passion *without* concluding that "the Jews killed Jesus?"

For Christians everywhere, this is a grave question. Reading the Bible literally as the word of God, rooted in simplistic notions of historicity and facticity, inevitably produces negative attitudes toward "the Jews" portrayed as villains. And the passion narratives are only the tip of the iceberg. An uncritical reading of the New Testament, taken as a whole, can so seem to put Jesus in ontological opposition to his own people as to make any sense of his authentic Jewishness impossible. Christian contempt for Jews begins in Christian contempt for the Judaism of Jesus, as if he were somehow not a faithful—we would say "orthodox"—Jew to the day he died. That contempt continues to be sacralized when the letters of Saint Paul are read as justifying a polarizing opposition that begins by setting grace against law or faith against works and ends by setting the church against the synagogue in an enmity willed by a Christian (New Testament) God of love in conflict with a Jewish (Old Testament) God of judgment. This us-against-them structure of thought, with Jews embodying a cosmic negative other, is a mutated gene in the DNA of the Western imagination. And no, its damaging consequences are not finished with.

Yes, Cardinal O'Malley was right to lift up, in Temple Emanuel in Newton, the hope for "a civilization of love." But that assumes a next phase of a massive Christian religious education that really has yet to begin. It matters urgently that young people—as a Catholic, I would insist, *Catholic* young people—not be ushered into the old room furnished with images of anti-Jewish contempt, no matter how readily those young people make themselves at home there. As the Holocaust made very clear, images of contempt are lethal. *Nostra*

Aetate renounced the most blatant of those images—"You killed Jesus!"—but it left unfinished the task of uprooting its source in the oppositional structure of mind just described. Jews will not be safe from the insult of anti-Judaism, or the violence of antisemitism, until this further project of theological transformation is much more fully undertaken throughout the Christian world.

Because of Fr. John Pawlikowski, and his partners in reconciliation so vividly represented in this book, that work is well begun. Indeed, the precious meaning of their accomplishment shows itself in nothing more powerfully than in the way it prophetically points to what must be undertaken now. In the name of God, and for the sake of right relations at long last.

CONTRIBUTORS

Mehnaz M. Afridi is associate professor of religious studies and director of the Holocaust, Genocide, and Interfaith Education Center at Manhattan College. She is the author of *Shoah through Muslim Eyes* (Academic Studies Press, 2017) and coeditor of *Global Perspectives on Orhan Pamuk: Existentialism and Politics* (Palgrave MacMillan, 2012). She is a member of the committee on Ethics, Religion, and the Holocaust at the United States Holocaust Memorial Museum.

Judith H. Banki was assistant director of the American Jewish Committee's Interreligious Affairs Department when she authored the first of three memoranda ("The Image of the Jews in Catholic Teaching") that the AJC sent to Cardinal Augustine Bea, documenting problems later addressed by *Nostra Aetate*. Over a half century, she has collaborated with John Pawlikowski on a number of projects, including conferences, side-by-side articles, and a coedited volume, *Ethics in the Shadow of the Holocaust: Christian and Jewish Perspectives* (Sheed and Ward, 2001).

Victoria J. Barnett is director of programs on Ethics, Religion, and the Holocaust of the Jack, Joseph and Morton Mandel Center for Advanced Holocaust Studies at the United States Holocaust Memorial Museum. Author of *For the Soul of the People: Protestant Protest against Hitler* (Oxford University Press, 1998) and *Bystanders: Conscience and Complicity during the Holocaust* (Praeger, 2000), she is a leading authority on Dietrich Bonhoeffer and is the editor and translator of the fifteen-volume Dietrich Bonhoeffer Works.

Mary C. Boys, SNJM, is dean of academic affairs and Skinner McAlpin Professor of Practical Theology at Union Theological Seminary, New York City. A prolific writer and editor, she is the author most recently of *Redeeming Our Sacred Story: The Death of*

Jesus and Relations between Jews and Christians (Paulist Press, 2013). She is the recipient of numerous awards and honorary doctorates, including the Sir Sigmund Sternberg Award from the ICCJ, the Nostra Aetate Award from Seton Hill University, and the Shevet Achim Award from the CCJR.

James Carroll is the author of eight works of nonfiction, most recently *Christ Actually*, and twelve novels, most recently *The Cloister*. Among his honors are the National Book Award, for *An American Requiem*; the National Jewish Book Award, for *Constantine's Sword*; The PEN-Galbraith Award for *House of War*. He is an associate of the Mahindra Humanities Center at Harvard University. He lives in Boston with his wife, the writer Alexandra Marshall.

Robert A. Cathey is professor of theology at McCormick Theological Seminary, Chicago, and the author of *God in Postliberal Perspective: Between Realism and Non-realism* (Ashgate, 2009). He is a member of the Christian Leadership Initiative of the American Jewish Committee and the Shalom Hartman Institute, Jerusalem, and a coauthor of *"...In Our Time..." A Statement on Relations between the Presbytery of Chicago and the Jewish Community in Metropolitan Chicago* (November 21, 2015). He is an elected member of the Christian Scholars Group on Jewish-Christian Relations.

Mary Doak is professor of theology and religious studies at the University of San Diego, where she specializes in liberation and political theologies, theologies of democracy and religious freedom, the goal of human life and history from a Christian perspective, and theologies of the church. She is the author of *Reclaiming Narrative for Public Theology* (SUNY Press, 2004), numerous journal articles, and, most recently, *Divine Harmony: Seeking Community in a Broken World* (Paulist Press, 2017).

Susannah Heschel is the Eli Black Professor of Jewish Studies at Dartmouth College. The author of over one hundred articles, her books include *Abraham Geiger and the Jewish Jesus* (University of Chicago Press, 1998), winner of a National Jewish Book Award, and *The Aryan Jesus: Christian Theologians and the Bible in Nazi Germany* (Princeton University Press, 2010). She is the recipient of four honorary doctorates, numerous grants, and in 2015 was elected a member of the American Society for the Study of Religion.

Steven Leonard Jacobs is professor of religious studies and the Aaron Aronov Endowed Chair in Judaic Studies at the University of Alabama. He has authored or edited fourteen books, including *In Search of Yesterday: The Holocaust and the Quest for Meaning* (University Press of America, 2006) and *Dismantling the Big Lie: The Protocols of the Elders of Zion* (Ktav Publishing House, 2003). He is on the board of advisors for the Aegis Trust for the Prevention of Genocide, England, and is an officer of the International Association of Genocide Scholars.

Edward Kessler, MBE, is the founding director of the Woolf Institute, Cambridge, England and an authority on the relationship between religion and society. He has written or edited nine books and dozens of articles, including *An Introduction to Jewish-Christian Relations* (Cambridge University Press, 2010) and *Jews, Christians and Muslims* (SCM, 2013). He was a consultant for the Vatican's Commission for Religious Relations with the Jews as it prepared "'The Gifts and Calling of God Are Irrevocable' (Rom 11:29): A Reflection on Theological Questions Pertaining to Catholic-Jewish Relations on the Occasion of the 50th Anniversary of Nostra Aetate (No. 4)."

Michael S. Kogan is professor emeritus of philosophy and religion at Montclair State University, where he taught for forty-two years and chaired the department of philosophy and religion for twenty-four years. In addition to articles in scholarly journals, he is the author of the thought-provoking *Opening the Covenant: A Jewish Theology of Christianity* (Oxford University Press, 2008). An avid spokesperson for interreligious understanding, he now writes and lectures from retirement in Charleston, South Carolina.

Yehezkel Landau, a dual Israeli-American citizen, is an interfaith educator, trainer, and consultant active in Jewish-Christian-Muslim relations and Israeli-Palestinian peacebuilding for more than thirty-five years. He is a board member of the Stimulus Foundation and contributed to two earlier volumes for Stimulus Books: *Voices from*

Jerusalem: Jews and Christians Reflect on the Holy Land (coeditor and contributor) and *John Paul II in the Holy Land: In His Own Words* (contributor). From 2002 to 2016, he was a professor of Jewish tradition and interfaith relations at Hartford Seminary and holder of the Abrahamic Partnerships Chair.

Ruth Langer is professor of Jewish studies and associate director of the Center for Christian-Jewish Learning at Boston College. She is the immediate past chair of the Council of Centers on Jewish-Christian Relations. Author of many articles, her books include *Cursing the Christians? A History of the Birkat HaMinim* (Oxford University Press, 2012), *To Worship God Properly: Tensions between Liturgical Custom and Halakhah in Judaism* (Hebrew Union College Press, 1998), and *Jewish Liturgy: A Guide to Research* (Rowman & Littlefield, 2015).

Amy-Jill Levine is University Professor of New Testament and Jewish Studies, Mary Jane Werthan Professor of Jewish Studies, and Professor of New Testament Studies at Vanderbilt Divinity School and College of Arts and Sciences. A prolific author and editor, her work in Jewish-Christian relations has been recognized with six honorary doctorates as well as numerous book awards, grants, and distinguished lectureships. Her most recent work is the revised second edition of the *Jewish Annotated New Testament* (Oxford University Press, 2017).

Martin M. Lintner, OSM, is professor of moral theology at the Philosophical-Theological College in Brixen/Bressanone South Tyrol, Italy. He is the former president of the European Society for Catholic Theology (2013–15) and since 2014, president of INSeCT (International Network of Societies for Catholic Theology). He is the coeditor of the journal *Brixner Theologisches Jahrbuch* and author of numerous articles on fundamental moral theology, bioethics, and sexual and family ethics.

Carmen M. Nanko-Fernández is professor of Hispanic theology and ministry, and director of the Hispanic Theology and Ministry Program at the Catholic Theological Union, Chicago. Past president of the Academy of Catholic Hispanic Theologians of the United States, she has numerous publications to her credit, including the forthcoming *¡El Santo! Baseball and the Canonization of Roberto Clemente* (Mercer University Press) and with Jean-Pierre Ruiz, "Dialogues in the Margins: The Biblia De Alba and the Future of Catholic-Jewish Understanding," in *Toward the Future: Essays on Catholic-Jewish Relations in Memory of Rabbi León Klenicki* (Paulist Press, 2013).

Jon Nilson is professor emeritus of theology at Loyola University, Chicago. Besides Loyola, he has taught at St. Procopius College, the University of Dallas, and has held visiting professorships at the Catholic Theological Union and the General Theological Seminary. He was a Catholic representative on the Anglican-Roman Catholic Consultation in the United States from 1984 to 2007. He served as President of the Catholic Theological Society of America in 2002–2003. Along with numerous articles and reviews, his most recent book is *Hearing Past the Pain: Why White Catholic Theologians Need Black Theology* (Paulist Press, 2007).

Elena G. Procario-Foley is the Driscoll Professor of Jewish-Catholic Studies at Iona College, New Rochelle, New York. She served as chair of the Council of Centers on Jewish-Christian Relations from 2006 to 2011 and is an elected member of the Christian Scholars Group on Jewish-Christian Relations. Along with articles in the area of Jewish-Christian relations, she is the coeditor of *Frontiers in Catholic Feminist Theology: Shoulder to Shoulder* (Fortress Press, 2009) and the editor of *Horizons: The Journal of the College Theology Society*.

Carol Rittner, RSM, is Distinguished Professor of Holocaust and Genocide Studies Emerita and Dr. Marsha Raticoff Grossman Professor of Holocaust Studies Emerita at Stockton University, New Jersey. She is the author or coeditor of numerous essays and fifteen books about the Holocaust and other genocides, including *The Courage to Care* (NYU Press, 1989), *Rape: Weapon of War and Genocide* (Paragon House, 2012), and forthcoming from Paulist Press, a revised edition of *The Holocaust and the Christian World*.

John K. Roth, Edward J. Sexton Professor Emeritus of Philosophy and Founding Director of the Center for the Study of the Holocaust, Genocide, and Human Rights (now the Mgrublian Center for Human

Rights) at Claremont McKenna College, has published hundreds of articles, and authored, coauthored, or edited more than fifty books. Named the 1988 U.S. National Professor of the Year by the Council for Advancement and Support of Education and the Carnegie Foundation for the Advancement of Teaching, Roth has also received the Holocaust Educational Foundation's Distinguished Achievement Award for Holocaust Studies and Research.

Jean-Pierre M. Ruiz is associate professor and senior research fellow of theology and religious studies at St. John's University, Queens, New York. He is past president of the Academy of Catholic Hispanic Theologians of the United States, has been an editor or on the board for a variety of biblical and theological journals, and is most recently the author of *Readings from the Edges: The Bible and People on the Move* (Orbis Books, 2011), winner of a Catholic Press Association Award. Ruiz serves on the Religion and Foreign Policy Working Group of the U.S. Department of State.

Katharina von Kellenbach is professor of religious studies and former chair of the department of philosophy and religious studies at St. Mary's College of Maryland. She is the author of *Anti-Judaism in Feminist Religious Writings* (Oxford University Press, 1994), articles on Rabbi Regina Jonas (1902–44), and *The Mark of Cain: Guilt and Denial in the Lives of Nazi Perpetrators* (Oxford University Press, 2013). Her current project is *Composting Guilt: An Ecofeminist Critique of Rituals of Purification of Past Wrongs*.